THE
DIVINE TRINUNITY

OF THE
Father, Son, and Holy Spirit
OR

The blessed doctrine of the three coessential subsistents in the eternal Godhead without any confusion or division of the distinct subsistences or multiplication of the most single and entire Godhead:

Acknowledged, believed, adored by Christians, in opposition to pagans, Jews, Mahometans, blasphemous and anti-Christian heretics, *who say they are Christians, but are not.*

Declared and published for the edification and satisfaction of all such as worship the only true God, Father, Son, and Holy Spirit, all three as one and the self-same God blessed forever.

By FRANCIS CHEYNELL, minister of that gospel which is revealed from heaven by Father, Son, and Holy Spirit in the holy Scriptures of truth.

Berith Press
P.O. Box 861, Kansas, OK 74347
(918) 896-2055
www.berithpress.com

The divine Trinunity of the Father, Son, and Holy Spirit, or, The blessed doctrine of the three coessential subsistents in the eternal Godhead without any confusion or division of the distinct subsistences or multiplication of the most single and entire Godhead acknowledged, believed, adored by Christians, in opposition to pagans, Jewes, Mahometans, blasphemous and antichristian heretics, who say they are Christians, but are not, was first published in 1650.

This Berith Press reprint, in which spelling, grammar, and formatting changes have been made, is a 2024 publication. With thanks to David Jonescue, Logan West, and Alex Sarrouf of Project Puritas for their endeavors, and to EEBO-TCP for the corpus of texts it has produced. Also with thanks to Mr. Charles Johnson, and the Facebook group Nerdy Language Majors, for their linguistic help with some of the Greek. The excerpt from Chapter 9 of Cheynell's original published by Reformed Books Online is very helpful too.[1]
Printed in the U.S.A.

ISBN 978-1-963516-02-9

---

[1] Francis Cheynell, *The Grounds of Christ the Mediator Receiving Divine Worship* <https://reformedbooksonline.com/wp-content/uploads/2014/07/cheynell-francis-how-worship-is-due-to-christ.pdf>
[Accessed 2/1/2024]

Table of Contents

Introduction to Francis Cheynell's *The Divine Trinunity of the Father, Son, & Holy Spirit*..1
The Epistle Dedicatory to Francis Rous...7

Chapter 1: The Godhead is spiritual, infinite, and incomprehensible...................1
Chapter 2: God is the first, eternal, and independent being, the fountain of all being and well-being, and therefore cannot but be, exist, and persist in being 5
Chapter 3: God has sufficiently and graciously revealed himself in his holy Word for our edification and salvation...9
Chapter 4: This single and eternal Godhead subsists in Father, Son, & Holy Spirit, without any multiplication of the Godhead...15
Chapter 5: The manner of God's being or subsisting in the Father, Son, and Holy Spirit, is the best manner of being that is or can be, and the single Godhead is thereby thrice illustrious throughout the world..41
Chapter 6: The divine subsistence, being the most excellent subsistence that is or can be. The word *subsistence* or *person* cannot be attributed after the same manner to God, Angels, and men...49
Chapter 7: The three uncreated, divine, and coessential subsistents are sufficiently distinguished, though they cannot be divided..127
Chapter 8: The grand mystery of three divine and coessential subsistents in the single Godhead is not problematic, but fundamental..171
Chapter 9: This grand mystery of faith has an effectual influence into the practical mystery of godliness and power of religion...185
Chapter 10: Christians who have a lively sense and sweet experience of this grand mystery of faith, and practical mystery of Godliness, are afraid to hold communion with such as pretend to be spiritual Christians, and yet deny the divine nature and distinct subsistences of Christ and his Holy Spirit.....................................285
The report made to the reverend assembly, March 8th, 1647-48, by Mr. Cheynell...309

Introduction to Francis Cheynell's
The Divine Trinunity of the Father, Son, & Holy Spirit

By Steven J. Carr

"I fear that atheism may soon become a national sin in England, if there be an indulgence (worse than any at Rome) vouchsafed to irregular phantasies, and appetites under pious pretenses." So writes Francis Cheynell (1608-1666) in the epistle dedicatory to Francis Rous of this very book. Cheynell was not talking about the radical and total denial of the existence of God which is what we think of atheism today. Rather, he was talking about the errors of the Socinians (precursors to the modern Unitarians), Familists (a mystical sect with some similarities to the Quakers), Muslims, Jews, and any others who denied the doctrine of the Trinity. Socinianism and Socinians, however, were the main target in much of his writings.

Socianianism was not properly an atheistic religion. It still taught the existence of one (non-triune) god. However, Cheynell wrote elsewhere that it "let open a wide gap to atheism,"[2] for not only was it guilty of denying the two natures, and therefore the mediatorship of Christ, but also it denied the soul's subsistence after death to enjoy the reward of life in heaven or the torment of death in hell. The issue for Cheynell was not that the denial of the Trinity and other fundamental doctrines of Christianity equalled a radical denial of the existence of God, but that it left one without Christ and, therefore, as the apostle Paul said, "without hope and without God (*atheoi*) in the world (Ephesians 2:12)." We can only know God through Christ. Jesus himself said, "No one cometh unto the Father, but by me (John 14:6)."

---

[2] *The Rise, Growth, and Danger, of Socinianisme.* Together with a plaine discovery of a desperate design of corrupting the Protestant Religion, whereby it appears that the religion which hath been so violently contended for (by the Archbishop of Canterbury and his adherents) is not the true Protestant Religion, but an hotchpotch of Arminianisme, Socinianisme, and Popery, etc. (London: For Samuel Gellibrand, 1643), 25.

Whoever does not believe that Jesus is the Christ, the Son of God will remain without God in this world and in the world to come.

Socinianism, though based upon the teachings of Lelio and Faustus Sozzini,[3] could also be used as a broader term for anyone who sought to revise Christianity along the lines of reason instead of biblical authority.[4] This is what the deists of the late seventeenth and early eighteenth centuries sought to do. What kind of god did these rationalistic thinkers discover? What form did their religion take? Theirs was a god who created the world, who had some governance over the world, but who did not, nor indeed could, demonstrate his love by sending his own Son to die for sinners (Romans 5:8). Theirs was a religion that was moralistic but had no doctrine of salvation for lost sinners. These were men who had the form of godliness but denied the power thereof (2 Timothy 3:5). A religion that knows God as Creator and Governor but not as Redeemer will leave men without hope and without God in the world and in the world to come.

Cheynell, like many orthodox divines, taught that man's reason was a gift of God and was able to discover truths concerning God, but what was discovered by reason were only "imperfect and obscure notions." And, because of man's sinful corruption, he was "very apt" to abuse these notions; thus, Cheynell wrote, reason must be regulated by the Word of God.[5] The doctrine of the Trinity, however, is not discoverable by reason, for, though the invisible attributes of God are "clearly seen" in creation (Romans 1:20), the knowledge of God needed for salvation, which is the knowledge of God through Christ, is revealed only in the Word of God by the Spirit of God. Cheynell wrote, "The saving knowledge of God in Christ is revealed by the Spirit speaking in the Scriptures of truth; nay, Father, Son, and Holy Spirit do all join in revealing to us the saving mystery of faith and godliness, that

---

[3] See Francis Cheynell, *The Rise, Growth, and Danger of Socinianism*, 1-21.

[4] David D. Hall, *The Puritans: A Transatlantic History* (Princeton, NJ: Princeton University Press, 2019), 305.

[5] *The Divine Triunity of the Father, Son, and Holy Spirit* (London: T. R. and E. M., 1650), 2.

by the grace of Christ, the love of God, and Communion of the Holy Spirit, we may have a glorious fellowship with all three as one God, the only true God, whom to know is life eternal (John 17:3)."[6] Any religion built solely upon human reason will, once again, leaves man without hope and without God in the world. Cheynell did not want this for his fellow Englishmen which is why he took up arms to fight the pernicious, soul-damning heresy known as Socinianism.

Francis Cheynell has been described by some as a heresy-hunting and bigoted fanatic who suffered from occasional bouts of an unknown mental disorder.[7] What should we say about this? Indeed, what can we say at all about this son of a physician, fellow at Merton College, avowed presbyterian, dedicated scholar, zealous preacher, chaplain in the army of the Earl of Sussex, patriot, Westminster divine, and controversialist? He was well-known in his own day, but the amount of biographical material available to us today is only able to give us no more than a fair bit of knowledge about him. We are not able to dig very deep into his life, but what is said of him in *The Non-Conformist's Memorial* of Edmund Calamy is, I believe, a fair and accurate summary of the man:

"From the writer's concessions, however, the reader will remain possessed of the idea that Dr. Cheynell's was a truly great character, tho' from undeniable facts he will be constrained to own it was not without its blemishes."[8]

Much, I believe, can be said about the man's character by looking at the account of his treatment of William Chillingworth. Chillingworth at one

---

[6] *The Divine Triunity of the Father, Son, and Holy Spirit* (USA: Berith Press, 2024), p. 30.
[7] Adriana McRea, *Constant Minds: Political Virtue and the Lipsian Paradigm in England, 1584-1650* (Toronto, ON: University of Toronto Press, 1997), 154; David D. Hall, *The Puritans*, 305; Augustus Charles Bickley, "Francis Cheynell" in *Dictionary of National Biography*, Vol. 10 (Oxford: Oxford University Press, 1885-1900),. 222-224.
[8] Edmund Calamy, *The Non-Conformist's Memorial:* Being an Account of the Ministers Who Were Ejected or Silenced after the Restoration, Particularly by the Act of Uniformity, which Took Place on Bartholomew Day, Aug. 24, 1662. Abridged and Corrected by Samuel Parker (London: W. Harris, 1775), II:467-468.

time studied at a Jesuit college but being dissatisfied with the Roman religion, returned to the Church of England and soon after published a treatise titled *The Religion of Protestants a Safe Way to Salvation*. His treatise, however, did not promote the true Protestant religion, as the title suggests, but instead, as James Reid notes, promoted his Arian views.[9] It was thought, however, that he was a Socinian, and it was inevitable that he should be caught in Cheynell's crosshairs.

Chillingworth, who served in the army of King Charles I during the English Civil War, was captured and made prisoner by Parliament's army but was later allowed to lodge in the house of the Bishop of Chichester. Cheynell took it upon himself to visit with him and, when he fell sick, attended to him making sure that he was able to get help from a physician. While attending to him, Cheynell tried to reason with him about his views hoping to convince him of the true faith. He fervently prayed that he would change his mind, and called others to pray as well. Sadly, Chillingworh died unconvinced. Nevertheless, Cheynell showed kindness even after his death by obtaining for him the rite of burial.

At Chillingworth's burial, however, Cheynell cast a copy of his book into his grave and said, "Get thee gone, thou cursed book, which hast seduced so many precious souls; get thee gone, thou corrupt rotten book, earth to earth, and dust to dust; get thee gone into the place of rottenness, that thou mayest rot with thy author, and see corruption."[10] This outburst has caused some to question his character and, perhaps, even his sanity. Cheynell found it necessary to write in defense of his actions in a short work entitled *Chillingworth Novissimi, Or, The Sickness, Heresy, Death, and Burial of William Chillingworth*. Chillingworth, though dead, yet was survived by those who agreed with his views and continued to propagate them. This was Cheynell's reason for his outburst. He could no longer do anything for Chillingworth, but he could still do something about his errors and those

---

[9] *Memoirs of the Westminster Divines* (Paisley: Stephen and Andrew Young, 1811), 1:229.
[10] James Reid, *Memoirs of the Westminster Divines*, 1:230.

who held them. Though we might concede his outburst was ill-suited for the moment, we have to say it was born out of a zeal for the truth of Scripture and out of a sincere desire for men's salvation.

What can we say about Francis Cheynell? If anything, this account of his dealings with Chillingworth argues for a man who both loved his Savior and cared for lost souls.

I am thankful that Cheynell's *The Divine Triunity of the Father, Son, and Holy Spirit* is being reprinted. Cheynell feared that atheism would soon be a national sin in England. He was more right about that than he could ever have known. We have seen a move in society beyond Socinianism to outright atheism not only in England but also here in the United States. We still however have many within the church who do not understand how essential the doctrine of the Trinity really is. If we are to bear witness to the truth of the gospel to these ungodly societies, we must be firm in our belief in the only true God and in Jesus Christ whom he has sent. We cannot afford now more than ever to neglect the precious doctrine of the Triunity of the Father, Son, and Holy Spirit.

My hope for this book is the opposite of Cheynell's express desire for Chillingworth's heretical book. May its message draw many precious souls to the Savior. May it continue long in bringing many sons to glory. May it deliver many unbelievers from corruption that they might be granted "an inheritance incorruptible and undefiled, and that fadeth not away" (1 Pet. 1:4). May it also be a testament to him who sat by the bedside of a dying man and pleaded with him to obey the truth so that those who are without hope and without God in the world may through Christ be reconciled to God.

The Epistle Dedicatory

To the worshipful Francis Rous Esq.,
the learned Provost of Eaton College.

Sir,

It was the sad complaint of Hilary in his time that there were as many creeds as wills,[11] and everyone presumed to alter the wholesome form of sound words, or else wrested it to a corrupt sense. And you know the sense of a creed is the creed. In these days of Libertinism, men account it a kind of bondage to confine themselves to a wholesome form of sound words, though they are consecrated words, and therefore such as cannot be condemned.

The devil has set good men at variance about secular affairs, private interests and public rights, and in the meantime robs or cheats us of what is spiritual and glorious, the purity of truth, the power and beauty of holiness. We live in sad times, in which atheism pleads for protection and intolerable errors contend for toleration.

They who blaspheme Christ and his gospel in jest, are atheists in good earnest (as Lucian and Rablais were) but God will plead his own cause if we will not. Lucian (as Soudas relates) was torn to pieces with dogs, and Rablais died drunk with wine and atheism. We have good cause to suppress and bewail the very first risings of natural atheism; we must not suffer any black suggestions or hovering thoughts which relish of atheism to roost and nestle in our hearts. These extemporary thoughts are sins which do proceed from us, but O! Let them not be familiars, and inmates which lodge, and dwell within us. I fear that atheism may soon become a national sin in England, if there be an indulgence (worse than any at Rome) vouchsafed to irregular

---

[11] "Periculosum nobis est tot nunc Fides existere, quot voluntates, dum aut ita Fides scribuntur ut volumus, aut ut volumus intelliguntur." Hilarius

fantasies and appetites under pious pretenses. They who deny the Godhead of Jesus Christ, and the Holy Spirit, hope to escape censure in England, if they can have the favor to be called devout Familists, although their blasphemy and wantonness declare them to be sensual Socinians, and beastly atheists. The Socinians and Familists have even already shamed the more modest Mahometans. Mr. Pocock (the learned and ingenuous professor of Hebrew and Arabic in this university, in his notes upon Gregory the Arabian Phoenix) assures me that the Al-Hayetians acknowledge the incarnation of the eternal Word, and that we shall all be judged by this Incarnate Word at the last day.[12] The more moderate Turks would stop their ears at the hearing of such blasphemies against Christ as has poisoned this English air. Some Mahometans hold that *Christus est Deus de novo ortus*, as the Socinians say, he is *Deus factus, Subordinatus*, etc. And the Mahometan sectaries talk just like our Familists, antinomians, etc., as will be evident to any one that will peruse Mr. Pocock's choice and learned annotations.[13] *Licitum pronuntiant vino and scortationi indulgere, and reliqua quae lege vetita sunt perpetrare; omittenda esse censent, quae lege mandata sunt, and oratione.*

I am ashamed to English that with my pen, which some professors have translated in broad and foul English by their gross neglect of duties, contempt of ordinances, and bold practice of abominable lewdness; I will not mention their dreams of a fantastical hell and heaven. But sure I am our Familists, and their Alshii speak the same dialect, when they discourse of their being godded with God, and salute one whom they reverence with this atheistic complement: "*Tu est tu, id est, tu es Deus.*" "Sir, you are what you are, you are God!" Henry Nicholas, the father of the Family of Love, said of himself, "I am God." A man would think that our Familists had met with some Mahometans at Poland or Constantinople, and some of the worst of them also. For Al Gazalius, a precise and learned Mahometan, would teach them better language and behavior also: he says that cleanliness is a part of

---

[12] D. Pocockii specimen Hist. Arab. pag. 21. Annot. pag. 218. & 219
[13] D. Pocock, Annot. pag. 219

faith and the key of prayer that we must have pure minds, clean hearts and hands. But enough of that.

Sir, being encouraged by the committee, for regulating this university, to undertake a service which I even tremble to repeat, and you being chairman of that committee, I conceived myself obliged to present you with this treatise. When the university was pleased to elect me the L. Margaret's Professor of Divinity, the revenue due to that professor by a grant made under the great seal of England, Caroli, was settled by special act.[14] And the university did purchase the lease of the house and meadows in Worcester, which belong to the said professor, and would (if they might have had the common privilege of leaseholders) have bought the inheritance of the premises outright forever; but the university is denied the benefit of the lease and the common privilege aforesaid. The house and meadows are sold to others, and no revenue paid to the professor. I desire that the university may be righted, and that my successor may not suffer as I have done.

Sir, notwithstanding these discouragements, I conceived it my duty either to read or write for the propagation of the Christian faith, and honor of the blessed Trinity according to the first grant. I consulted the university and yourself, and you both concurred that *rebus sic stantibus*, it was better to write than read, and that it did most conduce to the propagation of the Christian faith.

Finally, that it was most requisite that I should write in English, because since the beginning of the year 1645, there have been many blasphemous books to the great dishonor of the blessed Trinity printed in England. But I have found the task far more difficult because there are many Socinian subtleties which will hardly bear English, and I could not but take some notice of them, either by a formal answer, or else by a confirmation of that deep truth which they do with no less blasphemy than subtlety, reject and

---

[14] April 20th, 1649. This act shall not extend to the revenues of any public professor or reader in either of the universities. Ad laudem & honorem sanctae & individuae Trinitatis, ac Fidei & Christianorum augmentum.

deny. I have been forced sometimes to express my mind in Latin in the margin, merely upon that account, but the plainest reader may, if he is pleased to read the fourth, fifth, eighth, and ninth chapters, understand as much of this mystery as is necessary to be known; and I am confident that the happy union between the mystery of faith and the practical mystery of godliness is as plainly represented in this little treatise, as in any of the ancient or modern divines; for I have faithfully endeavored to give you the strength and quintessence of both in a familiar way with many experimental observations of mine own, which I shall now review and practice in my most retired condition.

But before I retire, give me leave to speak a word for my brethren who are eminent for all manner of learning, sound in the faith, holy in their life, and peaceable in their conversation. If men of such qualifications do not know how to rest in the present unsettledness of public affairs, and yet are ready to perform all lawful things required of them for the defense and preservation of the true religion and public liberties; why may not such be still employed for the promoting of such a just accommodation and reformation as may effectually advance the grand public interest, the power, purity and growth of religion in this land? you cannot look upon these men as enemies, and dare not deal with them as the worst of infidels (whom Christian princes have sometimes banished from their dominions)[15] if you desire to have the same common friends and enemies with Jesus Christ. Now which is the more tolerable penalty, to be outlawed or banished, is not hard to determine.

If you look upon them as Presbyterians, it is no dishonor to them to be true to their principles in the midst of changes; it is a sign that they were never friends to the fortune of the cause, but to the cause itself; forgive them if they know not how to pursue a new interest without new light or direction from the word of God. Besides they are such Presbyterians as all

---

[15] See Weemes, Volume 3, *Exposition of the Judicial Law*, chapter 15.

godly and prudent Independents will close within the highest and sweetest acts of church communion. For I am confident that no wise and godly men will practically separate from us in those very things in which they do doctrinally agree with us, because that text which they do so often cite (Philippians 3:15-16) is demonstratively clear in this very point, and manifestly condemns all causeless separation from lawful communion with the godly members of reforming churches.[16] Godly Presbyterians and Independents do:

(1) Receive the same officers, pastors, teachers, ruling elders, and of the same qualification required in the rule set forth by the parliament.

(2) Admit members of the same qualification held forth by the Assembly, namely visible saints, who being of age, do profess faith in, and obedience to the Lord Jesus Christ according to the rules of faith and life delivered in the Word.

(3) Desire that the above mentioned officers should be incorporated in one eldership, and join in all acts of government of the church.

(4) Hold the same censures of admonition and excommunication, and do likewise receive such as have been censured into communion again, as soon as they give testimony of their repentance to them.

(1) Godly Independents do acknowledge that parochial churches (wherein ministers and others endeavor to remove all things justly offensive, that so all ordinances may be administered in purity) are true churches of Christ.

(2) They retain communion with these parochial churches by baptizing their children, and receiving the Lord's Supper there, as occasion serves. And if occasional communion with us be lawful, constant communion with us would not be sinful.

(3) They receive the members of such parishes as aforesaid unto communion with themselves in their own congregations also occasionally.

---

[16] Si vultis vivere de Spiritu Sancto, tenete charitatem, amate veritatem, desiderate unitatem, ut perveniatis ad aeternitatem.

(4) They profess that they are ready to give an account to such parochial congregations, as to sister-churches, whensoever they are offended at any irregular administrations in independent churches.

(5) They esteem a sentence of non-communion passed by such parochial congregations, is churches against them, upon any scandal wherein they are unsatisfied, as a means to humble them, and as an ordinance of God to reduce them. Much more might be added, but it is clear from these premises, that prudent and godly Independents cannot conceive themselves obliged:

[1] To set up other churches with differing rules of constitution or worship; For Presbyterians and Independents did both agree in the same Confession of Faith and Directory for Worship, and resolved to practice most of the same things, and those the most substantial in respect of government also, as appears by those few transactions in the Assembly, and Committee for Accommodation, which have been printed.

[2] Nor can they say that they are forced to gather new churches out of true Reformed churches; for a circumstantial difference cannot be a sufficient ground for leaving all ordinary communion with true reforming churches. The prudent and godly Presbyterians have set no bounds to themselves in their reformation but the Word of God, and therefore if the Independents will set forth a complete model of their whole church way, and church order, fully, freely, and clearly, and prove it by plain texts out of the holy Scriptures, we shall thankfully receive whatsoever they shall convincingly impart. And I shall be bold to say, that there had been a judicious, affectionate and practical accommodation between us (notwithstanding some speculative differences in notional ideas) if there had been no interposition of statesmen or swordsmen, when the Committee of Accommodation had sadly considered and reviewed all material arguments on this side, and on that; and if you set aside all reasons of state and secular considerations, I do not see why men who agree in the substance of the service and worship of God, in the Directory according to the preface, in the Confession of Faith set forth by the Assembly, and in the doctrine contained

in the confessions and writings of the reformed churches, should not mind the same thing, and walk by the same rule, that there might be a practical communion between us in all points wherein there is a doctrinal agreement, and we might go hand in hand to heaven together, with meekness of wisdom, and sincerity of love.

Let men of both persuasions beware of such a superstitious tenderness as usually arises from some unconscionable error, and unmortified lust, because it is no privilege, but a judgment to be given up to error or lust; and from such ensnaring liberty, which is indeed perfect bondage, good Lord deliver us. No man is obliged to follow the positive prescript [command] of an erroneous conscience in any point or case whatsoever. Differences of judgment did not extinguish the relation of membership amongst the Romans and Corinthians. And it is certain that the substantials of church-government must not be changed in every age according to the gradual differences of light in several persons and congregations.

We humbly desire that there may be a strict and mutual obligation condescended to in some expedient by all godly men of both persuasions for mutual edification, and for the preservation of all the churches in these dominions in truth, godliness, and peace, that we may not pass unchristian censures upon our Christian brethren.[17]

Let all private quarrels then fall to the ground, and let us mind the common interest of the Lord Jesus, and seriously promote it in our respective places in faith and love. And let all statesmen beware: (1) That they do not fall into the same spiritual or civil evils which they themselves have condemned in the king and prelates. (2) Beware of Erastianism, which overthrows all church government, both Presbyterian and Independent. (3) Take heed of civil skepticism, which overthrows the fundamentals of public faith and public rights, and plucks up all civil government, by the roots. (4) Beware of Familistic polytheism, for the Familists affirm that there are as

---

[17] An expedient desired for a happy union between Presbyterians and Independents
Dum propter haec alter alteri Anathema esse caepit, nemo penè Christi est. Hilarius.

many christs, as many gods manifested in the flesh, as there are saints on earth. But to us there is but one God, and one Lord Jesus Christ; it is enough for blind pagans to talk of many gods and many mediators.[18] (5) Beware of atheism, the great monster of this age, compounded of Socinianism, Familism, Libertinism, and antinomianism. The Ephesians complain of none but robbers of churches, and blasphemers (Acts 19:37). But we have cause to complain of them, and apostates, idolaters, atheists, and what not? (6) Beware of a toleration of intolerable errors. Reverend Mr. Cotton is afraid that the antichristian whore will steal in at the backdoor of a toleration. The magistrates of England are engaged by the oath of God to root out whatsoever is contrary to sound doctrine, and the power of godliness. That man is seduced by a private spirit (as you observe well in your orthodox book) who "lusteth after envy," after sects and divisions; but the Holy Spirit is a catholic Spirit, a Spirit of catholic faith and catholic love, an unreserved and universal love to all that believe and love the Lord Jesus Christ.

Let us then all hold fast the wholesome form of sound words in faith and love. For they who waver against the credit of their own testimony, are not (as the Civilians say) to be heard or regarded, because they have lost their credit. We are reserved for some service in this declining age; and therefore it becomes us to be orthodox saints, steady Christians, that our posterity may imitate us, and see those glorious days, which some conceive are come already, because they have attained a little vainglory in this age of vanity.

The writers of this present time, who seem to contradict one another concerning the light and glory of these unhappy days, may as easily be reconciled as Sophocles and Euripides were concerning the goodness of women. Sophocles – being asked the reason why he did always represent women in his tragedies as very good, whereas Euripides did ever represent them as very bad – answered, that he and Euripides did not at all contradict one another; for says he, I do ever represent women just as they should be,

---

[18] Jeremiah 2:11-12, 28

and Euripides just as they are. In like manner some writers represent these times just as they should be, and others represent them just as they are. But I must condemn those, who draw a crooked conclusion from the corrupt doctrine and manners of this untoward and crooked generation, and infer that there is no church of God in England, because antichristian and blasphemous seducers are multiplied without number, and favored in the land, though all the magistrates and godly of the nation are by one confederate body, obliged by solemn oath to root out idolatry, blasphemy, heresy, schism, profaneness, and whatsoever else is contrary to sound doctrine, and the power of godliness. (1) It is not denied that there is a fry of Achans in the land. (2) The sins condemned are inexcusable, and so are all the foster-fathers of them. (3) We pray that they who have given their power to the beast, may give it to the lamb. (4) All faithful ministers do open heaven to the faithful, and shut it against unbelievers, as our master enjoins us (Mark 16:15, Luke 24:47) and therefore we are true and faithful to the king of saints and commonwealth of Israel. (5) There are thousands in England whose hearts bleed at their eyes for the abominations of the land; men that do seriously endeavor to save themselves and others from this untoward generation, according to Peter's direction (Acts 2:40). (6) The house of Jacob was the church of God, and yet there were foul faults, incest, and murder found amongst his sons. May the Lord persuade and encourage the fathers of this nation to be as zealous against the sins of the nation, as Jacob was against the sins of Reuben, Simeon, and Levi.

    I must go backwards here, as Shem and Japheth did.[19] I do not have time to mention other things, but let all such as have the power and bowels of fathers, take heed that they do not persecute or offend one of those little ones who believe in Christ, much less undo one of those great ones, who have much of Christ, and his Spirit reigning in them.[20]

---

[19] Genesis 9:23
[20] Matthew 18:6

Believe it Sir, there is a company (I put myself out of the number) of select men in Oxford; I know not whether there be, all things considered, the like in the world again, men able and willing to promote the commonwealth of true religion, public liberty, and ingenuous learning for the commonwealth and good of mankind in all nations; for they are acquainted with all necessary arts, sciences, and languages, and dare throw the gauntlet to the proudest champions in the antichristian world. Some few of these may perhaps be complained of by some weathercocks, who can rather turn than crow, some froward children who bite their mothers breasts, or vipers who would eat a way to their own preference through their mothers' bowels.

It is not for want of pride or ignorance that these afflict your doors and ears with unnecessary complaints, which they prove just as Erucius did his against Roscius, who when he was asked who told him so, he answered, No body; and when it was demanded how the accusation would be proved, answered, In truth I know not. What is this (says Tully, *Pro Sexto Roscio*) but to abuse the laws and judges, to object what you cannot prove, nay, do not so much as endeavor to prove? It may be you will reply as Hazael did: "Am I a dog that I should be accessory to any grievous or unrighteous decree?" You know what Hazael did; and you know that Asa was a good man, and yet a persecutor. But I hope that as you have been zealous for the Reformation, so you will be zealous for the preservation of the university, which is the earnest desire and prayer of,

Your thankful servant,

Francis Cheynell

Chapter 1

The Godhead is Spiritual, Infinite, & Incomprehensible.

We read of the eternal Godhead in the "Book of the Creature" (Romans 1:20), and therefore I prize philosophy because it is subservient to divinity; nay, that philosophy which manifests the eternal power and Godhead of our great Creator is in deed and truth nothing else but natural divinity. This natural divinity is called "the truth" (Romans 1:18). and it is a divine truth, because it does declare το γνωστον του θεου: all that can be known of God by the light of nature (Romans 1:19-20).

I subscribe to that of Clement of Alexandria: "We ought not to swear allegiance to any sect of philosophers, whether Stoics, Epicureans, Platonists, or Peripatetics, but we must select and embrace whatsoever is true and faithfully delivered concerning God by any sect,"[21] and the truth selected out of all sects is not vain philosophy, but natural divinity. There is something of the image of God and law of nature written in our hearts and consciences, as is evident by common experience and plain testimonies of the Word of God, and therefore the Scripture does not condemn all philosophy, but vain philosophy (Colossians 2).

These natural notions of the eternal Godhead should excite us to inquire further after God, as the apostle shows in Acts 17:27, because though our natural notions concerning God are true, yet they are such imperfect and obscure notions, or rather hints, that we are by reason of the corruption of our nature, very apt to abuse them, and therefore we must regulate them by the Word of God.

The Godhead is spiritual, and therefore, invisible. The professors of wisdom became fools when, upon a clear sight of some invisible things of God, they changed the glory of God into a visible image made like unto

---

[21] Proverbia etiani non Christianis

corruptible man, and unreasonable creatures. Such images are both artificial and real lies, for by making images of God, these learned fools changed the truth of God into a lie, and then adored and worshiped their own lies (Romans 1:20, 23, 25).

The Godhead is infinite, and the immensity of God's perfection cannot be measured by any created understanding. God is great, and his greatness is unsearchable (Psalm 145:3). The greatness of God is not a greatness of bulk and quantity, but of perfection and excellence. He is great in power, and his understanding is infinite (Psalm 147:5), and therefore his understanding is unsearchable (Isaiah 40:28). When men and angels search furthest into God's perfection, they do most of all discover their own imperfection, for God will make them know that the secrets of his wisdom are double to that which they behold, and that it is impossible by our most accurate disquisition to find out the Almighty unto perfection (Job 11:6-7), but we may find him out unto salvation in the holy Scriptures.

If we sum up all that the philosophers and scholars can attain to in their discourses of this first principle, it will amount to no more than this: men and angels can never comprehend that perfection which dwells in God, for the perfection of God is infinite, and therefore incomprehensible.

Let scholars examine this brief account: *Deus est ens, ens entium, essentia essentiarum, ens purum, ens simplex, ens simpliciter simplex, ens absolutum, ens necessarium, ens absolute necessarium. Ens primum, aeternum, independens, perfectum infinitum, infinite perfectum, and proinde immensum*. Let us therefore study, believe, and embrace the holy Scriptures, which may satisfy and save us.

I confess that I have been very much taken with some discourses in Aristotle's *Metaphysics* concerning the spiritual and eternal efficacy of the first principle, first mover or prime understanding, whose very essence, substance, nature, and being is a spiritual and eternal self-efficacy, from whence it was easy to demonstrate the self-sufficiency and all-sufficiency of this eternal understanding, and from thence to infer that this eternal Spirit, whose very being is efficacy (or as we say: a pure act), should be effectually obeyed and sincerely worshiped with pure and spiritual worship.

I shall not examine those passages which are usually cited out of Plato, Iamblichus, Trismegistus, and others upon this subject, because it is clear to me that those glorious mysteries which they did either discourse or treat of were discovered to them by a Hebrew light. Plato was not called "the Atticising Moses" in vain; Clemens Alexandrinus and several others have said enough of that, and saved me the labor of a learned digression upon that subject; and it is conceived that Christians have inserted such passages into the works of heathens.

The Platonists say "*Lumen est umbra Dei, Deus est lumen luminis.*" The apostle says: "God is light, and in him is no darkness at all," that is: God is perfection itself without any imperfection at all (1 John 1:5). God is a pure act. God is one single, infinite perfection. And therefore as Seneca said: "We need to compose our whole man into an argument of modesty when we discourse on the nature of God, lest we speak anything rashly, or affirm anything that is untrue."

The works of God are great, and his thoughts (decrees and counsels) very deep (Psalm 92:5). Who then is able to sound the depth of his natural perfection, whose immense perfection is like a sea (if there were any such) which has neither banks nor bottom? Who can sound a bottomless depth, or define an infinite perfection? God is near us, nay in us, and yet far off from us. There is an infinite distance between his excellency and our infirmity. He is far off from our senses and from our understanding; and therefore instead of begging for longer time as the philosopher did, I will conclude as the wise man does in Ecclesiastes 7:23-24: "All this have I proved by wisdom: I said I will be wise, but it was far from me; that which is far off and exceeding deep, who can find it out?" Heraclitus put forth a pretty riddle: "If you do not hope for something above hope, you shall never find out that which can never be found."

It is safer, as the poet said, to believe and worship God than to pry into him. *Nam praeter ipsum quaerere acquires nihil.* How much Raymundus de Sabunde, Agostino Steuchus Eugubinus, Pacardus and others would have found without the help of the Scripture, let such as are spiritually judicious judge.

Chapter 2

God is the First, Eternal, & Independent Being, the Fountain of All Being & Well-Being, & Therefore cannot but Be, Exist, & Persist in Being.

It is a rule generally received in the schools that all creatures have more of imperfection and nothingness than they have of being or perfection.[22] But all being, the whole of being is in God. God is *principium totius esse*, the fountain of all being, and well-being, the only self-being.

God is the first, eternal and independent being, and therefore can have no cause of his being without himself, or above himself, because he was before, and is above all causes (Isaiah 44:6).[23] God is the first and the last. He is everlasting, and therefore can have no efficient or final cause; and it is utterly impossible that God should have any matter or form, or anything answerable to either, because it is impossible that anything should set bounds to his boundless being and infinite perfection.

God is αυταιτιος,[24] says the philosopher, and αὐτόθεος says the divine, but we must (as the Scholastics state the point) understand both *sensu negativo*, because God has his being not from any other, but from himself; and God is said to have his being from himself, because his very nature and essence are necessary, and therefore we cannot conceive the divine essence to be void of existence; it is utterly impossible that God should not exist, because the divine nature is a pure act, an absolute, necessary, eternal,

---

[22] Omnes creaturae plus habent non-Entis. quā Entis.
[23] Deus solus est αυτοων, quia se, & per se est, a quo, in quo, per quem & propter quem sunt quaecunque sunt; omnia quippe Deus aut in tempore sustentat in ipsis, aut aeternùm in se.
[24] That is, "caused by himself," or possibly αναιτιος ("uncaused") is intended here.

infinite, independent, single being.[25] We must not conceive that God was first in a naked power of being, and was afterwards reduced unto actual being by his own effectuall power, as if his existence were really distinct from his essence, or did virtually flow from, and consequently depend upon his essence, as its proper cause. For it is manifestly absurd to conceive this pure, infinite and eternal being not to be in act, since it is a pure act. God declares the incomprehensible purity of his infinite and single being in that amazing and yet edifying text: "I am that I am (Exodus 3:14)," as if he had said: "There is nothing in your God which is not God – my attributes do not differ from myself, my being is absolutely necessary, every way perfect, altogether pure, single and infinite."

I do therefore conclude as Jerome, that the very nature of God is being itself, and therefore he ever was and cannot cease to be. He cannot borrow his being from anything, who gives being and well-being to all things.[26] The absolute and independent necessity of the divine being does demonstrate its eternity, and therefore all the differences of time are untied by the Talmudists, to connote the eternity of God in that text Exodus 3:14, according to that excellent commentary made by the apostle in Revelation 1:8: God is the Almighty, which is, and which was, and which is to come.[27]

Hence it is that some have thought fit to translate that text of Exodus 3:14 according to the full scope of the future tense amongst the Hebrews: "I am that I am that I was, and that I will be." For the future tense amongst the Hebrews, points at all differences of time past, present and to come; but others observing the strict and proper signification of the future, translate it thus: "I will be that I will be."[28] The angel of the waters unites all differences

---

[25] Qui verè, necessariò & absolutè est essentia primò & per se est, imò a seipso, & per seipsum existit, & proinde non potest non existere. χαρις απο του ο ων. Revelation 1:4. Vide Hieronym. Epist. ad Marcel. de X. Dei nominibus.

[26] See Jerome on Ephesians 3

[27] Omnia tempora conjuncti de Deo dicta aeternitatem connotant. (Revelation 1:8)

[28] Futurum trium temporum differentias in se continet. Qui erat, qui est, & semper est, uti Epiphanius contra Archonticos. Futurum perseverantiam essendi denotat & independentiam.

of time in that grateful acknowledgement (Revelation 16:5): "Thou art righteous O Lord, which art, and wast, and shalt be, because thou hast judged thus." And: "Jesus Christ (who is one and the same God with his Father) is the same yesterday, and today, and forever (Hebrews 13:8)." The rabbis upon Exodus 3:14 express themselves after this manner: "The blessed God said unto Moses, say unto them, "I that have been, and I the same now, and I the same for time to come," etc., or as others more agreeable to the Chaldee paraphrase: "I, he that is, and was, and hereafter will be, hath sent me unto you.""[29]

But enough of that: it is now time to conclude that this first and independent being cannot be measured in itself, because it is infinite, nor in its causes, for it has no causes, but is from itself, of itself, by itself and for itself; for as the apostle says: "All things are of him, and through him, and to him; to him be glory forever. Amen."[30]

---

[29] See Henry Ainsworth and Andre Rivet on Exodus 3:14
[30] Romans 11:36

Chapter 3

God has Sufficiently & Graciously Revealed Himself in his Holy Word for our Edification & Salvation.

This incomprehensible God, who is of himself and for himself, cannot be made known to his creatures but by himself. Men and angels cannot know him any further than he is pleased to reveal himself unto them.

The word of God is pure and perfect, fully discovering God's mind and our duty. The Scriptures direct us in all points of faith, in all parts of worship, and in all passages of our life and conversation. There is the whole body of religion, and the only right way to salvation sufficiently and graciously revealed unto us by God himself, for God is the author, object, end of true religion, and is the only happiness and salvation of his chosen people, and therefore God alone can direct us how to serve and enjoy his own blessed self in an acceptable and comfortable way, for his glory and our own everlasting satisfaction.[31]

The Jesuits tell us that the Scriptures are but a partial rule, and that we must be beholden to some unwritten word or tradition for the proof of some points, which are necessary to be known and believed for our everlasting salvation. Some instance in the doctrine of the Trinity; others in the worship of the Holy Spirit. The papists do generally acknowledge that it is necessary for the attainment of salvation to believe the number of the persons of the Trinity, and their consubstantiality, because no man can be saved who does not believe in the Father, Son, and Holy Spirit – in all three as in the only true God, one and the self-same God blessed forever. But some of them deny that this mystery is sufficiently revealed in the written word, and therefore I

---

[31] Dogmata theologica non sunt vera quia ecclesia ita testatur, sed quia Deus ita testatur in Scripturis aeternae veritatis.

shall make it my business to confute them, and all that adhere unto them in the following treatise.

The saving knowledge of God in Christ is revealed by the Spirit speaking in the Scriptures of truth; nay, Father, Son, and Holy Spirit do all join in revealing to us the saving mystery of faith and godliness, that by the grace of Christ, the love of God, and communion of the Holy Spirit, we may have a glorious fellowship with all three as one God, the only true God, whom to know is life eternal (John 17:3), we are taught by the Father to come to Christ for salvation (John 6:45), we are taught by the Son (John 1:18, Hebrews 1:2), and we are taught by the Spirit (Hebrews 3:7, Revelation 2:29. and 1 John 5:6).

The Spirit bears witness after an especial manner to this saving truth. It is the Spirit that bears witness, because the Spirit is truth, yet all three (and therefore the whole Trinity: the Father, the Son, and the Holy Spirit) do join in bearing record, and their record is written, for it stands upon record in the gospel, and their record is a saving record, and there can be no other record produced to prove that Christ is our Savior (1 John 5:7, 11, 12, 13, 20; John 20:31). If we study the Scriptures, believe, apply them, worship, and act according to them, then we shall be saved by our faith in the written Trinity: in Father, Son, and Holy Spirit, without the help of any unwritten tradition whatsoever, for the holy Scriptures are able to furnish the man of God unto perfection, and make the simple wise unto salvation (2 Timothy 3:15-17).[32]

Cyril, in his book of the Trinity and person of Christ, put forth not long since by Wegeline, says that he would not speak or think anything of God, but what is written in his Word.[33] Clemens Alexandrinus says that we ought to make good every point in question by the Word of God, because that is

---

[32] Vide Nazian. lib. 5. de Theologiâ Epiphanium Apostolicos redarguentem. Chrysost. in 1 Cor. cap. 2. Basilium in Ethicis.

[33] Cyrillus lib. de Trinit. & personâ Christi. a Wegel. edit.

the surest, nay, that's the only demonstration.[34] He speaks of theological demonstration: that nothing can be embraced with a divine faith but that which is delivered to us upon divine testimony, and we are to seek for the Testimony of God, nowhere but in the written Word of God. And therefore Basil disputes after this manner: "Whatsoever is not in the written Word of God is not of faith, and whatsoever is not of faith is sin, and therefore it is a sin to obtrude any doctrine upon the conscience as an article of faith, which is not written in the Word of God." Putean is bold to say that if Basil's meaning was according to his words, then he was a Huguenot, that is as we tend to say, a Puritan.[35]

When I read what the papists write on this argument, I stand amazed at their blasphemies, and am unwilling to stain my paper with the repetition of them. They who have read Cano, Hosius, Coster, Eck, Gaultier, Charronaeus, Stapleton, and the rest of that rabble, will not wonder that the Socinians call the doctrine of three persons and one God into question, when the papists – who were baptized in the name of the Trinity, and profess that they believe the equality of three distinct subsistences in the same divine essence – do yet notwithstanding in their writings grant as much as the Socinians need to prove, namely that the doctrine of the distinction and equality of persons in the same divine essence cannot be proven but by unwritten traditions, by the testimony of the church of Rome, and so on. And yet several papists undertake to defend the doctrine of the Trinity against the Socinians, though they know that the Socinians do not at all value traditions or the testimony of the church of Rome; and therefore, though several papists write against the Socinians, yet they do promote Socinianism by their vain doctrine of unwritten traditions. Stapleton is not

---

[34] Clement of Alexandria, *Stromata* 7
[35] Vide Basil. Ascet. Reg. 80; Nihil est de fide nisi quod Deus per Apostolos & Prophetas revelavit, aut quod inde evidenter deducitur. Bellarm. l 4. de verbo Dei c. 9.

ashamed to deny that it can be proven out of Scripture that the Holy Spirit is God, or that he is to be worshiped.

But Salmeron deserves commendation in this point: "The Scriptures," he says, "are therefore said to be written by divine inspiration, because they instruct us in divine mysteries concerning the unity of God and Trinity of persons."[36]

Photios in his *Bibliotheca* shows that Ephraeni did not dispute of the consubstantial Trinity out of the testimonies of fathers, but out of the Holy Scriptures.[37] Justin Martyr, Athanasius, Basil, Irenaeus, Cyril, Cyprian, Tertullian, Epiphanius, Theodoret, and many others of the fathers did assert the doctrine of the Trinity, and some of them did confute the Valentinians, Eunomians, Sabellians, Photinians, Arians, Macedonians. Samosatenians, etc. out of the holy Scriptures.

The Nicene Synod did urge Scripture for the maintenance of the truth, which they declared in the confession of their faith; and the synod which met at Constantinople did the like, as is most evident to such as have perused those learned and ancient records.[38] Athanasius confounded the Arians by clear testimonies of Scripture, and in his *Book of the Decrees of the Nicene Synod*, he says that the true disciples of Christ do clearly understand the doctrine of the holy Trinity preached by divine Scripture.

I shall not trouble or amuse the reader by quotations out of Cyril, Ambrose, Hilary, Augustine, Nyssen, Nazianzen, or any of those worthies but now mentioned, whose labors have been ever famous in the church of God, yet I must not omit one pregnant proof out of Augustine, who

---

[36] Vide Salmer. in 2 Epist. ad Timoth. Disput. 4.
[37] Photios, *Bibliotheca*
[38] Vide Cyrill. de Trinit. & pers. Christi c. 10. Theodoret. Epit. divin. dogm. c. de Spiritu Sancto. Damasc. orth. fid. l. 3. Naz. Orat. 23. in laudem Heronis. Athan. de Decret. Synod. Nicen. Eundem Epist. ad Serapion. & de sentent. Greg. Nyssen. Dyons. contra Eunom. Tertul. adversus Praxaean. Theodoret. Dialog. 2. cap. 4. Nazianzen. orat. 37. de Spiritu Sancto. Epiphan. contra Sabel. Basilium contra Eunomium, Sabellium, Arium. Cyprian. lib. 2. adversus Judaeos ad Quinirum, cap. 6. August. contra Maximin. Bellarm. de verbo dei l. 4. c. 11.

appealed from the Nicene and Ariminensian Synods, and challenged Maximinus to dispute with him about the great point of consubstantiality out of the Scriptures. Bellarmine himself is forced to confess that Augustine had good reason to do so, because that point is clear by Scripture. But then we must likewise consider what Augustine says upon this argument, that the thing (or sense of any word) may be in Scripture though the word itself be not to be found there, though the words *Trinity*, *Trin-unity*, and *consubstantial* are not found in Scripture, yet that which is signified by those words may be clearly proved by the holy Scriptures.[39] "These three are one;" "I and my Father are one" – behold a Trinity, Trin-unity, consubstantiality, and all quickly proven.

That rule is of great concern, and very pertinent to the point in hand, which Augustine delivers in his *Answer to Maximinus the Arian*, Book 3 Chapter 3. Out of those things which we read in Scripture, we may collect some things which we do not read, and so both understand and believe the thing which is delivered in other words in Scripture than those which we are now forced to use so that we may confirm the orthodox Christians and refute the gainsayers. But I am weary of this task, and therefore call upon my reader to join with me in searching the Scriptures that we may find out the truth, for reason cannot demonstrate or comprehend these mysteries of faith, and the rule is: *Rationum fulcro dissoluto humana concidit authoritas.*

---

[39] Quod expresse non habetur in Scripturis, potest tamen inde evidenter deduci. Vocabulum in Scripturis non legimus; rem cui hoc vocabulum recte adhibitum est, fideique sensum invenimus. Vide Augustinum Epist. 174. ubi contra Pascentium Arianum disputat. Eundem insuper in Ioannem Tract. 97. Ambrosium lib. de fide contra, Aria nos cap. 5. Augustinum contra Maximinum Arian. Theod. Hist. lib. 1. c. 8. Basil. contra Eunom. c. 4. Tractat. Definit. Tom. 2. Athanas.

Chapter 4

This Single & Eternal Godhead Subsists in Father, Son, & Holy Spirit, Without any Multiplication of the Godhead.

When Gregory of Nyssa undertook to confute the artificial blasphemy of Eunomius, he desired that the true God, the Son of the true God, and the Holy Spirit would direct him into all truth.[40] I have likewise implored the divine assistance of the Father, Son, and Holy Spirit, that I may open this mystery of the single Godhead in three distinct subsistences, with faith and prudence, perspicuity and reverence. I consider that the Godhead is spiritual, and therefore I desire to avoid all carnal expressions in a treatise of this nature.

There is a twofold knowledge of God: absolute and relative. The absolute knowledge of the eternal power and Godhead is in part discovered by the works of God, as has been shown in the first chapter; but the relative knowledge of God (I speak of inward relations between the three subsistences) is not, nay cannot be attained unto by the light of nature; no example can illustrate, no reason angelic or human, can comprehend the hidden excellency of this glorious mystery, but it is discovered to us by a divine revelation in the written word, and therefore our faith must receive, and our piety admire what our reason cannot comprehend. It is fit therefore that this grand mystery of the divine Trin-unity should be soberly explained, that it may be steadfastly believed, and reverently applied in all evangelical administrations.

We read of the Godhead, the nature and subsistence of God in the holy Scriptures.[41]

---

[40] Greg. Nyssen. contra Eunom. lib. 1
[41] Job 12:16, Proverbs 8:14, Isaiah 28:29, Galatians 4:8, Philippians 2:6, Colossians 2:9

(1) The Godhead: θειοτης (Romans 1:20), θεοτητος (Colossians 2:9), θειον (Acts 17:29). I am not at leisure to play the critic upon the words, it is enough for my purpose simply to declare the truth in the most plain and simple manner.

(2) The nature of God is held forth to us in the holy Scriptures, which forbid us to give divine honor to any of those things which are not gods by nature (Galatians 4:8). For the apostle in that place reproves their idolatry, and tells them, that when they knew not God (that is the only true God who is God by nature, because truly God) they did service to them which by nature are no gods; from whence it is easy to conclude that the only true God whom we ought to serve, is God by nature. And we read of the divine nature (2 Peter 1:4) of which all that are regenerate are said to be partakers, because they bear his image; for else it is evident that there is an infinite distance between God and grace, which is not only finite, but imperfect also, and if it were perfected is but an accident; nay, there is an infinite distance between the nature of God, and nature of man in respect of excellency, even then when the two natures are most intimately united as they are by a hypostatical union in the person of the Lord Jesus.

(3) This only true God, who is God by nature, subsists. And if we will seek after him, we shall find that he does not subsist very far from any of us (Acts 17:27). But the Godhead does not subsist out of the Father, Son, and Holy Spirit. For all the fullness of the self-same Godhead is in each one of the three. Therefore, the name of God is attributed to each one of the three, in holy Writ. [1] To the Father (Romans 7:25, 8:3). [2] To the Son (Acts 20:28, Titus 2:13; 1 Timothy 3:16, 6:15-16). [3] To the Holy Spirit (Acts 5:3-4, Psalm 95:3, 8-9 compared with Hebrews 3:1; 1 Corinthians 3:16-17, Hebrews 1:1 compared with 2 Peter 1:21; 1 Corinthians 12:5-6).

And when the name of God is especially attributed to the Father (in regard to order, and that gracious dispensation which is by consent of all three vouchsafed for our salvation) the Son and Spirit are not excluded, as we shall prove at large in this very chapter.

(1) The eternal Godhead subsists in the Father, for we read of his subsistence in Hebrews 1:3. Christ is the express image of his Father's subsistence or person, as we do commonly translate the word, but I do not hear that any but gross atheists have been so bold as to deny the subsistence of God the Father; and therefore I need not superadd anything to so plain a text.

(2) The same Godhead subsists in the Lord Jesus, who is equal to the Father because he subsists in the nature of God (Philippians 2:6).[42] The word υπαρχων is best rendered *subsisting* in that place, because there is a comparison there between two subsistences or persons, the Father and the Son; and therefore the Son counts it no robbery to be equal with the Father, because he subsists in the nature of God. He has the same divine nature, the same Godhead with the Father and all the fullness of the Godhead dwells truly, really, bodily in the Son, for *body* is opposed to *shadow*. Nay, it may be rendered thus: "The Godhead dwells personally in the Son," for σῶμα many times signifies a person. Therefore some learned men take σωματικός to be as much as υποστατικός: all the fullness of the Godhead dwells really in the subsistence or person of the Son (Colossians 2:9). Christ is the illustrious brightness of his Father's glory, the lively character of his Father's subsistence or person (Hebrews 1:3). Christ is not the character of his own subsistence, but of his Father's subsistence, and therefore the Son has a peculiar subsistence distinct from the subsistence of his Father. Christ is the express image of his Father's person, and therefore the person of the Son is distinct from the person of the Father, for no person is the image or character of itself. Concerning the word *subsistence* or *person*, I shall speak fully in the two next chapters, and make it evident that the divine subsistences or persons do infinitely excel the subsistences or persons of men and angels. In the meantime, I shall clearly prove that the Godhead subsists in the Son, and Holy Spirit.

---

[42] εν μορφη θεου υπαρχων

The Godhead subsists in Jesus Christ, who was before the beginning (John 1:1). *Was* notes what is past; and therefore had his being before the beginning of time. That his eternal being is a divine being, is clear, because eternal, and because it is not only said, that he was with God before the beginning, but he was God. Therefore it clearly follows that Jesus Christ is the same eternal God with his Father, for it is impossible that there should be more than one God, as I shall clearly demonstrate before I conclude this chapter.

I wonder at the impudent blasphemy of some who pretend to be saints in these days of error and vanity, and yet are bold to affirm that they themselves are as well and as truly God as Jesus Christ because it is said that they have their being in God (Acts 17:28) are partakers of the divine nature (2 Peter 1:4) and are one with Christ (John 17:21-23, 26).

I shall entreat the men of this persuasion to consider that "Jesus Christ is over all God blessed forever (Romans 9:5)," "God manifest in the flesh (1 Timothy 3:16)," "the blessed and only Potentate, the King of kings, and Lord of lords, who only hath immortality," etc., to whom honor and power everlasting is ascribed (1 Timothy 6:15-16). He is the great God (Titus 2:13); the true God (1 John 5:20). Does any mortal man dare to lay claim to these titles and this honor? To which of the saints or angels did God say at any time, "Thou art my Son, the heir of all things, the illustrious brightness of my glory, and lively character of my person. Thy throne, O God, is forever and ever, and all the angels of God shall worship thee (Hebrews 1)?" These things are so clear and plain, that I am even almost ashamed to write more upon this argument; and yet I am encouraged and even provoked to proceed. Jesus Christ was the wonderful child; a child, and yet a father, the father of eternity;[43] a child, and yet a counselor, the wisest of all counselors, for he is wisdom itself; a child, and yet a God, a mighty God (Isaiah 9:6).

---

[43] Isaiah 9:6 En infantem aeternitatis Patrem, En parvulum optimum maximum, Deum maximum.

Certainly this one text is sufficient to put them to the blush who presume to compare themselves with the Lord Jesus, the mighty God.

Jehovah is a title proper and peculiar unto God (Isaiah 43:11-12).[44] Jehovah is the only Savior and the only God, and Psalm 83:18 states: "That men may know that thou whose name alone is Jehovah, art the most High over all the earth." But the Lord Christ is Jehovah, and therefore the Lord Christ is God. Jehovah sits on a throne in majesty and glory (Isaiah 6:1, 3, 5, 8), but the Lord Christ is this Jehovah, as the apostle assures us (John. 12:41-42. The Lord Christ is that Jehovah to whom every knee must bow; as appears by comparing Isaiah 45:21-25 with Romans 14:9-12 and Philippians 2:6, 9-11. The like is clear by comparing Psalm 102:19, 22, 25-26 with Hebrews 1:10-12. Once more, compare Numbers 14:26-27 with 1 Corinthians 10:9-10 and Numbers 21:6. And hence it is that Christ is so gloriously described (Revelation 1:5-8). He is "Alpha and Omega, the beginning and the ending, which is which was, and which is to come, the Almighty." And therefore he is Jehovah. For the apostle in that place, and so to the end of that chapter, insists upon these and the like expressions which do comprise in them the sense and meaning of that divine and glorious title of Jehovah.

I might further insist upon this argument, and show that the title of *Lord* – so often given to Christ in the New Testament – answers to the title of *Jehovah* in the Old Testament. And as some reverend divines conceive, the apostles did purposely use the title of *Lord* so that they might not offend the Jews with the frequent pronouncing of the word *Jehovah*. "Thou shalt fear Jehovah thy God" (Deuteronomy 6:13. Deuteronomy 10:20) is rendered by the apostle, "Thou shalt worship the Lord thy God" (Matthew 4:10). And so (Deuteronomy 6:5): "Thou shalt love Jehovah thy God, is rendered in

---

[44] Christ is Jehovah and therefore he is God. "Ehié Jehovâ & quod ex eo contractum est Iah ab Hajâ vel havâ (Esse) derivantur, Essentiam infinitam notant. Nomen itaque Jehovae (cui reliqua duo sunt aequalia) Deo proprium est." Gomarus oper. par. 3. disp. 2. *De Deo Vero*.

Matthew 22:37: "Thou shalt love the Lord thy God." I hope no saint will presume to arrogate the title of *Jehovah* to himself, for he whose name alone is Jehovah is the mighty God, the Most High over all the earth.

Jesus Christ is Immanuel, God with us (Matthew 1:23), that God who took flesh and blood (1 Timothy 3:16), and that God who redeemed the church with his own blood (Acts 20:28).

The ancients insist much upon that proof in John 16:15: "All things that the Father hath are mine," compared with John 10:30: "I and my Father are one," and John 10:37, "If I do not the works of my Father, believe me not," for from hence they do conclude that Christ has the same divine nature and Godhead with the Father. They both have the same divine and essential titles and attributes, and perform the same inward operations in reference to all creatures whatsoever; and therefore they did further infer, that they had reason to use the word *consubstantial*; for though the word is not in Scripture, yet the sense and meaning of it is orthodox and canonical, because evidently deduced from these texts and some other Scriptures which we have insisted on before.[45]

I shall add one more Scripture to make it yet more clear: compare John 17:10 with John 16:15: "All things that the Father hath are mine." "Father, all mine are thine, and thine are mine (John 17:10)," that is, whatsoever belongs to the Father as God, belongs to Christ; for we speak not of personal, but essential properties.[46] Christ lays claim to all that is natural, to all that belongs to the Father as God, not to anything which belongs to him as the Father, as the first person of the blessed Trinity. In John 17, Christ proves that the apostles were his apostles because they were his Father's apostles, and given by the Father to him in verse 9, but he gives a more general reason for it in

---

[45] Epiphan. contra Apostolicos. Vide Cyril. lum in Ioh. cap. 3. & 8. Hiuro. in Zach. 2. Ambr. l. 5. de fide cap. 4. Aug. contra Pascen tium; nemo igitur jam calumniaturde verbo; et si enim verbum ipsum in Lege scriptum non reperitur, res tamen reperitur, ego et Pater unum sumus Epist. 174.

[46] παντα οσα εχει ο πατηρ εμα εστιν (John 16:15), τα εμα παντα σα εστιν (John 17:10). Vide D. Glassium in Explic orat. Christi.

verse 10: "And all mine are thine, and thine are mine." It is a general rule expressed in the neuter gender, and therefore cannot be restrained to the apostles, as the Socinians would limit the speech of Christ, but it must be taken in its full extent. But that I may give full weight and measure pressed down and running over, consider that the other text of John 16:15, which has a double note of universality, and therefore is very emphatic in proof of this point: "All things whatsoever that the Father hath (as God) are mine." But the Father has an eternal Godhead, infinite power and majesty; and therefore, says Christ, "they are mine." Epiphanius, disputing against the heresy of Sabellius, expounds this rule thus: "All that the Father has is mine. The Father is God and I am God. The Father is life and I am life, for whatever the Father has is mine."[47]

For the clearer demonstration of this truth, let us now descend to particulars. [1] The attributes of God, [2] the works of God, and [3] the worship of God are all ascribed and given to Jesus Christ, so that we may confess and acknowledge him to be God, the true God, the mighty God, the self-same only God with the Father and the Holy Spirit.

[1] The attributes of God are ascribed to the Lord Jesus. {1} The eternity of God (John 1:1): "In the beginning was the Word." *Was* notes some former duration, and therefore we conclude that he was before the beginning, before any creation or creature; for it is said that he was God in the beginning, and his divine nature whereby he works is eternal (Hebrews 9:14) He is the first and last (Revelation 1:17), hence it is that he is called "the firstborn of every creature," because he who created all, and upholds all, has power to command and dispose of all, as the firstborn had power to command the family or kingdom (Colossians 1:15-17).[48] Compare Isaiah 44:6 with Revelation 22:13 and Proverbs 8:22-23, and with my margin. {2} Jesus Christ is omnipotent (Philippians 3:21). He is called by a metonymy the power of God (1 Corinthians 1:24). He is the Almighty (Revelation 1:8).

---

[47] Epiphanius, *Contra Sabellium*
[48] Micah 5:2, *from the days of eternity*; John 17:5.

He made all things (John 1:3. Colossians 1:16-17, Psalm 102:26, compared with Hebrews 1:8:10, John 1:10). He upholds all things (Hebrews 1:3, Colossians 1:17). {3} Jesus Christ is unchangeable (Hebrews 1:12, cited out of Psalm 102:26-27). {4} Christ is omniscient (John 2:25). He is the searcher of hearts (Revelation 2:23). He knows all things (John 21:17). He is the wisdom of the Father (1 Corinthians 1:24). Of himself, he knows the Father (Matthew 1:27), and according to his own will, reveals the secrets of his Father's bosom, and therefore is called "the Word," and all the treasures of wisdom are in him (Colossians 2:3). {5} The immensity of God belongs to Christ; for he is not contained in any place, who was before there was any place, and did create all places by his own power (John 1:1, 3). Whilst he was on earth in respect of his bodily presence, he was in the bosom of the Father, which must be understood of his divine nature and person (John 1:18).[49] He did come down from heaven, and yet remained in heaven (John 3:13).

[2] Christ performed the works of God, such proper and peculiar, such divine and supernatural works as none but God can perform:[50] he did raise the dead by his own power at his own pleasure (John 5:21, 28-29, John 11:25). He is called the resurrection and the life, because he is the author of both: whatsoever the Father does, the Son does likewise (John 5:17, 19). He wrought miracles, he has the same nature and power with the Father, and therefore he does the same works: he regenerates our souls, pardons our sins, save our souls; he has appeased the wrath, and satisfied the justice of God, by his divine mediation; he gives temporal, spiritual, eternal life (2 Corinthians 5:17, John 6:38:40).[51]

[3] Divine honor is due to Jesus Christ.[52] For: {1} all the glorious angels are commanded to worship him (Hebrews 1:6). {2} All true Christians are described by their calling on and believing in the name of Christ (Acts 9:14,

---

[49] See also: Proverbs 8:22, John 1:1, 3, Matthew 18:20, 28:20
[50] See also: John 2:19, 21
[51] See also: Isaiah 53:4, Acts 20:28, Hebrews 9:12, 14, 26.
[52] See also: Romans 10:14; 1 Corinthians 1:2, John 14:1, Psalm 2:12, Romans 10:11

John 1:12). {3} All are obliged to give the same honor to Christ, which they are required to give to God the Father (John 5:23). {4} Examples every way warrantable, because agreeable to these precepts, are frequent in the Word (Acts 7:59-60; 1 Corinthians 1:2, Revelation 22:20). {5} Baptism is administered in the name and to the honor of Christ (Matthew 28:17-20). {6} At the Day of Judgment, every knee must bow to him, and acknowledge him to be equal to his Father (Isaiah 45:21-25 compared with Romans 14:10-12, Philippians 2:6, 9-11). {7} All that are justified do believe in him; and they who do believe in him shall not be ashamed (Romans 3:25-26; 1 Peter 2:6-7). {8} The apostolic benediction so often repeated in the epistles.

From whence I argue, since God will not give his glory to another, because he is true (Isaiah 48:11) and cannot because he is just, it follows that though Christ be a distinct person, yet he is not a distinct God from his Father, but one and the same God with him, God blessed forever. Much more might be produced upon this argument. That which has been said is abundantly sufficient, if God set it home upon our spirits by his own Spirit; but if men will not be persuaded by these Scriptures, neither would they be persuaded though one should rise from the dead. In the next place I am to demonstrate the divine nature, person, titles, attributes, works, and worship of the Holy Spirit.

(3) The same eternal Godhead subsists in the Holy Spirit, who is God blessed forever. The Holy Spirit is a spiritual and infinite substance, subsisting with peculiar properties, and acting according to the counsel of his divine will. The apostle – having distinguished between the Spirit, and the gifts of the Spirit – shows that the Spirit itself, that one Spirit, that one and self-same Spirit, works and distributes all those excellent gifts according as he pleases (1 Corinthians 12:4).[53]

---

[53] το εν και το αυτο πνευμα (1 Corinthians 12:4, 11); αυτο το πνευμα (Romans 8:4)

Now, [1] these particularizing and indigitating [indicative] terms, that one, that same Spirit. [2] The will of the Spirit. [3] The discriminating energy or efficacy of the Spirit, do all demonstrate the subsistence of the Spirit, and peculiarity of his subsistence. "When the Spirit of truth come, he will guide (John 16:13)." He says not *it*, but *he*, and therefore does not speak of an attribute, but a person, *he*, etc., which is the more to be observed, because the word in the original which signifies *Spirit* is of the neuter gender, and yet our Savior speaking of the Spirit, says *he*, to point out the peculiar subsistence or person of the Spirit, "When he, the Spirit of truth," etc. (John 16:13), and therefore we ought to take special notice of that expression.[54] And all those notes of particularity (1 Corinthians 12) applied to the Spirit, do show that he is a particular, and undivided substance, one Spirit, the same Spirit, the self-same Spirit, one and the self-same Spirit (1 Corinthians 12:4–12).

And that this spiritual particular undivided substance is a divine substance is evident, because it is said that the same Spirit who works all in all is the same Lord and the same God (1 Corinthians 12:5-6) and *Lord* in the New Testament answers to *Jehovah* in the Old, as has been proven above in this very chapter.

When Peter drew up a charge against Ananias, he puts this question to him: "Why hath Satan filled thy heart to lie to the Holy Spirit? thou hast not lied unto men, but unto God (Acts 5:3-4)." The black and unpardonable sin is after a more special manner committed against the Godhead subsisting in the Holy Spirit, and the peculiar office and dispensation of the Holy Spirit, than against the Father or the Son; and that sin is in some respects pronounced the most grievous sin (Matthew 12:32).

If the Holy Spirit were only the power of God, as Socinians love to dream, that sin would not be so highly aggravated, for it is not the highest and foulest aggravation of sin to say it is committed against the power of

---

[54] εκεινος το πνευμα (John 16:13)

God. The Father, Son, and Spirit have but one power, as they have one and the same nature; and therefore the Father is said to work in the Son, and by the Spirit; and hence it is that Christ is called "the power of God" (1 Corinthians 1:24),[55] and the Holy Spirit is called "the power of the Most High" (Luke 1:35) because the power of the Father (who is called "the Most High" in opposition to the highest of creature) resides in, is exercised, and is made manifest by the Holy Spirit, and especially manifested in that omnipotent work of the conception of our Lord and Savior. The very shadow of the Holy Spirit makes a virgin to conceive; this miracle declaring him to be God.

The Holy Spirit is Jehovah, the great God, and King above all gods, as is evident by comparing Psalm 95:3, 6-9 with Hebrews 3:7, 9. The Spirit of Jehovah is the God of Israel (2 Samuel 23:2-3). The people rebelled against Jehovah, and tempted him in the wilderness (Deuteronomy 6:16, Numbers 14:26-27, Deuteronomy 9:7, 24). Now that is meant of tempting and rebelling against the Holy Spirit, as well as against God the Father and Jesus Christ, as is clear, if you compare Isaiah 63:10 and Hebrews 3:7, 9 with the places alleged. The Holy Spirit is that Jehovah who made the New Covenant with his chosen people (Jeremiah 31:31 compared with Hebrews 10:15-16). The Holy Spirit is that Jehovah who spoke by Isaiah the prophet (compare Isaiah 6:8-9 with Acts 28:25-26). We might argue in like manner, from Leviticus 19:2 etc. compared with Hebrews 9:7-8 and several other places (Numbers 12:6, Hebrews 1:1; 2 Peter 1:21; 1 Corinthians 12:5-6).[56]

The *omnipotence* of the Spirit is clearly proven because he works all in all, according to the counsel of his will, and works miracles, which transcend not only the common course and order, but the whole power of nature (1 Corinthians 12:6, 9-11) such are the raising of the dead (Romans 8:11), the regeneration and sanctification of our souls (Titus 3:5; 1 Corinthians 6:11),

---

[55] Vide Gomarum Disp. de Trinit. Tom. 3. Disp. 7. & 8.
[56] See Numbers 12:6, Hebrews 1:1-2; 2 Peter 1:21; 1 Corinthians 3:16-17; 1 Corinthians 6:19 compared together; 1 Corinthians 12:5-6.

and therefore he is called "the Holy Spirit," because the Father and the Son do according to divine dispensation sanctify us by the operation of the Holy Spirit. Moreover, the Holy Spirit did teach the prophets and apostles, and lead them into all truth, he overshadowed the virgin, etc. (John 16:13, Acts 2:4; 1 Peter 1:11, and 2 Peter 1:21). The Holy Spirit is the great God and Creator of all things (Psalm 93:3, 5, Hebrews 3).

The Holy Spirit is *omniscient*, for he knows the deep things of God, and the secrets of men. He inspired the prophets and apostles, and moved them to reveal the mysteries of faith and godliness (1 Corinthians 2:10-11; 1 Peter 1:11; 2 Peter 1:21, Romans 9:1, Revelation 2:23).

The Holy Spirit is *omnipresent*. He dwells in all saints as in a temple, he repairs, adorns, beautifies his temple, and acts in every single saint, not as the spirit of disobedience acts in children of wrath, for we cannot fly from the presence of the Spirit because he is omnipresent (Psalm 139:7).[57]

By what has been already written, it is evident that the Holy Spirit has the titles and attributes of God,[58] and that he performs works proper to God.[59] And that divine honor is due unto him, I shall clearly prove because it is denied by the blasphemous wits of this discoursing age.[60]

The Holy Spirit – who spoke by Isaiah the prophet – is worshiped by the angels of God, as is most evident by comparing Isaiah 6:3 and 6:9 with Acts 28:25-26. The whole church of God is exhorted to worship the Holy Spirit as the Great God, as Jehovah, as our Maker; to bow down and kneel before him, that is, to give him divine worship both inward and outward, because he is our God, as appears by comparing, Psalm 95:3, 6-7 with Hebrews 3:7-9. The apostle gives divine honor to the Holy Spirit when he appeals to him as to the searcher of hearts (Romans 9:1), and the Holy Spirit

---

[57] Romans 8:9; 2 Timothy 1:14; 1 Corinthians 3:16, Romans 8:26-27
[58] 1 Corinthians 12:11
[59] 1 Thessalonians 2:13. Vide Basilium. lib. de Spiritu Sancto.
[60] See Nazianzen, Orat. 37 & testimoniorum examē de Deitate Spiritus Sancti inventes. Petrum Damianū lib. 3. Epi 1.

who speaks to the churches, joins with the Son of God (who speaks to them also) in searching of the heart and reins (Revelation 2:17-18, 23), and all the churches are commanded to hearken to both as unto God blessed forever. Our souls and bodies are said to be the temples of God because they are the temples of the Holy Spirit, and therefore we are commanded to worship and glorify the Holy Spirit with our souls and bodies; for the Spirit dwells in his temple so that he may be worshiped in his temple. The temple is a profane place if there is no worship there; and it is, and must be, pure, holy and spiritual worship, and sacrifice, such as the Holy Spirit delights in, else the temple will be defiled and destroyed. Compare 1 Corinthians 3:15:16, 17; 1 Corinthians 6, 19, 20; 2 Corinthians 6:16, 18, and 2 Corinthians 7:1.

The church is blessed in the name of the Holy Spirit as in the name of God, and the communion of the Holy Spirit is spiritual and saving as well as the special grace of Christ, and love of the Father, as appears by that solemn apostolical benediction (2 Corinthians 13:14).[61] And the beloved disciple proclaims the Spirit to be the fountain of grace and peace as well as the Father of Jesus Christ, and therefore begs grace and peace of the Spirit of grace (who purifies and pacifies our hearts) for all the churches (Revelation 1:4). The Holy Spirit regulates all churches and church affairs (Acts 13:2, 4; 15:28; 20:28). Baptism is administered in the name and for the honor of the Holy Spirit (Matthew 8:19). The Holy Spirit bestows upon us and works in us those spiritual and glorious blessings which are sealed in or conveyed by baptism, and therefore we are more especially baptized by the Holy Spirit (Matthew 3:11, John 3:5-6), for we are born of the Spirit, regenerated, washed, renewed by the Spirit, who purifies the soul as water does the body (Titus 3:5-6).

The violation of the honor and worship of the Holy Spirit is most severely punished (Mark 3:29, Hebrews 6:4, Hebrews 10:28-29),[62] and

---

[61] See also: 1 Corinthians 6:19-20, Romans 12:1-2; 1 Peter 2:5; 1 Corinthians 3:16-17, Ephesians 2:18, 22.
[62] See Augustine, *Contra Maximinium*

therefore there is special care taken in the holy Scriptures both for the preservation and vindication of the honor of the Holy Spirit.[63] We must not grieve, vex, resist, or quench the Holy Spirit, that is, we must not displease him, we must not disobey him, we must obey his dictates and his motions; we must be quickened, taught, led, ruled, governed by him. We must attribute all the glorious titles to the Holy Spirit given him in Scripture, of which we have so largely discoursed. We must acknowledge him to be the Spirit of truth, and therefore must believe in him, the Spirit of supplication, the Spirit of grace and holiness, and therefore love him and pray to him. We must either renounce our baptism in his name,[64] or else we must confess that we are obliged to believe in him, reverence, love, obey, glorify him with all inward and outward worship, for we are debtors to the Spirit to live to the Spirit, and glorify the Spirit of regeneration who works in us the instrument of justification, so that there may be an effectual application of Christ to our souls. Though Christ make the purchase, the Spirit of adoption makes the assurance: he seals us up to the day of redemption, and therefore good reason have we to offer up our souls and bodies in a spiritual sacrifice to him; for these temples were made for sacrifice (Romans 12:1-2; 1 Peter 2:5). Now if God, who will not give his glory to another because he is true and just, gives all this glory to the Holy Spirit, it concerns us to glorify him.

If there were not all, this and a great deal more to be said for the honor of the Holy Spirit, yet it were an invincible argument to me if I could only say that the Holy Spirit is God, and therefore to be worshiped as God with divine worship. The Holy Spirit is one with the Father and the Son, one God, and therefore all three are to be worshiped with the same divine worship. It were enough for such men as have not so much as heard whether there be any Holy Spirit or not (Acts 19:2), to talk as the filthy dreamers and blasphemous heretics of this rotten age usually do, who belch out the

---

[63] Acts 7:51, Isaiah 63:10, Ephesians 4:30, Hebrews 3:7-8, Galatians 5:18, 25, Romans 8:12-14, 1 Thessalonians 5:19

[64] 1 Corinthians 12:13, Matthew 3:11, John 3:5

language of hell against the Spirit of grace, and I cannot but wonder that subtle Jesuits, Arminians, and Socinians who pretend to study and search the Scriptures, should say that there is nothing to be found in Scripture concerning the worshiping of the Holy Spirit.

That the Spirit acts according to the counsel of his divine will, has been sufficiently proven; only it must be considered that as Father, Son, and Spirit have but one nature, so they have but one will.

Concerning the peculiar and personal properties of the Holy Spirit, I shall treat when I come to speak of the distinction of these subsistences.

For the conclusion of this chapter, I am to prove that the Godhead subsists in Father, Son, and Spirit – all three without any multiplication of the Godhead.

The Father and the Son are but one God (John 10:30): "I and my Father are one." The Father, Son, and Spirit, all three are but one God (1 John 5:7). There is but one God (Ephesians 4:6, Deuteronomy 6:4, Isaiah 44:6, 8; Isaiah 45:2, 1:22). Nay there can be but one God; there can be but one most perfect being, one infinite perfection; the most perfect being is the most single being, and therefore Father, Son, and Holy Spirit are all three but one only God; they are consubstantial, coequal, coeternal. They have one nature, mind, will, power, and Godhead. Some of the ancients who meant well said there were three substances, but they meant three subsistences or persons, as Hilary expounds them, for he says, "They did not intend to assert three different essences."[65]

Hence it is, that such as were more wary in their expressions, did use the word *subsistence*, and said that there were three subsistences, but one

---

[65] "Deus unus, trinunus, solus, unicus, simplicissime unús, unicissime unicus. The Father, Son, and Holy Spirit all three are but one only God (1 John 5:7, John 10:30). Unitatem essentiae contra Arianos, Trinitatem personarum contra Sabellianos tuemur. Tres substantias esse dixerunt, Subsistentium personas per Substantias edocentes, non Substantiam Patris et Filij et Spiritus Sancti diversitate dissimilis essentiae separantes ex concil." Antiochen. Hilar. de Synodo adversus Arianos.

substance or essence in this divine Trinunity. This is the first of all the commandments, to acknowledge one only God (Mark 12:29). As there is but one mediator to intercede, so there is but one God to justify, and intercede unto for justification (1 Timothy 2:5, Romans 3:30, Galatians 3:20). It is one and the same God who commands heaven and earth, (Deuteronomy 4:35, 39, Isaiah 37:16).

The gods of the heathens were false gods, dunghill-gods, or devil-gods: magistrates are but mortal gods; they must die, and rise to judgment, and hold up their hand at the tribunal of Jehovah (Psalm 86:8, 9:10, Psalm 82:6-7; 1 Corinthians 8:6). I prove this point at large, because I perceive by Mr. Fry's sad account that we are much misconstrued in this weighty point, as if by acknowledging three distinct subsistences, we did create two new gods, and affirmed Jesus Christ and the Holy Spirit to be two distinct gods both from the Father and from one another. But we are no Tritheites:[66] we acknowledge a Trinunity as well as a Trinity in opposition to the error of the Tritheites; we believe the unity of the Godhead; and I never read of the Trinity of the Godhead in English, until I read it in the title of Mr. Fry his opinion, which he delivered to the house, and has since printed and published to the world.[67]

We do believe that God is one, most singly and singularly one, and an only one.[68] The unity of the Godhead is neither a generic nor a specific unity, but a most singular unity, which I need not call a numerical unity, as some do. I had rather call it the most single, singular, and perfect unity, as

---

[66] We do not only acknowledge a Trinity, but a Trinunity in opposition to the error of the Tritheites. Unum & Trinum de monstrant trinunum Deum simplicissimè unicum (1 John 5:7). Hi tres sunt unus ille Deus, trinunus Deus, Infinitum, hoc est, summe & absolutè perfectum, non potest esse nisi unum. Si unus potest emnia, quid opus est pluribus diis? omnia autem potest Deus trinunus. Deus est trinunus, est unus absolute, trinus relate; unus quoad essentiam, trinus quoad subsistentiam.

[67] See Mr. Fry's *Answer to the Charge of Blasphemy and Error*, etc. p. 20, 22.

[68] Deus ita est unus, ut etiam fit solus, & ita solus ut non possit esse alius. En naturam infinitam summē unam, & unicissimè unicā.

some profound divines do, who have told me what I have read in others, that I had need be very curious in the delivery of this weighty point.[69]

All the three persons have one and the same single and infinite Godhead, and therefore must mutually subsist in one another, because they are all three one and the same infinite God. Three consubstantial, coessential, coeternal, coequal persons, are distinguished but not divided; are united but not confounded;[70] united in their one nature, not confounded in their distinct subsistences; nay, though their subsistence is in one another, yet their subsistences are distinct, but their nature most singularly the same;[71] nay, the divine nature is as singular as any one of the single subsistences, and yet whatever is proper to the divine nature is common to all three of these divine subsistences; and the divine nature does not subsist out of these three divine subsistences.[72]

But the more we deliver concerning the unity of the Godhead, the more advantage do the Socinians hope to gain for the justifying of their blasphemous dreams. For if this unity of the Godhead is not only notional but real, and God is most singly and singularly one, and an only one, as has been proven. "Why then," they say, "we will be bold to urge an invincible argument to prove that God the Father alone is God, and therefore neither Jesus Christ nor the Holy Spirit is truly and properly God by nature. God the Father alone is the only true God, but neither the Son nor the Holy Spirit is God the Father. Ergo, neither the Son nor the Holy Spirit is the only true God." For the proof of this proposition – that the Father alone is the only true God – they cite some of those places which I have alleged to prove the

---

[69] Deus non tam unus numero dicendus est, quàm unicus. Pater & filius sunt unum potius, quàm unus. (John 10:30). Sunt inquies unus Deus, imò potius sunt idem unicusque Deus.

[70] Personae coessentiiales & in se mutuò subsistentes inconfusè uniuntur, & indivisè discernuntur.

[71] Natura divina est singularissima, & simplicissimè unita.

[72] Natura divina est simplicissimè singularis, & tamen communis Patri, Filio & Spiritui Sancto. Nec mirum, cùm fit simplicissimè & perfectissimè infinita.

unity of the Godhead;[73] but they lay most weight upon John 17:3. "Behold," say they, "a plain acknowledgment from the mouth of Jesus Christ:"[74] Christ acknowledges his Father to be the only true God, and therefore excludes both himself and the Holy Spirit; for there is but one only God, and God the Father alone is that only true God.[75]

These subtle heretics are guilty of a pitiful piece of sophistry in the drawing up of this argument, which is more full of blasphemy than wit, for observe:

(1) Our Savior does not say "That we may know thee only to be the true God" but "That we may know *thee*:[76] the only true God." For as Athanasius said well, "We must know Jesus Christ to be the only true God also; because Christ, and so the Holy Spirit also, is one and the same God with the Father."[77] All three persons are the only true God; for though they differ in subsistence, they do not differ in nature, they have all of them one and the same singular Godhead, the self-same divine nature; the Father, Son and Holy Spirit, are but one and the same infinite Spirit, one Jehovah, one God, who is the only true God, God blessed forever.[78]

Now it does not follow that the Father, Son, and Spirit differ essentially because they differ personally, for these three are one (1 John 5:7). One God, who is the only true God. The Father is the only true God; behold, the predicate in that proposition is not personal, but essential, and every essential predicate belongs to each and every one of the three persons, because they

---

[73] 1 Corinthians 8:5-6; 1 Timothy 2:5, Ephesians 4:6

[74] Christus ipse dicit patrem suum esse illum unum solum verum Deum etiam respectu sui. Seipsum namque ibidem nominat atque à Patre distinguit. Socinus in tract. de Deo, Christo, & Spiritu Sancto. Catechis. Racoviens. cap 1. p. 37. Socin. libro quod Evangelici, etc.

[75] John 17:13

[76] En structuram Grammaticam {*ut cognoscant Te illum solū verum Deum*} non autem {*ut cognoscant solū Te, illum verum Deum*}.

[77] En structuram logicam, particula exclusiva Solum non cohaeret cum subjecto, sed cum praedicato, pater est ille Deus, qui solus verus Deus est.

[78] Distinctionem personalem concedimus, essentialem negamus. Hi qui tres sunt personaliter, sunt unum essentialiter.

have one and the same divine essence, and therefore the apostle says *these three are one*.[79]

(2) Observe how John 17:3 is expounded by John himself in 1 John 5:20. "And we know that the Son of God is come, and hath given us an understanding that we may know him that is true, and we are in him that is true, in his Son Jesus Christ. This is the true God and eternal life." Now add John 17: "This is life eternal to know thee the only true God," etc. and then put all together thus, "This is life eternal that they might know thee the only true God and Jesus Christ whom thou hast sent." "The only true God," for as John himself expounds, this Jesus Christ is the true God and eternal life (1 John 5:20).

(3) Observe that John himself expounds this also of the Holy Spirit;[80] for, Father, Son, and Holy Spirit are one only God (1 John 5:7): "These three are one," and therefore it does not at all follow that the Son and Spirit are not the true God because the Father is the only God; for they are all three one and the same God, who is the only God, the only true God.

(4) Observe that I do not (as some learned men do) only affirm that the word *only* is put there to exclude false gods, but I say that it also denies Jesus Christ and the Holy Spirit to be different gods – other gods from God the Father – because they are one and the same God with the Father, as is evident in those two places (1 John 5:7, 20) cited before.[81]

Those learned men do well to exclude false gods; the Socinians do ill to exclude the Son and Spirit who are the same God with the Father. *Only*

---

[79] Non enim sensus est, solus verus Pater est Deus, sed Pater est solus verus Deus praeter quem non est alius Deus.
[80] Spiritus Sanctus est αὐτόθεος non relate quá persona procedens, sed absolute quá Deus est per Essentiam perfectissimam á se ipsâ existentem; est enim Spiritus Elohim patri filioque coessentialis et coaequalis. (Genesis 1:2).
[81] Particula exclusiva {*Solum*} προς αντι διαςολην αντι διαιρεσιν non reliquarum Trinitatis personarum sed fictitiorum numinum usurpatur, ita ut excludat ea tantum quae extra naturam divinam sunt, et á Patre res essentiâ diversae sunt; eadem autem natura divina est in Patre, Filio et Spiritu Sancto.

excludes every false god; but the Son and Spirit are (as the Father is) the only true God, blessed forever.

The term *only* does not exclude any divine person,[82] but it does exclude each and every one of the creatures, because every divine person has the same divine nature, but no creature is capable of the divine nature, unless we do understand it as 2 Peter 1:4 is to be understood, of the image of God, or having such an interest in the divine attributes, that God will exercise and put forth his wisdom, power, and all, for their everlasting good, and be himself their all sufficient reward, portion, and objective happiness. And it is to be observed that the terms *only* and *true* are both applied to the same part of the proposition, namely to the predicate alone.

(5) "This is life eternal, to know thee." But the text says, "This is life eternal to know Jesus Christ" also; that is, this is the way and means for the obtaining of eternal life, and this is the beginning of eternal life, to know, believe, love and obey Jesus Christ.[83] But eternal life is perfected by knowing of God in heaven, not by faith but by sight. Now eternal life does not consist in the knowledge, belief, or love of any mere creature; and therefore the Godhead of Jesus Christ is proven out of this very text, which those who deny his Godhead urge in order to justify their blasphemy in the denial of it.[84]

(6) Eternal life consists in knowing of Jesus Christ, whom God has sent to be our mediator. This eternal life will be perfected in heaven, when the mediation of Christ will have an end. Therefore, it is the knowing of and believing in this mediator as God satisfying for us which makes us happy, for

---

[82] Ut cognoscant Te, qui es ille Deus, qui solus verus est, quoniam illa est sola Deitas vera, quae est in Patre, & sic non excluditur Filius, qui est in Patre unus idem que Deus cum Patre & Spiritu Sancto. Ioh. 1. 1. 1 Io. 5, 7.

[83] Vita aeterna hic inchoative habetur cognoscendo Deum per fidem, habetur autem in coelis perfecte cognoscendo Deum per visionem. Verba de [προποτισμω] vitae intelligenda. See Cyril *On John* Book 2, Hilary *On The Trinity* Book 9, & *Contra Julian* Book 5, and Ambrose, *Of Faith* Book 5.

[84] Vita aeterna est solummodo in vero & aeterno Deo, in summo bono, uti Ambrosius cont. Arianos.

he perfects the work of mediator as God by his eternal Spirit, that is his divine nature (Hebrews 9:14) and by the blood of God (Acts 20:28), by the sufferings of the Lord of glory (1 Corinthians 2:8), for he obtained eternal redemption for us by virtue of his eternal Spirit (Hebrews 9:12, 14).

(7) To know Jesus, that is, to know him as a Savior, as one that saves us from our sins, is to know him as a God,[85] as one God with his Father, as the true God and the only God; according to that which we read Isaiah 43:10-12, 25. "That ye may know and believe and understand that I am he; I even I am Jehovah, and beside me there is no Savior."[86] And Isaiah 45:21-25: "There is no God else beside me. A just God and a Savior, there is none beside me. Look unto me and be ye saved all the ends of the earth, for I am God, and there is none else. To me every knee shall bow. In Jehovah have I righteousness. In Jehovah shall the seed of Israel be justified."

Compare this with Romans 14:10-11, and the Socinians may as safely conclude that there is no other God but Jesus Christ, as they may conclude that there is no God but God the Father, from John 17. But they and we ought to conclude from these and the other Scriptures mentioned before, that Jesus Christ is not a different God from his Father, but is one and the same God with him.[87]

These exclusive and restrictive terms (*one* and *alone*, etc.) do not then exclude any of those three who are one in nature and essence, though they differ in their manner of subsistence. For I cannot conclude from 1 Corinthians 8:6 that "to us there is but one God, the Father," etc., that the Father only is God; any more than I can conclude from the words following in the very same verse – "and one Lord Jesus Christ" – that Christ only is Lord, and so exclude the Father from Lordship as the Socinians would

---

[85] Isaiah 43:10-11, 25. compared with Hebrews 1-3; 1 John 1:7, Act. 4:12
[86] O Jehovah justitia nostra. Jeremiah 23:6, Psalm 68:18-20 compared with Ephesians 4:8, Isaiah 8:14, 16 compared with Romans 9:30, 33.
[87] Secundum Philosophum Iolus. dem est quod non cum alio, & ideo tantummodo excludit illud quod alietatem dicit; Filius autem non est alius à Patre nessentia, sed tantum in persona. Lyranus in locum.

exclude the Son from the Godhead. 1 Timothy 6:14-16 is urged by some to prove that Jesus Christ only has immortality, but they dare not conclude from thence that God the Father is not immortal.[88] I read Matthew 23:10: "One is your Master, even Christ," but I must not conclude that the Father is not our Master; for the Father teaches (John 6:45) and the Holy Spirit was Doctor, Master, Teacher, even to the apostles themselves (John 14:26, 16:13).

If that text of 1 Timothy 6:15-16 should be meant, as some conceive it is, of God the Father, yet I find the same titles given to Jesus Christ in Revelation 19:16, and therefore I conclude that both are one and the same immortal God and King (1 Timothy 1:12, 16-17; 1 John 5:20).

I read in 1 Corinthians 12:4 that "the same God worketh all in all," and verse 11, that "one and the self same Spirit worketh all," but I dare not conclude from thence that the Spirit only is God, and that the Father and the Son work nothing at all.

From these and many other such like expressions, we may safely conclude:

(1) That these terms *one* and *only* are not always universally exclusive in the Scripture sense, if all circumstances are duly considered and the Scriptures rightly compared. In 1 Corinthians 9:6, we read: "I only and Barnabas." The word *only* does not exclude Barnabas, but includes him. Barnabas was joined with Paul, but Jesus Christ is more nearly joined with the Father. In John 8:9, Jesus was left alone; but the woman was with him, and all that were for her condemnation are excluded.[89] In 1 Kings 12:20, there are two exclusive terms found here: "There was *none* followed the house of David but the tribe of Judah *only*," and yet the tribe of Benjamin adhered to David, as you may read in the next verse. But surely the Father, Son, and Holy Spirit are more closely united than the tribe of Judah was

---

[88] See Augustine, Tractate 105 in John, Athanasius, *Disputation Against Artum in the Council of Nicea*, Nazianzen, Oration 36, Ambrose *On Faith* Book 5, Basil *Contra Eunomium* Book 4, Cyprian *Against the Jews, To Quirinus*.

[89] See Glassium on John 17

with the tribe of Benjamin. In Deuteronomy 1:36, we read that "None should see the good land save Caleb," but Joshua is joined with him in verse 38, and therefore he was not excluded. You see, here is some union or conjunction still between the persons that are included; but there is the highest union, nay, unity between the Father, Son, and Spirit, because these three are one in nature, and that nature most simply single, and singularly one.

(2) When the term *only*, or any like term, is applied to the divine nature, or to any divine title, attribute, or work, the Father, Son, and Holy Spirit – being one in nature[90] – cannot be divided or separated by that exclusive term, though there is a personal difference between them, and a special order and dispensation to be observed amongst them, as we shall hereafter prove.[91] But the intent of the Holy Spirit is to exclude all that are not gods by nature, as the apostle speaks (Galatians 4:8) from the Godhead, and from laying any claim to the natural attributes of God, or pretending to do any work that is proper and peculiar to God.

The true and living God is opposed to idols (1 Thessalonians 1:9). But Jesus Christ and the Holy Spirit are to be acknowledged and served as one true and living God with the Father. The living God, the God of truth, and King of eternity, is opposed to those counterfeit gods (Jeremiah 10:11-12). And therefore when the apostle says "There is no other God but one (1 Corinthians 8:4)," he tells you whom he excludes: such as are but conceited gods, so called and so reputed, equivocal gods (1 Corinthians 8:5-6). The Lord Jesus and the Holy Spirit are God by nature, the same God with the Father, and therefore they are not excluded.

In like manner, when it is said that Jehovah alone did lead the people in the wilderness, and conduct them unto Canaan, that exclusive particle is put

---

[90] See Augustine, *de Praedest. Sanct.*, Chapter 8. Quicquid est essentiae divine & denominationis abea, non unus de Filio & Spiritu Sancto, quam de ipso Patre enuntiatur.

[91] Omnia Trinitatis opera ad extra sunt inseparabilia.

to exclude strange gods, such as were then idolized, but were indeed no gods, as is most evident from Deuteronomy 32:12. So Jehovah alone did lead him, and there was no strange god with him. But these strange gods who are here excluded, were no gods, as is clear by comparing the 16th and 21st verses of the same chapter.

I have already proven that the title of *Jehovah* is given both to Christ and the Holy Spirit, and therefore when it is said "Jehovah alone did lead them in the wilderness," the Son and Spirit are not excluded; for the Spirit did instruct and guide them in the wilderness (Nehemiah 9:20), and the Spirit did instruct their teachers also, but they rebelled against the Spirit (Isaiah 63:10). And Jesus Christ, the angel of God's presence, was present with them to guide them (Exodus 23:21). The name of God and the nature of God is in him, for he is to pardon sin or punish as he pleases.[92] Our Savior is called "the only Lord" and "the only wise God" (Jude 4, 25), but the Father is not thereby excluded from being God, for he is the only wise God also (1 Timothy 1:17), and therefore by the same reason the Father is the only true God and the Son and Spirit are the very same only true God also.

When our Savior presses that text of Matthew 4:10: "Thou shalt worship the Lord thy God, and him only shalt thou serve," he does not exclude himself or the Holy Spirit, for both are to be worshiped with divine worship, as has been already proved at large in this very chapter. Many other proofs might be produced from other Scriptures, and several other arguments collected from John 17 to prove that Jesus Christ is not excluded from being

---

[92] Nomen Dei proprium in medio ejus h. e. est proprium ejus atqueintimum. D. Glassius de Trinitate p. 193. Christus nondum carne vestitus nomen Angeli assumpsit, propter familiarem cùm populocō municationem; nomen autem Jehovae retinuit. Jud. 6. 11. 14, 16, 20, 21, 25. c. 2, 7, 4, 5. cap. 13. 5. 13. [Hosea] 12:5. Genesis 32:29-30, Zechariah 2:3, 5, 10; 1 Corinthians 10:4. Calvin, *Institutes of the Christian Religion*, Book 1 Chapter 13.

the same only God with his Father.[93] To know Christ who is God, and anointed of God (Hebrews 1:8-9, Psalm 45). To know Christ whom thou hast sent, ergo he was a divine person before he was sent to take the human nature, and he had eternal glory with his Father before the world was (John 17:5). Nay, his calling of God *Father* makes him equal with God; nay, he is not only equal to, but one with his Father, (John. 5:18, John 10:30). Moreover, if the Father does not have a divine and eternal Son how is he a divine and eternal Father? Finally, if the Father, Son, and Holy Spirit are not all three the same true God, then there is no God, for these three are one, and therefore all three are one God, or else there is no God at all, from whence it will follow, that if we will be Socinians, we must be atheists. The Son and Spirit have the same nature with the Father; and therefore if his nature be divine, so is theirs.

---

[93] Isaiah 37:16. Christus est Deus in propitiatorio super Cherubim manifestatus. Romans 3:25. Rex Regum Revelation 19:16. qui fecit caelum, & terram. John 1:3, Hebrews 1:2-3, Colossians 1:16. Ergo Christus etiam est Deus ille solus, idem unicus que cum Patre Deus. Isaiah 25:8-9, Malachi 3:1, Jeremiah 33:15-16. & Jeremiah 23:6, Romans 14:10-12, John 20:28.

Chapter 5

The Manner of God's Being or Subsisting in the Father, Son, & Holy Spirit, is the Best Manner of Being that is or can be, & the Single Godhead is Thereby Thrice Illustrious Throughout the World.

Hitherto we have contended for the truth of this divine being or subsisting; now we shall demonstrate the excellency thereof. God is made known to us as the everlasting Father of our Lord Jesus Christ, and is to be adored and worshiped as the Father of our Lord Jesus (Romans 15:6, Ephesians 1:3; 2 Corinthians 1:3).[94] If God had been the Father of men and Father of angels only, and not the Father of our Lord Jesus, he would not have been so exceeding glorious as now he is, for angels have but a finite excellency; but when he begets a Son equal to himself, without any change in himself; and the begetting of this glorious person, is as eternal as the divine nature itself, this mystery is exceeding glorious and admirable, and – like the Godhead – incomprehensible.

Moreover, the Lord Jesus Christ, his own Son (Romans 8:32) and his only Son begotten by eternal generation (John 1:14), being the illustrious brightness of the Father's glory, and the express character of his subsistence, is so exceedingly glorious, that the most glorious angels above are commanded to adore and worship him (Hebrews 1:3-6).[95] "For to which of the angels said God at any time, Thou art my Son, this day have I begotten thee? And therefore when he brings his first-begotten, and his only begotten

---

[94] En cultum propriè Evangelicum, concordé, Deum ac Patrem Domini nostri Jesu Christi concorditer colimus, uno ore uti Christianos decet glorificamus

[95] En Patris Hypostasin in filio refulgentem: En Filii Hypostasin eum à Patre distinguentem.

Son into the world, he saith, And let all the angels of God worship him." Behold how the Godhead shines gloriously not only in one single person, but in Father and Son both, by this manner of subsistence, that every tongue may confess Jesus Christ to be God and Lord, to the glory of God the Father. And therefore the Father is not lessened or robbed of his glory, by the glory of his coequal Son (Philippians 2:6, 11).

But there is a pious acknowledgment made of this glorious mystery, which very much does redound to the glory of God the Father. For by this means, God the Father is acknowledged to be the first personal principle subsisting of himself, and by himself; for he received not his subsistence from any other, and he gives subsistence unto two glorious persons equal with himself. The Socinians seem to be very zealous for the glory of God the Father; and therefore they deny the Godhead of Christ and the Holy Spirit, to the glory of God the Father, as they pretend; but the Scripture teaches us the contrary, namely to confess the Godhead of Christ and the Holy Spirit to the glory of God the Father. For it does exceedingly redound to the glory of the Father, that he gives subsistence unto two glorious persons who are equal to himself, and yet receives no subsistence from them, or any other. "For as the Father hath life in himself, so hath he given to the Son to have life in himself (John 5:26)."

There is a subsisting life given to the Son by an eternal generation, and the Father has life in himself, and self-subsistence also. And yet on the other side, it is no dishonor to the Son to be begotten of the Father, and to receive subsisting life from the Father; for the Son has life in himself also,[96] and being God of himself, quickens whom he will by his divine power even as the Father does, for he has the very same power and will which the Father has, because they have both one and the same divine nature.[97] And therefore the Jews did conclude rightly when they said that our Lord Jesus made himself equal with God by saying he was the Son of God (John 5:18). It is no

---

[96] Vitam dedit Pater Filio vere subsistentem non Alicnat. one, sed Communicatione.
[97] John 10:30, 1:33-34

dishonor to Jesus Christ to receive subsisting life in such a glorious way from the Father, as that he is equal with the Father, nay, one with the Father, and therefore is to be worshiped with one and the same worship with the Father, with divine and spiritual worship, inward and outward worship the worship of our bodies and souls, of our whole man.[98] For all men are bound to honor the Son, as they honor the Father (John 5:23). And let all Socinians take special notice of what follows: "He that honoreth not the Son, honoreth not the Father which hath sent him (John 5:23)." Let them not then pretend that they dishonor the Son (by denying his Godhead) to the glory of God the Father; for the Father will maintain and vindicate the honor of his first-begotten, and only-begotten Son. And let them diligently consider that text of 2 John 9: "Whosoever transgresseth and abideth not in the doctrine of Christ, hath not God; he who abideth in the doctrine of Christ, he hath both the Father and the Son." It is for the honor of our great ruler Jesus Christ, that he was begotten from the days of eternity (Micah 5:2).

Finally, it much redounds to the glory of the Father and the Son that both do concur to give subsisting life to the coequal Spirit by eternal spiration. The Father and Son do both breathe forth this glorious Spirit, the Spirit of Elohim, of both persons (Genesis 1:2). The Spirit that proceeds from the Father (John 15:26) is sent by Christ from the Father, and the Spirit is given by Christ. Christ breathed upon the apostles when he gave the Holy Spirit to them, to show that the Spirit was breathed forth by himself as well as from the Father (John 20:22).[99] And he is often called "the Spirit of the Son." The Holy Spirit receives of that which is Christ's as well as the Father's (John 16:14-15), and Christ is glorified by the Spirit (John 16:14) as the

---

[98] Qui accipit vitā subsistentem, accipit vitam independentem: dare vitam non arguit ullam causalitatem, accipere vitam non arguit ullam dependentiam; & preinde in Deo non minoris perfectionis est esse Filium, quam esse Patrem. Pater enim necessitate naturali generat filium, filius eandem naturam habet cum Patre non ex gratiâ vel indolgentiâ Patris; non est enim precatio Deus; atura divina in filio est incausata, independens, & per omnia eadem natura divina quae est in Patre; ipsa etiam subsistentia quam accipit filius est sibi naturaliter debita.

[99] Temporalis operationis Sigillum, aeternae spirationis fignum (John 20:22).

Father is glorified by Christ. For Christ receives from the Father, and the Spirit from Christ, what they both reveal to the church of Christ. Nor is it any dishonor to the Spirit to proceed from the Father and the Son in such a glorious way as to be equal with them, nay one with the (1 John 5:7). For all the churches of Christ are obliged by the first sacrament of Christianity to honor the Holy Spirit with their bodies and souls, which are his holy temple, as they honor the Father and the Son.[100] The Spirit of Jehovah is the God of Israel (2 Samuel 23:2-3). The Holy Spirit, as he is one God with the Father and the Son, has an infinite essence, which exists of itself, though as he is the third person, he has not subsistence from himself, but by emanation, procession, spiration from the Father and the Son; and yet both concur to build a temple to the Holy Spirit that he may be worshiped as God.[101] These three – Father, Son, and Holy Spirit – do take mutual delight, content, and satisfaction in one another. The distinction between them is not absolute, but relative only. They do mutually subsist in one another, and all of them subsist in the same glorious Godhead,[102] which Godhead dwells equally in its fullness in all three, and is as truly the nature of the Holy Spirit, as it is the nature of the Father and the Son. And this divine nature is infinite, not included in or excluded from any place.[103]

The divine works whereby the glory of the Godhead is so much manifested unto us are performed by the Godhead subsisting in the Holy

---

[100] Si ex lignis & lapidibus templum Spiritui facete juberemur, quia cultus hic soli Deo debetur, clarum esset divinitatis ejus argumentum. Nunc ergo quanto clarius istad est, quod non Templum illi facere sed nos ipsi esse debemus? Augustin. ad Maximin. Epist. 66.

[101] Subtractâ subsistentia Spiritus Sancti Deus defineret esse Personaliter Spiritus Sanctus; & proinde ista subtractio est impossibilis, imo ipsa etiam suppositio futilis, quia tanta est tam essentiae divinae quàm personarum perfectio ut nec pauciores nec plures esse possint.

[102] Tres personae divinae non distinguuntur secundum esse Absolutum, sed per proprietates Relativas dignosountur; & proinde distinctio est tantum Respectiva, & Modalis.

[103] Deus ingenium nostrum admiratione suspēsam tenet & corda nostra efficaci sen su penitus afficit, ut deficientes sub ejus magnitudine ad opera intimiora respiciamus ejus{que} reficiamur bonitate Aug. in Ps. 144.

Spirit as well as in the Father and the Son.[104] For all the works of God upon or about the creature for their creation, sustentation or regulation are inseparably united, as Augustine often argues,[105] and the Schoolmen from him. All things are of the Father by the Son and through the Spirit (1 Corinthians 8:6. John 5:19, John 1:3, Genesis 1:2; 1 Corinthians 12:11, 13, Ephesians 2:18),[106] so that by the majesty of all three shining in the Word and the joint concurrence of all three in every work that is properly divine, the Godhead is made thrice illustrious throughout the world, and yet the Godhead remains singly and singularly one in all three subsistences.[107]

Finally, the natural and infinite perfection of the Godhead requires this wonderful communication of subsistence by the Father as the first personal principle to the Son, and by the Father and the Son to the Holy Spirit. For it is most certain that God is not capable of any other being, or any other manner of being or subsisting than what he has, for he has the best being that is, nay the best that can be, because the being of God and the manner of being or subsisting of the Godhead in these three – Father, Son, and Holy Spirit – is infinitely perfect, and there can be no better being, or manner of being or subsisting then that which is perfect, infinite, and infinitely perfect.[108]

The Father did not arbitrarily beget his Son, nor did the Father and the Son arbitrarily concur in breathing forth the Holy Spirit, but the natural and infinite perfection of the Godhead did require this wonderful

---

[104] Deus immensu est non voluntatis libertate sed naturae necessitate; essentia divina est tota intra omnia, tota extra omnia, nusquam inclusa, nusquam exclusa, omnia continens, à nullo contenta.
[105] Augustine, de Praedest. Sanct. c. 8.
[106] Actiones sunt suppositorum.
[107] Nazianzen, *On Baptism*, Oration 4..
[108] Quiquid De naturale est perfectissimū est; aequè necessariū est esse tres personas Deitatis, quàm est, essentiam divinam esse unicā, & proinde aeque perfectum est unum at{que} alterum, quia utrūque naturale & proinde substantiale; ipse etiam respectus inter personas divinasest substantialis, naturalis, mutuus, simultaneus, necessarius, aeternus, in singulis autem singularis.

communication of itself,[109] because such is the natural perfection of the divine nature or Godhead that it could not be fully communicated unless subsistence were communicated by the Father to the Son, and by both to the Spirit for their mutual, eternal, and infinite satisfaction and delight. And therefore the Father did not beget his Son, nor did the Father and Son breathe forth the Spirit arbitrarily, but naturally and necessarily, though voluntarily for the eternal satisfaction of all three subsistences, that the whole Godhead might be in every one of these three according to its infinite perfection, and all three subsist in the unity of the Godhead, and dwell in one another, mutually possess, love and glorify one another from everlasting to everlasting, because all three are coessential, coequal, and coeternal – each one of the persons, the third as well as the first, being God by nature (Galatians 4:8), and not by the mere favor of any one or more of the coessential persons.[110]

Therefore, both the generation of the Son and breathing forth of the Spirit must be eternal, because both are natural, for whatsoever is natural unto God must be eternal,[111] but because the Father is the first personal principle of subsisting life, all is from him by the Son (1 Corinthians 8:6),[112] and all is referred back again to him as the first personal principle, even by the Son (John 5:19) in regard to the Father's self-subsistence, his order of subsisting, and his communicating subsistence to the Son and Holy Spirit, though all things in the world are wrought by the Spirit also, as has been shown. Hence it is that the name of God is most familiarly given to the Father, both in the Old and the New Testament,[113] though Father, Son, and

---

[109] Divina essentia ad suam summam perfectionem sine personisesse ne quit, nec personatu una sine alterâ obintimam relationē. Bisterfell contra Crellium lib. 2. Sect. 1. cap. 4

[110] Qui naturá Deus est, verus Deus est: qui verus Deus est, naturá Deus est.

[111] Quicquid Deo naturale est aeternum est.

[112] Omnia à Patre tanquam primo principio Personali esse dicuntur, et proinde omnia ad ipsum ut primum principium Personale reteruntur.

[113] John 1:1, 17:3, Romans 15:6, John 14:1; 1 Peter 1:21; 2 Corinthians 1:3, Ephesians 1:3, Colossians 2:2.

Holy Spirit are all equally God, nay, are one and the same God, who is the only true God blessed forever.[114]

We may then look upon the Son, admire and bless the Father, look upon the Father and bless the Son, look upon Father and Son and bless the Spirit, look upon all three, admire and bless, adore and love, know, believe and obey all three coequal persons, subsisting in the same most single Godhead, and have access to the Father through the Son, and by the Spirit with reverence and confidence, zeal, and love.[115]

---

[114] Trinitas non est conjunctio Dei unius (scil. Dei Patris) cum duabus rebus creatis, Filio nimirum Spiritu{que} unus Deus est, unus est Baptismus, una fides in Patrem, Filium, Spiritum; Deum unum unicum unicissimum.

[115] Propius seipsum cognoscendum Deus exhibet, quando in unica essentia tres nobis personas considerandas proponit. Colonius.

Chapter 6

The Divine Subsistence,
Being the Most Excellent Subsistence That Is or Can Be.
The word 'Subsistence' or 'Person' Cannot be Attributed After the Same Manner to God, Angels, & Men.

It is not my business at this time to make any metaphysical distinction between the persons of men and angels; but I desire to distinguish between created and uncreated persons, because uncreated persons subsist in one single and infinite essence. It may seem strange to some metaphysical wits that one person, and much more than three distinct persons should subsist in one single and undivided essence; but these discoursing wits do not (1) distinguish between created and uncreated persons, (2) ground their faith on scholastical subtlety, or (3) study the holy Scriptures with humility and faith, and beg a blessing of their studies by fervent prayer.[116] For they might read in the Scriptures of a divine person subsisting in the divine nature (Philippians 2:6) being in the form of God, etc., that is subsisting in the nature of God, because it presently follows, that therefore he thought it no robbery to be equal with God; for persons that are coessential must needs be coequal; Christ and his Father do both subsist in the same divine essence, for Christ is the express image of his Father's subsistence, and he and his Father are one, one in essence (John 10:30, Hebrews 1:3). We find this interpretation was received in the time of Justinian the Emperor, and therefore it is not an interpretation lately coined.[117]

Because it is said "who being in the form of God," the Holy Spirit demonstrates the hypostasis or subsistence of the Word in the essence of God. And because it is said that he took upon him the form of a servant, it

---

[116] εν μορφη θεου υπαρχων Philippians 2:6
[117] Justinian. Edict. de Fide

signifies that God the Word (that is God the Son) is united with the nature, not the subsistence or person of man. He did subsist in the nature of God, but he did assume the nature of man, and therefore Christ has a divine subsistence, no human person;[118] no human person subsists in the nature of man; nor does the person of an angel subsist in the nature of an angel; but the divine person of Christ subsists in his divine nature, nay, all the three persons do subsist in the single and infinite nature of God.

From whence I conclude that there is not only a manifest, but an infinite difference between created and uncreated subsistences or persons. And I speak of *persons* rather than *personalities*,[119] because those abstract notions are not very well understood by the most discoursing men; for even they acknowledge that abstracts are not well, or not happily understood, unless you descend to the consideration of their subjects.[120] My purpose therefore upon most mature deliberation is: (1) to distinguish between created and uncreated persons, and (2) to treat of uncreated persons rather than personalities, that is to treat of the three persons not abstracted from, but subsisting in the divine nature.

I will not speak simply of the Son as a son in that abstract relation, or of the Son as a person, or as the second person, by abstracting his personality from the divine nature in which he subsists; but I desire to speak of Jesus Christ as subsisting in the nature of God, according to that expression of the apostle (Philippians 2:6), subsisting in the nature of God. For I am resolved to follow the Scripture, and I do not think it safe to abstract the incommunicable subsistence of Christ from the divine nature in which he subsists, lest I fall into vain speculations, as many learned men have done.

---

[118] Solis personis divinis ob infinitam & simplicem Essentiam convenit in Essentiâ subsistere. Nulla enim persona Angelica vel humana subsistit in Natura vel essentiâ.

[119] Persona propriè est quid concretum ex essentiâ intelligente & Personalitate.

[120] Abstracta faelicius intelliguntur mentione Subjectorum. Intellectus potiùs de Concretis omnia praedicit quàm de Abstractis, quia actiones sunt Suppositorum.

Now if you take in the divine nature of Christ (and there is the same reason for all three persons, because all have the same divine nature) there will be, I say, not only a manifest, but an infinite difference between the person of Christ, and the person of the most glorious angel in heaven. Those who have long studied the most refined and curious part of metaphysics, when they come to discourse of the distinction between a singular nature and a person, are forced to confess that they do confine their speech to created natures and persons because there is even almost nothing evident to them by the light of reason concerning the divine nature and uncreated persons.[121] And therefore on the other side, it well becomes me to confine my discourse to uncreated persons, because there is so vast a difference between them, and the most excellent of all created persons; only something I must say of created persons, that by comparing them with uncreated persons, I may demonstrate wherein they agree and wherein they differ.

Boetius relates that when there was an epistle of the Council of Chalcedon read, in which there was this orthodox position, that Jesus Christ is a single person, and yet there are two distinct natures in his single person, Boethius desired the learned men then present to assign the difference between a singular nature and a person, and no man, says he, was able to tell me the difference, or to declare what a person was. But though Boethius smiled at the ignorance of others, yet he was not wise enough to conceal his own,[122] for he defines a person thus: "A person is the undivided substance of a rational nature."[123] I am not at leisure to reckon up the defects of this imperfect definition.

Vasquez is bold to say that Aristotle knew not how to distinguish a person from a singular nature. And there is no doubt but very wise men have

---

[121] De Naturâ & Personis divinis ex lumine rationis fere nihil dici potest; mysterium de Deo Trinuno universam transcendit Philosophiam.

[122] Vide Chenitium *De Trinitate* c. 4.

[123] Persona est naturae rationalis individua Substantia; Boehbius l. de duabus naturis & una persona Christi

erred grossly in this point for want of studying:[124] (1) the state of the soul in its separation from the body. (2) The human nature of Christ assumed without any human person. (3) The difference between the divine nature, and persons which subsist in it. I believe Aristotle did not study the first so exactly as he should have done; and I am sure he knew nothing of these two last most considerable points.

I shall not stand to show the vanity of Laurentius Valla,[125] who seems to forget all his elegancies when he comes to discourse of a person, and draws his arguments from the flourishes of an orator, or the several passions, humors, relations, conditions, or offices of men that are personated upon a stage; and therefore this whiffler deserves to be hissed off from his stage, for he does only make sport for atheists and Familists by such ridiculous discourse. And he is sufficiently absurd, when he stoops so low as to say that a person is a quality, and that there is a triple quality in God. And Scaliger showed his critical skill in divinity to purpose, when he was so foolish as to say that a person does not signify a substance but a quality.[126] Bellarmine is orthodox in this point, and proves at large that the word *person* usually signifies a *substance*, in very approved authors both sacred and profane.[127]

Well may we then say that the church of God has not offended the curious ears of such as are the great masters of language the orators, civilians, grammarians, and others, when they say that a divine person at least connotes the substance or nature of God; and the self-same substance being in all three persons, it does not follow, as Gostavius or Mr. Fry would have it, that there are three substances in the Godhead because there are three

---

[124] Philos. distinctionem naturae & Personae vix intelligebant, quia nihil de mysterio Incarnationis audiebant.

[125] Laurentius Valla. lib. 6. Elegant. In Deo poni personam, quod verè Deo sit triplex qualitas, tales qualitates statuo in Deo & has dico esse personas.

[126] Vide sis Soaligerum in oratione de verbo Inepti satis inepte disserentem. in Epist. p. 374.

[127] Bellarm. lib 2. de Christo. cap. 5.

persons subsisting in the Godhead, for the substance or nature is the same in all three persons: Father, Son, and Holy Spirit.

And we speak of the substance of the persons, when we describe them, not that we may show wherein they differ, but that we may show wherein all three persons agree. And if we should abstract the personality of these uncreated persons from their divine substance or nature, when we describe them, we should seem to rob them of their divinity even in the very description of them. We must not say that a divine person is a mere relative propriety [*special characteristic, peculiarity*],[128] or a pure manner of being, existing, or subsisting, for every person is God, and all three persons but one Jehovah, one God. They do imprudently destroy the divine and coessential Trinunity, who affirm the holy Trinity to be nothing else but three proprieties or three manners of subsisting. For what is that consubstantial Trinunity, of which the ancients speak, but the single and infinite substance or essence of three divine subsistences or persons? If you leave out the divine essence or substance out of the definition, how is it a consubstantial or coessential Trinunity?

The Father, Son, and Holy Spirit: all three do naturally subsist in the same divine and undivided nature.[129] I must therefore describe divine persons as divine persons, when I am to put a difference between them and uncreated persons; and if I describe them as divine persons, I must not abstract their personal proprieties from their divine nature, though what is personal may in some sense be affirmed to be naturally due to that particular person.[130] But besides those personal proprieties or characteristics whereby the Father, Son and Holy Spirit do appear even to our weak understanding

---

[128] Nulla persona est purus putos [τεο πος] υπαρξεως sive existendimodus, & mera proprietas, vel relatio; Trinitatē imprudenter tollunt qui Patrē Filium & Spiritū Sanctum tres existendi modos definiunt; sunt enim Personae Coessentiales

[129] Carolus Magnus apud Genebrardū cap. 20. Liturgiae; Pater prima, est divinitatis persona in quâ caeterae duae naturaliter manentes existunt.

[130] Quicquid Patri proprium & peculiare est, Patri sano modo naturale dicitur; est enim perfectio Relativa Patri quà sic naturaliter debita, tanquam primo principio Personali.

to be three distinct subsistences,[131] the whole and undivided Godhead dwells in every one of these three subsistences, though it subsists after a different manner in each one of the three.[132] The Father is God subsisting after that peculiar manner, which is proper to the Father. Now that peculiar manner of subsisting superadded to the divine nature, makes a true distinction between the Father and the other two subsistences, but it makes no composition at all, either in the Father, or in the Godhead. Hence it is that various profound and orthodox writers maintain that a divine person is nothing else but the very divine essence itself modificated [*qualified*].[133] Give me leave to explain this abstruse [*difficult to understand*] notion a little, by giving an instance in the personal principle, God the Father.

God the Father is the first person of the Godhead distinguished from the Son and Spirit (who are one and the same God with him) by his peculiar manner of subsistence, singular relation, and incommunicable properties.

Here is, as they love to speak, the divine essence modificated with a peculiar manner of subsistence, a singular relation and incommunicable properties.[134] What this peculiar manner of subsistence, singular relation, and incommunicable properties are, I shall demonstrate when I come to treat of the distinction of these three divine subsistences in the very next chapter.

I hope I need say no more to prove that a divine person at least connotes the substance, essence, and nature of God; and therefore it will not be safe to abstract the personality of an uncreated subsistence from that single and

---

[131] Calvinus Personas divinas proprietates vocavit, sed nudas proprietates esse negavit

[132] υποσασις quicquid tribus commune est cum proprietate habet peculiari. Proprietatibus dignoscuntur personae, non constituuntur.

[133] Vide Bisterf. de uno Deo, etc. lib. 2. §. 1. cap. 4. Essentia divina est modo substantiali modificata; Subsistentia enim est modus substantialis, qui ab ipsa essentia divina separari nequit, imò persona divina est ipsam et essentia divina certo modo se habens. Est enim persona divina ipsissima Essentia Modificata. Persona autem non est essentia Simpliciter, sed cum modo subsistendi considerata. Vide D. Alting. Loc. Com. Part. 1. & Problem. Calv. Inst. l. 1. c. 13. Bezam. part. 1. quaest. & Homil. prima adversus Sacramentarios. Zanchium de tribus Elohim. Melancton. Loc. Com. Polanum in Syntag. Chamierum de Trinitate. lib. 1. cap 3.

[134] Persona divina est ipsamet natura divina peculiari modo se habens.

infinite nature which is one and the same in all three subsistences. I do not find the most raised metaphysical wits very forward to define or describe a personality; but they speak of a person *in concreto*, of a subsistent rather than a subsistence; and of a suppositum, rather than an abstract suppositality.[135] The imperfect definition of Boethius is all too commonly received in the Schools, and he says that a person is an undivided substance. Those who have studied the point more exactly, and correct his definition, do all agree that a person is an undivided substance, an understanding substance, a complete, incommunicable, independent substance, which does not depend upon anything else by way of inhesion, adhesion, union, or any other way for its sustentation. This is the general and common opinion.[136]

I know there are some private opinions, as I may call them, concerning the formality of a person, which I shall but point at, and easily confute with the light and gentle touch of a running pen. It is very absurd to say that a person is made complete in his subsistence by any accidents or any formality arising from a heap of accidents, because a person is the most perfect substance, and therefore cannot be made complete by any accidental subsistence; there is a manifest contradiction in that ridiculous expression.[137]

Aristotle says that singular substances do subsist κυριότατως και πρωτως και μαλιϛα: most properly, principally, and perfectly.[138] To subsist by itself, is the most perfect kind of subsistence; and that cannot be said to subsist by itself, which subsists by a heap of accidents. Others say that a

---

[135] Persona directè denotat subsistentiam, consequenter connotatnaturā. Vasquèz. Persona est individuum subsistens vivum, intelligens, incommunicabile, independendens, non sustentatū ab alio nec pars alterius. Persona est suppositū intelligens Persona in Concreto naturam includit, quia Persona naturam participat, & personalitas est substantiae sive naturae modus Substantialis & separabilis, rarissime autem separatus. Persona est substantia completa intelligens, per se subsistens, incommunicabilis, & independens.

[136] Persona conficitur ex essentia & proprietatibus distinctivis ita ut quaelibet persona in se sit perfecta substantia. vide Hilarii Sermon. in Fest. S. Trinitatis.

[137] Persona subsistit per se; accidentia autem sunt in alio; ex natura Substantiali & accidentibus non potest fieri unum per se. Vide Ferrariens. contra. Gen. 4. c. 39.

[138] Aristotle, *Categories*, Chapter 5.

person is completed by a mere negation, but subsistence is positive, though subsistence may be described by some expressions that are negative.[139]

The second person of the Trinity supplies and performs all that a human person can perform to the human nature of Christ. Now to say that the divine person of Christ supplies the room of a negation, and does all that a negation can do, is to say it does very little or nothing at all.[140] Finally, some say that a person is completed by the existence of its nature. But it is clear that a soul in the state of separation exists, and yet that soul is not a person, nay never was a person at the first instant of its creation or union.[141] And it will be most absurd to say that the human nature was assumed by Christ and hypostatically united without or before the existence of that nature, because it was united before it had any human subsistence, and consequently before it had any existence, if that subsistence be nothing else but existence, as these discoursers suppose. But it is high time to leave pursuing of these wanderers, for it is clear that subsistence is a positive and substantial mode, because [it is] the most perfect manner of being, which we express as well as we can, when we say that a person does subsist by itself, without union unto, or dependence upon anything else for its sustentation; nay, that it is incapable of any such union, though it be for the present in a state of separation. And

---

[139] Complementum Personae dicit negationem unionis cōmunicationis & dependentiae tum aptitudinalis tū actualis, ut omnes partes tam integrantes quàm essentiales ipsaque etiam anima separata à ratione Personae excludantur. Vide Joannem de Neapoli in Quodlibet.

[140] See Suarez, Disputation 34, Section 2 n. 8.

[141] Existentia communicabilis non potest este Subsistentia Personalis. Tria sunt in Supposito; Natura, Existentia, & Subsistentia, sive Personalitas. Pantusa. Natura humana existit in personâ divina sine propriâ personalitate, non sine propriâ existentiâ. Vasquez. Natura existens producitur non tantum in supposito proprio sed & in alieno, uti patet de natura humana in Christo; non est enim in Christo duplex Suppositum. Caietanus. Subsistentia est modus positivus & Substantialis incommunicabilis & Independens, naturae intellectivae, integrae, & completae conveniens. Anima rationalis separata habet Modum per se, quem non habebat in corpore, sed est incompleta, & habet non tantum obedientialem sed & Aptitudinalem dependentiam, quia ex naturâ suâ est forma materiae, & proinde non habet perfectissimum modum subsistondi per se.

therefore the Schoolmen usually say: "*Quod subsistit per se, nec est nec esse potest in alio, ullo modo; quia subsistere per se sumitur pro perfectissimo modo subsistendi per se.*"

It is evident by what has been said that even created persons are defined by their substance or nature which is instead of a genus when we define a person *in concreto*; and when we speak of the formality of a person, we say it is a substantial mode, and the most perfect manner of subsisting; and therefore a created person is not completed by any quality or accident whatsoever. Now if a created person be a substance, and the formality of a created person be substantial, I have no ground to abstract a divine person from the divine substance or essence, because a divine person cannot be separated from the divine nature; as the human nature may be from a human person; and though a precisive abstraction does not lay any ground either for a rational negation, or a real separation; yet if the divine nature be not considered and taken notice of in the description of every divine person, men will be apt to conceive that the divine nature and persons may be separated.

The Scripture does not present any such abstract notion of the Father, Son, or Holy Spirit unto us, but teaches us to consider them as divine persons, that is, persons that have a divine nature; for else we should make a trinity of modes, no Trinunity;[142] a trinity without God or Godhead,[143] and give our adversaries cause to say what they have said, without cause, contrary to their own principles as well as ours: "*En Trinitatem sine Deo!*" For even they themselves acknowledge the first person of the blessed Trinity to be God.

It is our wisest course therefore to describe every person as a divine person as God, and acknowledge all three persons to be one and the same God, according to the Scriptures. For we must not only consider three

---

[142] Non est Trinitas modorum, sed personarum coessentialiū trinunitas.

[143] Quod excipiunt Trinitatē igirur fore sine Deo, ex eadem insulsitate nascitur. See John Calvin, *Institutes of the Christian Religion*. 1.13.25

personalities, but three persons,[144] and the same single Godhead in all three persons, and all three persons in the Godhead. I must not treat of the first person simply as a Father, but as a divine and eternal Father, as God the Father (Romans 15:6, Ephesians 5:20, Colossians 2:2, John 17:3). For God is to be so considered as he is to be worshiped by us, and we are not to worship an abstract personality without reference to the Godhead.

We must consider what is common as well as what is incommunicable; we must treat of that which is absolute as well as of that which is relative; and whilst we speak of a trinity of persons, we must not forget the unity of the essence, that so we may not hold forth a trinity of modes without the Godhead, or tempt weak heads to dream of a trinity of gods. Judicious Mr. Calvin did not think fit to discourse much of created persons, and therefore described none but a divine person; and he would not adventure to abstract an uncreated personality from the divine nature in which every of the three uncreated persons subsists.[145] In our most accurate definition of any created nature, which we are best acquainted with, we judge it reasonable to take in that which the nature defined has common with other natures, as well as that which is proper to it alone.

And certainly it is very fit, in our description of every divine person, to take in the nature which is common to all three persons, and not only what is proper and peculiar to any one. "I call a person," says Calvin, "a subsistence in the essence of God." And then he descends to take notice of the relation of a divine person to the rest of the coessential persons, and his distinction from

---

[144] Nam Deus ita se praedicat unicu esse ut distinctè in tribus personis considerandum proponat quas nisi tenemus, nudum & inane duntaxat Dei nomen sine vero Deo in cerebro nostro volitat. Calvin. Instit. lib. 1. cap. 13. §. 2.

[145] Vide Calvinum Melanct. Oecolampadiū, Bucanura, D. Altingium, D. Gomarum. Wendelinum, Bislerfeldium. Persona divina est essenti. ae divinae subsistentia incommunicabilis. Personam voco subsistentiam in Dei essentiâ, quae ad alios relata, proprietate incommunicabili distinguitur. Calv. Instit. Vide Cyrillum Exposit. fidei Orthod. Anastasium Theopolit. Damascen. de Orth. fid. lib. 3. c. 4. 5, 6. Persona divina est substantia spiritualis ad alios sibi coestentiales relata, & tamen ab illis incommunicabili proprietate distincta.

them by some incommunicable property. It will be a very dangerous attempt then to treat of the divine persons in such abstract expressions as do only hold forth some curious notions about the relation of these persons to, and distinction from, one another, without taking notice that all three persons are coeternal and coequal, because coessential.[146]

If we will discourse soberly of the Godhead, we must speak of it as one single infinite perfection common to Father, Son, and Holy Spirit, to all three, and none other. The single Godhead, the whole Godhead is in every single person, and it is common to all three in a singular and glorious way. For the divine nature is not communicated to these three as a genus to its species, for it is undivided and indivisible; nor as a species to its individual, for it is not multiplicable nor as a totem or whole to its parts, for the Godhead has no parts, it is impartible, and as has been said, indivisible; nay the Godhead is not communicated so to any one person, as a created nature to a created person, which may be separated from a created subsistence; for the divine nature cannot possibly be separated from all, or any one of the divine subsistences or persons.

And therefore we must not discourse of the Godhead in such a notional way, as if the Godhead did exist out of the three persons without any relative subsistence; for that is clearly to dream of some strange, absolute God, who is neither Father, Son, nor Holy Spirit. When we describe the Godhead according to our best understanding, we dare not abstract it from the three persons, but say that the Godhead is one single, spiritual, infinite essence, in which the Father, Son, and Holy Spirit do subsist.

And when we describe a divine person, it is absurd to abstract the personality from the divine nature; for how can you describe a divine person, if you abstract his personality from his divinity? Every single person is God, nay every single person is the Godhead, the nature, the essence of

---

[146] The Godhead is not to be abstracted from the persons or the persons from it The Godhead described, not abstracted. De omnibus & singulis & solis his tribus personis tota Deitas perfecta & omnibus numeris una dicitur.

God, considered with that subsistence, relation, and propriety which is peculiar to that person. Every single person is God of himself. *Deus non est per aliud Deus.* Finally, take all the three persons together, and they are nothing else but one God; and they are one God, not absolutely considered in his abstract nature, but relatively considered with those peculiar relations and incommunicable properties whereby the three persons are distinguished from one another. When the name of God is taken essentially or commonly in Scripture, we say it belongs to all three persons, because it is spoken without any determination or restriction to any one particular person, as John 4:24: "God is a Spirit;" Matthew 4:10, and Matthew 19:17: "There is none good but God."[147] These places must be interpreted of all three persons, for it is certain that Christ did not by these speeches exclude himself or the Holy Spirit from being good or from being worshiped. And when the name of God is taken personally or singularly in Scripture, we say it is understood of one person by a synecdoche, because though the other persons may be excluded from what is proper and peculiar to any one person, because it is personal, and therefore incommunicable, yet they cannot be excluded from anything that is essential, because the same divine essence is common to all. Now the title of God is essential, and what has been said of that is true of all essential titles and attributes; but personal relations, properties, and actions, are all peculiar, as we shall show at large in the next chapter.

All that I need to infer from hence for the present is that when we describe the divine nature, we should not abstract it from the three persons; and when we describe a divine person, we should not abstract him from the divine nature. When the Scripture speaks of created persons, it does not

---

[147] Vox Deus de eo proprie dicitur qui naturâ Deus est, & de eo quidem vel ουσιώδης Communiter sine certae personae determinatione, vel, υποςατικως de una aliquâ personâ per Synecdochen. Nomen Deus sive Absolute dicatur de totâ simplicique Deitate, sive Relate de unâ aliquâ personâ unam eandemque essentiam designat; quaelibet enim persona est αὐτόθεος, & in Deo non distinguuntur *esse* & *essentia*; tota Deitas est ex se, & à se, & singulae personae sunt ipsissima essentia cum distinctis relationibus personalibus considerata.

abstract the personality from the singular substance or nature. When the apostle says in 2 Corinthians 1:11 that thanks shall be given by many persons, he does not mean many personalities, but many human singular substances; thanks should be given by a multitude of men, particular men. *Actiones sunt suppositorum, non suppositalitatum.* In like manner when we read that Christ is the character of his Father's person (Hebrews 1:3), the word is *subsistence.* The meaning is not that the Son is the character or express image of the Fatherhood of the first person, for Christ does not beget a son as the Father does, but Christ is the image of the subsistent, that is, of God the Father, and not of the mere subsistence or personality, as it is abstracted from the divine nature.

Jesus Christ has two natures in one single person. Now that person is a divine person, the second person of the Godhead, and if I describe the person of Jesus Christ, I may abstract his person from his human nature, and not mention that nature, which infinitely differs from his divine person, but I must not abstract the person of Christ from his divine nature, because he has no other than a divine person, which cannot be separated from (and should not be described without consideration, and mention of) the divine nature.[148]

For this second person is not barely considered as a person, or as a second person, but as a divine person, as the second person of the Godhead, as the natural, coessential, coequal, coeternal Son of God as his own Son, his first begotten Son, his only begotten Son (Romans 8:32, John 1:14). And therefore he must be considered as God, the true God, God blessed forever (John. 1:1, 14:18, Romans 9:5; 1 John 5:20), and therefore he must be described as God *of himself;* for the Son is Jehovah, as has been proven, and we are obliged to believe in the Son as well as in the Father (John 14:1), Jesus Christ is one and the same God with the Father.

---

[148] Christus non solùm officio Deus est, ut blasphemant Sociniani, sed Naturâ Deus est; coessētialis enim filius est. Consequens est, si in Deum credius, & in me credere debeatis, quod non esset consequēs si Christas non esset Deus. Iohan. 14 1. [αυτουσια] non est Patri peruliaris, sed tribus personis Cōmunis.

Now papists and Socinians will both confess that the Father is αὐτόθεος, God of himself; and therefore it will follow that the Son is God of himself. If the Godhead of the Son were begotten, and the Godhead of the Father unbegotten, there would be two distinct Godheads in the Father and the Son, the one begotten, and the other unbegotten. Take it thus then in brief: the second person of the Godhead is the only begotten Son of God subsisting in the unbegotten nature of God, because he is the natural and coessential Son of God the Father, and therefore has one and the same unbegotten nature with the Father; the subsistence of the Son is begotten, but the divine nature of the Son is unbegotten.

The Holy Spirit is an infinite Spirit, coessential with the Father and the Son, and not a mere subsistence proceeding from both; and yet he is distinguished from both by his personal relation and incommunicable property.

These grounds being laid for a foundation, it is easy to build on, and infer: (1) that the Father, Son, and Holy Spirit, are not mere personalities, but divine persons. (2) A divine person is not a quality or any other accident, but an infinite substance subsisting after the most perfect and glorious manner that is or can be. (3) The divine nature, being infinite, contains all manner of perfection within itself, both absolute and relative; and therefore the relations which are between the divine persons, are natural, perfect, and divine. (4) The divine nature cannot be separated from all or any one of the divine persons. (5) These three divine persons are one and the same God, one infinite Spirit; and therefore they are coessential, coequal, and coeternal. (6) These three divine persons are distinguished (as shall be shown in the next chapter) but cannot be divided or separated either from the divine nature, or from one another, because they do all three subsist in the divine nature, and in one another; for they have one and the same single and infinite nature, and are one infinite Spirit, the same omnipresent God. (7) The word *subsistence* is a consecrated word, which as we find upon record in the holy Scripture, is fit to be made use of when we speak of that divine manner of being which the Father, Son, and Holy Spirit have in the Godhead and in one another. The heathen orator could say: "*Verbis consecratis utendum.*" He meant words that were consecrated by the use and approbation of classical authors; but I mean, words consecrated by the Holy Spirit. The word ὑπόστασις, which we render *subsistence*, and by way of analogy, person; has many other significations;[149] but when it is used on this occasion, upon this subject, we may after so many disputes about this argument, easily understand the proper, and consecrated importance of the word.[150] We may take warning from the mistakes of others, and avoid those rocks on which others have suffered shipwreck. Some who understand that ὑπόστασις did signify essence, were offended with such as said there were three hypostases in God; because according to that signification of the word, to say that there are three hypostases in God, is to say that there are three essences in God and consequently, that there are three gods.

It is readily acknowledged that the word ὑπόστασις does sometimes signify the nature or essence of a thing,[151] not the generic or specific nature in their latitude and abstract universality, but the nature truly existing, and subsisting in the world.[152] This acceptance of the word may, all things duly considered and soberly expounded, be admitted, with some grains of allowance for the infinite difference which is between created, and uncreated subsistents. For if hypostasis be described *in concreto*, for which we have with

---

[149] ὑπόστασις in Scripturis frequēter sumitur probasi, seu fundamento quo aliquid nititur, 2 Cor. 9. 4. 2 Cor. 11. 17. Heb. 3. 14. fundamentum in quo spes nostra & gloria nititur. Fides etiam ὑπόστασις τον ελπιζομενων dicitur Heb. 11. 1. ut Hypostasis significat essentiam; haereticorum est tres Hypostases asserere in divinis. Vide Theodor. Hist. Eccles. lib. 2. c. 8. Patrum consensum hac de re videas apud Damascenum, Nazianz. &c.

[150] ὑπόστασις sumitur pro re per se Subsistente, pro supposito intelligente, pro divinâ Dei Patris Subsistenrià (Hebrews 1:3). Filius est imago Personae Patris, est enim filius essentiae ejusdem cū Patre, non imago essentiae.

[151] ὑπόστασις significat naturam verè Subsistentem & per se subsistentem hoc est modo perfectissimo subsistentem.

[152] Hypostatica Emphaticis opponuntur, quia omnia Hypostatica veram habent essentiam.

invincible reason contended all along this chapter, then hypostasis connotes the divine nature, and does not signify an abstract subsistence, but a complete subsistent.[153]

When I say that Jesus Christ is the character of his Father's subsistence, I do not (as I have formerly shown) understand it thus, that Jesus Christ is the character of his Father's abstract personality, but he is the character of God the Father; I take in the divine nature. But you must then consider that the glory of the Trinunity must be preserved in this acceptance; for there is not a new nature in each one of the three but the divine nature which is connoted in these three hypostases is the very same. There is the glory of the mystery which dazzles the eye of carnal reason, and therefore whatever we say on this argument must be taken *cum grano salis* and expounded θεοπρεπῶς,[154] because of the infinite difference between a finite and infinite nature, and between created and uncreated persons, as I shall (God-willing) show at large before I conclude this chapter.

Three persons may and do subsist in one and the same infinite nature, and therefore, though every hypostasis connotes the divine nature,[155] yet all here connote one and the same infinite nature[156] in which all three persons do subsist.[157] To subsist is (as Aristotle the great interpreter expounds it) to have the most perfect manner of being by itself that a substance – the best of beings – can attain to, and it is very proper to say that the Father, Son, and

---

[153] υποστασις est Essentia divina charactere hypostatico insignita, sive proprio subsistendi modo distincta. Magnum discrimen est inter Personam & proprietatem Personae: proprietas Patris Absoluta, est esse αγενητον, Respectiva esse Patrem; Persona autem Patris est Deus filium gignens in unitate essentiae ingenitae.

[154] Θεοπρεπῶς: After a divine manner.

[155] οὐσία significat naturam Absolutam Communem: υποστασις significat Naturam subsistentem cum proprietatibus Relativis & distinctivis.

[156] Personae divinae sunt per se subsistentes; nihil autem per se subsistit sine subsistentiâ.

[157] Subsistentia divina est ipsamet essentia divina peculiari modo se habens; unius autem essentiae sunt plures modi, sive respectus diversi juxta nostrum concipiendi modû Scripturis conformem. Singull autem modi singulas essentias non postulant in rebus creatis, & proinde ejusdem essentiae infinitae plures modi & respectus diversi esse possunt.

Holy Spirit have the most perfect manner of subsistence in the divine nature that is or can be. The divine nature considered with all absolute and relative perfection in Father, Son, and Holy Spirit, does most truly, properly, and perfectly subsist;[158] for there are three illustrious subsistences in that one undivided infinite nature; and therefore the Godhead thus considered, does subsist κυριστατως και πρωτως και μαλιςα.[159] Singular substances have the most perfect subsistence. A Spirit is the most perfect substance. God is the most single and singular substance, and he is the only infinite Spirit, the best of Spirits, and therefore he must have the most perfect subsistence.

Every single person [of the Godhead] is αυτόθεος and therefore I will be bold to infer that these three persons only do perfectly subsist by themselves, though in one another; for they have one independent, spiritual, infinite nature, which is of itself, and is complete in itself, because infinite in perfection, and therefore contains all absolute and relative perfection in itself. But when we speak of the relative perfection, we speak of three in one, because the relative properties are distinctive.[160] And when we treat of the absolute perfection, we speak of one in three, one essence in three persons, who do all three subsist with their relative and incommunicable properties, in that most perfect and single essence. This is that divine Trinunity which contains all absolute and relative perfection, and therefore has the most perfect and excellent subsistence, that is, or can be.

Finally, though these three persons do mutually subsist in one another,[161] yet they are said to subsist by themselves,

---

[158] ουσία apud Craecos Logicos Personam significat, & υποστασις non raro essentiam, sed vocum earum in Theol. jam fixa est & limitata significatio, & proinde Logicos istos nobis imitari non licet.

[159] Aristotle, *Categories*.

[160] Athanasius. Symb. Naz. orat 37. Sophron. act. 11. Concil. Oecum. sexti. Damas. Anasta. Syn.

[161] "If any man refuse," I cry, "to acknowledge three hypostases in the sense of three things hypostatized, that is three persons subsisting, let him be anathema." Jerome Letter 15 <https://earlychurchtexts.com/public/jerome_letter_15_to_damasus_three_hypostases.htm> [Accessed 1/25/2024]

(1) Because these persons do not subsist in one another, as accidents do exist in a subject; for accidents exist in another, because of their imperfection; but these subsist in one another because of their perfection, because they have the same single infinite nature, and are one infinite and omnipresent Spirit.

(2) They subsist mutually in one another; the Father subsists in the Son (John 14:10-11) as well as the Son in the Father; and therefore this subsisting in one another does not argue any imperfection, but does demonstrate the infinite perfection of all three subsistents, but there is no mutual inexistence of an accident in a subject, and a subject in that accident or any other.

(3) These three subsistents have one and the same spiritual, independent, infinite nature, which is complete of itself and in itself, and the whole creation does not afford one example to illustrate, much less to parallel these three illustrious subsistences in one undivided nature.[162] And it is impossible it should, for this one undivided nature in which these three glorious persons do subsist is an infinite nature, and there can be but one infinite. And therefore the Socinians seem to have lost what they do so much idolize – their reason – when they desire us to illustrate this mystery by an example.

(4) These three subsistents are coequal because they are coessential. The fathers, upon some of these considerations, did agree to use the phrase of "three hypostases and one essence," though the word *hypostasis* was not so plain and familiar at first, especially to Latin ears, and therefore Jerome complains that some were too rigorous in imposing that word without expounding of it to such whose judgment was orthodox, though their skill but small in the Greek.[163]

---

[162] Hypostases dicuntur, nulla tamen est in divinis personis suppositio vel subjectio, sed coessentialis aequalitas. Vide Aquin. p. 1. q. 39. art. 1.
[163] Hieronymus Epist. 57. Novel. lum a me homine Romano nomen exigitur—Interrogamus quid per tres Hypostases posse arbitrentur intelligi. Tres Personas subsistentes aiunt. Respondemus nos ita credere. Non sufficit sensus, expressum nomen efflagitant—& quia vocabulanon ediscimus haeretici judicamur Hieron. Epist. 57. si quis tres subsistentes personas non confitetur Anathema sit.

To conclude my discourse upon this word *subsistence*, be pleased to consider that we read of the nature of God, we read of the subsistence of the Father, and we read that these three, Father, Son, and Holy Spirit are one; having these two words *nature* and *subsistence* in Scripture, we are prompted by the Spirit speaking in the word to explain this mystery thus:

The Father, Son, and Holy Spirit
are three in subsistence,
but one in nature.

No mystery can be explained with less violence and more sobriety, for we are precise in keeping to the very words of Scripture in explaining this grand mystery to the plainest of men; and therefore they were sentenced of old that did not believe this plain truth.

(9) We have no reason to be offended with the use of the word *person*, when we treat of this argument if we add a fit epithet, and say the Father is a divine person, or an uncreated person, and say the same of the Son and Holy Spirit. The word *person* signifies the most excellent kind of subsistent, an understanding subsistent, as is acknowledged by all the masters of language, sacred and profane, as has been proven, and that place 2 Corinthians 1:11 is very clear: of all the derivations of *persona*, that pleases me best, *persona quasi per se una*, because it expresses the unity and excellency of a personal subsistence. *Per se* notes the excellency, because *subsistere per se* notes the most excellent kind of subsistence. Nay, the word *person* expresses more excellence than the word *subsistence* alone does import, for it is proper to say that a beast subsists, but it is absurd to say that a beast is a person because a person is an understanding subsistent.[164]

---

[164] υπoστασις quamvis substantiam primam significat, tam animatam quàm inanimatam, Persona verò, tantùm substantiam singularem intelligentem qualis Deus, Angelus, homo.

But neither of these words expresses the excellence of that subsistence which the Father, Son, and Holy Spirit have in the Godhead.[165] And therefore we do not only say that these three are persons or subsistences, but we say they are uncreated persons, divine subsistences, persons subsisting in the divine nature, persons of the Godhead, that so we may take in all the excellency which these words subsistence and person do afford; and then by other epithets superadd that excellency which is proper to Father, Son, and Holy Spirit, and leave out all that imperfection which is in created persons and subsistences.

The word *subsistence* is in the Scripture (Hebrews 1:3). The word *person* is in Scripture applied to men (2 Corinthians 1:11) who have a more excellent subsistence than beasts, an *understanding subsistence*, and therefore both Greek and Latin fathers did at last agree to use the word *person*, because it signifies an understanding subsistent.[166] And if you add *divine* or *uncreated person*, then there is no danger of any mistake; unless men will be so vain as to say the word *person* sometimes signifies a visible shape, an outward form or appearance, the countenance or gesture of a man, or else some office, relation, or quality; and say that we do make three shapes, countenances, etc., in the Godhead, as Sabellius, Servetus, and such bold atheists as have sucked in their poison, are wont to say.[167] We do therefore vindicate the church of God from these insolent and groundless aspersions, and freely declare what we mean by person, namely: *an understanding subsistent*.

Each of the three divine persons has an office and has a relation, but no divine person is an office or a mere relation. But the Godhead contains all

---

[165] Magnâ prorsus inopiâ humanum laborat eloquium. Dictum est tamen tres personae, non ut illud diceretur, sed ne taceretur omnino. Non enim rei in, effabilis eminentia hoc vocabulo explicari valet. Aug. lib. 5 de Trinitate cap. 9.

[166] Damascen. in Dialog. cap. 43. Nazianzen. orat. 31. in laudem Athanasii.

[167] Vocibus non semper cum respectu suae originis, sed ex receptà consuetudine utendum. Anti-Trinitarians equivocate in abusing the various significations of the word *Person*.

relative as well as absolute perfection within itself, as has been said.[168] God, as represented to us in Scripture, does as it were take upon him the person of a displeased father, and sometimes of a well-pleased father; but we do not say there are three such persons in the Godhead. For one divine person may sustain the person of a well-pleased father at one time, and the person of a displeased father at another. And if any man will be so ridiculous as to conclude from thence that then one person may be two persons, I hope that he will see his own vanity and be sensible of the equivocation, by considering what has been said already in this very chapter.

When we say, God takes upon him the person of a well-pleased Father, we speak ανθρωποπαθως after the manner of men; just as when we speak of the eyes and hands of God, but we must be understood θεοπρεπως after such a manner as becomes the infinite dignity and pure majesty of God.[169]

If men do not willfully mistake, they may then know what we mean by person, when we say there are three uncreated persons in the Godhead. The word person is in Scripture; and if it were not, yet as long as the thing signified by it is there, we have no reason to account that word, or any other such like, an exotic word, because we find it very proper and pertinent to the point in hand, in the sense which we have so often declared, that there might be no mistake, but a full agreement in such a high and weighty point.[170] It is out of question that we may expound the Scripture by words and phrases which are not in those very letters and syllables to be found in Scripture, as long as we do not affect a needless curiosity in inventing new

---

[168] Persona significat Relationē prout est Subsistens in naturâ divinâ. Aquin. p. 1. q 39. art. 1. In creaturis relationes sunt accidentales, & proinde accidentaliter insunt, relationes autem in Deo sunt subsistentes, & ipsamet essentia divina, Aquinas ibidem. Pater non genuit meram nudamque relationem, sed correlatum, Filium subsistentem, nec non coessentialem.

[169] Locutiones Impropriae Dei essentiam non exprimunt, sed ejus notitiam tenuitati nostrae accommodant.

[170] Voces tanquam consecratas omni jure judicamus, si earum conjugata, & Synonyma in Sacrâ paginâ reperiantur. Si enim talibus vocibus sensum mentemque Scripturae exprimentibus uti non liceret, nec explicare Scripturam pro concione liceret, neque in alias linguas vertere.

and obscure phrases, and a rigid superstition in defending them, for that would not conduce to edification, but beget or foment an endless contention.[171] Our expressions must be sober and plain; grave and useful, such as may hold forth the godly and prudent simplicity of the Scripture. That is all that needs to be said for the use of such words and phrases as are fit and necessary to be used in this and various other obscure points.

There are some that mistake the attributes of God for persons, and they make more than three persons; and therefore I shall not go about to reckon up the innumerable absurdities which follow upon that one mistake. *Uno absurdo dato, mille sequuntur.* I read, indeed, that Sabellius conceived the Father, Son, and Holy Spirit to be different attributes of God, but the orthodox Christians desired him to remember that there were more than three divine attributes, and pressed him to acknowledge that a trinity of persons do subsist in the unity of the nature of God, and then they would close with him and give the right hand of fellowship unto him.

The fraud and subtlety of Arius, Sabellius, and the rest of the old heretics, gave the reverend doctors of the church cause to use the words *Trinity, coessential, consubstantial,* and the like, so that they might more clearly and fully manifest this profound and glorious mystery.[172] And those who did wrangle about these words, did indeed deny the mystery and thing itself; and therefore did but manifest their pride, fraud, obstinacy, for the maintenance of their damnable heresy, when they quarreled with those eminent writers, for making use of unwritten words and phrases, upon so just and necessary occasion, that the written truth might be more clearly

---

[171] Temerè non sunt inventa nomina quae per evidentem consequentiam mentem Domini in Scripturis loquentis fideliter exprimūt; cavendum est ne vocabula repudiando, ipsam repudiemus veritatem, superbaeque temeritatis simul & haereseos arguamur.

[172] Cùm Scriptura testetur tres dici quorum quisque in solidum sit Deus, nec tamen plures esse Deos, nimis morosum est de voce contendere, cùm res in aperto sit. Colon. Anal. Paraphrast. Calv. Inst. pag. 34. In Scripturis occurrit vox Trinitatis numero namerante. 1 Iohan 5. 7. & numero numerato passim, ut in Baptismo Christi. Matth. 3 & in Baptismo nostro Matth. 28.

explained and fully defended.[173] It is not in the judgment of any man, any fault at all, to make truth plain, unless in the deluded judgment of such who are enemies to truth. Now we have removed the rubbish, we begin to build:

A divine person is a spiritual and infinite subsistent, related indeed to those other uncreated persons that subsist in the same divine nature with it, but distinguished from those coessential persons by its peculiar manner of subsistence, order of subsisting singular relation, and incommunicable property.

In these few lines, there is matter enough to fill many sheets, and I am to treat of the distinction of persons at large in the next chapter.

A divine person is spiritual, for God is a Spirit, the Father of spirits, the Spirit of spirits, an infinite Spirit, and therefore has life, the best of lives, nay *is life itself in perfection*, and therefore we read of the understanding and will of God. An understanding life is the best life that we are acquainted with, and the life of God is a subsisting life, everyone of the divine persons is subsistent, and therefore, each one of them has subsisting life. We may then safely conclude that each one of the divine persons is a spiritual and infinite subsistent. I say *subsistent* in order to show that I do not abstract the subsistence of the person from the divine nature in which the person subsists; herein all the three persons do agree.

Moreover, every divine person has some relative perfection, for they are mutually related to one another.

Finally, every divine person has some peculiar and incommunicable property. But if we come to treat of any peculiar manner of subsisting, or the order of subsisting, or that singular relation which is proper to every one of the three, or any certain incommunicable property, whereby any one person is distinguished from the rest, then we must leave treating of what is

---

[173] Hilar. lib. de Synodis. Inane enim est calumniam verbi pertimescere ubi res ipsa cujus verbum est non habeat difficultatem—expertus pridem sum & quidem saepius quicun{que} de verbis pertinacius litigant fovere occultum virus, ut magis expediat ultrò provocare, quàm in corum gratiā obscuriùs loqui.

common to all three persons, and show wherein these coessential persons differ, or whereby it appears to us, that they are distinguished. We will therefore for order's sake inquire: (1) what distinction there is between the divine nature, and the divine persons: Father, Son, and Holy Spirit. (2) What difference there is between created and uncreated persons. (3) How these three uncreated persons are distinguished from one another.

This question concerning the distinction of the divine nature and these three most glorious persons which subsist in it, is the most difficult point in all divinity, and therefore I humbly beg the assistance of all these glorious persons, that I may conceive and write judiciously and reverently of this profound and glorious mystery of faith. I remember that excellent speech of judicious Calvin: "*Non minori religione de Deo nobis loquendum quam cogitandum sentio; quicquid autem de Deo a nobis cogitamus stultum est, and quicquid loquimur insulsum.*" "Whatever we think or speak of our own heads concerning God, will be like ourselves unsavory, foolish, and vain. No language is rich enough, no words are significant enough to declare this profound mystery, which the understanding of men and angels cannot comprehend, nor the tongue of men and angels express, if all the saints and angels in heaven and earth should sit in council and communicate their notions to one another about this argument, they would acknowledge this mystery to be not only inexplicable and unspeakable, but inconceivable and incomprehensible."

(1) Concerning the distinction which is between the divine nature and a divine person, it is to be considered that I have most studiously declined the describing of a divine person *in abstracto* for the reasons mentioned above, and I might add many others. But it is enough to say that the cleanest abstraction does but suggest an inadequate conceit of a divine person; and when you abstract the nature of God from the personalities, men are apt to dream of some strange God that is neither Father, Son, nor Holy Spirit, and so to create a new God, or to conceive that the divine nature may, as the human nature of Christ subsists *in alieno supposito*.

(2) Those who deny the Trinity must, if they are not worse than Turks or Socinians, acknowledge that God the Father subsists, and therefore they are engaged to show the difference between the essence and subsistence of the Father, as well as we are, who believe the Trinity. But there is no greater a distinction between the person of the Father and the nature of the Holy Spirit than there is between the person of the Father and the nature of the Father, for the nature of the Father and the Holy Spirit is one and the same divine nature, which is as impossible to be divided or multiplied in two or three persons, as it is in one single and undivided person, because the divine nature is single and infinite, and the divine persons do mutually subsist in one another, and all three persons subsist in this single and undivided nature, which is indivisible, unmultipliable, and most purely and singularly one and the same infinite perfection in all three persons, and there can be but one most single absolute and infinite perfection.

(3) The divine nature is subsistent, necessarily, and perfectly subsistent; the most perfect manner of subsisting by and of itself is due to the most perfect nature.

(4) The divine nature is not indifferent to subsist in the Father, Son, and Holy Spirit, or out of them; for in regard to its infinite perfection and actuality, it can neither subsist without or otherwise than in the Father, Son, and Holy Spirit, because the divine nature cannot subsist without all, or any of that relative perfection, which shines in these three glorious persons, who do all subsist in the same divine nature, and yet mutually subsist in one another with all relative perfection. The reason is most clear, because the divine nature being infinite in perfection must contain and comprehend all relative as well as all absolute perfection.

(5) God is not compounded (as angels are) of nature and subsistence; for whatsoever belongs to the perfection of God, belongs to the nature of God, and therefore God does not subsist by the superadding of anything or manner of a thing, any *modus* that is (as the Schools speak) extra-essential, or really distinct, and separable from the essence and nature of God. And we

have formerly shown that the essence of God is intrinsically necessary and infinitely perfect, and therefore the most perfect manner of subsisting by and of itself is due to the most perfect nature.

(6) Although men and angels are not able to comprehend, much less express this incomprehensible mystery, yet we may set satisfactory bounds to our thoughts and discourses by the analogy of faith, for the Scripture says that the Father and the Son are one, and that all three persons are one, and therefore we do conclude that as the infinite perfection and actuality of the divine nature requires three subsistences, because this infinite perfection contains all relative, as well as all absolute perfection, so does the single and most singular nature of God require that these three glorious persons subsist in the unity of the Godhead. Now we are sure that the oneness or singleness of God's nature does well agree with the infiniteness of his nature, because there can be no multiplication of that which is infinites; there cannot be two or three infinites, and therefore we must conclude, that these three subsistents are one infinite God subsisting with all absolute and relative perfection. This is the sum and substance of all that can be said *a parte rei*, as we tend to speak; but because we are not able distinctly to apprehend the absolute and relative perfection of God, God makes himself known to us in a way most suitable to our weak apprehensions in representing himself to be an eternal Father, and then we are ready to inquire after and willing to hear of an eternal Son.

Now according to our weak manner of conceiving, we must apprehend that there is a divine relation between the eternal Father and his coeternal Son, and conclude that these two are distinguished from, and in a well-qualified sense opposed to, one another with a mere relative opposition, for there can be no contrary opposition between the persons. But this relative and friendly opposition assures us that the Father is not the Son, and that the Father did not beget himself, but did beget his Son. But then we consider again, that this Son is an eternal Son, and therefore is God, and we are sure God did not beget another God, for the power of God is not, nay cannot, be exercised about anything repugnant to the nature of God, and nothing is more repugnant to the Godhead than a plurality of gods; and therefore we must conclude, that the Father and Son are one and the same God. Now we are come to the mystery which faith must receive and reason admire.

(7) We may best resemble all that difference which is between the essence of God and the divine subsistences, by considering the transcendent affections of *Ens simpliciter* and the attributes of God, who infinitely transcends not only a predicamental substance, but a metaphysical entity, as the most metaphysical men who are sound in the faith do honestly confess.

[1] Concerning the transcendent affections of *Ens*,[174] which are *unum, verum, et bonum*; we say, these three affections, and *Ens in latitudine*, do not make four things really distinct; and yet we say they are real and positive affections; for our metaphysical science has too much serious majesty, to be pleased with the pretty fictions of reason, when our understanding has got leave to play, and recreate itself with its own artificial inventions. The thing is most clear and evident to all at the very first proposal, because the things which God has made, are not beholding to God only for their entity, and to us for their goodness, for the things do not cease to be good when our understanding ceases to work, but the things are truly and really good whether we think them to be so or not.

Moreover we say that these positive and real affections of *Ens* do not make any composition at all in *Ens* transcendently considered, because then the most simple and uncompounded being would lose its being. For simplicity would be repugnant to entity, if that entity itself did involve any composition. And therefore it is agreed on all sides, that this proposition, *Ens simplex est Ens*, is a true proposition. Finally, from what has been said it is reasonably and commonly inferred, that entity, truth, goodness, and unity, make but one real thing, though they do all four differ *quoad modum*

---

[174] That is: God considered as the most perfect or real being.

significandi: because the thing adequately signified by all those four words is but one real thing, namely the very entity of *Ens* transcendently considered. For when I say "*Ens est unum*," this predicate *unum* does not superadd any new entity, but does imply and connote the very entity of *ens*. Nay more, if you ask these metaphysical men what this transcendent unity is; they will not answer, that unity is indivision, but unity is the very undivided entity itself; not that unity alone signifies simply and adequately the same that *ens* does *in tota latitudine*, as *res* or *aliquid* do; for unity does not signify truth and goodness, which are the two other transcendent affections of *ens*, but *ens* in its complete compass and adequate signification imports entity, truth, unity, and goodness also. Truth is a single affection of *ens*, and therefore it signifies, or rather connotes, entity under an inadequate conceit or notion, for it does not represent *ens* in its full latitude, but as considered with respect to the understanding.

If we may now make so bold as to compare the essence of essences with these metaphysical notions, we may in some weak measure resemble that difference which is between the essence of God and divine subsistences, at least in some few particulars. For if when we compare creatures with creatures, there appears to be some dissimilitude even in the most apt similitude, and no similitude runs (as we say) upon four feet; it is not to be wondered at, if this comparison be rather a resemblance than an illustration. When divine revelation has gone before, and we have built upon that as the groundwork and foundation by a serious faith, these metaphysical notions may be subservient helps in a subordinate way.

{1} The Father, Son, and Holy Spirit do all three really, positively, truly subsist in the divine essence; and yet these three subsistences, and the divine essence, do not make four, no nor two things really distinct; even as entity, truth, goodness, and unity, do not make four things really distinct, as you heard but now, but are one real thing and no more.

{2} *Ens* is not compounded of entity and its three affections, nor is God compounded of the Godhead and three subsistences, and nor is any one person compounded of the divine nature and subsistence.

{3} As truth is not goodness nor goodness truth, nor either of them unity, and yet all three are entity, so the Father is not the Son, nor is the Son the Father, nor is either of them the Holy Spirit, and yet all three are God, for they are all three but one God subsisting with all absolute and relative perfection, as has been shown.

{4} Each one of the three affections of *ens* connotes entity. Each one of the three subsistences connotes the Godhead, the divine nature, as has been proven at large.

{5} Not any one of the three affections of *ens* does, nor do all three together superadd a new entity; not any one of the three subsistences does, nor do all three together superadd a new deity, a new divine nature, or Godhead, for *ens* is one:[175] *Ens est trinum, non triplex, trinum et unum Ens trinunum: Deus est trinus non triplex, trinus et unus, Deus trinunus.* This instance in some measure resembles the mystery of the Trinunity.

{6} No affection of *ens* can be really separated from *ens*, nor can one of the divine persons be separated from the divine nature, or the divine nature from any one of the divine persons, or any one of the persons from either of the other two.

{7} All the affections of *ens* are distinguished, but none divided; all the three subsistences are distinguished, but they cannot be divided.

{8} Truth and goodness, which are two of the affections of *ens*, are distinguished by their several and peculiar relations. Truth has relation to the

---

[175] Ens est unum, verum, bonum. Ens est essentiâ unicum, affectionibus autem trinū, trinum & unum, Ens trinunum. Unum est quod prius de unoquoque ente cognoscitur: Verum quod proxime cognoscitur; intellectus enim est prior potentia, quàm intellectus; & verum dicit ordinem ad intellectum; bonum ad voluntatem. Denique si res sit ficta, non est bona; & proinde bonitas quodammodo fundatur in veritate; omnes autem tres passiones sunt à parte rei. Entitas quoad significatum intrinsecum; entitas est bonitas & è converso.

understanding, and goodness to the will. The Father, Son, and Holy Spirit are known to be distinguished by their several and peculiar relations, and if it is not unreasonable to say that there is in entity three affections, and two relations *in ente simplicissimo*, without any composition in, or multiplication of the entity, why should it seem unreasonable, or at least why should it seem incredible that there are three subsistences and several relations in the Godhead, without any composition in, or multiplication of the Godhead?

{9} One affection, nay all the affections *in abstracto*, do but inadequately represent *ens*, unless you take notice of the entity itself, as well as the three affections. One single subsistence, nay all three subsistences *in abstracto*, do but inadequately represent God, unless you take notice of the Godhead in which they subsist; and therefore this precisive abstraction of the subsistences from the divine nature, is but an inadequate conceit of God, as has been demonstrated above in this very chapter. For we must not dream of a trinity of modes, but assert and believe the glorious and coessential Trinunity.

The Father is truly God, that God who is the only true God; but the Father alone does not adequately represent God to us as he is described in the Holy Scriptures.[176] It is true that the divine essence is by the subsistence of the Father adequately the Father, but as God is represented by that divine subsistence only, he is not *Deus Trinunus*, he is not Father, Son and Holy Spirit. The Father alone is not all those three witnesses who are one God. And therefore the acute Socinians with their precise abstractions do but

---

[176] Una subsistentia divina non plane prastat idem quod praestat altera; est enim inter personas divinas differentia relativa numerica Nec est essentia divina bis aut pluries id quod est, per tres subsistentias. Nam per subsistentiam Patris essentia divina est Pater, non Filius: per subsistentiam verò Filii nec Pater est nec Spiritus Sanctus: non itaque bis est Pater, vel bis Filius, vel bis Spiritus Sanctus; nec possibile est ut eodem respectu essentia divina sit Pater, quo est Filius. Tanta autem est essentiae divinae perfectio, ut una subsistentia ipsi non possit esse adaequata. Per subsistentiam itaque Patris divina essentia adaequatè est Pater, non verò adaequatè Deus. vid. Bisterfeld. lib. 2. sect. 1. cap. 5.

suggest an inadequate conceit of God: that the only true God, whom we worship, does not subsist only in the person of the Father.

We worship God subsisting with all absolute and relative perfection in Father, Son, and Holy Spirit, for these three are that one God who is the only true God blessed forever. This is the adequate representation of God in the Scriptures of truth. And we are resolved to regulate all our metaphysical notions by the holy Scriptures, so that we may make the highest of sciences to acknowledge the supremacy of that divine science which is nowhere to be learnt but in the Word of God, for the purest reason must be elevated by the Word and Spirit of God for the discovery of this mystery.[177]

{10} These affections of *ens* represent the manner of that being which *ens* has as it is transcendently considered; and the three divine subsistences do represent that manner of being which God has as he is most transcendently considered, namely as subsisting after the most glorious manner with all absolute and relative perfection.[178] It is the manner of a transcendent entity to be one, and true, and good, and it is the manner of God's being to be one God in three subsistences. These three are one single God, there is no composition or multiplication imaginable in this single and infinite being.

I was bold to adventure upon this enquiry because so many reverend learned orthodox and pious doctors of the church have declared that the divine essence differs from the divine subsistences as the manner of the thing does from the thing itself, and the persons differ from one another, *tanquam modi a modis*.[179] I conceived that there was something more in the expression

---

[177] In quibus ratio est integra, religionis nostrae mysteria cum ratione consentiunt: in quibus corrupta, cum ratione pugnant mysteria, ut rationem corrigant potius quàm superent. In omnibus enim mysteria supra rationem sunt omnino re, ratione, & modo.

[178] Deus est essentia univocè sive Ens entium, transcendens transcendentium, & proinde essentias non solùm Physicas, sed & Metaphysicas omnes infinitè omnibus modis superat; & proinde discrimina multa incidere ne mireris propter similium istorum inaequalitatem maximam.

[179] Veritatem convenienter Naturae ex sacris Scripturis asserimus; exiguum autem lumen tam est simile maximo, ut prout natura unum sunt, ita conjunctione in unm transeant, & in majore ac perfectiore minus sorbeatur, vide I unium Trinit. defens. 1

than was commonly known. Moreover, I considered that if there might be so great simplicity or singleness in a created and finite entity, notwithstanding there are three affections and two relations which do affect that entity, it seemed to me somewhat easy to believe that there are three subsistences in one infinite Godhead without any composition in, or multiplication of the single Godhead.

Finally, I perceive that some youthful towering wits are drawn away from the simplicity of the gospel by some frothy speculations presented to them as most sublime curiosities and metaphysical notions; and therefore I humbly submit what has been said to the judgment of the learned, and conclude this discourse with the same prayer wherewith Augustine shuts up his books of the Trinity: "*Domine, Deus unus, Deus Trinitas, quaecunque dixi in hoc libro de tuo agnoscant et tui; si quid de meo, et tu ignosce & tui.*" "O Lord, who art one God, O God, who art a whole Trinity of persons in the Godhead, what ever I have said (in this discourse) of thine, let all that are thine acknowledge, whatever I have said of mine own, Lord let it be pardoned by thee and thine."[180]

[2] Concerning the attributes of God, we may observe that they are all perfect, glorious, infinite, because they do signify and declare the infinite perfection, happiness, majesty, and glory of God; and to speak higher yet, these glorious attributes though they be very many, are nothing else but the single undivided indivisible essence of God, we may be instructed, but are even confounded with the glory of this mystery.[181]

---

[180] Curandum est quod mentem errantium occupat, tumor rationis humanae inani Philosophiae Metaphysicae specie abreptae; unu aut alterum Scripturae locum in transcursu vellicat, ne sine Christo aut Scripturâ (quod vel imperitis foret odiosum) videantur esse: et proinde quia ratione humanâ intumescunt, ex ijs ipsis principijs quae natura docet, et approbat, falsas esse ipsorum hypotheses, et Argumentationes demonstravi. Ab ijs quae nobis notiora sunt explicatio petenda est, et proinde explicatio Metaphysica non contemnenda est; quae enim docet Natura minimè cum verbo Dei pugnantia, docet Deus.

[181] Quanto diutius cogito, tanto mihi res videtur obscurior. Cicero de Simonide lib. 1. de Natura Deorum.

There are three reasons why we do not readily apprehend this truth.

{1} The defect of words to express it, especially in English, but indeed the most rich and copious languages are only happy in the confession of their penury [*paucity*] when we come to treat of this argument, because the mystery of the Godhead transcends all our eloquence, and teaches us to admire and adore with silence what we cannot express without a manifest demonstration of our ignorance.[182]

{2} The imperfect manner of signifying is easy to be observed in our most significant words, and therefore we must confess that the excellency of God transcends the significance of the most significant words in the most rich and copious tongues.

{3} The imperfection of our own understanding,[183] and of our manner of apprehending and judging of things while we are in the body.[184] If any man desire to know a reason why he cannot readily apprehend these divine mysteries, let him consider the perfection of the mystery, and the imperfection of his own reason, and he has a sufficient reason, a reason from whence he may draw a most invincible argument against idolizing of his own reason, so far as to make his reason judge of the mysteries of faith.

Let us then prudently consider that we are not able to apprehend the infinite and impartible essence of God but as it were by parts, by many incomplete and inadequate conceits and apprehensions.[185] The most

---

[182] Quam admirabilis est Deus, cum omnibus linguis fit indicibilis, omnibus cordibus incogitabilis! Aug. de cognitine verae vitae. cap. 3. Lombard. 1. sent. distinct. 8. Homo imbecillitatis Soboles, ignorantiae alumnus, in tantâ mysteriorum caligine Dei ignarus vocibus tenebrosis utitur ad lucem significandam; in verbo veritatis tenebrae appellamur, est cato in nobis tenebrarum interiorum subjectum, exteriorum illex: est peccatum in nobis depascens carnem ut hedera parietem, mentem obscurans, et voluntatem à vera luce abripiens tanquam unco Carnifex.

[183] Paucae lectionis, nullius intellectionis mancipia, intellectione satis mutilâ perfectonem metiuntur infinitam.

[184] Visio quae caelestis Reip. cives beat, non fit per principia nobis connaturalia: ibi intellectio sine ratiocinatione, scientia sine disciplina, quies sine motu: istius coeli Sol ipse Deus est sine occasu & sine ortu.

[185] Intellectus finitus quod est simplex & infinitū unico simplici{que} actu non capit.

profound and serious schoolmen have fairly expressed this truth. "There are not," say they, "many attributal perfections, nay, there is but one perfection in God; for all the essential attributes of God are nothing else but that single and undivided essence which is singularly and altogether the same essence in all three subsistences."[186] Nay, to speak properly the divine essence is one single infinite perfection, and we cannot say that perfection is in the essence of God; but rather that the highest perfection, even infinite perfection is the essence of God; it is every way his essence, and no way at all distinguished from it.[187]

Finally, if by *attributal perfections*, you mean the conceits or signs of perfection, they say these signs do indeed signify the divine essence, but the signs themselves are so far from being the essence of God, that they do not all of them signify the same divine essence after the same way and manner of signifying; for it is clear, that some of the attributal terms are affirmative, some are negative, some are absolute, some connotative, and relative.[188]

For observe that, when the perfection of God is declared *per viam negationis*, by negative expressions, as when we say God is immaterial, incorporeal, invisible, immortal, immutable, immense, and the like, we intend to remove all imperfection from the essence of God, and leave his pure essence single and alone, because it is one single and infinite perfection.[189] We deny that there is anything in God which might make him like to the creature in imperfection: for whatever there is which betokens matter, change, privation, or imperfection, we deny that to be in God,

---

[186] Accipiendo Perfectionem prore ipia quae perfecta est, non sunt in divinis plures perfectiones Attributales; omnia enim in divinis quae sunt Communia tribus non plurificantur, sed sunt unum simpliciter & una simplex Essentia. Biel 1. Sent. dist. 2. quaest. 2.

[187] Propriè & de virtute sermonis loquēdo non est concedendum quod in Deo vel divinâ Essentiâ sit perfectio, sed perfectio summa est omnibus modis divina essentia ipsa ab eâ penitus indistincta. Biel. 1. Sent. dist. 2 quaest. 2.

[188] Multi termini Attributales Affirmativi, Negativi, Absoluti, Connotative, & Relativi ipsam eandamque Essentiam Divinam simplissimam sed diversimode significant.

[189] Vide Basil. lib. 1. contr. Eunomium.

because God is one entire, infinite perfection. Therefore we say as Isidore Clarius does, that in these negatives there lays hidden not only a positive but an infinite perfection, and what is infinite must be single.[190] You see still the perfection is a single perfection. And when the perfection of God is declared *per viam eminentiae*, as the Schools speak, by attributing all perfection which we find in the creatures unto God, after we have removed all imperfection, we say the perfection signified is most perfectly and properly in God;[191] but the manner of signifying of that perfection by attributes taken from the creatures, does somewhat relish of that imperfection which is in the creature; and therefore we say such attributes in respect of the imperfect manner of signifying do not clearly hold forth that single and infinite perfection which is in God.

Hence it is that reverend divines have laid down so many rules as cautions to direct us in this weighty point:

(1) A finite and compounded understanding cannot apprehend the glorious perfection of a single and infinite essence, but by distinct properties or attributes.

(2) The essential attributes are all of them common to all the three persons of the Godhead, and to them only.[192]

(3) These essential attributes are not distinguished from the divine essence, but are the very divine essence or Godhead itself.

(4) All these essential attributes are infinite and eternal, because they are the infinite and eternal essence of God.

---

[190] Isidore Clarius Orat. 5. tom. 1. pag. 21.
[191] Attributa illa quoad rem significatam magis proprie Deo quam creaturis attribuuntur; accipiendo autem perfectiones Attributales prosignis vel conceptibus, perfectionem significāt, sed imperfecto modo significant, & proinde modus significandi creaturis proprie convenit, perfectio significata Deo convenit, sed secundum modum Eminentiorem. Vide Th, pag. 1. quaest. 13. art. 2. 3. 6. Zanch. de Naturâ Dei. cap. 8. quaest. 3.
[192] Omnes proprieta tes Dei nō possunt creaturis communicari, quia sic multiplicaretur essentia: necaliquae, quia sic divideretur.

(5) These essential attributes do not differ from one another, because the essence of God is single, uncompounded, undivided, indivisible, and one of these attributes essentially predicates of the other.[193] The power, wisdom, goodness of God, are single, eternal, immutable, infinite.

(6) These essential attributes do differ from one another only according to our weak apprehension, for our finite and compounded understanding – not being able to comprehend what is single and infinite – frames different conceits of the properties of God, according to the different objects and effects of these attributes.

Now because our understanding grounds all its conceits upon the several objects and effects of these attributes, we say, the difference is not purely rational, or a mere fiction of reason, but we call it a virtual or eminent distinction, framed by reason upon the grounds aforesaid, for the help of our weak understandings. For we must consider that this virtual distinction is not a real distinction;[194] because it does not import that the attributes of God are actually many or really different, but it signifies that the infinite essence of God does eminently contain all real perfections which are many indeed in the creatures. But all perfection in God is but one single and infinite perfection, which single and infinite perfection in regard to its eminency,[195] and our weakness cannot be expressed by one single act, or by one formal and adequate conceit of ours, because we do apprehend things according to those several objects about which they are exercised, and those several effects which are by their virtue and influence really produced.

---

[193] Attributa Divina non distinguuntur actualiter in reipsa, neque à Dei Essentiâ neque inter se, quia perfectio Divina est simpliciter infinita. vide Irenaeum l. 2. contr. haeres. cap. 8. Iust. Mart. q. 144. August. de Civ. Dei l. 12. cap. 2. Hen. quodlibet. l. 5. q. 1. Durand. Ocham. in 1. d. 2. q. 2.

[194] Perfectiones omnes creaturarum quatenus sunt in Deo nihil aliud sunt, quam ipsamet creatrix Essentia Dei. Vide August. lib. 4. Gen. ad lit. cap. 24. lib. 4. de Trinitate. Anselm. Monolog. cap. 34. 35.

[195] Deus solâ & suâ eminenti virtute omnes creatas perfectiones creaturis communicat, & quicquid est perfectionis in creaturis eminenter continet.

Now no effect in the world is adequate to the infinite virtue and eminent perfection of the divine nature, and therefore we cannot apprehend the eminent and infinite virtue of the divine nature,[196] but by considering of those many objects and manifold effects in the world, which do all represent the eminent and infinite virtue of the divine nature; and hence it is that we call it a virtual and eminent distinction, whereas indeed it is rather an eminence than a distinction, because the divine nature eminently contains all perfection in its infinite perfection, and the divine virtue manifests itself upon different objects and various effects; and therefore our weak understanding frames different conceits of it according to those different objects and effects, and consequently gives so many different attributes to God.[197] And God has so far condescended to our weakness in Scripture as to declare his single perfection by several names and attributes, answerable to those different objects and effects, in which the eminent and infinite virtue of God gloriously shines throughout the world. I have insisted long upon this virtual and eminent distinction, that I might by so many several expressions beat this grand mystery into the heads of the meanest Christians.

(7) When one attribute of God is abstractly considered from the rest of the attributes, that abstraction must be purely precisive not exclusive. I must not consider God's justice alone, so as to exclude his mercy, or any other of the divine attributes, from being comprehended within the single and undivided perfection of the divine essence. When the justice of God is considered abstractly, and the abstraction is purely precisive, all the attributes of God are at least implicitly included within the abstract consideration of

---

[196] Nullus effectus est infinitus, & proinde nullus effectus est Divinae Virtuti adaequatus.

[197] Eminens & virtualis distinctio in re, non est distinctio sed eminentia; est tamen respectu nostricon cipiendi virtutem eminentem secundum distinctos respectus ad diversa objecta & effectus distinctos.

divine justice;[198] for divine justice is essential justice, infinite justice; God is just by his essence, not by any virtue, or good quality; and he that is just by his essence, is perfectly just, infinitely just; you see that infinite perfection is implied, and infinite perfection is essentially all perfection, and therefore all the other attributes of God are implied, when I do consider one single attribute within an abstraction purely precisive; for there is the same reason of all other attributes of God; because God is essentially good, wise, merciful, etc., as well as just.

(8) The attributes which are called communicable attributes, are as truly the single and undivided essence of God, as those attributes, which we call incommunicable; for if we speak properly and strictly, no attribute of God can be communicated to a creature, anymore than the divine essence itself (Isaiah 42:8, Matthew 19:17; 1 Timothy 1:17). For all the attributes of God are his name, his perfection, his glory, his essence, his Godhead; and if any of the attributes were communicated, the essence of God must be multiplied, divided, or distracted from itself. The communicable attributes are infinite, and there cannot be more infinites than one, and therefore they must all signify one single and infinite perfection. For if any of the attributal perfections were finite, then the perfection of God would be made up of many finite perfections;[199] and God would not be infinitely perfect in himself, of himself, and by himself, but by some finite perfections superadded to his essence, which is utterly repugnant to the single and infinite perfection of God.[200] Yet true it is, that some attributes of God are said to be

---

[198] Quodlibet attributum divinum est infinitum simpliciter in genere entis, & proinde essentiam divinam & reliqua omnia Essentialia Attributa in suâ Essentiali ratione includit. Vide Caietan. de ente & essentiâ, cap. 6. quaest. 12. Communicable Attributes.

[199] Perfectio simplex & infinita non est ex multis & finitis perfectionibus conflata.

[200] Perfectiones quae sunt in creaturis distinctae sunt in Deo simpliciter & unitè; perfectio enim divina est infinita, & proinde simplex & unicissima.

communicable by analogical accommodation,[201] not in respect of the properties themselves, which are all infinite, but in respect of the effects of those properties; there is something in the creature by the bounty of our creator, and grace of our redeemer, which resembles after a weak manner the perfection of God, and therefore we are said to be partakers of the divine nature (2 Peter 1:4) when we bear the image of God in righteousness and holiness of truth.

For we are still to remember that God is to be known *per viam eminentiae*, when we make an eminent distinction between one divine attribute and another, or ascribe any of the perfections which are found in the creatures by way of attributal perfection unto God. For God is not great in quantity, or good by a quality, but by his own infinite essence.[202]

We must remove all imperfection from God, that we may know him *per viam negationis*. Therefore we say mercy and goodness are not accidents in God, his understanding and his will are not faculties, his anger and hatred are not passions, his many attributes are but one single perfection; the perfections which are in the creature are imperfect, but the perfection of God is infinite.[203] Finally, we must consider God as the cause of all perfection in the creature, that we may know him *per viam causalitatis*.

These grounds being laid, let us consider what great difference there does to our weak understanding appear to be between the divine attributes, whether they be compared with the divine nature, or with one another, and

---

[201] Quicquid est perfectionis in creaturis Deo attribuitur, salva Analogiâ quae inter Deum & creaturam perfectissimam semper intercedit. Perfectio creata ut sic non est Formaliter in Deo seclusis imperfectionibus creaturae; nam seclusâ omni imperfectione non remanet Formalis perfectio creaturae ut sic. Vide Suar. Metaph. Disp. 30.

[202] In his quae non mole magna sunt idem est majus esse, quod melius esse. Aug. Trinit. lib. 6. cap. 8.

[203] Nulla perfectio creata est in Deo Formaliter secundum adaequatam rationem quam habet in creaturâ, sed eminenter tantùm, quia imperfectio includitur in intrinseca ratione & conceptu creaturae; Sapientia creata est accidens, Sapientia creata est finita, & imperfecta. Perfectio itaque est in Deo Formaliter secundum proprium conceptum Dei.

yet that indeed and truth there is no real difference between the attributes and the divine nature, or between the divine attributes themselves, and we shall more easily conceive what great difference there is between the Father, Son, and Holy Spirit, without any essential difference between them.

The holy Scriptures – speaking to our weak capacity – describe God and his attributes after such a distinct manner to us, that we cannot but conceive, that there is some ground even in the word of God for this virtual and eminent distinction between the attributes, as will be most evident to any that observe the usual phrase and language of the Scriptures in these and the like places (Exodus 34:6-7; 1 Timothy 1:17, Psalm 103:8-10; 1 Timothy 6:15-16).[204] But it is as clear that God herein graciously condescends to our weakness, because we know that the divine nature is single and infinite, and therefore contains in it all actual perfection eminently, and all possible perfection both singly and actually,[205] because all true and pure perfection is most formally included in the nature and essence of God. Therefore, this eminent distinction grounded on the phrase of Scripture, and upon visible objects and effects, gives us no ground at all to conceive that the divine nature is not one single infinite perfection, because the Scripture speaks distinctly of God, and of his several attributes, only to teach us to apprehend the impartible perfection of God by degrees rather than parts, because we cannot apprehend it altogether.

Our conceits of God are inadequate, and collected by way of analogy from the perfection of the creatures; but we must consider that what the creatures do perform by many and distinct qualities and acts, God performs

---

[204] Distinctio non est Pura fed eminens, quia formatur & fundatur in verbo Dei quod distinctè de iis loquitur ad captum nostrum. D. Alting. Problem. part. 1. Prob. 10. pag. 49. D. Voet. pag. de unica & simplicissimâ Dei Essentia. Vide. Wallaeum. Gomarum.

[205] Deus est ex seipso Ens essentialiter summe perfectum & proinde essentia divina includit omnem possibilem perfectionem; nam perfectiones illae, quae sunt in Deo tantum eminenter prout in ipso, sunt Formalissime de conceptu Essentiali Dei. Vide Suarez. Met. Disp. 30. Sect. 6. Id circo ne quaeramus qui sit, cū sit omnia, & super omnia, & praeter omnia, αυταυτος. Vide Iul. Scalig. Exercitat. 365. p. 2. de Deo.

by his own essence which is one most single and most pure act. And therefore we conclude that this distinction is not really grounded upon God himself, upon his nature, or essence, but upon the effects of God. The objective conceits or things conceived are not really or actually different in themselves, but virtually and eminently in the several effects, egresses, terminations of God's eminent virtue, and single power, which is every way boundless and infinite, and therefore never works according to its full and adequate virtue.

The Scotists do indeed seem to say more, because they say that this distinction of the attributes is formal and *ex natura rei*; but then they come off again in their explication of these terms, and say that their meaning is that they are distinguished formally, not actually, but virtually and eminently, and therefore we mean the same thing.[206] For the divine essence is not only a single unity, but the first unity, which is incapable of any difference or number whatsoever;[207] only we cannot by a single act comprehend God's single perfection, because our understanding is finite, and his perfection is infinite.[208]

But it will be said that the attributes of God have to our apprehension not only different, but contrary effects: the justice of God punishes, and the mercy of God spares.

The answer is easy: the effects are to our apprehension contrary, nay they are contrary in themselves, but the attributes are not contrary; for the attributes do both belong to the same God, nay they are the same God, and

---

[206] Hanc distinctionē vocant rationis ratiocinatae virtualem aut Eminentem. Nonnulli autem distinctionē appellant ex Natura Rei Formalem, non Actu, sed virtute, aut Eminenter. Vide sis Rhadam Controvers. inter Thomam & Scotum part. 1. Contro. 4.

[207] Quicquid in Deo est essentiale unum est: à primâ autem unitate omnis differentia, omnisque numerus abesse debet.

[208] Pluribus conceptibus Formalibus inadae quatis realiter destinctis unam eandémque essentiam simplicissimam divisim vel potius gradatim concipimus. Conceptus autem ejusmodi Analogicè desumimus à rebus creatis, quae per multas distinctasque qualitates praestant ea, quae essentia divina per se.

these attributes do not overthrow but preserve one another. Now we readily grant that the effects are really different, nay contrary; but we deny that the attributes of justice and mercy are really different, or contrary in themselves.

Finally, we grant that according to our manner of apprehension, it is very improper to say that the attribute of God's mercy is the attribute of his punitive justice, because the terms are here taken *in sensu formali*, as we use to speak, and therefore that manner of predication is improper; yet if you take the terms *in sensu identico*, the thing is true, because mercy and justice are the same thing, the same essence. We may say that the same God, the same essence, which is mercy itself, punishes, but it is very improper and absurd to say that God forgives by his punitive justice, because God who speaks distinctly of his own attributes in his word, so that he might help our weak understanding, will not give us leave to speak so confusedly of his glorious attributes, as to puzzle the understanding of our weak brethren.

What I have said concerning the justice and mercy of God might, *consideratis considerandis*, be applied to his other attributes; and I might discourse in like manner concerning the understanding and will of God, concerning the acts and decrees of God, and inquire whether they are distinct from the essence of God, so that we may better understand the distinction that is between the divine subsistences and the divine essence, by comparing the divine attributes, acts, decrees, subsistences and essence altogether; but I shall be brief in that.

(9) The decrees of God, which we, according to our weak apprehension, are apt to conceive as many, are but one single and pure act in God;[209] nay, to speak strictly, they are nothing else but God himself decreeing; for the

---

[209] Deus in seipso semper agit intellectu & voluntate ut purus Actus.

divine essence is one pure and single act.²¹⁰ *In Deo non distinguuntur esse posse & operari,*. The decrees and acts of God, his knowing, willing, etc., are not many in their own absolute nature, for they are the nature of God considered as a pure and vital act; and hence it is that we say the decrees of God (in their absolute nature, or as they are considered with reference to God's own uncreated truth and goodness) are all essential and necessary, they did not begin to be, they cannot cease to be; God did not begin to know or love himself, he cannot cease to know his own almighty power, or to love his own uncreated goodness.

The decrees of God upon this account, and in this consideration, are not capable of multiplicity or division, opposition or succession, dependence or order.²¹¹ For here is nothing but one pure, vital, eternal, unchangeable act, which is God himself, knowing and loving of himself for himself. Take it all thus in brief, in a few short conclusions.

[1] God is a pure act, and therefore he cannot but act vitally;²¹² he must understand, and will. Here is no such liberty or mutability as Vorstius dreamt of, opposed to unchangeable necessity, for as God cannot cease to be because

---

²¹⁰ De actionibus Dei quas Decreta vocamus rotundè dicimus, Decreta Dei secundum perfectionem quam dicunt in Deo esse necessaria, aeterna & essentialia. Decreta autem quoad speciem, terminationem & extensionem ad externa esse libera, nec deo estentialia esse, nec ipsum Deum. Voluntas enim divina liberè terminatur ad creaturas sine ullâ sui mutatione, vel reali additione; accedit autem externa quaedam denominatio, & respectus rationis ex parte Dei in ipso decreto jam liberè terminato fundatus, ex parte creaturae in ipsa futuritione seu existentia illius.

²¹¹ Voluntas & volitio divina una est & simplex; nec multiplicitatē aut divisionem & distractionem, nedum oppositionem, nec prius & posterius aut successionem, nec dependentiam causalitatis & effectus aut cujuscunque alterius ordinis admittens; haec autem omnia rebus volitis competere possunt; res autem volitae à voluntate & volitione divina realissimè & infinitè distinguuntur; de rebus enim externis libere volitis loquimur. Vide Maccovium Miscell. qu. Disp. 17. 20. 23, 24, 25, 26. Voetium. ubi supra.

²¹² Actus divini considerati secundum id sunt, quod nil differūt ab essentia divina, & proinde nulla est in illis vel mutatio, vel libertas, sed summa necessitas. Sicut enim Deus non potest non esse, sic neque potest non velle, non intelligere. Imo actus divini considerati secundum respectum quem dicunt ad objectum Primum ac principale, ad ipsissimam nimirum Dei essentiam, sunt etiam necessarii; quia Deus non potest non essentiam suam scire, & tanquam summum bonum amare.

he is the first, necessary and independent being, and his necessity of being speaks his infinite perfection, so he cannot cease to act because he is a pure act. He must act vitally, who is life itself; he must know and will because he is the best life, and purest act; and this necessity speaks his purity and perfection also.

[2] If this pure and vital act be considered with reference to God's own essence, they cannot be distinguished, because God's essence is a pure act.[213] The self-same divine essence is both the act, and object in these immanent actions, which do not pass out of God towards, and therefore have no relation at all to, or denomination from, any external object.[214] God knows and wills all things within himself naturally, and necessarily; it's his nature to love himself; here is no distinction imaginable.

[3] Personal acts (such as the begetting of the Son and the breathing forth of the Spirit) are not arbitrary, but necessary and natural acts, and therefore eternal; now acts that are absolutely necessary *sine potentia ad oppositum*, as we use to say, being natural and eternal, are nothing else but God acting in and by some one or more of the three divine subsistences.[215] Nothing that is eternal can be out of God, and there is nothing in God that is not God, and therefore I need say no more of those personal acts in this place, because I am to treat of them at large in the very next chapter.

[4] The intrinsic acts of God which do connote some habitude and respect to something that is out of the Godhead, are the will of God, or the essence of God considered after the manner of an act of his will, *essentia ex se actuosa* (as the Schools speak) *concepta per modum actus volendi*. If this act be considered in itself, it is nothing else but the will or essence of God, because

---

[213] Vita divina est intellectu, voluntate, & potentiâ actuosa. Deus novit seipsū ut primum & infinitū objectum, amat seipsum necessariò, necessitate naturae, sed absque coactione, quia non potest nolle gloriam suam, aut seipsum negare.

[214] Actus immanentes nullum dicunt respectum ad, quia non transeunt in objectum externum.

[215] Actus Personales sunt aeterni, & proinde horū est absoluta necessitas absque potentiâ ad oppositum.

it is an intrinsic and vital act.[216] But now if this act be considered as relative, and as related to something that is out of God, we say this act is not necessary, but free in respect of all those things which God decrees to produce or permit in the world, for God arbitrarily decrees to permit or produce this, and not that, according to the counsel of his own will, it being as truly and fully in his power to permit or produce that, as this. Both were alike possible, but this is made future, and will in the fullness of time be present in act by virtue of the free decree of God, for all creatures are produced and do exist by the will of God. It is most evident that the will of God is the same whether it acts upon himself or something that is out of the Godhead.

[5] The relation which is between the will of God and the creature, whether in futurition, or existence, is extrinsic.

[6] The denominations grounded upon the termination, or relation of the will of God towards the creatures, is extrinsic also.

[7] These actions of God which are said to be rather from God than in God, as to create, govern, redeem or the like, are called extrinsic, and therefore the denomination of God from them must be extrinsic.[217]

[8] We have no ground to conceive that the essence of God is compounded with extrinsic terminations, relations, or denominations.

[9] Though the objects which God wills are very different, and their production is successive, yet the will of God is the self same, and is one single and pure act. The power of willing and the act of willing are not distinct in God; nay God wills his own happiness necessarily, and the

---

[216] Actus intrinseci in Deo connotantes respectum ad extra sunt ipsa Essentia Dei concepta per modum actus, sed relativi, & quidem ad extra. Omnia enim novit Deus quae sunt extra se, substantias, & accidentia. Genesis 1:31. Universalia, & singularia, Psalm 33:13-14, Job 1-2. Magna & parva. Matthew 6:25. bona & mala. Psalm 33:15. Genesis 6:5. interna & externa. Matthew 6:4. praeterita. Isaiah 38:3. futura. Isaiah 41:23. praesentia: possibilia denique 1. Samuel 23:11. & impossibilia. Titus 1:2. Omnia etiam liberè vult extra se, quaecunque nimirum statuit vel permittere vel producere; non enim quicquid potest facit.

[217] Actus extrinseci sunt a Deo effectivè, non sunt in Deo Subjectivé.

happiness of men and angels freely by the same will; necessity and liberty do not make distinct powers or wills in God.[218]

[10] There is no *potentia executiva* in God, and therefore all those conceits of Vorstius concerning any change or composition in God by several acts or decrees are but mere dreams, and vain conceits, though they be now published to the world, not with less blasphemy than impudence in this licentious age.

It is evident by what has been said that the eminent virtue of God (notwithstanding its several objects, egresses, terminations, relations, denominations and effects) is one single and infinite perfection. This will be the constant result and conclusion of all sober debates and Christian discussions. For if the perfection of God be not single, then it must be compounded, but it cannot be compounded either of things that are finite, or of things that are infinite. The perfection of God cannot be compounded of finite things, because it is infinite; for many nay all finite things cannot make up one infinite; and God cannot be compounded of many infinite things, because there can be but one thing that's infinite, and that is God. And therefore since God's perfection is his essence, and his essence is single, uncompounded, undivided, indivisible, it must follow that whatsoever is in God, is God, and God is (as has been often shown) one single infinite perfection. This is our first principle and last conclusion into which all our debates, and by which all our doubts about this argument may and ought to be resolved.

The distinction between the divine nature and persons may be considered:

{1} In respect of predication, the divine essence is predicated of every person, because everyone of the three subsistences is God, nay is the divine nature considered with this or that personal propriety and relation

---

[218] τό naturale & τό liberum nō constituūt diversas potentias in Deo.

respectively. But one person is not predicated of another, the Father is not the Son, nor is the Son the Father, or the Holy Spirit.

{2} In respect of communication, the divine nature is not only communicable but communicated to all three persons; but it is of the formal reason of a person to be incommunicable.

{3} In respect of relation. The divine nature does indeed eminently contain all absolute and relative perfection; but the formal relations whereby the persons are not only distinguished from, but opposed to one another, cannot be essential under that consideration, because they are peculiar to the several persons, and not common to all three persons, as the essence and nature is.[219] Peculiar and distinctive relations are not essential, because the persons who are relatively distinguished, are not essentially distinguished. The divine nature of the Father is not his fatherhood, for if it were, then each one of the three persons would be God the Father, all three persons would be one person, which is a manifest contradiction.[220]

{4} In respect of generation and procession, the divine essence does not beget, nor is it begotten. It does not proceed, and yet the Father does beget. The Son is begotten, and the Holy Spirit proceeds; the person of Christ is begotten, but his divine nature unbegotten.

{5} In respect of number: the persons are three, the divine nature most simply single, and singularly one.

{6} In respect of order: there is an order to be observed amongst the divine persons; the Father is the first personal principle, the Son the second, and the Holy Spirit who is breathed forth by the Father and the Son, is the third. The Scripture says there are three, and commonly reckons them in that order, and we have no ground to reckon the Holy Spirit before the Son

---

[219] Distinctio in Deo nascitur ex relationibus propriis sive personalibus quales sunt paternitas, filiatio, spiratio, processio; quaedam enim relationes sunt omnibus personis communes quales sunt Identitas fundata super Vnitatem Essentiae, similitudo fundata super Vnitatem Attributorum, & aequalitas fundata super unitatem magnitudinis.

[220] Essentia & paternitas virtute & eminenter Formalem distinctionem continent, quia ita se habent ac si Formaliter distinguerentur.

because he proceeds from the Son, but the divine nature being a single unity, and the first unity, is as incapable of order as it is of number.

[11] Notwithstanding all these and some other distinct considerations, I shall be bold to make this peremptory determination: the three divine subsistences are not really distinguished from the divine nature, or essence. The Scripture says that Christ and his Father are one (John 10:30) and that all three are one (1 John 5:7), essentially one, and therefore really one.[221] I have said enough above to prove all three persons to be essentially one. The three persons are one God subsisting with all possible perfection, relative as well absolute in one pure act *ex parte rei*. The three divine persons do not differ from the divine nature, as a human person does from the human nature singularly considered, for a singular human nature may be separated from a human person as is evident in the incarnation of our Lord and Savior. But the divine nature cannot subsist *in alieno supposito*, the nature of God cannot subsist in any other or any fewer than these three persons, who are one and the same God; And therefore the divine nature does not differ really from the persons, *tanquam res à re*, as we say, nor *tanquam res à modo separabili*; they do not differ really either way; nor do the persons differ really, that is *realiter separabiliter* from one another, as shall be proven when we come to speak of the distinction of the divine persons in the next chapter.

[12] The distinction between the divine nature and three divine subsistences is not a groundless conceit or a mere fiction of reason, because it is grounded on the word of God.[222] For our apprehension of God must be

---

[221] Ego & Paterunū sumus nempe Essentiâ, Potentiâ & Gloriâ. Ergo Christus deducit fidem nostram ad hoc fundamentum, nimirum ut ipse sit unus cum Patre Deus—necesle habemus ut videamus in Christo Deitatem, in facie ejus personam Patris, cum sit Character Personae ipsius; in facie ejus gloriam Dei, cum sit splendor gloriae ipsius: in manu ipsius manum & potentiam Patris; denique in illo totam Dei Patris majestatem. Rollock in John 10:30.

[222] Credimus tres esse Hypostases nobis in Scripturâ significatas per nomina quae relationem significant. Non est enim Pater nisi Filii, nec Filius nisi Patris, nec Spiritus nisi Spirantis. Itaque relationes quidem ipsas habemus in divinis literis. Chamier. de Canone lib. 9. cap. 10.

agreeable to that divine revelation, which God has vouchsafed us of himself in Scripture. Now it is most clear and evident, by what has been said in this whole discourse, that the holy Scriptures teach us to conceive distinctly of some things in God, which are not really distinguished in him. And therefore Mr. Fry may do well to consider, and retract that rash censure which he passes upon this doctrine of God, when he says that the doctrine of three distinct persons or subsistences in the Godhead is a chaffy, gross, carnal, and absurd opinion, in the title and 22nd page of his blasphemous book, for this distinction is not only grounded on a phrase of Scripture, but is eternal.[223]

[13] The distinction between the divine nature and persons is an eminent distinction. I have told you above what we mean by that expression. The persons are the essence of God, and not anything separated or divided from it; everyone of the three persons is a person of the Godhead, nay everyone of the three persons is the Godhead considered with some particular property and relation; and the Godhead being absolutely single, we must conclude that the divine nature and a divine person is the same essential real thing, though they are eminently distinguished by sundry considerations, as has been shown.

But it is objected that each one of the three persons is a substance, and if there are three substances subsisting in the Godhead under sundry formal considerations, then there will be three divine substances, three substantial relations and properties, and therefore the Godhead will be compounded by these three substances, substantial properties and relations, or else there will be three substantial and formal gods.

To this grand objection, I make these few returns by way of answer.

---

[223] Haec distinctio habet fundamentum non tantum in effect is aut phraseologiâ Scripturae, quia fuit ab aeterno. Nam ab aeterno Essentia fuit non tantùm Communicabilis sed Communicata, persona autem incommunicabilis; persona filii, genita, essentia ingenita.

{1} Each one of the three persons is a substance, a divine substance, but they are the same divine substance, because they are the same God. These three are one, they are unum, one divine substance, one God; they are all three divine persons, but they are coessential persons, and inessential persons of the same Godhead.

{2} The peculiar relations do distinguish, but they do not compound, for they do not superadd any new entity, much less any new Godhead, because all these relations are natural, eternal, and therefore they are God. Absolute and relative perfection in God, are but one single perfection.

(i) The parts or extremes wherewith any thing is compounded must be really, or at least modally and separably distinct; for all created natures and persons being compounded, are not only modally, but separably distinct.

(ii) The parts compounding must be united by some efficient cause,[224] and one of the parts must be a mere power or passive potentiality that is capable of further perfection, and the other an act to make that power perfect and complete.[225]

(iii) There must be by virtue of this union and perfection some dependence, multiplicity and change. Now it is clear that the nature of God in which the persons subsist is not capable of these imperfections, for: (a) There are no compounding parts in God. (b) The persons are not made one person by their inessential subsistence, but remain three distinct persons. (c) The persons are not separably distinct from the divine nature, or from one another. (d) The persons do not perfect the divine nature, for it is infinitely perfect of itself, and the three persons are by virtue of the same divine

---

[224] Quae actu ex naturâ rei distinguuntur, non possunt inter se uniri nisi per actionem causae efficientis: nulla autem causa essiciens prior Deo est; ergo.

[225] Essentia in creatis est divisibilis & perfectibilis; persona enim creata actuat et perficit essentiam perfectibilem; personalitates autem increatae non sunt actus naturae divinae ut sic & praecise consideratae eam perficientes vel informantes.

essence essentially the same God, and really one, as has been laid down.[226] The divine nature is not like a created nature, which is (*imperfectae actualitatis,* as we say) so imperfectly actuated, as that it is capable of further perfection; for the divine nature has no weak, imperfect, defective, passive potentiality in it, and therefore cannot be contracted, determined, actuated by any personal properties or relations. If God be essentially considered, he has a singular existence of himself by his own essence, and has most perfect unity and quidditative or essential actuality, because his essence is the most perfect essence that is, or can be. If God be personally considered, he has the most perfect personality that is, or can be, and every person has a perfect, proper and peculiar subsistence, which is not capable of any farther perfection *in esse personali.* Every person is complete *in esse quidditativo per essentiam, in esse personali per propriam subsistentiam.* I need say no more on that argument, because I have upon several occasions said so much already.

{3} The essence of God is not multiplied by sundry considerations of the same essence.

{4} The three formal considerations are not essential but personal considerations, and we grant that there are three formal persons in, and of the Godhead; but it will not follow from thence that there are three gods, for these three persons are one God.[227]

---

[226] Essentia in creatis est imperfectae actualitatis & proinde perfectibilis. Essentia autem divina non habet se ad modum potentiae perfectibilis, nec persona divina ad modum actus naturam divinam infinitam simplicissimam perficientis. Ratio quidditativa, & ratio Relativa in Deo tanquam diversae rationes Formales à nobis concipiuntur, sed ambae illae rationes Formales sunt in Deo secundum ultimám unitatem & actualitatem propriam. Nihil enim perficit essentiam divinam in actu quidditativo praeter ipsissimam essentiam; nihil perficit personam in esse Personali praeter propriam Subsistentiam, nihil perficit personam in esse Relativo praeter propriam relationem: Pater per ipsam paternitatem perficitur in esse Relativo.

[227] In Deo est essentia & tres relationes, sed non sunt tres essentiae relativae. Proprietates personales praecisè & formaliter sumptae non uniuntur inter se, & in se: nam unio in & cum essentiâ est in aliquo tertio.

{5} A divine person may be presented to our most serious thoughts under a threefold consideration, as learned Junius observes.[228]

(i) The first consideration of a person is common or essential, because the same divine essence is common to all three persons; when a person then is considered as God, we call this an essential or common consideration, because the persons are no way distinguished under this first consideration, but are one thing, the choicest and chiefest of things, and are one with the most single and singular kind of unity: Father, Son, and Spirit are one Jehovah, one God and the same God.[229]

(ii) The second consideration is personal, and yet absolute, whereby the person is considered as subsisting in the unity of the divine essence.[230] This consideration is more singular, because every person has its proper and peculiar subsistence; for the Father subsists of himself, but the Son has subsistence from his Father. Now the self-subsistence of the Father is proper, peculiar, personal, that is, proper and peculiar to his person, and yet this self-subsistence is absolute, for his self-subsistence is not his fatherhood, and therefore it cannot be esteemed relative. But though this consideration is more singular, because every person has his peculiar subsistence, yet herein all three persons agree, that they do all three subsist in the unity of the same Godhead, though every person has his proper subsistence, and his peculiar way of subsisting. Here are indeed three subsistences under this

---

[228] Vide Junium contra Bellarminum, Controv. 2. lib. 1. Praefat. Ut res planior sit, id praemittendum est personae considerandae triplicem rationem esse; Communem in essentiâ quà Deus est: Singularem Absolutam in Persona quà subsistit in unitate Essentiae; & Relativam in distinctione & ordine personae unius ad alteram.

[229] Ratione Communis Deitatis & communium essentialiumque attributorum, nulla distinctio cogitari debet, sed tantùm ratione Personae & proprietatum personalium.

[230] Essentia notat naturam divinam cum proprietatibus communibus: Persona notat naturam divinam cum proprietati bus dist inctivis, sive istae proprietates sint Absolutae, sive sint Relativae; habere subsistentiam à seest quid Absolutū: [...] est quid Positivum Nomen autem Personae, nomen Relativum communiter dicitur originationis aut originis respectum includens, quo Persona divina à se, vel ab aliâ subsistentiam habere significatur. Habere autem subsistentiam à se, quantum mihi videtur non dicit respectum ad aliud, vel alium.

consideration, and yet but one divine substance, essence, nature, Godhead, because all three do subsist in the unity of the same Godhead, for we must still keep our eye fixed upon that text: "These three are one."[231]

(iii) The third consideration is relative in the order of one person to, and distinction of one person from another. This distinction of persons is to be handled at large in the next chapter; our point in question here in this chapter does not concern the distinction of one person from another, but the distinction of all three persons from the divine nature.[232]

Now they who speak most largely of the distinction between the persons, and say it is in some sense a real distinction,[233] do yet confess that the real distinction which they treat of is not essential,[234] and therefore still here is an essentially union of the three persons under all these three considerations. We do still make much of 1 John 5:7, and hold it fast for our direction and support.

{6} This argument will be best answered by showing the vast difference between created and uncreated persons, and I have with a great deal of patience waded through all these perplex disputes, that I might make way for the clearing of this grand mystery, and glad I am that I am now got within sight of it, though I have had as hard a passage as Hannibal had over or through the Alps, and yet I have made my way without fire or vinegar.

(2) Concerning the difference between created and uncreated persons, we may observe that: [1] All created persons have a finite and dependent nature. [2] They have a compounded nature. [3] They have a different

---

[231] Tres sunt in eadem naturâ divinâ indivisâ Coexistentiâ Coessentialiter subsistentes; tres enim personae inconfusè uniuntur & indivisè discernuntur.

[232] Est aliquid in persona Absolutum quod est Proprium, est aliquid in Deo relativum quod est Commune. Identitas, similitudo, aequalitas, mutua praesentia personarum inter se propter inconfusam in se mutuò comprehensionem, sunt relationes ad intra omnibus personis communes; relationes autē distinctivae sunt propriae.

[233] Omnis distinctio essentialis est realis, sed omnis distinctio realis non est essentialis. D. Voetius.

[234] Personae divinae non differunt realiter essentialiter, nec realiter separabiliter, sed proprietatibus realibus personalibus; tales autem sunt istae reales proprietates quae essentiae divinae non superaddunt novam entitatem. Vide D. Alting. Problem. X.

nature. [4] They have a different understanding, will, and power. [5] They have a different place and presence. [6] They have different accidents, and are distinguished by a heap of accidents. [7] Human persons with whom we are best acquainted, may differ in time also; one human person may subsist a long time after another is dissolved.

Having laid down these positions, let us now make the comparison, and observe the difference between created and uncreated persons:

(1) **All created persons have a finite and dependent nature, but the nature of all uncreated persons is independent and infinite.** This one difference is an infinite difference, and surely if there were no other difference, that would suffice to discover and overthrow all the arguments of Socinians and Familists. I do often admire that the acute Socinians who pretend to be wholly ruled by reason, should have no more reason in them than to argue after this absurd manner. Three human persons are thus and thus distinguished, ergo if there be three divine persons, they must be thus and thus distinguished also, even just as human persons are. Is not this a gross fallacy,[235] because of the imparity and infinite inequality?[236] If the divine persons must be called into question, let them be tried by their peers. They say they cannot comprehend this mystery; I say the reason is because it is a mystery, and if they cannot comprehend it, they may the better believe it to be incomprehensible. The single nature of these three persons is infinite, and if men wonder that they cannot comprehend what is infinite, it is because they do not consider that they themselves are finite.

---

[235] Vide Nazian, orat. de Spiritu Sancto. Damasc. orthod. sid. lib. 3. c. 5. Athanas. Dialog. de Trinitate & in Mat. 11. Nazian. orat de pace Orat. 37, & 51.

[236] Absurdum est personas coessentiales & infinitas ad creatarum quae finitae & diversae essentiae sunt modulum redigere.

(2) **The nature of these three glorious subsistences is independent.** The nature of all created subsistences is dependent, and therefore it is no wonder if a dependent nature do subsist in its proper person, and depend upon its proper person for sustentation; but the divine nature does not depend upon the three subsistences for its sustentation or subsistence, but all three persons do subsist in this independent and infinite nature (Philippians 2:6), subsisting in the nature of God.[237] So the Scripture expresses it, and we must apprehend and believe these holy mysteries according to the holy Scriptures, because no man has seen God, and God is the only all-sufficient witness concerning his own essence and subsistence, concerning himself; and therefore we must not think or speak otherwise of God than according to the Scriptures of truth, in which God has sufficiently and graciously revealed himself (John 1:18, Matthew 16:17, Matthew 11:26-27).

The Scriptures direct us how to distinguish uncreated persons from created persons. Our finite and dependent nature subsists in a created person, but uncreated persons do subsist in an infinite and independent nature; there is a manifest difference. Our nature indeed subsists in the divine and uncreated person of the Son of God, but that is not according to the common course of nature, there is a peculiar reason and another mystery in that wonderful subsistence. And yet even in that wonderful mystery our dependent nature subsists in a person, which notes its dependence; and our nature is more satisfied and quieted by subsistence in a divine than in a human person, because it has a more glorious sustentation, and is more powerfully upheld by that divine and uncreated person. The divine person of Christ subsists in his divine nature, and the human nature of Christ subsists in his divine and only person.

(3) **All created persons have a compounded and divisible nature, but uncreated persons have a single undivided and indivisible nature.** The Socinians, Arminians, and Vorstians of this age do not love to hear any

---

[237] Natura creata est dependēs; persona creata est Independens, quia non est in alio per dependentiam ab illo tanquam sustentante.

discourse of the single nature of God, in Father, Son, and Holy Spirit; this doctrine, they say, is philosophical, scholastic, metaphysical, and therefore there is nothing which concerns faith, piety, or manners in it.

But it is most clear and evident that all the glorious attributes of God are united by an eternal bond which cannot be dissolved, and we have invincibly proven that they do all signify but one single and infinite perfection. If you take away the singleness of God's being, you take away his incommunicable, unchangeable, incomprehensible, independent and infinite perfection. This point is excellently discussed and opened by Damascene.[238] "Composition, he says, "begets strife. Strife may well cause a separation, and separation dissolution, which all who know anything of God will acknowledge to be repugnant to the perfection of the Godhead."

The learned doctors of old did consider that God is a most pure and perfect act, the first and independent being, that he is what he is by his own essence, and not by participation.[239] But Vorstius was bold to publish his dreams contrary to the analogy of faith and unanimous judgment of the reverend doctors of the ancient church.[240] The Socinians in their catechism,[241] and the Arminians in their confession and apology, are exceedingly to blame in this point.[242] The Socinians expunge the single and infinite perfection of God's spiritual nature out of their catechism,[243] that they may more securely deny the coessential Trinunity of Father, Son and

---

[238] Damascen. Orth fid. lib. 1. c. 4.

[239] Vide Irenaeum lib. 2. cap. 16. Athanas. in decret. Synod. Nicen. Nazian. lib. de Fide. Cyrill. lib. 10. contra Iulian. Euseb. Praeparat. Evangel. lib. 8. c. 2. Athenagoram, Talianum, Augustin. de Trinit. & passim.

[240] Vorstius Deum contemnendum pingit Corporeum, visibilem, mutabilem, accidentibus subjectum, in quo sunt plures res, &c. Vide Eglisem. Cris. & Hypocris. Bogerman contra Grotium. Synod. Nat. Dodrac.

[241] Racov. Catechis. de cognitione Dei cap. 1.

[242] Remonstrant. Confess. Apolog. p. 41. 42.

[243] Deus est Spiritus. Joh. 4. 24. Jehovah Exod. 33. 19. Eheje. Exod. 3. 14, 15 ο ων Revelation 1:4. Summe perfectus Genesis 17:1. summeque unus. Deuteronomy 6:4. & proinde omnem de Deo compositionem imò & quasi compositionē de Deo negamus. vide Rhadā Episcop. Pact. Controvers. infter Thomam & Scotum, part. 1. Controv. 4. append. 2. pag. 82. 83, 84.

Holy Spirit; and therefore I do insist upon this difference between created and uncreated persons, because if the doctrine concerning the single and infinite perfection of God's spiritual nature be overthrown,[244] all the fundamentals of the Christian religion will be overturned.[245]

God is Jehovah, he is what he is by his own essence, he can neither cease to be, or to be what he is; for he cannot be any other thing, or any otherwise than now he is, and ever was (Exodus 3:14-15, Revelation 1:8, James 1:17, Psalm 10:2, 27). God is called *light* and *love* and *life* in Scripture, to note the singleness of his being, because whatsoever is in him, is himself, and he himself is one single infinite perfection, he is light itself, and in him is no darkness at all (1 John 1:5).

God has not such an imperfect singleness of being, as we say, is in the first matter of last difference and the like; nor such a singleness as is in angels, or the souls of men, for theirs is but a comparative singleness, there is some kind of composition even in the most glorious angels.[246] God is not compounded of a nature, attributes, and relations, as has been shown, nor is any of the divine persons compounded; nor can the Godhead be said to be compounded of three persons; for though the persons be distinguished, they do not compound, nor can they be compounded.[247] Distinction connotes perfection, because it is opposite to confusion, but composition denotes multiplicity and imperfection. We must then consider that: [1] The essence

---

[244] Eglisem. contra Vorstium.

[245] Maccov. Mis. quaest. Disp. 17. 20, 23, 24, 25. 26. Vasquez. disp. 16. Deus est liber ab omni compositione etiam improprie dictâ, qualis est ex essentiâ & esse, ex natura & supposito seu ex essentia & subsistentiâ, ex genere & differentia: & proinde liber ab omni distinctione in essentia suá. Nam distinctionis & multitudinis transcendentalis personarum atque adeo modorum & relationum longe alia est ratio. D. Voet.

[246] Mareria Prima formae, differentiae ultimae, &c. simpliciter simplices dicuntur; Angeli sunt Comparative simplices; essentia autem divina est Absolutè & simplex. Ens summum est summe unum, & proinde essentitiae unitate unum, simplicissimè unicum. Vide. D. Voetium de Natura Dei saimpl.

[247] Non debemus proprietates Dei ab essentia ejus vel cogitatione scparare, quia in essentiae forma & virtute omnes continentur, & Deus sine proprietatibus ejus cogitari non potest. D. Wallaeus de Deo. pag. 127

of God is most perfect, and therefore nothing can be added to it to make it more perfect, because it is infinitely perfect.[248] [2] Whatsoever is compounded may be dissolved into the parts whereof it is compounded. The Godhead cannot be dissolved, because it cannot be changed. [3] Whatsoever is compounded, must be dependent both in being and in working. But God is independent.[249] Ergo: [4] the parts compounding are before the whole that is compounded; but God is the former of all things, and therefore nothing can be before God.[250] The divine essence cannot be later than itself, or later than anything else, because it is the first and eternal being.

Now if neither of the nature or attributes of these uncreated persons, nor the persons themselves be compounded, nor God compounded of the nature and persons; here is another very great difference between created and uncreated persons, who have life, and are life itself, because they are one single perfection.[251]

(4) **Three created persons have three different natures, but these three uncreated persons have the self-same most single and singular nature.**[252] Three created persons may have the same specifical nature, but they have not the same singular nature; created persons in respect of their specifical nature which is universal, are ὁμοιούσιοι of like nature, but in respect of their singular nature they are ετερουσιοι. But now these uncreated persons are ομοουσιοι in respect of their singular essence.[253] Look how

---

[248] Essentia divina non est in potentiâ, quia est paras actus, non est perfectibilis, quia omnes perfectiones complectitur.

[249] Deus non depender à subjecto à causis vel internis, vel externis, à principio quocunque priori aut superieri.

[250] Essentia divina non est in se composita, nec aliquid ipsi componibile, nec ipsa alicui componibili. Essentia aeterna nec scipsâ nec ullâ realiâ posterior esse potest.

[251] Proprietates Dei non minùs infinitae sunt quàm ejus essentia; mul a itaque infinita in Deo essent si attributa non essent ipsissima Dei essentia simpliccisma, Joh, 5. 26. est vita; Joh. 11. 25.

[252] Unius personae in creatae tota est essentia divina, sed non solius.

[253] Singula sunt in singulis, & omnia in singulis, & singula in omnibus, & omnia in omnibus, unum omnia. August. lib. 6. de Trinitate cap. ultimo. Nec major est essentia in tribus quàm in duabus, nec in duabus quàm in unâ, quia tota est in singulis. August. ubi supra.

many created persons there are of the same species: so many singular substances there are of that species.²⁵⁴ For a finite nature cannot be communicated to several proper persons of the same species without a multiplication of singular natures or substances, because every finite nature is imperfect and divisible.²⁵⁵

The human nature is communicated to Paul, Peter, and John. Now these three persons are three men, for they have three distinct singular natures, though they have one universal nature; and no wonder, for their nature is imperfect and divisible; their universal nature is *unum multiplicabile*. But the nature which is common to these three divine persons is not universal but singular; it is *unum immultiplicabile*, because the divine nature is infinite, and that which is infinite cannot be multiplied; the unity of the divine nature is real and most perfectly singular.²⁵⁶

The same singular nature, the whole nature being of bound less perfection is really and eternally communicated to all three persons without any division of the nature, separation of the persons or composition of nature and persons. The persons are distinguished, but not separated; and if we speak properly and strictly, the divine nature, as it is common to all three persons, is neither distinguished nor multiplied;²⁵⁷ for the nature is not

---

[254] Tot sunt sustantiae singulares quot personae creatae.

[255] Essentia creata est finita, circumscripta, imperfecta, divisibilis, perfectibilis: per differentiam enim individualem sive personalem contrahitur, perficitur. Essentia partibilis per partes & separatim inest singulis individuis Angelicis & humanis. Essentia autem divina est perfecta infinita simplex, & proinde eadem etiam numero & individuo (quod aiunt) tribus personis communis citra omnem multiplicationem, divisionem aut separationem; eadem quippe natura singularis est tota in singulis personis divinis.

[256] Unitas specifica non est rei sed rationis extra men tem enim nostram non est unitas naturae humanae in personis diversis sed pluralitas. Unitas autem essentiae divinae est realis, & singularissima, quia ita Deus est unus ut etiam sit solus, & ita solus ut non possit esse alius.

[257] Persona multiplicatur & proinde distinguitur; essentia autem divina nec distinguitur, nec multiplicatur.

distinguished from itself,[258] nor are the persons distinguished from one another by the nature, or natural properties, but by personal properties, which are not naturally common to all three, as the attributes are (which we call natural because they are essential) for these personal properties are naturally peculiar and incommunicable, and yet they do nor superadd any new nature; because the divine nature contains all relative as well as absolute perfection in it; and the Godhead considered with all these incommunicable properties is but one single Godhead, as has been shown: this is a transcendent mystery indeed.[259]

(5) **Created persons have a different understanding, a different will, a different power, because they have a different nature.** But uncreated persons who have one and the same undivided and infinite nature, must have one and the same understanding, will and power. For, we cannot comprehend God as one pure vital act, but as his life is actuous or active in his understanding and will, in his essential and almighty power.[260] Now, what is essential, that must be common to all three persons.[261]

Whatsoever the Father is as he is substance, as he is life, as he is eternity, as he is perfection, as he is God, the same is the Son of God, and the Holy Spirit, as Augustine frequently discourses. When the attribute or predicate is essential, whatsoever is affirmed of the attribute or predicate, that must be true of the subject, as the philosopher and all that have any reason in them, do unanimously conclude.[262]

The essential power of God is the very essence of God. God acts by, and of himself, and not by any faculty or power superadded to his essence.

---

[258] Unitas ad essentiam proprie pertinet, distinctio autem personarum non ad essentiam propriè & per se, sed ad rationem in essentiâ respicit. Iunius contra error. Samosat.

[259] In omnibus mysteria supra rationem sunt Re, Ratione, & Modo.

[260] Vita Dei est actuosa intellectu, voluntate, & potentiâ.

[261] Quod essentiae proprium est hypostasibus commune est.

[262] Quicquid dicitur de praedicato essentiali, dicitur de Subjecto.

Christ is called "the power of God,"²⁶³ and the Holy Spirit is called "the power of the Most High" (1 Corinthians 1:8, 24, Luke 1:35)²⁶⁴ in order to show that they have the same essential power that the Father has. Christ says that none can take his sheep out of his hand, because none can take them out of his Father's hand, for he says: "I and my Father are one (John 5:28-30)." We have one nature, one hand, that is one power. For the hand of God can be nothing else but the power of God. Therefore since all the three divine persons are one God, because they have one and the same divine nature, these three are one with the most perfect and singular manner of unity.²⁶⁵ Finally, since the power of God is the essence of God, it must follow that all three persons have the same power, because they have the same divine essence, and they have the self-same essence by nature, not by mere indulgence or grace.

But then some who have a great mind to cavil, tell us that we do but equivocate when we say these three persons have the same essential power, because we do conceal the other member of the distinction, which is relative or personal power.²⁶⁶ Now it is impossible, say they, that these three should have the same personal or relative power, because the Father begets a Son as he is God the Father, as he is the first personal principle, and not simply and absolutely as he is God. But the Son has not power to beget himself, or to beget another Son, because there can be but three divine persons, and there

---

²⁶³ Filius αυτοδύναμος dicitur ab Epiphanio contra Marcellianos haeresi. 72 pag. 358. [Vide] Basilius de Filio contra Eunomium lib 2 pag. 339.

²⁶⁴ Vide D. Gomari Diatriben de Christo αυτόθεος & D. Voetii notas in select. Disp. D. Voetii par. 1. pag. 442. 445. 449.

²⁶⁵ Omnes tres personae sunt Coessentiales, & proinde essentialiter unum sunt; *tres enim persone non sunt tres essentiae*, sed ipsissima & unicissima essentia, quia simplicissima. Personae autem Coessentiales sunt coaequiles; licet enim filius & Spiritus Sanctus vitam, potentiam, omnia habeant à Patre, omnia habent per naturam, nihil per gratiam.

²⁶⁶ Potentia divina distinguitur in Personalem & Essentialē Personalis est quâ Pater generat filium, &c. Essentialis est quae cōmunis est tribus personis. Potentia Patris videtur esse Activa, quia Pater est gignens; generatio autem filii videtur esse Passiva, quia filius est genitus Psal. 2. 7. Joan. 1. 14.

is but one of the three called a Son in Scripture. Moreover, the Son is begotten, and therefore his power is rather a passive than an active power. But the power of the Father whereby he did beget his Son is an active power. Nor did the Holy Spirit breathe forth himself by his own power, for he did not proceed from himself, but from the Father and the Son; and therefore though there be but one essential power, it should seem that there are three personal or relative powers truly distinct in the Godhead.

This argument is the most plausible argument which is urged by them, and therefore it must be most warily answered.

[1] We do not equivocate in this or any other point, but do readily acknowledge that God the Father begets a Son as he is God the Father, and not simply and absolutely as he is God; because this eternal generation points at a personal property considered after the manner of a vital act. But then as this personal property and relation does not differ really from the divine essence, so this personal power of begetting does not differ really from the essential power, because God begets a Son in the unity of his own divine essence; his Son is equal to him,[267] and therefore not essentially[268] different from him (John 5:18, 26, John 10:30).[269] *Nulla fuit mutatio essentialis in filio, cujus essentia est immutablis.*

[2] We deny that there is an active power in the Father and a passive power in the Son in respect of generation,[270] because a passive power notes materiality and imperfection, but this eternal generation cannot be material,

---

[267] Nullus horum alium aut praecedit aeternitate aut excedit magnitudine aut superat potestate August. lib. 6. de trinitate cap. ultimo.

[268] Ideo non est Pater major filio, quia aequalem sibi genuit. Originis enim quaestio ista est, quis de quo sit; aequalitatis autem qualis aut quantus sit. Aug. Cont. Max. l. 3. c. 18.

[269] Pater non genuit filium exse per seminalem rationem, nec extra se per Physicam productionem, sed in se, hoc est in unitate essentiae genuit. Philip. 2. 6.

[270] Potentia passiva est propria materiae, ex quâ producitur genitum. In deo autem nulla est generatio Materialis. In passiva generatione genitum à non esse ad esse producitur; Filius autem semper actu exticit; genitus non est gignente posterior, quia ab aeterno genitus.

for God is a Spirit infinitely more spiritual than the most glorious angel. *Pater genuit filium et filius genitus est – spiritualiter, immutabiliter.*

[3] The two words of *begetting* and *being begotten* which are used in Scripture do not point at two different powers, an active and a passive, but at two different persons;[271] the Father who did beget, and the Son who was never unbegotten (Micah 5:2), for he was of old, from the days of eternity.

[4] It was not in the power of the Father to forbear the begetting of his Son, because the Son is *ens sum necessarium*,[272] as well as the Father, the Son is αυτοθεος, God of himself, and not God by participation, nor a different God from the Father, but the same God with the Father, and therefore an independent, eternal God, who did not begin to be God, who cannot cease to be God, but has life in himself as well as the Father (John 5:20) and has the self-same divine life, divine nature, divine power which the Father has; and therefore the Schools conclude well that *the Father and the Son have the same power, but with a different relation*;[273] but these different relations do not superadd a new essence, a new divine nature; and they who have the same essence, must have the same power, because the power of God is not distinguished from the essence of God, and the Father communicates the same essence and power which the Son receives.

---

[271] Generatio considerata respectu filii geniti est filiatio sive proprietas filii; generatio autē respectu Patris est Communicatio vitae subsistentis; per hanc autem communicationem filius est unum cum Patre ab aeterno. Mich, 5. 2. non sunt itaque duae generationes sed duae personae gignens, & genita. Vide D. Alting. Problem. XI. par. 1.

[272] Quod est in potentia gignentis, id non semper extitit, sed potest esse vel non esse. Filius autem semper exticit imò non potest non esse, quia est αυτοθεος Ens summe necessarium non minus quàm ipse Pater.

[273] Eadem essentia quae in Patre est paternitas, in filio est filiatio; eâdem potentiâ generat Pater, filiusque generatur. Habetitaque silius eandem potentiam quam Pater, sed cum alia relatione; Pater ut commuicans, filius ut accipiens, Johan. 5. 26. Tó generare est dare potentiam, τό gènerari est accipere potentiam vide. Aquin. Sum. part. 1. qu. 42. art. 6.

[5] There is the same reason of the Son and Holy Spirit; for these three are equal, nay one,[274] essentially one, one God with the most perfect kind of unity, as has been shown. And some that are metaphysical acknowledge that nothing is simply one,[275] but that which is most singly one and nothing is most singly one but God, who has nothing in himself but that which is himself. Aristotle, discoursing of six kinds of unity,[276] says that things may be said to be one: {1} in respect of continuity, because they are one continued body. {2} In respect of their subject, as two accidents in the same subject. {3} Because they are under the same genus. {4} Because they are of the same species. {5} Because they have the same definition; but then he concludes that all these are but imperfect kinds of unity, if compared with the last unity, which is {6} when a thing is one in respect of its single and indivisible essence.[277]

Now the Father and Son are one (John 10:30), the Father, Son, and Holy Spirit are one (1 John 5:7), and they are one after the most perfect manner, they are one in respect of the most single and indivisible essence, because the divine essence is most single and perfectly one.[278] And therefore since essence and power are not distinguished in God, it follows undeniably that these three who have one essence, have one and the same power, but with different properties and relations.[279]

---

[274] Non potest autem qui accepit ei qui dedit esse inequalis, quia & hoc accepit ut esset aequalis. Aug. lib. 3. contra Maximinum. cap. 14.

[275] Id solum simplicitur unum est, quod simplicissimum est; Solus itaque Deus simpliciter unus est in quo nihil omnino est quod Deus non est. Vide Fonsecam in Metaphys. Aristot. lib. 4. cap. 2. qu. 5. Sect. 7.

[276] Aristotle in *Metaphysics* Book 4 on the six kinds of unity.

[277] Omnia habet filius à Patre, sed Pater & filius unum sunt: filius itaque nihil accipīt ab ilio, qui est a Filio aliud; filius enim est idem cum Patre unicusque Deus.

[278] Pater & Filius spirando communicant vitam subsistentem Spiritui Sancto per quam Spiritus Sanctus est unum cum Patre & Filio. 1 Joan. 5. 7. Spiritus itaque spiratus vitam accipit subsistentem, nec non potentiam Coessentialem; eandem itaque potentiam habet Spiritus, sed cum diversa proprietate sive ratione personali.

[279] Patres dicunt essentiam generare, hoc est essentia relative accepta, essentia cum modo & proprietate personali considerata generat, hoc est Deus Pater generat Filium.

This truth will be more evident when we have discoursed of the distinction of these three divine persons, of which we are to treat in the next chapter.

(6) **Created persons have a different place and presence, but uncreated persons are omnipresent, they cannot be separated or divided from one another in respect of place or presence, but do subsist in one another.** The Father did beget the Son in the unity of the divine nature,[280] and the Son subsists in the nature of God (Philippians 2:6). and all three persons subsisting in the same single and omnipresent nature, they must subsist in one another.[281] The divine nature of the Father is in the Son, and therefore the Father is in the Son; the divine nature of the Son is in the Father, and therefore the Son is in the Father, and the like may be said of the Holy Spirit, for the divine nature of the Holy Spirit is in the Father and the Son. These three glorious persons are distinguished from one another, and yet they do subsist in one another. They do subsist in one another without any contraction, commixture, or confusion,[282] as Damascene taught the Schoolmen to speak.[283] When Philip desired Christ to show him the Father, our Savior answers: "He that hath seen me hath seen the Father (John 14:9)," because he is the image of his Father's person, and the illustrious brightness of his Father's glory; nay, because the nature of his Father is in him, and the person of his Father is in him; and therefore he calls upon Philip to believe that his Father is in him (John 14:10): "Believest thou not that I am in the Father and the Father in me?" As if he had said, "I wonder you should not

---

[280] Essentia non generat essentiam quia est unica, simplicissima: persona non generat personam extra essentiam, quia essentia infinita extra se fundi non potest.

[281] Tota natura divina est in tribus personis, tota in singulis singularissime unica, servatis tum essentialibus essentiae, tum relativis personarum in unitate essentiae proprietatibus.

[282] δι ασυγχτον αλληλαις [ἡ] εμπεριχω-ρησιν propter in confusam in se mutuo cōprehensionem & praesentiā potius quam circumincessionem ut satis barbare loquuntur. Vide Gomari Diatribé de Trinit. Inconfuse uniuntur indivise discernuntur.

[283] Vide Damascen lib. 1. Orth. fid. cap 19. Vide Biel. in sent, dist 19. q. 2. Thom p. 1. q. 42. art. 5. John 14. 10, 11.

believe this truth, it is a special article of your faith if you be a Christian, and it is a very plain article, for you have some sensible arguments to confirm your faith in this point, both from my words, and from my works; you may hear the Father speaking in me, and see my Father working in me." "The words that I speak unto you, I speak not of myself, but the Father that dwelleth in me, he doeth the works (John 14:10)."

And then he presses the point home upon him by a peremptory injunction in the eleventh verse: "Believe me that I am in the Father, and the Father in me, or else believe me for the very works' sake." Philip might hear what was truly divine in the saving words of Christ, and see what was divine in the miraculous works of Christ, and by the words and works (and Spirit of Christ making both effectual) he might be brought to believe this necessary point, that the nature of God the Father, and the person of God the Father is in Christ. Give me leave to insist upon this point, for there is more in it than we can well observe at first view, and therefore our Savior did press this point home very frequently, and require that men would expressly believe it – (John 10:38) "believe the works" – but to what end? Why? "That ye may know and believe that the Father is in me, and I in him." This is the end of Christ's working so many miracles amongst them: to bring them to believe that he and the Father did mutually subsist in one another. "*Credite operibus*: believe my works," he says, "they speak me to be God, and the Son of God, and therefore I am not guilty of blasphemy, because I say I am the Son of God, and equal to God, for I am God, I and my Father are one God; and if you believe that I and my Father are one God, you must believe that I am in the Father, and the Father in me."

This is the sum and substance of our Savior's discourse in John 10:25-39, and our Savior did enter into this discourse at the request of the Jews, who came round about him, and desired him not to hold them in suspense any longer, but to tell them plainly whether he were the Christ or not (John 10:24). All then who believe Jesus Christ to be the Christ, the true Messiah, the only Savior, and an all sufficient Savior, must believe, confess, and acknowledge this truth: that the Father is in Christ, and Christ in the Father.

From what has been spoken, it is clear and evident, that this is a point of life and death, as we say, a fundamental point, a point necessary to salvation, and therefore our Savior did so often insist upon it. In John 8, our Savior tells them more than once that he was not alone, and therefore his testimony of himself was not a single testimony, but his Father who was with him and in him did bear witness with him, and of him (John 8:16): "for I am not alone, but I and the Father that sent me; I am one that bear witness of myself, and the Father that sent me beareth witness of me (John 8:18), and he that sent me is with me, the Father hath not left me alone (John 8:29)."[284]

This point is difficult to believe, that Christ who is man is very God, the same God with the Father, a different person from the Father, yet subsisting in the Father, who is the only true God; but as Rollock says well,[285] though this point be most difficult, yet it is most necessary, and therefore we must beg the Spirit of God that we may get above nature, and see the Father in Christ, and Christ in the Father, for the natural man does not relish, receive, or perceive the things of God (1 Corinthians 2:14).

Our Savior told his disciples that when the Spirit was poured out more plentifully upon them, then they should know him to be in his Father. "The Father will give you another Comforter even the Spirit of truth, and at that day ye shall know that I am in my Father (John 14:16, 17, 20)," and in John 16, the Spirit had convinced the disciples of this weighty truth; for they say: "By this we believe that thou camest forth from God; Jesus answered them, Do you now believe? Behold the hour cometh, yea is now come, that ye shall be scattered every man to his own, and shall leave me alone, and yet I

---

[284] John 8:16, 18, 29; 14:10-11, 21; 10:38; 16:27, 30, 32; 17:21

[285] Ut autem difficillimum sit hoc credere, & naturam longè exuperat: ita necessarium est adeo ad salutem, ut sine fide illâ non sit salus. Hinc sequitur quòd cum à naturâ alienum sit, & tamen necessariū, oportere nos ex naturâ exire & supra na turam efferri, ad hoc ut videamus Deum in Christo habitantem. Rolloc. Cō. in Iohan. 14. v. 10, 11

am not alone, because the Father is with me (John 16:30-32)." In these and several other places, our Savior declares this truth unto us, that he is in his Father; and if it were not a weighty truth of very great consequence and high concernment, he would not insist so much upon it. It is the mutual insubsistence and coessential omnipresence of the Father and the Son.[286]

And the Spirit, being coessential with the Father and the Son,[287] must be in them both, from whom he proceeds in the unity of the divine nature;[288] for it is clear that an infinite nature cannot be poured forth beyond itself, because it is boundless, and therefore when we read (1 Corinthians 2:11) "What man knoweth the things of a man, save the spirit of man, which is in him? Even so the things of God knoweth no man, but the Spirit of God." We may safely add:[289] "which is in God, because he did proceed in the unity of the divine indivisible and boundless nature."[290]

The Holy Spirit has the same nature with the Father and the Son; and a nature of infinite and boundless perfection cannot be communicated to anything that is not infinite, to anything that is not itself, because there can be no other infinite thing but itself, there can be but one infinite, and everyone of the three glorious persons is one and the same infinite God. Upon these grounds we may answer many questions.

---

[286] Deus est ubique totus in seipso: quõmodo ubi{que} si in seipso? ubique quia nusquam est absens: in seipso autem quia non Continetur ab eis, quibus est praesens; anquā sine eis esse non possit. August. Epist. 57. ad Dardanum.

[287] Qui ubi que est in seipso est; qui in seipso est, in omnibus sibi Coessentialibus necessario est, volens tamen gaudensque.

[288] Naturae est in tribus personis non [ενος] tantùm, sed & ενωτης: personatum non μεταγγισμος quasi vas esset in vase, sed περιχώρησις, neinaequalitas inveheretur.

[289] Spiritus Dei dicitur esse in Deo, 1 Cor. 2. 11. qui tamen est Deus ipse, 1 Cor. 6. 20. nempe ad intimam inexistentiam trium personarum in seipsis exprimendam. D. Wallaeus de Simplicitate Dei pag, 128.

[290] In processionibus divinis nulla est partitio απορροια, vel [περιβολη] quibus tribus modis res creatae producuntur, quia eadem natura singularis simplex, indivisibilis & infinita sine divisione vel multiplicatione communicatur.

If you ask where God was before the world was made? I answer that he was then, just where he is now, in himself.²⁹¹

Dic ubi tunc esset, cum praeter eum nihil esset;
Tunc ubi nunc, in se, quoniam sibi sufficit ipse.

If you ask where the Father was, I answer: in the Son; if you ask where the Son was, I answer, in the Father; if you ask where the Spirit was, I answer: he was both in the Father and in the Son, and they both in him. God was in all three persons, and all three persons in the Godhead, and in one another,²⁹² and so they do, and will remain to all eternity, because they are coessential, because they are one omnipresent and eternal God.

The Godhead is not shut up in the narrow circle of the universe, the whole Godhead is in the world, and the whole Godhead is out the world, for the world cannot contain the true God, who did create, and upholds the world, and the single Godhead cannot be divided; and therefore we must not conceive that part of the Godhead is in the world, and part of it out of the world, but the whole Godhead is everywhere, it is not included in any place, or excluded from any place; the heaven and heaven of heavens cannot contain him (1 Kings 8:27), his perfection is higher than heaven, and deeper than hell (Job 11:8).²⁹³

---

²⁹¹ Totus in seipso ubique est Deus noster omnipraesentissimus, totus in mundo, totùs extra mundum totus super mundum, totus & unus in omnibus & singulis, nusquam inclusus, nusquam exclusus, ubique immensus, non per essentiae multiplicationem, extensionem aut divisionem, sed per infinitatem simplicissimam.

²⁹² Ante omnia Deus erat solus ipse sibi & locus, & mundus & omnia. Uti Tertullianus contra Prax.

²⁹³ Essentia Dei non miscetur cumsplen didis, nec a sordidis contaminatur, sed in utero virginis fuit hypostatice unita cum carne nostrâ sine ullâ commixtione, confusione, contaminatione, vel diminutione. [ουσια περουσιος ουσια εντελεχεια απλως απειρας] Si homo tantummodo Christus, quomodo adest ubique invocatus, cum haec hominis natura non sit, sed Dei ut adesse omni loco possit? Tertulian. de Trinitate. [Vide] Anastasius Antiochenus. Angeli sunt substantiae spirituales separaim & per se subsistentes, & proinde sunt alicubi definitive.

From what has been said, it is most clear, that since the essence of God is omnipresent, and the self-same indivisible essence is in Father, Son, and Holy Spirit, then all three must mutually subsist in one another. Though the persons be distinguished, they cannot be separated, divided, or contracted;[294] and therefore this sixth difference between created and uncreated persons, is so remarkable that I need not go about to prove that human persons are separated as well as distinguished: *tot sunt humanitates quot homines.* And it is most certain that angelic persons have a limited presence, because they have a finite essence. But it is otherwise in divine persons, for the Father works in the Son, and by the Spirit the Father subsists in the Son and in the Spirit, and cannot be separated from these coessential and omnipresent persons, who do subsist with him (as they are both from him) in the unity of the Godhead.

I need say no more concerning angels than what is commonly said, "*Angeli sunt alicuoi definitive; sunt enim in suo ubi non per operationem vel circumscriptionem, sed per designationem definitivam*:" angels are naturally somewhere, though they are not in any place by extension of parts yet their finite nature is contained within certain bounds and limits. Hence it is that some learned men affirm[295] that it is improper to say that God is somewhere because he is everywhere; *somewhere* being a definitive word.[296]

(7) **Created persons have many other different accidents besides place, of which we have spoken; and time or duration, of which we are**

---

[294] Tres personae sunt ενουσιοι quia ομοουσιοι, & non tantum ὁμοιούσιοι. Tres homines quibus una competit definitio, sunt tantum ὁμοιούσιοι, quia natura eorum est finita, & divisa; non enim tota essencia patris creati sed pars tantum filio communicatur, & hypostases eorum sunt separatae. Non sunt itaque ejusdem naturae indivisae, ejusdem naturae singularis, & proinde licèt communi ratione homines dicantur, tamen reipsa non sunt unus homo. Personae autem divinae ομοουσιοι sunt propter unius communis, & tamen singularis naturae identi tatem, quam simul & pariter, & totam habent Pater Filius & Spiritus Sanctus.

[295] Immensa Dei prae sentia non est accidés vel modus essentiae ejus sed ipsamet essentia. Deus non est alicubi sed ubique; quod est Alicubi est in ubi Definitivo. Vide Aug. qu. lib. 83. qu. 20. & lib. 8. Geres. ad lit. cap. 26. Chrysost. Homil. 5. ad Coloss. Damascen. Nazian. orat. 34. Basil. Hom. 16. Hieronym. in Isa. 66.

[296] Qui est ubique Repletive non est Alicubi Definitive. Vide Scalig. Exercit. 159. §. 5.

to speak. It will not be necessary or useful to discourse of every particular; but that which I intend to insist upon under this head is, that created persons are distinguished from one another by a heap of accidents, and therefore it will be sufficient for the making good of this seventh difference, to show that divine persons are not distinguished by a congeries [jumble], or heap of accidents,[297] because there is no accident at all in God. For the being of God is infinitely perfect, and singularly single, as has been proven; and therefore it is infinitely below the single perfection of God to be compounded of a substance and accidents for the adorning or perfecting of his glorious being. Relations are not accidents in God. The relation of one coessential person to another is agreeable to the essence of God. It is a necessary relation which did never begin to be, and cannot cease to be.[298]

[1] The relation of God to the creature cannot be real, because it is such a relation as might not have been; but there is no real thing in God which might not have been.

[2] There can be no real relation between two extremes, one of which two extremes is unchangeable, and the other might not have been.

[3] God was not in any passive potentiality or power, before he did create the world, to receive any real act, because he is really a pure act;[299] and it is evident that a new real relation is a kind of act whereof the pure, single, perfect and unchangeable essence is uncapable.

[4] Our weak understanding comparing God with the creatures, is apt to frame many denominations, which according to the manner of

---

[297] Personae creatae differunt intelligentia voluntate, potentiâ, essentiâ, operatione, locorum intervallis imo propriâ accidentium congerie. Vide Gomarum de Trinitate Tom. 3. pag. 24.

[298] Personae divinae non dicuntur Relativae propter essentias Relativas, sed propter modos sive proprietates Relativas, quae quidem proprietates non differunt realiter essentialiter, imo nec realiter separabiliter ab essentiâ divinâ. Personae autem divinae sunt extra omne genus omnemque dependentiam.

[299] Vide Metaphys. Fonsec. lib. 5. cap. 15. Sect. 7.

signifying, seem to import as if God were *in potentia ad multa*.[300] Yet if we do consider the thing signified, as we ought in a way agreeable to the pure, single, and infinite perfection of God, we shall find that these are but extrinsic denominations. This point is much beaten upon by the most acute Schoolmen and writers of metaphysics, and therefore I need not insist upon it; only observe that when I say created persons are distinguished by a heap of accidents, I do not mean that a person is made complete in his subsistence by any accident, or a heap of accidents, for I have refuted that conceit in this present chapter, and I hasten to the eighth difference.

(8) **Human persons with whom we are best acquainted, may exist in a very different time as well as in different places.** Some lived before, some since the flood; some before the incarnation, others since the death and resurrection of our Lord and Savior; but herein all agree that time is the measure of them all. Their duration is very imperfect; their duration is not always contemporary, never coessential. But all three uncreated persons are coeternal, because they are coessential, because they have the same divine eternal essence: angels are said to have an eternal duration, but they are not eternal in the same sense that the Father, Son, and Holy Spirit are eternal.[301]

[1] Because they were created (Colossians 1:16) and therefore did begin to be, they have not (as the Schools say) an interminable or interminated duration *a parte ante*.

[2] If they had been created from eternity, yet they could not have been esteemed coeternal with their Creator, who did create them out of nothing, and did not beget or breath them forth in the unity of his own divine essence.

---

[300] Vide Scotum, Estium &c. in 1. sent. dist. 30. Omnis quae ut denominatio respectiva concipitur in Deo ad creaturam est tantùm secundum rationem, & modum concipiendi nostrum, quia divina natura est Absoluta in se, & ab omni ordine creaturarum independens, sive creaturae existunt sive non. Vide Suarez. Disp. 47. Sect. 15. Num 25.

[301] Aeternitas proprie dicta est increata; duratio itaque Angelorum non est vera aeternitas. Aeternum dicitur quod est extra terminum, & ex se incapax termini, quia in sua intrinseca ratione infinitatem in durando includit.

[3] There can be no less than an infinite difference between the finite, dependent, changeable, defective duration of an angel,[302] and the infinite, independent, and immutable duration of these three uncreated, and all creating persons, who are one independent, unchangeable, eternal, and infinite God the eternity of the three glorious persons is interminable, indefectible, and immutable.

[4] If angels had been created from eternity, yet they would not have been essentially or intrinsically eternal, because their essence does not include any repugnancy to an actual beginning.[303]

[5] If angels had been created from eternity, yet God might have annihilated them afterwards, and then they had actually ceased to be.

[6] Although they were not actually annihilated, yet the very possibility of being annihilated is enough to prove their duration terminable, changeable, defectible; and therefore though they had been created from all eternity, they would not have been coeternal with their maker, nor would three angels have been coessentially coeternal with one another.[304]

[7] If angels had been created from eternity, they would have been eternal, not by any intrinsical or natural duration, as has been proven; and therefore they would have been eternal only by an extrinsic denomination, taken from the eternity of God.[305]

---

[302] Aliud est esse aeternum, aliud sempiternum, quia omne aeternum est immutabile. Richard. Victor. lib. 2. de Trinitate. c. 4. Ratio aeternitatis consequitur immutabilitatem sicut ratio temporis motum. Th. p. 1. qu. 10. art 2. c.

[303] Deus est aeternus, imo & sua aeternitas; Deus enim est infinita perfectio, & proinde simul, & ex se, atque immutabiliter habet totam perfectionem suam, ratione cujus ex se sit sufficiens ad coexistendum omni durationi, quantacunque illa sit; & proinde sicut Deus est sua essentia & perfectio, ita est sua aeternitat. Vide Suarez. Metaph Disp 50. Sect. 4. Th. p. 1. qu. 10, a. 2.

[304] Est in Angelis potentia Obedientialis ad corruptionem, quae naturalis dicipotest, quia in natura Angelorum quae à creatore dependet τό definere posse ad nutum creatoris fundatur. Omnis enim potentia Naturalis est quae in rerum naturis fundatur. Vide fis Suarez. Disp. 43. Sect. 4. n. 2.

[305] Si Angeli ab aeterno creati essent à Deo, non sequeretur eos esse Deo coaeternos per durationem intrinsecam, sed potius ab aeterno esse, & aeternitati coexistere per denominationem extrinsecam à Dei aeternitate sumptam; durarent enim ex

[8] Upon consideration of the premises, many reverend doctors of the church conclude, that angels are eternal only *à parte post*; and they are eternal *à parte post*, not by their own nature, but by the free favor and appointment of God; and therefore there is an infinite difference between the duration of these three uncreated persons, and the duration of the most glorious angels in heaven. Angels are mutable, and God is a free agent both in respect of creation, and in respect of preservation; and therefore God and angels are not coeternal as the Peripatetics dreamt.[306] God did voluntarily engage himself to create and preserve angels by his own decree; and therefore that subordinate eternity which they have *à parte post*, is vouchsafed unto them by the free and undeserved favor of God. For (as Damascene says well)[307] whatsoever had a beginning would soon have an ending, if he who gave a beginning to it by his infinite power should think fit to suspend his upholding and preserving influence, or put forth his almighty and irresistible power against it in a destructive way.

I will not take this fair occasion to speak of the acts or motions of angels to make this difference seem greater; for that which has been said is sufficient to make it evident that angels do not coexist with God the Father with the same duration wherewith God the Son and God the Holy Spirit do coexist

---

aeternitate, non tamen duratione quae sit aeternitas, quia aeternitas est duratio per se, & abintrinseco necessaria, independens, immutabilis, quae nullam variationem aut successionem admittit neque in esse, neque in propriis & internis actibus aut motibus; vel per internam capacitatem, vel extrinsecam potentiam. Angeli non sunt Deo coaeterni, multo minus aequaeterni, sed sunt potius aeviterni quàm aeterni.

[306] Unum est primum, alia dependent igitur. Ergo suâ naturâ omnia praeter unum corruptibilia. Tametsi enim sunt entia absoluta a subjecto & a termino: tamen haud sunt absoluta à causa. Sunt igitur per aliud, & ab alio; at omne dependens ab eo, à quo dependet, si est voluntarium principium, mutari potest; ergo ipsae quoque mentes immateriales etsi ponantur, à Peripateticis coaeternae Deo, tamen ut à Primo pendent à Primi nutu deponi possunt ab eâ essentiâ, in quâ sunt ab illo constitutae. Vide Scalig. exerc. 307.

[307] Damasc. Orth. fid. lib. 2. cap. 3. & 12. Iust. Mart. qu. 13, 14. Hieron. contra Pelagium lib. 2. Cyrill. 8. Thes. c. 2 Angelus auem non potest destrui per Physicam corruptionem, quia non componitur ex partibus Physicis. Viri itaque gravissimi ideo dicunt Angelos natura incorruptibiles esse, quia Angelus non habet aliquid intra naturam sui corruptivum.

with him, because these three coessential persons are coeternal; they are all three one God, who is his own essence, his own eternity; the Scripture calls the God of Israel the eternity of Israel (1 Samuel 15:29) and Aristotle[308] calls him life itself, the best life, an eternal life, that has neither beginning nor ending, nor succession; and therefore it is evident that he did not believe God to be subject to change or variation.[309] God is (he says)[310] a self-sufficient and eternal life. God is truly self-sufficient, because he is all-sufficient, he is infinite in perfection, and therefore infinite in duration; his infinite perfection and duration is nothing else but but his infinite essence; and this infinite essence is the self-same in all three coessential, coeternal and coequal persons, as has been proven. And therefore we have good cause to rejoice and triumph in this glorious difference between created and uncreated persons.

Give me leave to sweeten this dispute with some devotion. We have an everlasting Father, an everlasting Savior, and an everlasting Comforter. And we have good cause to lay a charge upon our immortal souls to bless and praise all three coeternal persons, for their eternal love, our eternal redemption and salvation.

"Praise the Lord O my soul, while I live will I praise the Lord; whilst I have any being will I sing praises to my God, and put confidence in him, for with the Lord there is plenteous and eternal redemption. But O put not your trust in princes, nor in those sons of men in whom there is no salvation, for their breath goeth forth, they return to their first earth, and in that day all

---

[308] φαμὲν δὴ τὸν θεὸν εἶναι ζῷον ἀΐδιον ἄριστον, ὥστε ζωὴ καὶ αἰὼν συνεχὴς καὶ ἀΐδιος ὑπάρχει τῷ θεῷ· τοῦτο γὰρ ὁ θεός. Aristot. lib. 12 Metaphys. cap. 7.

[309] Id enim Deus est (inquit Aristoteles) & proinde Deum ipsam vitam esse intulit; aeternitatem ae vum continuum, aeternumque vocat sine successione, sine terminis.

[310] Αιων dicitur [δπο] του α ει ειναι Legimus αυταρκεστάτη ζωην [και] αιωνα Aristot. 1. de Caelo text. 100. αιων αει ων inquit Phavorinus. Ο μηδεποτε αρξαμενος μηδε ληγων, aevum semper existens, quod numquam caepit, neque definit. Plutarchus insuper αιωνα Deo tribuit. [...] Deus est, secundum aevum immutabile, qui unus in uno nunc aeternitatem implevit. Psalm 146:1-6, Daniel 9:24, Hebrews 9:12, 15, Hebrews 5:9; 1 John 3:9; 1 Peter 1:20 23-25.

their thoughts and counsels perish. Happy is he that hath the God of Jacob for his help, whose hope is in the Lord his God, which made heaven and earth, the sea and all that therein is, which keepeth truth forever."

Read and consider the six first verses of Psalm 146: there is a great emphasis in the sixth verse: "which keepeth truth forever." O let us declare it to the following generation that this God is "our God forever and ever, and he will be our guide even unto death (Psalm 48:13-14)." Happy it is for us that we are redeemed by the precious blood of Christ, who offered up himself by by his eternal Spirit, his divine and eternal nature (Hebrews 9:14) that he might bring in everlasting righteousness (Daniel 9:24), obtain eternal redemption, and purchase an eternal inheritance for us (Hebrews 9:12, 15). Happy, thrice happy it is for us that we are born of incorruptible seed, which will abide in us forever. For we are born of the eternal Spirit, who will perfect his work in us, and be our everlasting Comforter. Finally, all three uncreated persons will be our all-sufficient and satisfactory portion and reward forevermore.

(9) **Three created persons have different actions and operations, because they have different singular natures, different powers, etc., as has been shown in this very chapter. All actions of Father, Son and Holy Spirit upon the creatures are undivided, nay, indivisible.** How personal actions *ad infra* differ, I am to declare at large in the next chapter, where I am to show how these three glorious persons who cannot be divided, are truly distinguished from one another; only before I conclude this chapter, it will be requisite to note that, though the Son cannot be said to beget himself, yet he is not passive in that eternal generation, as has been proven above. The divine nature which is communicated to the Son by generation, is the nature of the Son as well as of the Father. The Father does necessarily beget the Son in the power of that nature, and in the unity of that self-same single and indivisible nature; and that divine nature which is communicated to the Son, is not begotten by the Father, but is of itself; and therefore we say that Christ is God of himself, though he be not a Son of

himself, but of the Father by eternal generation, because the Father is the first principle of subsisting life.

I might proceed to treat of other differences: that common rule "*Actiones sunt suppositorum*"[311] is true of divine actions and uncreated persons; but it is manifest that there are many actions of the soul of man, both when it is in a state of union with, and when it is in a state of separation from the body, which cannot be properly and truly called actions of a person, but I shall not descend so low, as to take notice of such differences.

The nine differences which have been insisted on are all considerable. And from them all we may safely conclude that the word subsistence or person cannot be attributed after the same manner to God, angels and men. A divine person is a spiritual and infinite subsistent, which must not be considered as abstracted from, but as subsisting in the divine nature, and as related to those other coessential persons, from which he is sufficiently distinguished by some personal and incommunicable property. Therefore, subsistence is attributed to God after the most excellent and glorious manner. A person signifies the most excellent kind of subsistent, an understanding subsistent, as has been shown; but then an uncreated person, a divine person infinitely excels and transcends the person of the most glorious angel in heaven; and therefore we must remove all those imperfections from our thoughts, which are in created persons, when we meditate or discourse of these divine and uncreated persons, that we may think and speak according to the analogy of faith.

---

[311] "Actions are of the individual."
<https://www.encyclopedia.com/religion/encyclopedias-almanacs-transcripts-and-maps/scholastic-terms-and-axioms> [Accessed 1/26/2024]

Chapter 7

The Three Uncreated, Divine, & Coessential Subsistents are Sufficiently Distinguished, Though They Cannot be Divided.

We are now come to treat of that profound mystery, at which men and angels stand amazed. "How can three be one?" says the disputer of this world, "Or one be three? Can one be distinguished again and again from himself?" "O bold fools," says Athanasius, "Why do you not lay aside your curiosity, and inquire no further after a Trinity than to believe that there is a Trinity?" The Scripture says there is but one God, and the Scripture says that the Father, Son, and Holy Spirit are this one God; and yet the Scripture says that the Father, Son, and Holy Spirit are three; three and yet one; three persons and yet one God. We have shown above that the Godhead cannot be multiplied; now we are to show that the persons are distinguished, and what kind of distinction there is between these three divine and uncreated persons.

(1) These divine and uncreated persons are sufficiently distinguished to our apprehension, who ought to judge, believe, speak, worship, according to the Word of God.[312]

(2) These uncreated persons were truly distinguished from one another before there was any Scripture; any world. For the coexistence and distinction of these glorious persons is eternal, and therefore this distinction cannot be grounded upon the mere phrase of Scripture. It is the true intent of God in several plain expressions of Scripture to declare unto us the distinction of these divine and uncreated persons. I shall prove this point fully and clearly by certain steps and degrees.

---

[312] Trinitatis divinum dogma est; In Deo sic est ut dicit; in Scripturâ sic dicit ut est; in Ecclesiâ sic creditur ut Scriptura dicit. Iunius contra errores Samosit.

[1] These uncreated persons have distinct and proper names in the Word of God. The Father, the Son (or the *Word*), and the Holy Ghost (or *Spirit*). Now that we may not be Tritheites or Sabellians, let us consider that these three names do not signify three different natures, and yet they do signify three different persons, for it is evident that one person cannot be predicated of another.[313] The Father is not the Son, nor is the Son the Father; the Holy Spirit is not either of them, nor is either of them the Holy Spirit; and therefore they are three distinct persons of the Godhead.

[2] These uncreated persons are coequal, and therefore they are distinct. It is most absurd to say that the same person is equal to himself. But the Son is said to be equal to the Father (Philippians 2), therefore the Son is not the Father.[314] We do usually say that the Father, Son and Holy Spirit are equal in power to note a distinction of persons, but then when we speak strictly, we do not say the power of the persons is equal, but we say the power of the persons is the same, to note the unity of their essence.

We say the persons are equal in power, goodness, wisdom, and so on to note that one person does not exceed another in degrees of wisdom, power, and so on because it is impossible that there should be any degrees in that which is infinite; and the power, wisdom, etc., of all the three persons is the same infinite perfection, because all three have the same infinite essence. And therefore when we look upon power in a common notion, as referred to the divine essence which is common to all three persons, we say it is the same power. But when we look upon power in a singular notion as it is communicated after a singular manner to this, or that person, we say this person is equal to that in power, the Father equal to the Son, the Spirit equal to both, to note the distinction of the persons, and not the distinction of the

---

[313] Negamus Deum esse unicam personam tribus nominibus appellatam contra Praxean Sabellium, &c. Negamus tres personas divinas esse tres Deos contra Tritheitas ad unum omnes. Vide Tertull. contra Praxean. Calvinum contra Servetum. & Aug. Haeres. c. 41.

[314] See the Treatise of Reverend Mr. Estwick in his Refutation of Mr. Bidles Argumēts pag 89. 92. 93.

power, because the self-same Almighty power is communicated to the several persons in a several way; power is in the Father of and from himself, [that is] not from any other person; the same power is communicated to the Son, but it is communicated to him by eternal generation, and to the Spirit by eternal procession; the same power then is communicated to different coequal persons in a different way, as we shall more fully declare before we conclude this seventh chapter.

[3] **The uncreated persons are sufficiently distinguished by their number.** The nature of God is the first entity, the first unity, and therefore it is incapable of number, because it is most singularly single, and actually infinite.[315] It is not proper (if we speak strictly) to say that God is one in number; we should rather say that God is one, and an only one. *Deus non est unus numero, sed unicus*. But the persons of the Godhead are three in number: the Scripture speaks expressly of three: "these three (1 John 5:7)."[316]

If any man in Athanasius' time asked how many persons subsist in the Godhead, they were wont to send him to Jordan: "Go," say they, "to Jordan and there you may hear and see the blessed Trinity" – or if you will believe the holy Scriptures, read Matthew 3:16-17, for there:

{1} The Father speaks in a voice from heaven, and owns his only begotten Son, saying, "This is my beloved Son," etc.

{2} The Son went down into the water and was baptized.

{3} The Holy Spirit did visibly descend upon Jesus Christ.

In John 14, we have a plain demonstration of this truth. "I," says the Son, "will pray the Father, and he shall give you another Comforter (John 14:16-17)." May we not safely conclude from hence that the Spirit is a distinct person; another person from the Father and the Son? For the text is clear: the Son will pray, and the Father will give another Comforter; we

---

[315] Deitas est perfectio infinita simplicis sime unica Unitas ad essentiam pertinet, distinctio vero personarum non ad essentiam propiè & per se, sed ad rationem in essentiâ pertinet. Iunius contra errores Samosat.

[316] 1 John 5:7 Pater auditur in voce, Filius manifestatur in Homine, Spiritus dignoscitur in columbâ.

know the Holy Spirit is not another God; he is the same God with the Father and the Son, and therefore we must confess that it is meant of another person: "he shall give you another Comforter, even the Spirit of truth (John 14:16-17)." And again, in John 14:26: "But when the Comforter is come whom I will send unto you from the Father, even the Spirit of truth." What can there be more express or clear? The Scripture teaches us to reckon rightly, and we see the divine persons are reckoned three in number. One person is not another, there are diverse persons, there are three persons, the number numbered, the persons numbered are named by their distinct and proper names, the number numbering is expressly set down in sacred records. We are not more exact in any accounts than we are in reckoning of witnesses, whose testimony is produced in a business of great consequence and high concernment [*importance*].

Now in the great question about the Messiah, witnesses are produced to assure us that Jesus Christ, the son of the virgin, and the only begotten Son of God, is the true Messiah, the only all-sufficient Savior of his people from their sins. And there are three witnesses named and produced for the proof of this weighty point.

Now, one person that has three names, or two persons, and an attribute of one or both persons cannot pass for three witnesses in any fair and reasonable account. We are sure God reckons right, and he reckons Father, Son, and Holy Spirit for three witnesses, and he does not reckon these three and the Godhead for four (as they do who dream of a quaternity) because these three are one and the same God blessed forever.

Let us then be exact in observing, since the Holy Spirit is so exact in making of the account. In John 8, the Pharisees object that our Savior did bear record of himself, and did conclude from thence that therefore his record was not true (John 8:13). Our Savior answers in the next verses: "Though I bear record of myself, yet my record is true; for I am not alone, but I and the Father that sent me. And it is written in your law, that the testimony of two men is true. I am one that bear witness of myself, and the

Father that sent me beareth witness of me." It is most clear and evident by this discourse that our blessed Lord did make a fair legal just account, for he cites the law concerning the validity of a testimony given in by two witnesses. Then he reckons his Father for one witness, and himself for another. "I am one," he says, "and my Father is another:" I and my Father make two sufficient witnesses in a just and legal account. "There is another," (he) "that beareth witness of me, and I know that the witness which he witnesseth of me is true (John 5:32)." "There is another," he says. He does not mean another God, for when he speaks of his power and Godhead, he says, "I and my Father are one" (John 10:30). Christ and his Father are one God, but Christ and his Father are two distinct persons, for they are reckoned as two distinct witnesses; and one person must not be reckoned for two witnesses.

"There is another that beareth witness" (John 5:32) and "the Father himself (John 5:37) beareth witness of me." Well then, Christ is one witness, the Father is another, and the Holy Spirit is a third witness (1 John 5:7). We see the Holy Spirit speaks as plainly in this point as we do when we teach a child to tell one, two, and three. "For there are three that bear record in Heaven, the Father, the Word, and the Holy Spirit: and these three are one." If we peruse the Scriptures diligently as we ought, we shall find that these witnesses are three persons, who are one and the same blessed God. They are one in nature, though three in subsistence, to show that these three persons are not to be reckoned as three men are, who have three distinct singular natures really divided and separated; for these three glorious persons subsist in one another, and have one and the same single undivided and indivisible nature; and they are three witnesses, three persons truly distinct (John 1:14, 18; 5:38; 14:16).

(4) **The divine persons are distinguished by their inward and personal actions.** The Father did from all eternity communicate the living

essence of God to the Son, in a most wonderful and glorious way.[317] Now it is clear that the Father did not beget himself, and therefore the Son is another person truly distinct from the Father, and yet equal to the Father, because he is begotten in the unity of the same Godhead, and has life in himself (John 5:26): the living essence of God who is life itself being communicated to him by an eternal generation. The unbegotten Father is clearly distinguished from the only begotten Son. But I dare not say as some do, that the Father is active and the Son passive in this eternal generation because this generation is eternal. For nothing which is eternal can be truly said to be in a passive power to anything; much less can it be said to be in a passive power to be.[318]

The Son has life in himself, is life itself, has life essentially, and as he is the same essence with the Father, is of himself, and has all that is essential from that very essence; but that essence is communicated to the Son by the Father, and therefore the Son is said to receive all from the Father.[319]

But then we must consider that the Son receives nothing from the Father as from an external cause but as from an intrinsic principle rather the cause, for the Son does not depend upon the Father as an effect upon its cause; And I call the Father *an intrinsic principle of the Son's subsistence* because the Father begets the Son of and in himself in the unity of the same Godhead.[320] Their divine nature is one and the same, and their persons are coequal and coeternal because they are coessential. This is the very mystery

---

[317] Vita Dei est essentia vivens, vita subsistens, quae vita ut in Patre à nullo est, sic in Filio à Patre est.

[318] Nihil simpliciter aeternum dici potest fuisse in potentiâ, & proinde generatio aeterna non est distinguenda in activam & passivā.

[319] Communicatio est Essentiae objectivè, quia est id quod communicatur: Patris autem Activè, quia Pater generando Essentiam communicat.

[320] Filium à Patre, imò ex ipso Patre, & in ipso Patre genitū intelligimus est enim Filius Consubstantialis, Coessentialis, & proinde Patri coaequalis. Si Filius sit par Deo, par Patri ergo est ei coaequalis: si unum cum Patre, ergo etiam Coessentialis, 1 Iohan. 5:7.

of mysteries which corrupt and wanton reason derides, but prudent faith admires and adores.

The Socinians tell us that they cannot believe that the Father did beget a Son of his own substance, because God is eternal and unchangeable; the single essence of God is indivisible, and being most singularly one is incommunicable, part of the divine essence could not be communicated (say they) to the Son, because the essence is impartible, indivisible; and the self-same whole essence cannot be communicated, because it is most singularly one, and therefore incommunicable: *essentia quae est una numero est incommunicabilis.*

To this grand objection, I shall return a plain answer out of pure Scripture, and deliver it in certain propositions or conclusions, so that the answer may be more direct, clear, and satisfactory.

Conclusions concerning the eternal generation

(1) The Father did beget his Son. The Father himself bears witness to this truth, and his witness is full, and clear, and true. "Jehovah hath said unto me, Thou art my Son, this day have I begotten thee" (Psalm 2:7). Nay, the Father declares this truth to men and angels as a practical truth so that they may direct and regulate their worship according to this mystery. The apostle proves that Christ is more excellent than angels because "he hath a more excellent name than they; For, unto which of the angels said he at any time, thou art my Son, this day have I begotten thee? And again, I will be to him a Father, and he shall be to me a Son (Hebrews 1:4-5)."

Here's a double proof of the point: he has a more excellent name because he is the Son of God in a peculiar sense, and has the divine nature communicated to him, as shall be fully proven before we conclude this point. For the name of Son is not an empty title, he has the divine nature of his Father in him. Now, that he is the Son of God is testified again, and again, says the apostle (Hebrews 1:5). And he begins the sixth verse thus: "And again," etc. You see how he does inculcate this point, how he beats upon it again and again; and the reason is, because this truth is fundamental both of faith and worship, as is most evident in the sixth verse of that chapter. "And again when he brings in the first-begotten into the world, he saith, And let all the angels of God worship him (Hebrews 1:6)."

You see this mystery of the unbegotten Father and the only begotten Son is held forth to men and angels in order to worship, so that their worship may be directed to Jesus Christ as the Son of the living God, and to God the Father as the Father of our Lord Jesus Christ. God declared this truth after a glorious manner from heaven so that it might be more diligently considered. "And lo a voice from heaven, saying, "This is my beloved Son" (Matthew 3:17)" when he was baptized, and the like we read of when he was transfigured in the presence of the disciples in the holy mount. And the apostle takes notice of these solemn declarations from heaven, and lays them down as fundamentals of the Christian religion (2 Peter 1:16-20). All the glorious miracles wrought by our Savior, John 5:36 and his resurrection from the Dead bear witness to this fundamental truth, that Christ is the first begotten, and the only begotten Son of the living God; be pleased to compare, Acts. 13:32, 33. with Romans 1:4. and it will be evident that he was not made, but only declared to be the Son of God at the time of his resurrection.

(2) **The Father did beget his Son from all eternity before his works of old.** "I," (says the Son who is the wisdom of the Father) "was set up from everlasting, when as the highest part of the dust of the earth was not made, when he prepared the heavens I was there, etc. (Proverbs 8:21-31)."[321] His "goings forth were of old from the days of eternity (Micah 5:2)." (John 1:1-3): he was with God, he was God, before the beginning he had glory with his Father before the world was (John 17:5). *Relata simul sunt.*[322]

(3) **The Father begat his Son in the unity of the Godhead.** The Scripture speaks expressly that Christ is the proper or natural Son of God;[323] he spared not his own Son, or his Proper Son (Romans 8:32). God is the Father of Christ, his own Father (John 5:18). The Jews did well understand the importance and force of that expression, for say they, "in that he said God is his own Father, he hath made himself equal with God;" and therefore that phrase imports that he is the natural and coessential Son of God, else he could not be coequal with his Father (John 5:18, Philippians 2:6).

All those texts which prove that Christ is God, and that there is but one God, do prove that Christ is the natural and coessential Son of God. God has but one coessential Son, to whom he has given to have life in himself (John 5:26) because the divine nature, which is life itself is communicated to the

---

[321] Revel. 1. 18. Colos. 1. 15. primogenitus omnis creaturae phrasi Hebraea dicitur, qui ante omnes creaturas genitus.

[322] Relata simul sunt: Deus Pater & Deus filius sunt relata coaeterna; Pater aeternus generat filium coaeternum.

[323] πατερα ιδιον. Iohan 5. 18. του ιδιου Rom. 8 32. Proprium opponitur alieno quod est extra essentiam Act. 3. 12, Vide D. Alting Expli. Cacec. par. 2. qu. 33. pag. 177.

Son by this eternal and ineffable generation. It is proper to living creatures to communicate their nature by generation in their low and imperfect way; but the great God who is not subject to imperfection, after the most glorious and perfect manner begets a Son in the unity of his own living essence, who is therefore called "the Son of the living God," that is the natural and coessential Son of God, who has the same divine life, nature, essence with the Father. And therefore Peter is so highly commended for confessing that Christ is the Son of the living God: "Blessed art thou," says our Savior, "for flesh and blood hath not revealed it unto thee, but my Father which is in heaven." Upon this fundamental truth, Christ has built the Christian church as on a rock (Matthew 16:16-18). He who has life in himself is the natural and coessential Son of the living God. He has the same will, power, nature, essence, and life with his Father (John 5:18, 26, John 16:15. John 10:30; 1 John 5:7).[324] The same single and infinite essence is in Father, Son, and Holy Spirit. The whole undivided and indivisible essence of God dwells in the Son in its fullness and infinite perfection (Colossians 2:9).

(4) **The Father did beget his Son without change or motion after a most glorious and wonderful manner. There can be no change, motion, or succession in this eternal and most perfect generation.**[325] The essence of God is spiritual (John 4:24), and therefore the Son is not begotten of the Father's seed or any material substance, because God is a single and pure act, who begets Son within himself essentially one with himself and therefore his Son does not subsist out of himself (John 14:10, John 10:30) for an infinite nature cannot be poured forth beyond itself.

There can be no essential change in the Son by this generation, because the generation is eternal, and the nature which is communicated by generation is unchangeable. The Father did unchangeably beget his Son,

---

[324] Totam habet essentiam Patris qui dicitomnia quaecun{que} pater habet mea sunt. Iohan. 16. 15. nisi velint haeretici etiam patrem duntaxat partem essentiae divinae habere. Et situt Pater habet vitam in seipso, sic dedit filio habere vitam in seipso. Iohan. 5. 26.

[325] Generatio divina est omnis materiae motus mutationis nec non successionis expers,

and his Son is unchangeably begotten, there is no shadow of changing or turning either in the Father of lights, or the Son of righteousness, because they are one and the same unchangeable Jehovah (James 1:17, Malachi 3:6).

They are too carnal and base who make an unworthy and odious comparison between the material generation of a weak man, and this more than spiritual and supernatural generation.[326] The eternal and unchangeable Father begets an eternal and unchangeable Son according to the perfection of his eternal, unchangeable, infinite nature. The Father begets his Son naturally, and therefore in a way agreeable to his unchangeable nature. If the Son were not necessarily begotten, his being would not be necessary, and then his essence would not be divine.

(5) Jesus Christ is truly and properly the only-begotten Son of God, and therefore the only natural Son of God. Jesus Christ is called the Son of David according to his human nature, but the Lord of David, and the Son of the living God according to his divine nature, as appears by our Savior's discourse with the Pharisees (Matthew 22:41-46). And the Jews sought to kill Christ because he called God his proper Father, as appears by the original text, for our English translation omits that most observable emphasis. The words are: ιδιον ελεγεν τον θεον (John 5:18), and Christ is called God's proper Son: ιδιου υιου (Romans 8:32).

And the apostle gives the reason why he is called the proper Son of God in a more excellent way than the most glorious angel is the Son of God, because Christ is begotten by the Father, but the angels were only created by

---

[326] Homo generat modo physico, spiritus creatus modo Meta hysico, spiritus increatus modo plusquam Hyperphysico; Homo gignit filium à se efficienter, exse Materialiter, extra se Terminative. Substantia producit accidens à se efficienter, in se subjective. Deus non gignit filium efficienter, quia filius non dependet a patre tanquam effectus a causâ; dependentia enim in esse de creaturis tantum propriè dicitur, quarun essentia est sinita. Deus non gignit in se subjectivè, nec extra se Terminativè, nec ex se Materialiter; gignit autem in se & ex se Immutabiliter, & ut ita dicam Inessentialiter, quia genitus non est extra gignentem, sed in eo, & cum eo sabsistit in unâ uniicâque essentia indivisâ. Particula [Ex] Johan. 1. 14. non significat Materiam ex quâ, sed principlum à quo. Generatio filii non est libera, sed necessaria; filius enim Deus est, & proinde ens summè necessarium.

him. Observe the words of the apostle: "For unto which of the angels said he at any time, Thou art my Son, this day have I begotten thee." So that the proper reason why he is called the proper Son of God is because he is begotten of God. There is the most excellent reason why Christ is said to obtain a more excellent name than angels: Christ was begotten in the unity of the Godhead, and therefore he alone is properly the Son of God with a supereminent excellency.

The angels are not such excellent sons as Christ is: [1] Because Christ is begotten of God (Hebrews 1:5). [2] Christ is worshiped by angels with divine honor and worshiped as God (Hebrews 1:6). [3] He has the throne, scepter, and kingdom of God (Hebrews 1:8). [4] He has the sovereign and proper title of God (Hebrews 1:8). [5] The attributes of God, eternity (Hebrews 1:8, 10-12). [6] He sits at the right hand of God (Hebrews 1:13). All these excellencies are due to Christ as the proper Son of God (Hebrews 1), whereas the angels – the most excellent sons by creation – are but ministering spirits.

From these proper and excellent reasons we infer that Christ is the only proper or natural Son of God, because he is the only-begotten Son of God. "We," says John, "beheld his glory as of the only begotten Son of God." The word *as* is not assimilative, but declarative, and demonstrative in that place, for it declares to us that the glory of Christ is agreeable to his divine nature, he being the only natural Son of God, because he is the only begotten Son of God; just as if when we see a king sitting in his royal robes on his throne with a crown on his head and a scepter in his hand, we should say now we see him as a king, that is, now he is like himself. His state is agreeable to his majesty. Even so was the glory of Christ which the apostles beheld agreeable to the majesty of the only begotten Son of God (John 1:14). Therefore the word *as* was not inserted *tanquam terminus diminuens*: to diminish the glory of the only begotten Son of God; for the word *as* is left out in the eighteenth verse of this very chapter: "The only begotten Son which is in the bosom of the Father (John 1:18)." The Scripture abounds with several expressions to the same purpose. But we are specially to observe that the only begotten Son of God is propounded to us as the object of saving faith, and therefore this point ought to be diligently studied and considered by us. "For so God loved the world, that he gave his only begotten Son, that whosoever believes in him should not perish but have everlasting life (John 3:16)."

The Socinians – observing how much it concerns us to stand steadfast, and not yield one whit of ground in this point – have tried their wit to deceive and seduce us, and therefore they object that Isaac is called the only son of Abraham (Genesis 22:2, 12).

To this we answer without any great study that Isaac was the only son which Abraham had by Sarah. He was the only begotten son of the promise, though Ishmael was the son of Abraham by Hagar the bondwoman in an unworthy and dishonorable way. Therefore, this example will not serve the turn, and we reject it for its impertinency and dissimilitude.

Christ is the only begotten Son of God. He is absolutely and simply considered his only begotten Son, and not only in some respect as Isaac was the only son of Abraham. Christ (as Gregory Nazianzen said) is truly the Son of God, he alone is the Son, and the only Son of the Father, and his Son in an only or singular way, and he is the Son only, he is not the Father also, or the Holy Spirit. Jesus Christ is the proper natural true Son of God, begotten by the Father without a mother in the unity of the Godhead, from all eternity, equal to the Father, one and the same God with the Father, as the Scripture sets it forth. And therefore we conclude that he is simply and absolutely the only begotten Son of God, a more excellent son than all the other sons of God, not only more excellent in degree, for *gradus non mutat speciem*; but a super-excellent son, who differs from all his other sons, *plusquam genere aut specie*, because he is one God with the Father.

Jesus Christ is truly the Son of God because he is the true God (1 John 5:20) begotten of the Father (Hebrews 1:5), begotten without a mother (Hebrews 7:3), begotten from the days of eternity (Micah 5:2), a son equal to his Father, who begat him (John 5:18, Philippians 2:6), the Son of God,

(Matthew 16:16) the first begotten, and the only begotten Son of God, the natural and proper Son of God. For he is as the Father is, God by nature, (Galatians 4:8) and therefore naturally, necessarily, eternally begotten of the Father in the unity of the Godhead. Therefore, there is more than a gradual, nay, more than a specific or generic difference between this and all other sons of God. We see by all these various expressions, and by those divine and glorious attributes which are ascribed to Christ in Scripture, that God has wonderfully declared his love to us in sending his only begotten to redeem us according to that of the apostle (1 John 4:9): "In this was manifest the love of God towards us, because that God sent his only begotten Son into the world that we might live through him."

When our Savior called God his *Father*, the Jews did very well understand that he meant it in a proper and peculiar sense, and therefore told him that he did make himself equal with God (John 5:17-18) and that being but a man he made himself God (John 10:33). And though the Jews accused him of blasphemy, and endeavored to stone him as they pretended for his blasphemy, yet our Savior does not excuse his speech, or say he meant it in a metaphorical sense, but defends it by many arguments both in John 5 and 10, though he did thereby endanger his life; he says that he is equal to the Father, nay one with the Father (John 5:18, 10:30), and when the High Priest asked him whether he was the Son of the blessed (Mark 14:61), our Savior answers: "I am." There's a punctual and positive affirmation of it (Mark 14:62-63), and you may easily know in what sense the high priest meant it, by his renting of his clothes, and condemning our Savior to death for blasphemy (Mark 14:64).

And yet our Savior did not endeavor to allay their heat and rage with any retractation. He would not say that he spoke metaphorically, for he spoke properly, he meant that he was the proper and natural Son of God, who had the same nature and power with the Father, and therefore was able to do, and actually did the same works with his Father. And the Jews did understand him so, and therefore urged the law against him, and condemned him to death for blasphemy (John 19:7). The Jews answered him, "We have a law, and by our law he ought to die, because he made himself the Son of God." Mark the reason: "because he made himself the Son of God." If our Savior had not meant that he was the proper and natural Son of God, a Son equal to the Father, and one God with the Father, the Jews would not have accused him of blasphemy.

Moreover, the Jews do generally hold that those words of the second Psalm, "This day have I begotten thee," are meant of the Messiah, as Rabbi Solomon acknowledges in his commentary upon the place. "Whatsoever," says he, "is sung in this Psalm, our Masters have interpreted of King Messiah, but," (says he, and he whispers it as a secret) "in regard to the sound of the words, and for the refutation of heretics," (for so the Jew calls us Christians) "we think fit to expound it of David himself."

Here's a Jew who would fain [*gladly*] conceal a confessed truth from Christians, and there are some others it seems that would conceal this malicious concealment, for these words are expunged out of the great Hebrew Bibles set forth at Basel, but they are to be found in the Hebrew Bibles set forth with the commentaries of the rabbis at Venice by Bombergius, or else I had not insisted upon the words. I hope the detecting of this fraud may be very useful, but I must hasten to some other arguments.

The Socinians tell us that there are five causes of Christ's Sonship assigned in Scripture, which are all temporal causes, and therefore they see no reason why we should assert, or they believe, this eternal generation of the Son of God, since Christ may be called the Son of God upon another, and far different account. We desire to know whether each one of these five causes is a total or a perpetual cause. If they are each one a total cause, then there will be as many sonships as there are causes, no less than five sonships; for that rule is certain, where there is a total and sufficient cause in act, there the effect must follow. If they are partial causes, then the causes which succeed in order, do not produce their complete effect, until the last cause is in act. This we premise; that the vanity of this invention may be more evident in the whole contexture of their discourse. I shall now give them leave to speak their mind freely, and fully.

(1) The first cause of this divine sonship is (as they conceive) the conception of Christ by the Holy Spirit, whereby (say they) Christ is said to be begotten of God in an excellent and peculiar way. They urge that testimony of the angel, which stands upon record (Luke 1:35), to make good their conceit: "And the angel answered, and said unto her: The Holy Spirit shall come upon thee, and the power of the Highest shall overshadow thee: therefore also that holy thing which shall be borne of thee shall be called the Son of God." These words of the angel have reference to the prophecy of Isaiah mentioned in Luke 1:31. The words of Isaiah are: "Behold a virgin shall conceive and bear a Son, and shall call his name Immanuel (Isaiah 7:14);" "they shall call his name Jesus (Matthew 1:21);" "he shall be called the Son of the highest, the Son of God (Luke 1)." You see the words are different, and therefore we must have special respect to the thing signified. Observe then:

[1] That the prophet did foretell two particulars: {1} that a virgin should bear a son, and {2} that the son born of her should be called the Son of God. The virgin doubts of the first particular, and enquires how that could be without the knowledge of a man? The angel informs her that she should conceive after a peculiar and admirable manner by the overshadowing of the Holy Spirit, and from thence infers the second particular, that she should bring forth a Son, who was to be called the Son of God; and he gives the very same reason which was given by saint Matthew, because it was so foretold by the prophet Isaiah (Matthew 1:20-22). For the particle *therefore* (Luke 1:35) is not to be referred to the conception of Christ as the cause of this divine sonship, but to the prophecy of Isaiah recorded (Luke 1:31). "For all this was done that it might be fulfilled which was spoken by the prophet (Matthew 1:22)."

[2] They shall call his name Immanuel, God with us, and therefore he, the same person shall be called the Son of God; this is a higher reason than that which the Socinians allege.

[3] The Socinians put a fallacy upon us by assigning that to be the cause which is not the true cause.³²⁷ "He shall be called:" that is, declared and acknowledged to be the Son of God. This declaration or manifestation of the Son of God in the flesh was temporal (1 Timothy 3:16), but his generation was eternal (Micah 5:2). The Son of God was sent, manifested, incarnate, in the fullness of time (Galatians 4:4), but he was the Son of God before his incarnation, and therefore his incarnation is not the cause of his divine sonship, the effect cannot be before the cause, but the divine Sonship of Christ was before the world was.

The Holy Spirit is never called "the Father of Christ," and he could not be the principle of the subsistence or the Word, and therefore not the cause of this divine Sonship. The apostle states the point, and puts it past all dispute (Romans 1:3-4). Christ was made of the seed of David according to the flesh, but determined and declared to be the Son of God with power according to the Spirit of holiness by the resurrection from the dead, from whence it follows directly that Christ is not properly the Son of God according to the flesh, but is in that consideration rather to be called the Son of David as we observed above, because Christ came of David as concerning the flesh, but the eternal Son of God is God blessed forever (Romans 9:5).

When the Jews said that our Savior blasphemed because he made himself God (John 10:33), Christ asks them whether they did accuse him of blasphemy, because he said he was the son of God? (John 10:36). Whereby he declared that he was the Son of God according to his person which is truly divine: "Believe," he says, "that the Father is in me and I in him (John 10:38)." The force of his answer is evident: "I am in the Father, and the Father in me, and therefore I am a divine person; I am the Son of God, and

---

³²⁷ Fallacia non causae, quum non causa pro causâ ponitur.

therefore the divine nature is communicated to my person, I am begotten in the unity of the Godhead, I am in the Father, and therefore if it be no blasphemy for me to say that I am the Son of God, it is no blasphemy at all to say that I am God, because the divine nature is communicated to the natural and proper Son of God." There's the proper reason why Christ is called *the Son of God*: because the divine nature was communicated to him by an eternal generation.

(2) The second cause assigned by the Socinians why Christ is called the Son of God, is the sanctification of Christ, for which they cite John 10:35-36. "Behold," say they, "the second cause of this divine sonship plainly set forth unto us: Christ has obtained an excellent portion of the Spirit, he is sanctified and sent with a divine power into the world to save mankind."

To which we answer, that here is the same fallacy obtruded again, because [1] Christ was the Son of God before he was sent into the world. [2] God did not give the Spirit by measure to him (John 3:34). [3] Christ proves in John 10 that he is one with his Father in power, and therefore in nature, as appears: {1} because he does the same works that his Father does (verse 37), {2} because he is in his Father, and his Father in him (verse 38), and {3} because he is the natural Son of God, and therefore might truly call himself God (verses 33 and 36). {4} Because they themselves called magistrates *gods* upon a cheaper account, only in regard of their commission and office; much more might he call himself God because he was sanctified without measure, had a higher office and commission, being sent to do the work of God, to satisfy the justice of God, and save the elect of God, which he could not have done if he had not had the nature of God, and been thereby fully enabled to perfect this work of God. The argument is grounded upon the infinite distance and imparity between the office of a mediator and the office of a magistrate; between the only begotten Son of God, who is one with his Father who begat him, and the sons of men who are but the deputies of God.

(3) The third cause which they assign of this divine Sonship is the special love of the Father to this excellent Son (Matthew 3:17).

To this we answer, that God did not make Christ his Son because he loved him, but he loves him because he is his Son, a Son equal to himself, one with himself, the express image of his person, the illustrious brightness of his glory. That very place which they cite makes much against them. God does from heaven own Christ for his proper and natural Son in that very place (Matthew 3:17). God said not so to the best of angels (Hebrews 1:4-5): "To which of the angels said he at any time, "Thou art my Son this day have I begotten thee?"" That one place is sufficient to discover the fraud of the Socinians in this point.

(4) The fourth cause which they assign is the resurrection of Jesus Christ, because when Christ was raised from the dead he was as it were begotten again from the dead (Acts 13:32-33).[328]

To which we answer that Christ was the natural and proper Son of God before his resurrection, only he was declared to be the Son of God by his resurrection, according to that of the apostle (Romans 1:4):[329] "Declared to be the Son of God with power according to the spirit of holiness," (that is his divine nature) "by the resurrection from the dead." Christ was not made but declared to be the Son of God by his resurrection. His divine sonship lay hidden under the form of a servant before; only they who had spiritual eyes did discern it (John 1:14). "We have seen, and beheld the glory of the only begotten Son of God." Moreover, it is observable that the apostle endeavors to make the mystery of Christ's divine Sonship manifest in Acts 13, not

---

[328] Caelitus clamavit Pater Hic est filius ille meus, ut testatum faceret hunc esse proprium suum naturalem filium, è numero aliorum filiorum eo ipso exemptum.

[329] Genui Ps. 2. propriè significat generationem aeternam. Genui Act 13. significat Metonymi ce, hoc est genitum *patefeci* hodie, cum te excitavi amertius, Rom. 1. 4. explicitè dicuntur verba ista Psal. 2. de generatione, implicitè & consequenter autem resurrectioni accommodantur; consequenter inquam non ratione consequentis sed consequentiae. Vide D. Gomari Analys. Epist. ad Hebraeos pag. 299.

simply by his resurrection, but by the manner of his resurrection, and the state whereunto he was raised.

[1] For the manner, he was raised by his own Almighty and most glorious power in an irresistible way. He did offer violence to all the forces of death and powers of the grave, because it was not possible that he should be holden of them (Acts 2:24) when he came to declare himself to be the Son of God with power (Romans 1:4).

[2] For the state whereunto he was raised, he did not rise to return to the grave again, as Lazarus did, but he raised himself to an immortal life. And as concerning that he raised him up from the dead, now no more to return to corruption (Acts 13:34, Romans 6:9).

Now God, by raising Christ after such a manner to such a state, did declare him to be his only begotten Son, of whom David speaks in Psalm 2. Therefore, it was evident by the resurrection of Christ that God had fulfilled his promise by sending his only begotten Son to be a Savior unto Israel, so that we might have forgiveness of sins and all sure mercies by him who died for our sins, and rose again for our justification. This is the scope of the apostles discourse in Acts 13:23-29. Psalm 2 is cited here by accommodation to make good a remote and implicit consequence; as those words, "I am the God of Abraham, Isaac," etc., are cited to prove a resurrection by an implicit consequence (Matthew 22:31-32). "Thou art my Son, mine own proper Son, whom I own for my only begotten Son by raising thee to a never dying life."

(5) The fifth cause which they assign, is the exaltation of our Lord and Savior to glory, and the conferring of a name and power upon him above all creatures; for the apostle, as they conceive, speaks of this Sonship (Hebrews 5:5). "So also Christ glorified not himself to be made an high priest, but he that said unto him: "Thou art my Son, today have I begotten thee.""

I cannot but admire that the acute Socinians should cite every place where Psalm 2 is named to prove that there are so many several causes of the divine sonship of Christ, but I do more admire that they should cite this text of all the rest; for if their fifth argument have any force in it, it overthrows and disproves their four first arguments. If Christ was not begotten before his exaltation to glory, then he was not the Son of God before his exaltation. For surely these men of reason will easily grant that the effect cannot be before its proper and complete cause was in its causal actuality, or actual causality.

The words of God in Psalm 2 are so often repeated in order to teach us to keep our eye constantly fixed upon the divine Sonship of Christ whenever we discourse of his conception, birth, resurrection, transfiguration, and exaltation to glory, and conclude that the self-same person who was begotten of God from the days of eternity took our flesh, died for our sins, and rose for our justification.

For this is that great and fundamental truth which runs quite thorough the gospel, that the son of Mary who did and suffered all for us, is the proper, the natural Son of God, the only and all-sufficient Savior of his people from their sins. We must not part with this truth, for this is all our salvation.

It was very proper for the apostle to speak of his divine sonship when ever he spake of him as a mediator, as a priest, etc., because he could not have undertaken or gone through with any such office unless he had been the natural and proper Son of God equal to God; and therefore we do readily grant, that the divine offices of Christ do declare and make manifest the divine sonship, and nature of Jesus Christ, and this truth is most evident from the connection of Psalm 2:7-8.

I have with the more patience and content waded through this large and deep sea that I might come to the haven where we desire to be, so that we might come to take harbor and sanctuary in the merit and satisfaction of Jesus Christ, who is the natural and proper Son of God.

The eternal procession of the Holy Spirit

In the next place I am to prove the eternal procession of the Holy Spirit, whereby I shall make the distinction of the persons more clear and evident, and therefore I hasten to discuss that mysterious but useful point.

The Holy Spirit is not called a *Spirit* because of his spiritual nature only, for the same spiritual nature is common to all the three blessed persons, but he is called a *Spirit* upon a special and peculiar reason: because he is breathed forth by the Father and the Son.[330] The Holy Spirit is called "the Spirit which is of God (1 Corinthians 2:12):" το πνευμα το εκ του θεου.

The Spirit who proceeds from the Father is sent by the Son from the Father, John 15:26. The Greek church acknowledges that the Spirit proceeds from the Father by the Son. "All things that the Father hath are mine," says our Savior (John 16:15). But the Spirit did receive all from the Father, and Christ and his Father are essentially one (John 10:30). The Spirit is said to receive of the Son, and to glorify the Son (John 16:14). Whatever things the Father does, the Son does; and as the Son can do nothing without the Father, so the Father can do nothing without the Son; not that there is a defect of power in either, but an unity of power and nature in both.[331] The divine nature of both the Father and the Son was communicated to the Spirit by

---

[330] Spiritus dicitur non respectu spiritualis essentiae, sed Incommunicabilis subsistentiae, quia à Patre & Filio unà quasi spirantibus procedit.

[331] Omnia quae de unâ persona dicuntur, de altis etiã dicutur, exceptis relationibus oppositis, quia nihil in Deo multiplicatur nisi relatio opposita; spiratio autem quâ Pater spirat, non opponitur spirationi quâ spirat Filius. Pater enim unâ eadeque cum Filio spiratione spirat. Omnia quaecunque habet Pater, eadem etiam Filius haber, Iohn 16. 15. Iohn 17. 10. Exceptis tantum iis, in quibus ei opponitur. Non opponitur autem Patri *quoad spirationem*; Habet enim spiritus vitam subsistentem à Patre nec non filio unicissima spiratione. Vide D. Alting. Lo. Com. pag. 42. D. Maccovii Disput. 37. de Processione Spiritus. D. Brochmanum de S. sancto, qu. 8. Stegman. Photin. Disp. 6. wendelin. Christ. Th. lib. 1. cap. 2. Gomar. Disp. de Trinitate, Tom. 3. Disp. 7, 8. Junium Trin. Defens. contra Samosat. Polanum, Zanchium. Synop. Pur. Theol.

this eternal spiration. Therefore he is sent by both, and he receives of both, and he glorifies both, and he is the Spirit of both the Father and the Son.

He is called "the Spirit of the Father" (Matthew 10:20) because he proceeds from the Father (John 15:26), and he is called "the Spirit of the Son of God" (Galatians 4:6), "the Spirit of Christ" (Romans 8:9), "the Spirit of Jesus Christ" (Philippians 1:19), and "the Spirit of Christ," (1 Peter 1:11) because he receives of Christ, is sent from Christ, and is breathed forth by Christ; the Father and the Son breathe forth the subsistence of the Spirit with one and the same spiration.

When Christ breathed upon his disciples, he said, "Receive ye the Holy Ghost," to show that he had power to dispose of the Spirit, who did from all eternity breathe forth the Spirit. The Holy Spirit was breathed forth necessarily by both; I say, necessarily, because eternally there was a double and eternal necessity of it both in respect of the persons breathing and the person breathed. The Spirit was not breathed forth as a creature, but as a divine person: a person of the Godhead. He was breathed forth by procession, and subsists in the unity of the Godhead. He proceeds from both, and yet in both; for one divine person cannot subsist out of another, but all three subsist in the same undivided and infinite nature.

But the Socinians tell us that the Holy Spirit is nothing else but the power and virtue of God the Father – to which we answer that the Spirit is the natural virtue of the Father no more than he is the natural virtue of the Son, or of himself. For the virtue of God is the essence of God, the Holy Spirit is his own essence, and all three persons have one and the same essence. The Holy Spirit, who proceeds from the Father, is called "the power of the Father" (Luke 1:35), because the Spirit works as he proceeds in order. The Father works in the Son and by the Spirit.

But the Spirit who proceeds from the Father is distinguished from the Father. The Spirit did not breath forth himself, or proceed from himself. The Holy Spirit does not speak of himself (John 16:13), but the Father speaks of himself, because he is of himself, he is begotten of none, proceeds from none of the divine persons, is sent by none of them. The Holy Spirit receives of Christ and is sent by Christ, therefore the Holy Spirit is not the Father, but clearly distinguished from him (John 16:14-15, John 15:26, John 14:16-17, Matthew 3:16-17, Matthew 28:19; 2 Corinthians 13:14, and in several other places).

The Father and the Spirit are personally distinguished, but they are essentially one (1 John 5:7). They are one in power, nature, will, and yet are three persons, three witnesses who deliver one and the same divine testimony; The testimony of the Holy Spirit is as divine as the testimony of God the Father.[332] "The witness of God is greater" (1 John 5:9) must refer to the witness of the Father, Word, and Spirit (1 John 5:7), though the testimony of the Father is especially insisted on in the following words. For all the three witnesses in heaven give one and the same testimony, and that testimony is divine.

The Holy Spirit is the Spirit of God,[333] and the Spirit which is of God, "the Spirit of Elohim" (Genesis 1:2), "the Spirit of Jehovah" (Isaiah 11:2), the Spirit which is Jehovah and the God of Israel, as has been proven at large in Chapter 4. The distinction between the Father and the Spirit will be more evident when we come to treat of the personal properties.

The Socinians are so confounded in this point that they are forced to acknowledge that the Holy Spirit is no accidental virtue, no finite substance, no creature, but the uncreated and substantial virtue or power of God, because whatsoever is in God is the substance of God, as Eniedinus confesses. And Smalcius acknowledges that it may be granted that the Holy Spirit is God, because whatsoever is naturally in God may be called God. But I shall prove that the Holy Spirit is not only God, but a person of the Godhead distinct from the Father and the Son. Jesus Christ is called "the power of God" (1 Corinthians 1:24) and the Holy Spirit "the power of God" (Luke

---

[332] το πνευμα του θεου 1 Corinthians 2:11; το πνευμα το εκ του θεου 1 Corinthians 2:12; 1 Corinthians 12:5-6, Acts 5:3-4; 1 Corinthians 3:16-17
[333] Romans 8:11, 14; 1 Corinthians 12:3, Isaiah 6:1, Isaiah 63:14

1:35, Luke 24:49). The Son is a distinct person from the Father, and the Holy Spirit is as the ancients used to call him, the personal virtue or power of the Father proceeding from the Father, by whom he declares and put forth his power, and therefore the Spirit is said to work and distribute all gifts and graces as he will. Father, Son, and Holy Spirit have one and the same will and power. Still, we must bottom upon [*have as a foundation*] that truth: "These three are one" (1 John 5:7). That this procession of the Holy Spirit is mysterious, and for the manner of it unsearchable we do readily grant; and therefore I shall not presume to define after what manner the Holy Spirit is breathed forth from the Father and the Son, but we are sure that it cannot be any corporeal procession. The ancients did constantly distinguish between procession and generation, but the eternal generation of Christ being spiritual, the procession of the Spirit must be spiritual, for the Spirit is not only essentially a Spirit as the Father, and God the Son are, but he is personally a Spirit.[334] The more perfect and spiritual this procession is, the more evident it is that the Spirit was breathed forth in the unity of the Godhead.

(1) They who say that the Son proceeds from the Father use that term *proceed* in a general and very large signification, but then they say that the Son did proceed by generation, the Spirit by spiration thereby endeavoring to distinguish the manner of proceeding.

(2) They say the Son did proceed from the Father alone, and therefore is said to be sent by the Father only; but the Holy Spirit did proceed from the Father and the Son both, and therefore is said to be sent by the Son as well as the Father (Luke 24:49, John 15:26, John 14:26, John 16:14). But Christ is sent by the Father only, because he is of the Father only, and was not begotten of the Spirit; and the Father is not sent by any because he is of himself; hereby they endeavor to distinguish the principle of these divine processions.

---

[334] Non omne quod procedit Nascitur, quāvis omne procedat quod nascitur. Vide August. contra Maximin. lib. 3. cap. 14.

(3) The Son did proceed as the second person, the Holy Spirit as the third person of the Godhead, and hereby they endeavor to distinguish the order of these divine processions. We know this divine procession is [1] spiritual, [2] eternal because [it is] divine, and [3] immutable. This procession is not a change of the Spirit from not being to being, or from an imperfect being to a more perfect being.[335] We know that procession cannot be a motion from one place to another, for the Spirit is omnipresent, fills all places, and therefore cannot change its place. [4] Necessary. The Father and Son did from all eternity breathe forth the Spirit in the unity of the Godhead, not by any alienation of the Godhead from themselves, but by an unspeakable communication of the same divine nature to a third person of the Godhead. And this communication is natural. Therefore necessary it is, but not involuntary.

The Father and Son did not breathe forth the Spirit by any coaction or compulsion,[336] and yet we cannot say that the Father and the Son did arbitrarily or freely breathe forth the Spirit as all three persons did create the world, for they did create the world with such liberty and freedom as that they might not have created it; but they did naturally and necessarily breathe forth the Spirit, and could not but breathe him forth. This inward and personal act is natural. Such is the perfection of the Godhead that it must be communicated to all three persons, and such is the coessential unity of the

---

[335] Pater & filius spirando spiritū naturam divinam communicant spiritui, ita ut tribus Deitatis personis communis sit: non est haec Alienatio sed Communicatio.

[336] Spiritus Sanctus procedit nonvoluntate ut Scholastici, & post eos Catechismus Romanus ambigue docuerunt, sed necessitate naturae quéadmodum & filius naturâ genitus est. Paternon spirat sine filio, non ob defectum potentiae sed ob unitatem essentiae. Spiritus Procedit ab utro{que} subsistit in utro{que} quia est coessentialis utrique, 1 Iohan. 5. 7. & proinde haec aeterna Spiratio non est contingens sed necessaria; nec libera est nec Involuntaria. Neque enim necessitas haec vim infert, nec voluntas novum concilium designat ex deliberatione superveniens. Vide Athanas. Basilium, Cyrillum, Nazianzenum, Theodoretum, Damascenum. Vide Gomarum, D. Altingium, Maccovium, Zanchium, Tilenum, Crocium, Stegmanum, Polan. Syntag. lib. 3. de Trinitate cap. 6.

Father, Son, and Holy Spirit, as that all three do necessarily and naturally subsist in the self-same entire and infinite Godhead.

True it is that the will of God is the nature of God, but nature is a more comprehensive Word. Therefore, according to our manner of apprehension and in strictness of speech, it is more proper to say that the Father and the Son did breathe forth the Spirit by the perfection of their nature, than to say they breathed him forth of their own will, or by some arbitrary decree, for then it will follow that there might have been but two persons of, and in the Godhead, that the Holy Spirit exists and subsists contingently, and by consequence, that the Spirit is no person of the Godhead.

The acute Samosatenian, whom learned Junius confutes, desired to know whether the Holy Spirit was produced by an action of the will. Junius answers:[337] "If you oppose the will of God to the nature of God, we cannot say that the Spirit proceeds from the Father and the Son by their will but by their nature, because the Father, Son and Spirit are coessential, for as the Father did beget his natural Son by his nature, so do the Father and the Son breathe forth the coessential Spirit by their nature." "Nor is it safe to say," says Junius, "that the nature of the Father breathes forth the Spirit by an action of his will, but rather according to that manner (the infinite distance being observed between what is human and divine) after which the will does proceed in man," and this he says is but a weak resemblance of the Scholastics, which we are not bound to defend. For the nature of God is pure, single, infinite, and therefore we must not follow those resemblances too far which are grounded upon the distinction of the understanding and the will in creatures, because even that point is very disputable, and the most

---

[337] Iunius Cathol. Doct. de Trinitdefen. contra Samosat. pag. 36 Spiritus Sanctus procedit Naturaliter, hoc est actione Naturae, non autem voluntatis. Periculosé dicitur spiritum procedere naturâ quidē sed per actionem voluntatis: Non procedit actione voluntatis propriè, sed secundum actionem voluntatis procedere dicitur, id est secundum eamactionem, vel potius secundùm eum modum quo naturaliter procedunt voluntas & charitas. De hac re igitur possemus tacere, & rem Scholasticis defendendam permittere, aut ad libros eorum reijcere.

single and perfect nature of God infinitely transcends the perfection of angels.

I believe that you are, as I am, willing to get out of the dark. But enough of that, for we read that the saints are begotten by the will of God (James 1:18). But we must not conceive that Christ is begotten, or the Spirit breathed forth after the same manner as we are regenerated. The Spirit is breathed forth in a connatural and coessential way in the unity of the single and entire Godhead, but we are regenerated by the graces of God.

The Spirit proceeds equally from the Father and the Son, for the unity of the divine nature, and equality of divine persons cannot be maintained if that principle is denied. Peter Lombard and his adherents did mince the point with a very dangerous distinction: that the Spirit proceeds principally from the Father, and less principally from the Son. But it is clear and evident that the Holy Spirit being a coessential person has the self-same divine nature and essence entirely communicated unto him which is in the Father and the Son without any alienation of it from them or multiplication of it in him, and therefore the Spirit does not proceed from the Father and Son as they stand in relative opposition, but as they are essentially and naturally one; and therefore the Spirit did proceed from both equally, *aeque primo ac per se*, as we use to say. The Spirit receives from Christ (John 16:14-15), but the Spirit being God could not receive anything but subsistence from the Father or the Son. The Spirit glorifies the Son (John 16:14) in no other way than the Son as God glorifies the Father, because the Son did receive his subsistence from the Father as the Spirit receives his subsistence from the Father and the Son.

We must carefully distinguish:

(1) Between the generation of the Son and the procession of the Holy Spirit, though as we have shown above, the Son proceeds, if you take that word in a general notion. The most exact critics will not take upon them to distinguish between τό ἐξελθεῖν and τό ἐκπορεύομαι. Yet because we want words to express ourselves, the reverend doctors of the church thought fit to appropriate procession to the Holy Spirit for distinction's sake. The Scripture

says that Christ is the only begotten Son of God. God the Father is never called the Father of the Holy Spirit; nor is the Holy Spirit called the Son of God. Moreover, the Schoolmen have given advantage to the enemies of the Trinity by discoursing of divine processions at large in a general notion; and for these reasons I did endeavor to distinguish the procession of the Son from the Spirit in this chapter, in respect of the manner, principle, and order of procession.

(2) We must carefully distinguish between the eternal procession of the Spirit, and the temporal mission of the Spirit; but the natural and eternal procession of the Spirit may be evinced by the temporal mission of the Spirit. The Greek church acknowledges: [1] that the Holy Spirit is God, and [2] that he is one and the same God with the Father and the Son, and from hence we infer:

[1] That the Son did not send the Spirit by way of command as if he were greater than the Spirit.

[2] That the Son did not send the Spirit by way of counsel and advice, as if he were wiser than the Spirit. Therefore, the only reason why he did temporally send him is because the Spirit did naturally and eternally proceed from him, and receive his glorious subsistence of him. I might discourse more largely upon this subject,[338] but I consider what Athanasius, Damascene, and various other reverend divines who did long study these mysterious points, have acknowledged after many perplexed debates. The Son (say they) was begotten, and the Spirit proceeded. This we are sure of, because it is written. If you inquire after the manner how the one was begotten, and how the other did proceed, we answer that the Son was begotten, and the Spirit did proceed eternally, unchangeably, and unspeakably.

---

[338] Vide Athanasium 1. Dialog. de Trimtate Damasc. n. de fide Orthod. Modom Curiositati imponat Lector, nec molestas & perplexas disputationes cupidiùs quàm par sit sibi accersat. Calv. Instit. lib. 1. cap. 13.

Those places of Scripture which are spoken of God in the Old Testament are said to be spoken of the Son, and the Spirit in the New Testament, and therefore do by consent of both testaments, declare that the Father, Son, and Holy Spirit are one and the same God. For instance, Isaiah 6 is spoken of Jehovah, the God of Israel, whom the Mahometans, Sabellians, and Arians do acknowledge to be the true God. But this is spoken of Christ, says John (John 12:41): "These things said Esaias when he saw his glory and spake of him." But the Holy Spirit has his share in this prophecy (Acts 28:25), therefore those who believe both Testaments must conclude that the Father, Son, and the Holy Spirit are one and the same God.

Finally, the personal actions and properties of these three declare them to be distinct persons; therefore it is easy to conclude that Father, Son, and Holy Spirit are three distinct persons, and yet one and the same God.

That the Spirit is a person of the Godhead, has been proven in the fourth chapter of this book. That he is a distinct person from the Father and the Son is most clear by that which has been said both in that chapter and in this. All those places might be heaped up which prove the personal appearance of the Spirit, when he did assume the shape of a dove, and appeared as in tongues of fire,[339] his teaching, leading, acting, ruling, comforting, distributing of gifts and the like, together with the several phrases of him in Scripture, and frequent joining him with the Father and Son as their equal in power and authority in bestowing all spiritual and eternal blessings do evince the same.

The notes of distinction: "another," "even the Spirit," "these three," etc. The change of the gender in relative articles, which must necessarily be referred to the Spirit, is very considerable.[340] But I have said more than enough upon this point, and therefore proceed to make the distinction of these three uncreated persons yet more evident.

---

[339] Scriptura Neutro Antecedenti relativum masculini generis statim subjicit Iohan. 15:26 εκεινος non εκεινο: item Johan. 16, 13. 14.

[340] Ephesians 1:13–14.

(3) These uncreated persons are sufficiently distinguished by their order. The Scripture most commonly places the Father first in order, the Son second, and the Holy Spirit third, when all three are named. And by the inward and personal actions (which have been mentioned), it does appear that this is the natural order of these uncreated persons; for the Son cannot be placed in order before the Father, because he is naturally begotten of the Father; the Holy Spirit cannot be placed in order before the Son, because he does naturally proceed from the Son. This is the proper and natural order.[341]

Basil the Great in his αντιγραφον πιστεως complains that some in his time did place the Son in order before the Father, and the Holy Spirit before the Son, that they might gain some advantage by that device. Basil tells them that he had received order from the Lord to baptize in the name of the Father, Son, and Holy Spirit, and therefore was resolved to preserve that inviolable order, notwithstanding any devices or attempts to prevent it. When the witnesses in heaven are reckoned up in a business of the highest consequence, they are reckoned in this very order (1 John 5:7): the Father, the Word, and the Spirit. But it is confessed that sometimes it is most agreeable to the scope and purpose of the Holy Spirit to place the Son before the Father, as appears in 2 Corinthians 13:13 and Galatians 1:1, and hence it is likewise, that the Holy Spirit is sometimes placed before the Son, as Revelation 1:4-5, and sometimes before the Father and the Son (1 Corinthians 12:4-6). But the natural order does not overthrow either the equality or coeternity of the persons, nor does that order of enumeration which is *pro instituto*, overthrow the natural order, and both do sufficiently prove the distinction of the three uncreated persons.

(4) The divine persons are sufficiently distinguished by their personal properties. The property of the Father is to subsist of himself, that is, to receive subsistence or subsisting life from none but himself. I shall not enter into that sad dispute whether this personal property be absolute or relative;

---

[341] Vide Basilei Magni Epistolam quae in scribitur αντιγραφον πιστεως Edit. Basil. Gr. p. 330.

whether αὐθυπόστατος does not import something as positive and absolute as αὐτόθεος.[342] It is pleaded that the self-subsistence of the Father is not his Fatherhood, and that that rule is beyond dispute: "*Habere subsistentiam à se non dicit respectum ad aliud, vel alium.*" Therefore, I humbly offer it to the consideration of the learned, whether that self subsistence whereby the first person is distinguished from the Son and the Spirit is absolute, or relative. I will not take upon myself to determine anything in so deep a point, or suffer my reason to wax wild and wanton in discoursing of so great a mystery. Therefore, though there be something hinted which may amount to a *videtur quod sic* in the behalf of the less common opinion in this book, and it is clear that all three persons are nothing else but the Godhead considered with all absolute and relative perfection, yet I conceive it safest to waive that point, and conclude with that learned divine: "*Nos fidelem ignorantiae professionem temerariae assertioni praeferendam judicamus.*"[343] Whether then this self-subsistence is absolute or relative, it is enough for our present purpose to prove that the first person of the Godhead is distinguished by his self-subsistence from the blessed Son and Holy Spirit.

The self-subsistence of the Father is incommunicable. It is proper and peculiar to the first person to have subsistence from none but himself, and to be the first personal principle which gives subsistence to the other two coessential and coequal persons. The Son receives subsistence from the Father, and the Spirit receives subsistence from the Father and the Son, as has been proven above. Therefore, this self-subsistence makes a very remarkable, and undeniable difference between the Father and the two other uncreated persons.

Some learned men have from hence inferred that because the Father alone has subsistence from himself, therefore the Father alone is God of

---

[342] Pater αυτοφυης [...] a Doctoribus Orthodoxis dicitur Negative, quia à nullo est sed à seipso, & per seipsum ab omni aeternitate subsistit.

[343] "We judge that an honest admission of ignorance is to be preferred to an all too daring assertion."*Synopsis of a Purer Theology* (Den Boer & Faber, Ed.), 2023, Volume 1, pp.81-82

himself. But the consequence is absurd, for they do not distinguish between the essence of God and the peculiar subsistences in the Godhead. The essence of God is one and the same in all, and everyone of the uncreated persons: it is (if I may so speak) a self-essence and essence itself a self-deity, because everyone of the persons is truly, properly, essentially God, God himself; and therefore if the essence of the Father be a self-deity, so is the essence of the Son and Spirit.

The divine essence of the Son is neither begotten, caused, nor produced any more than the essence of the Father. The subsistence of the Son is begotten, but not caused; the divine essence is communicated to the Son, but it is not begotten by the Father. For the Father communicates that self-same divine and entire essence which is in himself, by begetting the personal subsistence of the Son in the unity of the Godhead from the days of eternity. Christ is not God by grace, but by nature; and the will of the Father did not precede and produce the Godhead in Christ, but accompany and approve the natural communication of the Godhead to Christ, even as his will approves his own natural and eternal goodness; and therefore Christ is both his natural Son, as has been proven, and the Son of his love (Colossians 1:13).[344]

Genebrardus was to blame to fall foul upon Calvin and Beza and other Reformed writers whom he condemns as guilty of a new heresy called *autotheanism*, because they said that Christ was God of himself, but he was not the Son of himself. Calvin and Beza did not deny that the Godhead was from all eternity communicated to the Son by the Father; only they say:

[1] That the Godhead which is communicated is in itself, of itself truly, properly, essentially divine; because the self-same Godhead is in the Father and Son whole and entire in both.

---

[344] Vide Genebrardum lib. 1. de Trinitate

[2] Because the Godhead which is communicated is not begotten, the unbegotten Godhead is communicated to the only begotten Son by an eternal generation.

[3] Because the Godhead which is communicated is not caused, produced, or created by the Father, as Valentinus Gentilis dreamt.[345]

Therefore, Genebrardus, Canisius, Gifford, Stapleton, Faber Fevardentius, and the rest are extremely mistaken when they say that Calvin and Beza deny that the Father did beget his Son in the unity of his own divine essence, for the meaning of Calvin was plainly this: the Son has the self-same divine nature with the Father, they are coessential: one and the same God who is the only true God, God of himself, not God by participation, or creation, but God by nature and essence. For Calvin speaks in opposition to Valentinus Gentilis, who denies the Son and Spirit to be coessential with the Father, but says that the Father did essentiate the Son with another manner of essence than his own divine essence, namely with a created and produced essence. Gentilis says that the Father only is truly God, because he only has an increated Godhead, and the Son has not the self-same Godhead with the Father.

I would not have said so much on this argument, but I find papists, Arminians, Socinians, and some bitter Lutherans do all join their forces to abuse Calvin, Beza, Viret, Farrell, Simler, Volanus, Gwalther, Bullinger, Lavater, the orthodox Helvetians, and many other Reformed writers upon this argument. Some say these reverend divines are guilty of heresy, blasphemy, and atheism, because they say Christ is God of himself, though they clearly mean that he is one God with his Father, and that the Godhead which is communicated to the Son by generation is an unbegotten Godhead – a self-deity. If anyone desires to read more upon this argument, he may consult Valentinus Gentilis, and all that write against him, especially Calvin, and the rest of the Reformed writers named. But now he may read the

---

[345] Solus Pater est αὐτόθεος id est ànullo superiore Numine Essentiatus sed à seipso Deus. Val. Gen. Pro thes. 8. 12. 40. & ultimâ.

ancients, with whom Arminius was not well acquainted. For if he had read them, he would not have said that the word αὐτόθεος is not to be found in the writings of the Fathers.

Those who are taken with Platonic raptures may read Dionysius, Plato's corrival; Maximus Pachymerius and the rest, will give them some light therein. Athanasius, Basil, Epiphanius, Nazianzen, Damascene, speak the same thing either [rhetorically or discursively], to whom I might add Justin Martyr, Anastasius and Cyril. As for Origen, I know his writings have been extremely corrupted by the iniquity of his antagonists, and yet there are many things that are excellent in him, which I am in charity obliged to conceive to be his genuine and proper judgment, and to impute many of his errors to the fraud, ignorance, or malice of such as made too bold with his works, or else to a kind of liberty of speaking, which good wits are not free from, when they have no adversary in sight who is like to call them to an account for their irregular phrases.

Bellarmine is as modest as we could expect such a sophister to be;[346] only he did not take notice of the controversy between Calvin and Gentilis. but we will pardon that error; for we know the cardinal was not at leisure, and therefore did many times pass sentence upon the Protestants for expedition sake before he had heard their cause. Gregory de Valentia is very ingenuous in this point, and makes a fair apology for the Autotheans.[347] If any desire to take a shorter cut, I shall refer them to three most eminent divines who have studied this point exactly, and are very critical both in state of the question, and their phrases, Chamier, Gomarus and Voetius. And now, I crave leave to proceed without begging pardon for this necessary digression, because I hope it may be very useful to learned men.

It is now easy upon the due consideration of the premises to state the point right. It is proper to the Father to have:

---

[346] Bellar. l. 2. de Christ. c. 19.
[347] Greg. Valent. part. 1. disp. 2. quaest. 1. punct. 1. pag. 718

(1) The Godhead without any communication of it to him from any other uncreated person.

(2) To have subsistence from, and of himself as he is the first person, and the first personal principle of giving subsisting life unto the other two coessential persons. For the first uncreated person cannot receive subsistence from any person, because he is the first person in order, though all three be equal in respect of dignity and duration. There can be no person in order before the first person to communicate his Godhead, or give personal subsistence to him either by generation or spiration, and this must be a characteristic and distinctive property which declares the subsistence of the Father to be incommunicable. For though all three uncreated persons do subsist in the Godhead, yet self-subsistence is proper to the Father. The Father alone is the first personal principle of subsisting life. The Father is distinguished from the Son, because the Father is unbegotten, and because he did beget the Son; the Father is distinguished from the Spirit, because he did breath forth the Spirit.[348] But I have said enough of that when I treated above of the inward and personal actions.

I need not take notice of their nice exception who say the Father is not his own Father, and therefore cannot be said to be begotten of himself, or to have subsistence from himself; yet because some take advantage thereby to censure the reverend doctors of the church, I shall stop the critics mouths with one criticism out of Hesychius and Soudas. "To be begotten of one's self," (says Hesychius) "is to be begotten of none." God is said to be begotten of himself because he is unbegotten; and Soudas concurs, and does either transcribe or subscribe. No man ever dreamt that the Father did beget either his Godhead, or his own personal subsistence, for the Godhead were no Godhead if it were begotten, and we know the Father is not his own Father though Synesius and some such poetical wits who meant well have adventured upon such dangerous expressions. It implies a contradiction that

---

[348] Eadem essentia est in Patre ἀγέννητος, in Filio γέννητος, in Spiritu Sancto [spirata]

anything should be the cause of itself, or its own effect, for the cause is before the effect, and nothing can be before and after itself; and there is a friendly opposition between correlates; the Father cannot be his own Son.³⁴⁹

But notwithstanding all that has been alleged by these critical disputants, still it holds good that the Godhead was not communicated to God the Father by any person created or uncreated, and the first person did not receive his personal subsistence from any other person by generation, spiration, or any other way. But I must not dwell upon this argument.

(5) The uncreated persons are sufficiently distinguished by their personal and inward relations; but we must not conceive that there are as many persons in the Godhead, as there are relations; for the Father is related to the Son and to the Spirit; and the Son is related to the Father and to the Spirit; and the Spirit is related to the Father and the Son.³⁵⁰ But there is a friendly opposition evidenced by some relations which do help together with the actions, order and properties mentioned above to demonstrate some kind of distinction between the persons. The Son as he is a Son is relatively opposed to the Father who begat him, and so the Spirit as proceeding by spiration is relatively opposed to the Father and the Son who did both join in breathing forth the Holy Spirit. Relations distinguish as proper and opposite.

I might discourse concerning the order of these persons in working, as well as of their order in subsisting. Something might be spoken of the peculiar manner of their working *ad extra*, and much might be said of the incarnation of the Son to declare him to be distinct from the Father and the Spirit; and something of the effusion of the Spirit. But I have said enough to

---

[349] Vocis sono ἀγέννητος negativus terminus est sed reipsa affirmat. D. Gerrard de Tribus Elohim. cap. 8. Sect. 50. pag. 175.

[350] Spiratio non est fundamentum relationis personalis hoc est propriae & peculiaaris; relatio autem distinguit vel quà propriavel quà opposita; paternitas & spiratio, Item filiatio & spiratio non opponuntur, non sunt proprietates peculiaries & incommunicabiles, & proinde non distingunt; relationes dicunt, sed non Personales proprias & oppositas. Vide Tho. part. 1. quest. 30. art. 2. An distinctio inter essentiam & relationem fit Realis, formalis, vel rationis. Vide Biol. 1. sent. dist. 2. qu. 11. & dist. 26. qu. 1. art. 3. Vide Basilium etiam contra Eunomium. lib. 2. p. 134.

evidence that these uncreated persons are distinguished; what kind of distinction there is between them, I am now to show, and that I may be brief and plain in the opening of this weighty point, I shall lay down the truth clearly in some few propositions.

(1) The Father, Son, and Holy Spirit are not essentially distinguished, for Christ and his Father are one (John 10:30) and all three are essentially one (1 John 5:7).[351] The Synod of Chalcedon determined that Christ was coessential with his Father according to his divinity, and coessential with us according to his humanity, but the natural union between us and Christ only proves a specifical unity. But Christ and his Father have one and the self-same divine and undivided essence. He must acknowledge more gods, who holds that the Son and Spirit have another or different kind of Godhead from the Father.[352] The Arians did divide the nature of the Trinity, and the Sabellians did confound their persons, but Christians acknowledge and maintain that there are three persons and but one single divine nature in the blessed Trinity. Only the second person did assume the nature of man that he might heal our nature and save our persons.

(2) These three divine persons are not distinguished *realiter separabiliter* – that is: they are not so distinguished that they can be divided or separated one from another, as created persons and things may.[353] These three coessential persons are omnipresent. They do all three subsist in the self-same omnipresent nature; nay, they do all three subsist in one another, without any contraction, commixtion, or confusion, as has been proven at large in this book. These coessential subsistences cannot be separated or divided any

---

[351] Trinitas est. unus solus immensus naturaliter Deus, praeter quem non est alius Deus. Vide Fulgentium de fide Orthod.

[352] Essentiam divinam exinanire ut distincti onem personarum demonstre mus est impium; essentiam autē in ipsâ distincti one complecti absurdum.

[353] Consequetiam negamus

more than their indivisible and infinite essence can be divided or multiplied.[354]

(3) These three uncreated persons are truly distinguished. This proposition is fully proven already in this very chapter.[355] I know it will be expected by some, that I should say that these three persons are distinguished really, but I shall humbly desire them to consider, that some have by that expression taken occasion to exercise their wanton wits in caviling against this deep and glorious mystery to the great prejudice of this weighty truth. If they are really distinguished, say some, then they differ essentially, or *tanquam res & res*, then they may be separated, say others, then there are three gods, say a third. It is too well known what sport atheists have made upon this advantage, and truly it is much at one whether men do profess themselves atheists or tritheites, for he who believes that there are three gods may, when he pleases, believe that there is no God at all.

Vorstius presses those that call the distinction between the persons *real* after this manner:[356] "If the three persons be really distinguished, then they are *tres res*, three real things; for the multiplication of persons is real, and therefore the Son being really distinct from the Father, and the Spirit from both, they must have three essences really distinct. And if they are *tres res*, then either three substances, or three accidents.[357] But the Reformed divines cannot," says Vorstius, "grant that they are three accidents, because they deny that there is any accident in God; and if they are three substances, then there are," he says, "three gods."[358] Valentinus Gentilis and some ministers of

---

[354] In illâ Trinitatis naturâ sic totum unum est ut nihil ibi possit separari vel dividi: sic totum aequale est ut nihil ibi majus aut minus valeat inveniri.
[355] Fulgentius lib. de fide Orthodox. ad Donatū.
[356] Quid quid est aliquid seu quod habet aliquam entitatem seu formalitatem inquit Vorstius habet essentiam.
[357] Consequetiam negamus
[358] Tum enim in creatis subsistentia & suppositalitas quia non sunt nihil sed aliquid haberent essentiam; & consequenter essentiae esset essentia & hujus rursum essentia, & sic in infinitum. Vide Eglisemnium in Crisi, pag. 20, 21. vide etiam Bisterfeldium, Smiglecium, Stegmannum, Kesterum in examine Metaphys. Photinianae. D. Voetium de unica & simplic. Dei natura, p. 236. Wendelinum, &c.

Transylvania reason much after the same manner. I know not whether Master Fry did ever read any of their writings, but I am sure that he has conversed with some of that persuasion, or else, his carnal reason is of near kin to theirs.

For upon this very ground Mr. Fry ventures to explode three distinct persons or subsistences out of his creed, but he will never be able to explode them out of the Godhead.[359] He may sooner explode himself out of the number of Christians, for if he takes away the divine person of Christ, he takes away the foundation of Christianity. But having shown him his danger, I desire to satisfy his reason, awaken his faith, and settle his conscience in this weighty point.[360] If he will deny his carnal reason, and not require any example to illustrate a mystery above reason and beyond example, Master Fry will tell us news indeed, if he can make it good that any ministers or members of the church of God in England do make Jesus Christ a distinct God from God the Father.[361]

(2) He may do well to publish those reasons, which move him and the others he speaks of, to be of that opinion.[362]

(3) He acknowledges that these three, the Father, the Son, and the Holy Spirit are equally God (page 21). Let him consider his own confession: "these three" – what are these three? Are they three gods? No, that he abominates. Are they three accidents? No, that is absurd. Are they three substances? If so,

---

[359] See Mr. Fry's blasphemy and error blown up & down the kingdom with his own bellows, p. 22, 23.
[360] Si hic ratio quaeritur, non est mirabile: si exemplum poscitur, non est singulare, Aug. Ep. 3. & li. 15. de Civ. Dei. cap. 13. lib. 15. de Trin. cap. 7. & Iob. Damas. Orth. fid. lib. 1. cap. 9,
[361] Mr. Fry his Bell. 22.
[362] Personae divinae Realiter distinguntur quia Scriptura alium dicit Patrem, alium filium, alium Spiritum Sanctum. Iohan. 5. 32. Iohan. 14. 16. & quia Relative opponuntur: atqui opposita, quà talia, non possunt esse idem; nō tamen distinguuntur essentialiter: omnis quidem distinctio essentialis est realis, sed non è contra. Personae ita sunt realiter idem cum essentia divinâ ut tamen Relative inter se opponantur; ad haec non sint praedicata Essentialia; distinguuntur itaque ab essentia divinâ ex natura rei eminenter. Vide D. Voet deunicâ & simplicis. Dei essentiâ, p. 234, 235, 236.

then created or uncreated? "Not created, for that," he says, "none will affirm." Are they three uncreated substances? "No," says he, "for then they would consequently be three gods (page 23)."

I hope by this time he sees how easy it is to retort his own argument. And if this retortion may help him to answer it, I shall be glad that I have retorted it.

His only answer ought to be: "I do believe that these three are three subsistents in the same single and infinite Godhead" (Philippians 2:6. John 10:30; 1 John 5:7, Hebrews 1:3).

Vorstius, Valentinus Gentilis, and the Transylvanians require some more curious answer, but I shall be as plain and as brief as the weight and depth of this mystery will permit me to be. I remember that Aristotle says: "He does make a truth sufficiently plain, who brings such proofs as the point in question will bear."

Now it is most evident that supernatural mysteries cannot be expounded according to the rules of art.[363]

Some return this answer: that if by *tres res*, three real things, you mean three persons, there are three real persons in the Godhead. They are not made three by a fiction of reason; they are declared three by the plain words of Scripture. But they were three before any Scripture was written, even from the days of eternity. But if by *tres res*, three real things, you mean three divine essences, we do deny that three persons are three divine essences, or three gods, for these three persons are but one God blessed forever.

If you ask others, they will say that these three are one being, but they are three proper and peculiar manners of being subsisting in the same

---

[363] Pater Filius & Spiritus Sanctus sunt tres Res, & non sunt tres Res diverso respectu: tres Res respectu relationum oppositarum. non sunt tres Res secundum essentiam. Wendelin. Christian, Theolog. lib. 1. cap. 2. pag. 105. Proprietates Personales essentiam divinam nec componant, nec multiplicant, personas autem faeliciter distinguunt. [Vide] Justin Martyr.

Godhead.[364] They have one essential subsistence, say others, but they have three incommunicable manners of subsisting. Some express it thus: these three are really distinct, but not essentially; modally, but not separably; truly, but relatively; formally, and yet but personally. Others that mean the same thing, say they are distinguished *secundum esse personale, non secundum esse quidditativum*.

They then that say the persons are really distinct, should explain themselves warily according to some of these or the like safe expressions: namely that by *really*, [1] they do not mean essentially, [2] they do not mean separably, and [3] that by *really*, they do mean that the relations and personal properties, whereby the three persons are known to be distinguished, are real relations and real properties, and not fictions of reason.

The relations are opposite, the properties incommunicable, and much might be said of the personal actions to the self-same purpose; but I must hasten.

Some do adventure to call this distinction *natural*,[365] but that is a very dangerous expression. It must not pass without some favorable grains of

---

[364] Non distinguuntur το πραγματι hoc est essentiâ, sed [τη πινοια] hoc est Formaliter, sivé τροπω υπαρξεως Personaliter. vide Damascen. lib. 1. de side Orthod Modi in divinis non sunt separabiles, sunt autem reales, & modi reales distinguunt realiter quamvis modaliter. Nonnulli distinguunt inter esse Patris, & esse Patrē. Inter esse Quidditativum & esse Personale. Personalitas divina est realis; distinguuntur itaque Realiter quia distinguuntur Personaliter. Relationes in divinis non componunt sed distinguunt: relationes autem reales realiter distinguunt. Proprietates reales propriè simul & realiter distinguunt.

[365] Richardus Bonavent. & Ioh. de Rip; personas distingui dicunt per proprietates Absolutas primò, & per Relationes Originis ex Consequenti. Discrimen [εννοητικοί] tantùm sinxerunt Noëtiani. Epiphan. Haeres. 57. Distinctio personarū naturalis essè videtur, licèt non sit essentia lis inter Patrem & Filium naturalem intercedit enim relatio naturalis. Personae per nihil quomodocunque distinctum à personis primariò distinguuntur. Frustra sunt autem qui ideo personas eodem modo distinctas esse somniant quo primò diversa distinguuntur; illa enim essentialiter distinguuntur. Vide Biel. 1 Sent. dist. 24. & 26. Vide Greg. Nyssen. contra Eu-Eunomium lib. 1. Athanas. Basil, Eunomium cont. Naz. D. Alting. Gomarum, Gerrard. Voetium, Maccov. Wendeli. Glassium, Rhadam, Capreolū, Becanum, Eglisemnium in Crisi, Meisuerum, Iunium, Calovium.

allowance, nor can it then pass unless it is seasoned with some grains of salt, and be mollified with some fair and orthodox interpretation. By natural distinction, they mean relative, because say they the relations which are between these uncreated persons are not only real, but natural also. The relation between God the Father and his own natural Son is a natural relation, grounded upon a natural and personal action, namely: the eternal generation of the Son. The Greek fathers speak much of the familiar and proper emphasis of this natural relation between the Father and the Son.

By *natural distinction* then, they do not mean an essential distinction, as if the three uncreated persons did differ in nature; but natural, in that sound and orthodox sense recited above.

I had rather leave my margin to relate the curiosities of others than to perplex a mere English reader with any scholastic difficulties. I have said enough for the explication of those terms which are most usual, and yet likely to give offense to such as do not understand the importance of them. I shall therefore conclude this point with Fulgentius' commentary, which is an excellent contexture of some pertinent Scriptures for the proof of the point.[366] "When you read," says he, "of Father, Son, and Spirit, understand that there are three persons of one essence, omnipotence, eternity," etc. For our Savior says: "I am not alone, but I and the Father that sent me (John 8:16)." And concerning the Spirit, he says: "And I will pray the Father, and he will give you another Comforter, even the Spirit of truth (John 14:16-17)." Moreover, he commanded his apostles to baptize all nations in the name of the Father, Son and Holy Spirit. And the equality of the persons proves the unity of the nature (Philippians 2:6, John 5:18)" – and from hence, he concludes that there are three persons, and not three natures in the blessed Trinity.

From what has been said, it is evident that these three uncreated persons are truly distinguished, but they cannot be divided, and it is not so safe to

---

[366] Vide Fulgentium lib. de fide Orthod. ad Donatum.

express the distinction of uncreated persons by terms of art. They who say the distinction is natural, real, absolute, or relative, do deny that the distinction is essential, or that the persons are separable.[367] They who speak most tenderly, say it is modal, formal, personal. They who say it is natural in respect of personal relations and natural Actions, confess that it is supernatural and mysterious, because the unity of the Godhead is unquestionable; the Trinity of persons subsisting in that Godhead admirable; both put together undeniable and inexplicable, and yet most necessarily and highly credible.

They who say the persons are formally distinct, do mean that they are truly distinct. They do not conceive that the distinction of the uncreated persons is grounded upon a mere fiction of reason, or upon the weakness of our apprehension, as if we did conceive one person to be three persons, because he is called by three names, as Praxeas, Sabellius, and some others dreamt. Nor do they believe that this distinction of these three uncreated persons is only grounded upon the phrase of Scripture, but they do acknowledge that there is a true and proper, not an improper and figurative distinction between these uncreated persons. Nay, they all confess that this true and proper distinction is an eternal distinction. It was from and it will last to all eternity, and therefore is not grounded only upon some offices and external dispensations which have respect unto the creature.

---

[367] Vide D. Voetium de unica & simp. Dei natura pag. 235. En Mysterium quod nec capit Ratio, nec demōstrat exemplum Sola enim revelatione divinâ nititur, & proinde fide divinâ suscipiendum est & pietate suspiciendum. Vide D. Alting. de Cognitione Dei Relativa. Incomprehensibilis rei imaginem in rebus creatis frustra quaerin us. Aug. lib. 15. de civ. Dei cap. 13. [Vide] Damas. Orth. fid. lib. 1. c. 9

Chapter 8

The Grand Mystery of Three Divine & Coessential Subsistents in the Single Godhead is not Problematic, but Fundamental.

All points of doctrine revealed in Scripture are profitable, and precious truths; and every man is obliged to receive, believe, and embrace every truth made known to him in, and by the holy Scriptures, because all truths contained in Scripture are of equal credit in respect of the authority of the revealer; but all truths are not of equal necessity, weight and importance in respect of the nature and matter of the points revealed. There is a vast difference between the nature, matter, weight and importance of these two propositions:

(1) Paul left his cloak, books, and parchments at Troas (2 Timothy 4:13).

(2) Jesus Christ is God and man, the only mediator between God and man, the only and all-sufficient Savior of his people from their sins.

The first of these propositions cannot be refused because it is grounded upon clear Scripture, and he who rejects a point of the least concernment, which he knows to be revealed in Scripture, does not in deed and truth believe and embrace any truth at all, no not truths which are of the highest concernment, upon the right ground and true reason, namely because God has revealed them to us in the holy Scriptures of truth.

A fundamental point is of such high concernment that whosoever is ignorant of it is condemned for his mere negative infidelity; and whosoever refuses to believe it, is condemned for his positive infidelity, because he rejects a truth delivered upon the authority of God, and a truth so highly credible, that it is necessary to be known, and believed for his own salvation. Our faith, piety, hope, charity, and salvation are all grounded upon these necessary and fundamental truths.

Those truths or points of doctrine are fundamental, without the plain and express knowledge whereof we can neither savingly believe in Christ, nor rightly worship God in Christ to the obtaining of eternal life.

The grand mystery of three divine and coessential subsistents in the single Godhead is a fundamental point.

I desire to make this point very plain, for the (1) satisfaction of the weak, (2) information of the ignorant, (3) conviction of the obstinate, and (4) edification of the meek and humble.

It is most clear and evident that it indeed highly concerns Christians to acknowledge: (1) a deity against the atheists, (2) the unity of this deity against the Pagans, and (3) a Trinity in this unity against Turks, Jews, and heretics, both ancient and modern.

We must (1) know, (2) believe, (3) acknowledge, (4) worship, (5) obey, (6) trust to, and (7) depend upon three persons, and one God.

Our blessed Lord, in that excellent prayer of his which is most largely recorded in John 17, says that this is life eternal to know the Father the only true God, and Jesus Christ, whom he has sent (John 17:3). This text has been opened and vindicated at large in this book already, therefore I shall make quick work now, and desire you but to compare this text with 1 John 5:20: "We are in him that is true, even in his Son Jesus Christ." This is the true God and eternal life; both texts tell us that it is eternal life for to believe that the Father and the Son are the only true God, and therefore this is a fundamental point. And the Scripture speaks expressly that these three, the Father, the Word, and the Holy Spirit are one, one God; for the witness or testimony delivered by these three is the witness of God (1 John 5:7, 9).

But it is objected by some that the words "These three are one" (1 John 5:7) are not to be found in some ancient copies, and therefore it will not be safe to build a point of such weight and consequence upon such a weak foundation.

To which we answer, it is true that these words are not to be found in the Syriac edition, but those who speak most modestly, do acknowledge that the Syriac edition is not authentic.[368] Learned Heinsius is much offended with that edition, as appears by his annotations upon 1 John 5:7. And if we consult the Scriptures, and compare this text with the following verses, and with some other places of Scripture, which are more plain, and then add the testimony and interpretations of the ancient and reverend doctors of the church, concerning the words in question, we shall be able to pass a right judgment upon the point in hand.

(1) The equality of the number of witnesses suits very rightly three witnesses on earth and three in heaven.

(2) The opposition between the quality of the witnesses, witnesses on earth, and witnesses in heaven; and yet their sweet harmony and agreement in one testimony. All six bear witness to one and the same truth.

(3) The diversity of the very nature of those three who bear witness on earth, and the unity of their divine nature who bear witness in heaven, is very considerable, and it is excellently expressed in the variation of the phrase, "These three are one (verse 7)," and "these three agree in one;" namely, *in* one testimony (verse 8).[369] Though their nature be different, yet their testimony is the same.

But it is objected that the Complutensian Bible says of the heavenly witnesses that these "three agree in one (verse 7)." I humbly offer this satisfaction to pious and learned men: that we have good reason to believe that there is an imprudent addition in the Complutensian Bible, rather than an omission of so many ancient and approved Bibles, and therefore it is fit that that addition should be expunged out of that one copy by the concurrent testimony of so many copies. Moreover, it is clear by the joint testimony of other copies that the words εν εισιν are omitted in the seventh verse, and the words εις το εν εισιν belong to the eighth verse, and therefore

---

[368] Si Syrum caeteros{que} sequimur, vel hiatus admittitur, vel ακολουθία quae imprimis elegans turbatur. Mihi qui talem primò usurparunt in Sacris licentiam θεομάχοι videntur. Heinsius, in locum.

[369] Bib. edit Complut. εις το εν εισιν v. 7.

there is an inexcusable omission, and an imprudent transposition in that corrupt edition.[370] But then it is further objected that these words "These three are one" are lacking in some other Greek copies; for answer I proceed in my observations.

(4) If we look upon the Scripture account in other places, we shall find it exactly agreeable to the account in this place, 1 John. 5:7. In John 8, our Savior pleads that two witnesses in law were sufficient for the proof of any point (John 8:17), and in verse 10 he says, "I am one, and my Father that sent me is another:" they are two witnesses, and yet but one God. "I and my Father are one (John 10:30)." One in power, and therefore one in nature. He speaks not of the Spirit, because Christ was not yet glorified, nor was the Spirit yet manifested by that eminent and glorious mission and effusion which was to follow after the ascension of our blessed Lord. But he did foretell that the third witness was to be sent from the Father by the Son (John 15:26): "But when the Comforter is come, whom I will send unto you from the Father, even the Spirit of truth, which proceedeth from the Father, he shall testify of me." I might add to these testimonies all other places of Scripture, wherein all the three witnesses are named together, and then produce all the places which have been formerly cited in this book to prove the coessential Trin-unity of those heavenly witnesses.

(5) The copulative *and* in the beginning of the verse of 1 John 5:8 very fitly connects the whole seventh verse with the eighth, as they are printed in our ordinary translation.

(6) Jerome assures us that the words in question were expunged by the Arians, because these few words do hold forth an undeniable proof of the divine and coessential Trinunity of these heavenly witnesses. And divers other learned and judicious men conceive that these words were blotted out in the time of Constantius and Valens the emperors who were sworn enemies of the blessed Trinity, and professed patrons of Arianism.

---

[370] Merces satis fallaces vendit officina Chr. Plantini Antverpiae in editione 1584 excusa & cum Bib. Ar. Mont. vulgat

(7) The heretics did blot out those words in (John 4:24), "God is a Spirit," as Ambrose assures us,[371] and therefore this practice of expunging such words in the Scripture as did refute their errors was too common amongst the heretics of old, as we might prove by witnesses enough, if that were our business.[372]

(8) These words of 1 John 5:7 are to be found in copies of great antiquity and best credit.

(9) This text is cited by the ancient fathers, by Athanasius in his dispute with Arius at the council of Nicaea, and Arius never denied it for to be Scripture, which certainly he would have done, if there had been any doubt made of it in the primitive times.[373]

It is cited by Cyprian also in his book *De Unitate Ecclesiae*. Paxillus in his book *De Monomachia* proves by an induction of the learned doctors of the church both before and since Athanasius that the doctrine of the coessential Trin-unity of these heavenly witnesses was generally received by all that were esteemed orthodox and pious in the church of Christ. Calovius also in his *Fides Patrum Ante Concilium Nicenum*, gives in a catalog for the satisfaction of all that desire resolution in this weighty point.

(10) These three heavenly witnesses are one in power, nature and will; all three bear witness to the same truth, and their testimony is divine (1 John 5:9). And the truth which they bear witness to is a fundamental truth, a saving truth, that we may believe on the Son of God and have eternal life (1 John 5:11-13). And if the authority of any one of these three heavenly witnesses be called into question, all may be questioned upon the same grounds, because their testimony is of equal authority. Their testimony is

---

[371] Vide Ambros. lib. 3. de Spiritu Sancto. cap. 11.

[372] Jurati veritatis hostes lucem hanc non tulerunt ideoque eraserunt. Vide Heinsium in 1 Joh. 5. 7.

[373] Athanas. Tom. 1. pag. 91, 92. 93. Cyprian lib. de Unitate Ecclesiae Paxillus de Monomachia. Calovius lib. de Fide Patrum ante Concilium Nicenum. See Mr. Estwick's learned discourse of the Godhead of the Holy Ghost. Dr. Alting. his vindication of this text in his confutation of the Racovian Catechism.

personal and divine; and if the testimony and authority of these witnesses were not divine, our faith which is built upon their testimony and authority, would not be a divine faith. *Quale est testimonium, talis est fides.*

All three heavenly witnesses join with one consent and will in propounding this fundamental truth, and therefore if we do not believe and embrace it, we give the lie to all the three witnesses in heaven (1 John 5:10). And if we do believe that Jesus is the natural Son of God, in and by whom all believers have eternal life, then we must acknowledge that Jesus Christ is one God with his Father, the true God and eternal life (1 John 5:20). Christ is God attributive (John 1:1), subjective (Acts 20:28; 1 Timothy 3:16).

This one proposition – that Jesus Christ is the natural and proper Son of God – is that fundamental confession of faith upon which the Christian church is built (Matthew 16:16-18): "Thou art Christ the Son of the living God." This is the rock upon which Christ has so firmly built his church, that the gates of hell shall never prevail against it, or this fundamental truth. We are all built upon Christ through the Spirit for a habitation of God (Ephesians 2:20-22). Father, Son, and Holy Spirit. All three join in laying this foundation, and all three are one and the self-same great God, who is the only true God blessed for ever, as has been fully proven already in this book, and therefore I may be the briefer in the discussion of this weighty point.

The form of baptism contains in it a short creed, or rule of faith (Matthew 28:19). And when the ancient fathers speak such high things of the creed, they understand it of this short creed which is part of canonical Scripture, and not of that form which is commonly called the Apostles' Creed. In like manner when they expound Ephesians 4:5 – "One Lord, one faith, one baptism" – they say, there is one faith and one baptism, because the sum of our faith is contained in the form of baptism.

When Epiphanius had reckoned up all the heresies in his *Anakephalaiosis*, he opposed this one Scripture – Matthew 28:19 – to them all, to show that he looked upon the doctrine of the Trinity as a breviary or at least prime fundamental of the Christian faith,[374] and Eusebius Pamphilus does the like.[375] I might produce many pertinent places out of Irenaeus, Tertullian, Athanasius, Basil, Nazianzen, Augustine and others to make good this useful observation: that the prime fundamental of the Christian faith is contained in the form of baptism, and founded on Matthew 28:19.[376] It were easy to show upon what occasion other articles were added to the public confessions of faith[377] in the most renowned churches in several ages.[378] And it is as easy to prove that the doctrine of the coessential Trinunity was for the matter and substance, if not in express terms, *in terminis terminantibus* as we say, constantly maintained:

(1) In public confessions of faith composed, explained, confirmed by the first general councils, published by the decrees, and edicts of pious Emperors, and ratified by their civil sanctions from time to time. I need not instance in the Nicene Creed, or that Creed which was composed by Athanasius who studied this point, defended and suffered for it above forty years. The confession published by the Synod of Constantinople does not differ in substance from the other creeds concerning this grand mystery of the blessed Trinity. I am not willing to expatiate [*write at length*] upon this argument, because I should then be engaged to cite very many testimonies of the ancients, which would swell up my book beyond its due proportion. But if any man desires to read more upon this argument for his own satisfaction,[379]

---

[374] Irenaeus lib. 1. cap. 2.
[375] Tertullian de Praescript. c. 14 & 20.
[376] Athanas. Epist. ad ubique Orthodox & Orat. C. G. Sab & contra Arian.
[377] See Dr. Ussher's sermon on the unity of the Faith.
[378] Author libri de Spiritu Sancto lib. 1. cap. 2. Greg. Nyssen. de Resur. Orat. 2. Epiphanius Anacephal. Euseb. Pamphilus Epist. ad Palestin. Augustin. contra Donatist, lib. 6. cap. 25, & Sermone in Symbolum. Hanc fidei normam—Christus ascensurus reliquit. Ait enim eunies baptizate &c.
Damascen. de fide Orthod. lib. 1. cap. 8. Concil. Ancyran. de Spiritu Sancto. 2. Didymus Alexander.
[379] Vide Parkerum de Desc. ad inferos Dr. Usher his learned Sermon of the Unity of Faith. D. Voet. de Symbolo Apostolico. D. Gomarum de Symbolo, de Trinitate. Glassium, Zanchium de Trinitate.

and has not so much time as to peruse the ancient records, he may read Master Parker's book *De Desc. Ad Inferos*, more especially his fourth book; the learned sermon of Reverend Doctor Ussher concerning the unity of faith, who gives a brief and satisfactory account of the ancient confessions of faith with a special reference to baptism; [and also] Doctor Voetius, Gomarus, and the rest who have written *De Symbolo Apostolico*, or of the mystery of the Trinity. The juggling of the Arians is so plainly set forth in the most faithful writers of ecclesiastical story, that I need not relate how they made use of their interest at court, and all their carnal policy in every considerable place to pack councils, forge or corrupt creeds, seduce all sorts of men, who were led more by interest than Scripture, and then to evade, or comply with subtle distinctions, mental reservations, equivocations, and such unworthy shifts for to save themselves from censure in a time of reformation.

(2) The catechisms of the ancients hold forth this doctrine; the catechumen were trained up in the knowledge of it. Lucian, who lived in Trajan's time, brings in a Christian catechising the heathens in the doctrine of the Trinity.[380]

(3) The form of baptism strictly observed in the churches notwithstanding the great ignorance and contention in the East, and the grand apostasy in the West, sufficiently proves that this doctrine of the Trinity had taken deep root in the minds of men, and that they were by the providence and special grace of God very diligent and faithful in communicating of it to their posterity from time to time.

(4) The doxology, or as some call it, *the hymn of glory*, evinces the same, and therefore the Arians endeavored to make an alteration in the doxology and instead of saying, "Glory be to the Father, and to the Son, and to the Holy Spirit," they said, "Glory be to the Father, by the Son, and in the Spirit," from whence we may observe by the way, that if we suffer the

---

Damascen. de fide Orthod. lib. 1. cap. 8. Concil. Ancyran. de Spiritu Sancto. 2. Didymus Alexander.

[380] Lucian. in Philopat.

fundamental doctrine of our faith to be corrupted, we shall not be able to preserve the fundamentals of our worship pure, and uncorrupt.

(5) The form of apostolic benediction which stands upon record (2 Corinthians 13:14) clearly holds forth the doctrine of the Trinity to be a fundamental both of faith and worship. And all who desire the grace of our Lord Jesus Christ, the love of God, the communion of the Holy Spirit, for their everlasting comfort and salvation, must believe and adore all three as one God, blessed forever.

(6) All who believe in God are commanded to believe in Christ as God, as one and the same God with the Father. "Ye believe in God, believe also in me (John 14:1)." They are commanded to honor the Son as they honor the Father (John 5:23). Therefore, the doctrine of the divine person of Christ as coessential with his Father is a fundamental both of faith and worship.

(7) The doctrine of the incarnation of the Word, the natural and proper Son of God, and the doctrines of Christ's satisfaction, of our redemption, and justification by Christ as an all-sufficient Savior, are fundamental doctrines necessary to be known, believed and embraced for our eternal salvation, for we know the blood of a mere man cannot give satisfaction to the justice of God for those gross affronts, injuries and abuses which have been offered by man to the infinite majesty of God.[381] The church of God is purchased with the blood of God (Acts 20:28). And if Christ has not redeemed the church with the blood of God, then the church is not redeemed, your faith and our preaching are both vain, because you and we are yet in our sins; for then God has not received satisfaction for our sins, nor a sufficient ransom for our souls. If the Son of God did not take flesh, then God was not manifested in the flesh. Then the whole mystery of godliness – which should be without controversy great and precious in the eyes of Christians – will be cheap, and

---

[381] Divinitas Christi est ipsum Fundamentale hujus dogmatis; est enim Articulus fidei necessarius necessitate finis respectu communionis internae & invisibilis cum Christo, hoc est cum Dei gratiâ & gloriâ: nec non respectu communionis Ecclesiasticae in visibili caetu.

vile, and of no account; for the whole mystery of godliness (1 Timothy 3:16) depends upon the manifestation of God in the flesh; Now the divine person of the Son took flesh; the person of the Father was not incarnate.

(8) It is not enough to believe that the son of Mary is risen from the dead; we must believe that the Son of God is risen (Romans 1:3-4). It is Jesus our Lord that rose for our justification (Romans 4:24-25, Romans 10:9).

(9) It is not sufficient to believe that there is a man sitting at the right hand of God; we must believe that Jehovah sits there (Psalm 110:1, Matthew 22:43-45). And the like must be said of our Advocate: he must be such a one as can plead the worthiness of his person, the merit of his obedience and sufferings, one who is able to save us to the uttermost (Hebrews 7:25; 1 John 2:1-2); one who can plead with some authority and majesty: "Father, I will that they also whom thou hast given me, be with me where I am (John 17:24)." He speaks with authority: "I will." He speaks like a coessential and coequal person; and it is for the glory of the Father to believe that the Father is in the Son, and the Son in the Father, that the Son is Lord, equal to the Father (John 14:10-11, Philippians 2:6, 11). Many more arguments might be collected from several places of Scripture cited above in the fourth chapter of this book, and I shall enlarge upon this argument in the ninth chapter.

(10) The Holy Spirit is the same God with the Father and Son, the same object of divine faith and evangelical worship, the same author of the Scriptures, and all-saving grace (Matthew 28:19; 1 Corinthians 12:6, 11; 2 Corinthians 13:14). Through the Son and by the Spirit we have access to the Father (Ephesians 2:18). All church administrations are to be performed in the power of the Holy Spirit, and are made acceptable by the merit of the Lord Jesus Christ. If we will hear the Spirit speaking in the Scriptures to the churches, if we feel the Spirit sanctifying of our hearts, if we do not desire to undermine the foundation of the Christian church, and so overthrow the church of Christ, if we do not renounce our Christian faith, and our baptism the sacrament thereof, if we do not reject the fundamental blessing (the best portion of ourselves and little ones) the grace of Christ, the love of God and

communion of the Spirit, why then, I beseech you, as the apostle does, for the Lord Jesus Christ's sake and for the love of the Spirit (Romans 15:30) and for the glory of God the Father, (Philippians 2:11) that you will believe, adore, embrace, love and obey the Father, Son, and Holy Spirit, as three divine and coessential subsistents in the single Godhead, as one God blessed forever, the adequate object, and author of your faith, hope, love, and happiness.

I do not desire to obtrude anything upon the acutest disputant as fundamental that is curious or unnecessary. Nay, there are many things necessary for the maintenance of this truth, and refutation of contrary errors, when we are to deal with subtle heretics, which I do not set before the common people as food fit to nourish them. For that reason, I do desire that they will look upon much of my sixth chapter, and of some other chapters in this book,[382] as fit for the direction of young scholars in this weighty point; for I find young wits apt to be seduced by logical subtleties, or rather fallacies, metaphysical notions, poetical raptures, nice distinctions and vain curiosities, from the simplicity of the gospel of Christ. Therefore, I have taken some pains in several chapters, but especially in the margin for the direction of hopeful youths, who have been too often entangled and ensnared by Socinian fallacies, and at last tempted into loud and hideous blasphemies. We do therefore lay down these plain truths as necessary to be known and believed for the maintaining of saving communion with God:

(1) That God is. "For he who cometh unto God must believe that God is." (Hebrews 11:6).

(2) That there is but one God (Deuteronomy 6:4).

---

[382] Dogma de Trinitate notat non tam negativam & Elencticam Theologiam quàm Positivam; & Theses Principales non tam modum, & methodum Gramatice, Rhetorice, & Logice dogma illud explicandi quàm ipsam rem explicatam, non tam formam ac modum per Philosophicas & Logicas notiones, distinctiones, & Axiomata dogma hoc contra Pseudo-rationarios quoscunque tutandi, eorum subtilitates persequendo, & ad absurdum redigendo. D. Voetius de Trinitate, pag. 467.

(3) That the Father, Son, and Holy Spirit are this one God, because they are all three coessential subsistents in this most single Godhead (1 Corinthians 8:5-6, Philippians 2:6; 1 John 5:7, John 10:30, Matthew 3:16-17, Matthew 28:19, Acts 5:4; 1 Corinthians 12:6, 11; 2 Corinthians 13:14, John 15:26, Revelation 1:4-5).

Reverend Calvin was not so morose and austere in this point as to contend about unnecessary words, or curious phrases, so there were such words used as did fitly and fully express the whole mystery of faith in this weighty point, and sufficiently refute the damnable errors of Arius and Sabellius.[383] If men will but acknowledge:

(1) That the Father, Son, and Spirit are one God and the self-same God.

(2) That the Son is not the Father, nor the Spirit the Son, but that these three are distinguished by special relations, incommunicable and unchangeable properties, so that there is a Trinity of coessential subsistents in the self-same divine essence, we are all agreed.

Arius would acknowledge that Christ is God,[384] but not consubstantial or coessential with his Father, for he did deny Christ to be the same God with his Father. And in like manner the Socinians will say that they acknowledge and maintain the true divinity of the Son and Holy Spirit, but they do deny that the Son and Spirit are one and the same God with the Father, and affirm that the Reformed churches who believe that all three persons have the self-same Godhead, and ascribe a false and imaginary Godhead to the Son and Spirit, which the Holy Scriptures nowhere acknowledge or declare. And this is the true reason why the orthodox doctors of the church have been so unanimous, especially of late years in

---

[383] Vide Cal. Inst. lib. 1. cap. 13. Sect. 5. & Colonii Anal. Praph. Instit. pa. 36.

[384] Vide Apologiam Voidovij & Ostorodi ad decret. in illustr. D. D. Ord. Belg. an. 1598. Non negamus Dei gratiâ veram filij Dei divinitatem, sed falsam imaginariam, & quam nusquam Sacrae Literae, agnoscunt. Smalcius etiam Zelum suum in propugnanda verâ divinitate Iesu Christi praedicat in libro de divinitate Christi cap. 25.

maintaining this proposition: *Pater, Filius, et Spiritus Sanctus sunt* αυτοθεος: The Father, Son, and Holy Spirit are one and the self-same God.

On the other side, Sabellius acknowledged that the Father, Son, and Holy Spirit are one God;[385] but if you say that the Father, Son, and Holy Spirit are three different subsistents, then he cried out as Mr. Fry does, that you acknowledge three gods.

The best way to avoid these (says judicious Calvin) is to say that there is a Trinity of persons in one and the same essence of God. For we must acknowledge the unity of the divine nature, because we read that the Father, Son, and Spirit are one, and we must acknowledge the Trinity of these coessential subsistents or persons, because we read that they are three. Now the Trinity and unity make a coessential Trinunity; and if the unity of the Godhead and Trinity of the subsistents or persons be acknowledged, we shall not wrangle about curious phrases, or unnecessary words. The most judicious and moderate men amongst the orthodox doctors of the church agree in this.[386]

The learned and reverend Doctor Davenant, in his judicious exhortation to brotherly communion between the Protestant churches, teaches us how to distinguish between points that are fundamental, and problems or propositions that are not fundamental. And when he comes to reckon up fundamentals, he instances in the Trinity, and expresses himself after this manner: "That God is one in essence, three in persons distinguished between themselves. That the Son is begotten of the Father. That the Holy Spirit is the Spirit of the Father and the Son. That these three persons are coeternal and coequal." "All these," says he, "are deservedly determined and ranked

---

[385] Dicit Sabellius patrem, Filium & spiritum nihil in Deo distinctum sonare.

[386] Dic tres esse, vociferabitur te nominare tres Deos. Dic in una Dei Essentiâ Personarum Trinitatem: dixeris uno verbo quod Scripturae loquuntur, & inanem loquacitatem compresseris. Cal. inst. l. 1 c. 13 sect. 6. Vide D. Voetium de necessitate, & utilitate dogmatis de SS. Trinitate page 467, 468. D. Crocium Synt. nec non Gomarum.

amongst the fundamental articles." Now if any should contend that all those things which are disputed by the Schoolmen, of the manner of proceeding and begetting, are also fundamental, and necessary to be determined on one side, verily he by this his rash judgment, would gain no favor with Christ.

But it is objected by some who do acknowledge Christ to be God, that they have no reason to close with us, when we say that Jesus Christ is coessential with God his eternal Father, because we impose a new word upon them, and so make a new fundamental of our own invention, to which I answer:

(1) That if we make an old truth plain by a new word, they ought to forgive us that injury.

(2) We explain our new term.

(3) We save them the trouble of an artificial and tedious deduction; for as soon as they do but understand the word, they must necessarily embrace the sense, and acknowledge that though the word seem new to them, yet the doctrine is old; for if the persons be of a different divine essence, then there would be more gods than one.

(4) We do hereby secure them against the subtlety of pernicious heretics who endeavor to seduce them into damnable heresies. For if the Father, Son, and Spirit have not the same divine essence, then either there will be more gods than one, or else the Son and Spirit are no gods at all, but such petty inferior gods as the Socinians make them.

(5) No man that has a sound brain and a single eye can conceive that there are several gods in the same essence, and therefore the expression is necessary and safe. The Father, Son, and Spirit are three coessential subsistents in the same single Godhead. They are all three one and the self-same God, who is God by nature, the only true God blessed forever. In this faith we will live, and in this we will die, as it becomes orthodox Christians who were baptized in the name of the Father, Son, and Holy Spirit.

Chapter 9

This Grand Mystery of Faith has an Effectual Influence into the Practical Mystery of Godliness & Power of Religion.

It is the great design, and faithful endeavor of sincere Christians to attain unto all riches of the full assurance of understanding to the acknowledgement of the mystery of God, and of the Father, and of Christ (Colossians 2:2). They who have but a form of godliness – μορφωσιν ανευ Μεταμόρφωσεως – a kind of painted powerless shadow of piety may look upon the doctrine of the Trinity as a scholastic point, a mere speculative doctrine which men receive by tradition from their forefathers; but they who live in the Spirit, and walk in the Spirit, Galatians 5:25. have a life that is hid with Christ in God – (Colossians 3:3) hidden from formal men, as colors are hidden from blind men; and these spiritual Christians do account the love of the Father,[387] the grace of Christ, and the communion of the Spirit to be their heaven upon earth. They receive Jesus Christ so as to live by him, walk in him, and live to him (Colossians 2:6, Philippians 1:21, 1 John. 5:12; 2 Corinthians 5:15).

What is a godly life, but a life of faith, and love, of joy and thankfulness, of self-denial, and devotion; of patience and obedience, hope and perseverance, victory, and triumph? This is the life of God, or that godly life, to which the Ephesians were all strangers till they had learned the truth as it is in Jesus (Ephesians 4:20-21). And how come we to be quickened to this godly life, but by being begotten of the Father (James 1:17-18), born of the Spirit (John 3:6), and hearing the voice of the Son of God (John. 5:25-26)? When we have learnt of the Father, and are drawn by the Spirit, we come unto the Son, who is "the way, the truth, and the life" (John 6:44-45, John

---

[387] 2 Corinthians 13:14

14:6). And how is this Spiritual life maintained, but by the supply of the Spirit of Jesus Christ? (Philippians 1:19).

Let us take the whole frame of a godly life to pieces, and view every part and spring, and wheel and pin, and then put it together again, and then we shall be able to judge what effectual influence these three coessential persons (considered as one and the same God, or as three distinct persons subsisting in the single Godhead) have into the practical mystery of godliness, and power of religion.

The doctrine of godliness contains: (1) our faith in God, (2) worship of God, and (3) obedience to God.

(1) *Our faith in God*

I have spoken of this grand mystery of faith, and shown that it is necessary to be known and believed in the eighth chapter at large, but I shall now treat of it in a more practical way. Adam in his innocence was bound for to believe in the Father, Son, and Holy Spirit, who are one Almighty God, creator, upholder and governor of heaven and earth, self-sufficient and all-sufficient, blessed in, and of himself, the only cause, and adequate object of the blessedness of his creatures.

Adam was created by all three, after the image of all three, for God said: "Let us make man in our image, after our likeness (Genesis 1:26)," and therefore we cannot conceive, but that all three were revealed to Adam, that he might know and believe in all three. Surely Adam was better catechized than Jews, Turks, and Pagans are in this great point, and therefore did know, believe, and worship all three. There is no question but he entered into covenant with all three, and therefore believed in all three. I cannot believe that two of the divine persons had no worship or service from Adam their creature before his fall; And doubtless Adam knew whom he believed, and whom he worshiped as his Almighty Creator and all-sufficient God. Adam under the first covenant was bound to believe in the second person as God, but not as God-man, the mediator between God and sinful man.[388] Adam did owe the right of subjection to all three, from whom he received the honor of dominion. The world was made for man, man for the honor and glory of Father, Son, and Holy Spirit. Adam's original righteousness did incline and enable him to believe in all three, and surely Adam understood that severe rebuke which was given him presently after his fall (Genesis 3:22). "And the Lord God said, Behold the man is become as one of *us*." But because I will forbear disputes, I will not proceed further upon this argument.

---

[388] Mercur. Trismegist.

[1] The faith of Christians' delights to exercise itself upon God the Father, Son, and Holy Spirit.

God the Father is pleased to be our tutor, to condescend so far as to teach us, and *oportet discentem credere*: scholars must believe their teachers. It is written in the prophets: "and they shall be all taught of God. Every man therefore that hath heard, and hath learnt of the Father cometh unto me (John 6:45)." We must believe the record that God the Father gives of his Son (1 John 5:10). When we look upon God as the Father of our Lord and Savior Jesus Christ, and look upon him as our God and Father in Christ, these near and dear relations do encourage us to believe him, and believe in him, to believe his truth, to believe his love; his fatherly and tender bowels do persuade and even constrain us to fix our belief and place our confidence in God the Father.

The heirs of promise have good encouragement to believe their Father, who gives them all they have and hope for, when he declares the immutability of his counsel in a faithful promise, and confirms it by an unchangeable oath (Hebrews 6:17-18). Surely the Father will not deceive his own children of their inheritance which he has made over to them by promise and oath. This is the ground of all our hope and comfort; we may safely cast anchor here (Hebrews 6:18-19). In the Old Testament, the Covenant runs in the names of Abraham, Isaac and Jacob; but in the New Testament it runs in the name of Christ. There we read "the God of Abraham, Isaac and Jacob;" but here we read: "God our Father, the God and Father of our Lord Jesus Christ," that is our God and Father in Christ, and for Christ; our Father because Christ's Father. "Grace be to you, and peace from God our Father; and blessed be the God and Father of our Lord Jesus Christ who hath blessed us with all Spiritual blessings in heavenly things in Christ (Ephesians 1:2-3)." We cannot but look up with faith and confidence to the Father of our Lord Jesus Christ and our Father as the fountain of all blessing, the fountain of grace and peace and glory.

This dear fatherly relation of God to Christ, and in Christ to us, is sometimes darkly intimated and but hinted, and sometimes clearly and fully expressed to encourage our faith. The disciples were very sad because they heard our Savior speak of going to his Father. "Go," says Christ, "to my brethren and say unto them (John 20:17)." What should Mary say for their consolation? Was it enough to tell them my Lord is alive, and calls you his brethren? No, that were too dark an intimation, and therefore our Savior gives her her message in words at length: "Go to my brethren, and say unto them I ascend unto my Father, and your Father and to my God, and your God (John 20:17)."

Here's an evangelical ground of faith, hope, and comfort in the time of the saddest distress. The great argument used to encourage poor trembling believers to come to Christ when they have interrupted their fellowship with God the Father, Christ and the Holy Comforter by any grievous wounding sin is this: "if any man sin, we have an advocate with the Father, Jesus Christ the righteous." God is a Father both to us and our advocate, therefore renew the sense of your justification by faith at a throne of grace. You see our faith is encouraged in the saddest trials by this argument. The Father of our Lord Jesus Christ is the Father of mercies, and the God of all comfort (2 Corinthians 1:3), the fountain of grace and peace (Romans 1:7, Galatians 1:3). Jesus Christ makes it his business to persuade poor tempted souls to believe that his Father loves them, and bears good will to them. "The Father himself loves you" (John 16:27) and Christ gave himself to deliver us from sin and the world, death, and hell, according to the will of God and our Father (Galatians 1:4). "And God so loved the world, that he gave his only begotten Son, that whosoever believeth, etc."

[2] God the Son is the object of our faith.[389]

John 14:1 reads: "Ye believe in God, believe also in me." Even the very Jews did believe in God; they who are Christians indeed believe in Christ also. For this end, the whole gospel was written that men might be persuaded to believe that Jesus is the Christ the Son of God (John 20:31), and that the belief of this grand point is necessary and effectual unto salvation is presently declared in the very same verse, and "that believing ye might have life through his name (John 20:31)."

"And this is the record that God hath given to us eternal life, and this life is in his Son. He that hath the Son hath life, and he that hath not the Son hath not life. These things have I written to you that believe on the name of the Son of God, that ye may know that ye have eternal life, and that ye may believe on the name of the Son of God (1 John 5:11-13)." And if God gives us an understanding to know this, the knowing of, believing and living in Jesus Christ the Son of God, the true God, will be effectual unto life eternal. "And we know that the Son of God is come, and hath given us an understanding, that we may know him that is true: and we are in him that is true, even in his Son Jesus Christ. This is the true God, and eternal life (1 John 5:20)." It is for want of spiritual understanding if we do not discern that all our hopes of salvation are built upon the Sonship and Godhead of Jesus. We must believe in Christ as he is the natural and proper Son of God as he is the true God, the self-same God with the Father.

{1} We must believe in Christ as he is the natural and proper Son of God, because this is exactly answerable to that dear and fatherly relation of God the Father, of which we have discoursed so largely in this chapter.[390] For as we are encouraged to believe in God as the Father of Christ, so are we encouraged to believe in Christ as the natural Son of God. Therefore, I have purposely insisted on such Scriptures as do evidently demonstrate this truth: that we are to believe on the name of the Son of God and to have life

---

[389] John 3:16
[390] 1 John 5:5, Acts 8:37, Matthew 16:16; 1 John 2:22-24

through his name (1 John 5:11-13, 20; John 20:31). We are to believe in Christ as a mediator, that our faith and hope may be settled in God: "who by him do believe in God, that raised him up from the dead, that your faith and hope might be in God (1 Peter 1:21)."

Now the great encouragement to believe in Christ as an all-sufficient mediator is this: Jesus Christ is the natural Son of God. Therefore, if Christ will but present us to his Father, we are confident that the Son of God, his natural Son, his proper Son, his only begotten Son will prevail with his Father for us; his relation to God, and his interest in God assures us that the intercession of our high priest will be irresistible, undeniable. "Christ glorified not himself to be made an high priest, but he that said unto him Thou art my Son, today have I begotten thee. As he saith also in another place, Thou art a Priest forever, after the order of Melchisedek (Hebrews 5:5-6)." We must, for the understanding of this Scripture, compare three places together: Psalm 110:1, 4, Psalm 22:7-8, and Hebrews 7:25, 28. "The LORD said unto my Lord, sit thou at my right hand. Thou art a priest (Psalm 110:1, 4)." "The LORD said, Thou art my Son, ask of me (Psalm 2:7-8)." "Ask what thou wilt, I can deny thee nothing, thou art my Son, it is thy birthright to be a priest, and it is proper for a priest to ask, and intercede." Other high priests were men of infirmity, but the Son who is consecrated and perfected for evermore, is able by his powerful intercession, to save those to the uttermost who come unto God by him (Hebrews 7:25, 28).

Nay, all the offices of Christ are grounded on his Sonship: his kingly power in Psalm 2 – "I have set my king," etc. "Thou art my Son (verses 6-7)." His prophetic power is grounded on his Sonship also. Matthew 17:5: "and behold a voice out of the cloud, which said, This is my beloved Son in whom I am well pleased: hear ye him."[391] "I have promised that ye shall be all taught of God, and therefore I send my own natural Son to teach and

---

[391] Matthew 17:5

instruct you; he is the great prophet and tutor of the church; hear ye him, and believe in him; for he is the true Messiah who is to teach you all things, and I have sent him on purpose for to instruct you." "And this is the work of God that ye believe on him whom he hath sent (John 6:29)."

But enough of this,[392] because I have spoken something of it already in the seventh chapter of this book,[393] and clearly proved that Christ could not have gone through with any of his divine offices[394] if he had not been the natural and proper Son of God, equal to God.[395] Read Nathaniel's creed (John. 1:49) and Paul's life of faith (Galatians 2:20).

{2} We must believe in Christ as God, the self-same God with the Father. When we know Christ to be God, we must glorify him as God by believing in him.[396] Now I have by many undeniable arguments proved Christ to be God, and therefore I may safely conclude that we ought to believe in him as God; for cursed is he who believes in an arm of flesh. When Peter preached to Cornelius, he told them that Jesus Christ was Lord of all (Acts 10:36) and judge of all (Acts 10:42). And that all the prophets gave witness to him, that through his name, whosoever believes in him, shall receive remission of sins (Acts 10:43).[397] I need say no more but this: "He that abideth in the doctrine of Christ, he hath both the Father and the Son (2 John 9)."[398] "Every tongue must confess that Jesus Christ is Lord to the glory of God the Father (Philippians 2:11)." "The Father is glorified in the Son (John 14:13)." And the Son is to be glorified in all them whom the Father has given him (John 17:10), and Christ is to be glorified by their believing in him (John 17:23). And the Father himself loves them, because they believe in the Son (John 16:27). And "he who honoreth not the Son, honoreth not the

---

[392] John 7:29
[393] John 5:23
[394] John 6:68, 17:8, 16:27, Matthew 16:16
[395] Acts 8:37, John 1:49, Galatians 2:20; 1 John 5:5
[396] Romans 1:21
[397] Acts 10:36, 42-43; 2 John 9, Philippians 2:11
[398] John 1:13, 17:10, 20, 16:27, John 5:23; 1 John 2:24

Father (John 5:23)." The great mystery of uniting the soul to Christ by faith (Ephesians 5:32) and making of it one Spirit with the Lord Jesus (1 Corinthians 6:17) is a main fundamental of the mystery of godliness, as shall be proved clearly before I conclude this chapter.

[3] **God the Holy Spirit is the object of a Christian's divine faith.**

The Holy Spirit, speaking in the Holy Scriptures, teaches us to believe not only in the Father, and in the Son, but in himself also. "It is the Spirit that beareth witness, because the Spirit is truth (1 John 5:6)." There are three that bear witness in heaven,[399] but here is special testimony given of the Spirit,[400] that we might be moved to believe the Spirit, who is to testify the whole truth concerning the Father, the Son and himself. It is the Spirit (says he) whose special office it is to bear witness, and therefore there is this special testimony given of him that the Spirit is truth. And then it follows that the Spirit is one with the Father and the Son: one in nature, and one and the same God with them both. "These three are one (1 John 5:7)," and the witness of God must without controversy be received, unless we will make God a liar, as the apostle reasons the point from verses 9-12. The Spirit is truth, the Spirit is God, therefore the Spirit is the object of divine faith; he that tells a lie to the Holy Spirit, tells a lie to God (Acts 5:3-4). He that then gives the lie to the Holy Spirit, gives the lie to God. The testimony of the Spirit is a divine testimony (1 Corinthians 2:1, 4), the demonstration of the Spirit, a divine demonstration, the power of the Holy Spirit, a divine power.

Paul says that his preaching was not with enticing words of man's wisdom, but in demonstration of the Spirit and of power; that our faith might not stand in the wisdom of men, but in the power of God. The wisdom, power, and testimony of the Spirit, are all of them divine. The wisdom of the Spirit is infallible, the power of the Spirit is irresistible, and therefore our most divine faith is built, and stands fast; grounded and

---

[399] 1 John 5:6
[400] 1 Peter 1:11-12, Acts 5:32

established upon the wisdom of the Spirit, because the wisdom of the Spirit is the wisdom of God (1 Corinthians 2:4-5).

We read in the prophets that all the children of God shall be taught of God (Isaiah 54:13) of all three persons; for the Father teaches (Matthew 16:17, John 5:45), and the Son who came out of the bosom of his Father, and yet remained in the bosom of his Father teaches (Hebrews 1:2).[401] But the Father and the Son, especially since the ascension of Christ, and the effusion of the Spirit, do teach the children of God – all his elect – by the Holy Spirit.[402] And therefore the apostle showing how God teaches his elect after a more peculiar manner, so that even babes in Christ, those whom he calls *little children*, are preserved even in seducing times, and led into all necessary truths, notwithstanding all the diligence and subtlety of those many antichrists, who are industrious to deceive.[403]

He says they have an unction from the Holy One and know all things: all things necessary to be known and believed for the obtaining the remission of sins, etc. (1 John 2:20). But more especially, he shows that the Spirit teaches them to continue in the Son and in the Father (1 John 2:24), and therefore in the doctrine concerning the Father and the Son, as it is more expressly set down in 2 John 9.[404] And then he shows that the Spirit should abide constantly in them, to give them clear and certain direction in all necessary points. 1 John 2:27 reads: "But the anointing which ye have received of him abideth in you, and ye need not that any man teach you: but as the same anointing teacheth you of all things, and is truth and is no lie, and even as it hath taught you, ye shall abide in him, or it." "Ye shall abide in Christ and abide in the truth, which has been taught you by the Holy Spirit; and the teaching of the Spirit is clear and certain, for," says he, "the Spirit is truth and is no lie." Here is the peculiar teaching of God: the Spirit teaches

---

[401] Matthew 11:25
[402] John 1:18, Matthew 11:27, John 15:15, Luke 4:18, Acts 1:3
[403] 1 John 2:20; 1 Corinthians 2:10-12; 1 Corinthians 12:3
[404] Proverbs 1:23, Isaiah 59:21, 30:21, Psalm 119:102, 1 John 2:27, 2 John 9

us to believe in himself, as well as in the Father and the Son. And the Spirit was sent by the Father in the name of the Son for this very purpose.

Moreover it is evident that the Spirit not only teaches babes in Christ, but he taught even the apostles of Christ. "But the Comforter which is the Holy Spirit, whom the Father will send in my name, he shall teach you all things (John 14:26)."[405] Nay, the Holy Spirit did indite [*compose*] all the Holy Scriptures, and inspire the prophets, apostles and all the holy men of God in the writing of them. The Scriptures were not written by the will of men, but by the motion of the Holy Spirit (2 Peter 1:21), where the motion of the Holy Spirit is opposed to the will of men, to show that the motion and will of the Holy Spirit is the motion and will of God.[406] Many other places and arguments might be superadded; but for the better instruction of ordinary readers, I shall draw out my arguments into rank and file.

{1} The Spirit is God. The testimony of the Spirit is the testimony of God (1 Corinthians 2:1, 4). The wisdom of the Spirit, the wisdom of God;[407] and the power of the Spirit the power of God (1 Corinthians 2:4-5, 13). The teaching of the Spirit is the teaching of God; the will of the Spirit is the will of God (2 Peter 1:21; 1 Corinthians 12:6:11).

{2} The Spirit is the author of the Scriptures (2 Timothy 3:16; 1 Peter 1:11-12, Revelation 2:29).

{3} The Spirit is the interpreter of the Scriptures, and his interpretation is clear, certain and infallible.[408] The Spirit discovers the hidden wisdom of God; the wisdom of God in a mystery, the deep things of God, which could not have entered into the heart of man, if the Spirit had not revealed them, and therefore the deep things of God (1 Corinthians 2:10) are called the things of the Spirit of God (1 Corinthians 2:4) and things which are spiritually discerned. Therefore, they are such things as the spiritual man by

---

[405] John 14:26, Acts 2:3-4, John 16:13
[406] 1 Peter 1:11; 2 Peter 1:21
[407] 1 John 5:6, 10
[408] 1 Corinthians 2:7, 10, 14-15

the help of the Spirit is able to perceive, discern, receive, and to say with truth and comfort: "Now I have the mind of Christ, now I know the things that are freely given me of God, because the Spirit has revealed them to me."[409] Consider the discourse of the apostle quite throughout 1 Corinthians 2, and this point will be very clear.

{4} The Spirit is the author of faith. He gives us supernatural light, and spiritual eyes (1 Corinthians 2:8-10, Ephesians 1:17-18). "He that believeth on the Son of God hath the witness in himself."[410] The Spirit is called *the witness* (1 John 5:6, 10). And the apostle assures us that none can say, with faith and full persuasion of heart that Jesus is the Lord until he has been taught to say so by the Holy Spirit (1 Corinthians 12:3).

They who are sensual and have not the Spirit (Jude 19) do slight the testimony of the Spirit, because the world cannot receive the Spirit or the things of the Spirit. It is a natural man's pride and folly to account those things below him which are above him; for he accounts spiritual wisdom foolishness, whereas indeed it is too excellent for him to understand because he is a mere natural sensual man but these spiritual things are spiritually discerned. He does not receive them; he cannot know them (1 Corinthians 2:14). This is the true reason why men do not believe in the Spirit, and adore the Spirit, because he is the Spirit of truth, whom the world cannot receive, because it neither sees nor knows him (John 14:17). But Christ says to his disciples: "Ye know him for he dwelleth with you and shall be in you (John 14:17 & Acts 5:32)."[411]

{5} The Spirit is the supreme judge of truth, even of controverted truths in matters of religion.[412] We need not speak of a private judgment of discretion, such as spiritual men may pass by the help of the Spirit and word of truth; nor of that public and ministerial judgment which may be passed in

---

[409] 1 John 3:24; 1 Corinthians 2:12, John 6:69, Isaiah 30:21; 1 Corinthians 2:15
[410] 1 John 5:6, 10
[411] 1 John 3:24; 1 Corinthians 2:12, Romans 8:9.
[412] Judicium discretionis non arguit Officium Judicis.

greater or lesser synods where pastors and elders are assembled by the ordinance of Christ, and therefore may pray in faith for the direction and assistance of the Holy Spirit in all their ministerial determinations.[413]

But I speak of the supremacy and sovereignty of judgment, which belongs to the Holy Spirit. True it is that Christ is king and head of the church, and therefore he is our master, doctor, and lawgiver (Matthew 23:10, James 4:12). But the Father has sent the Spirit in the name of Christ to teach us the meaning of the Word of Christ, and to lead us into all truth and holiness by the holy Scriptures of truth. The Spirit did indite the whole Scripture; and it is agreeable to the light of nature, that he who made the law should expound it.[414]

This Holy Spirit is a public Spirit. He governs the whole body of Christ, the whole church, and speaks in the whole body of the Scriptures and every part thereof, and if we do compare one place of Scripture with another, we shall by comparing of Spiritual things with Spiritual, come to understand the saving wisdom which the Holy Spirit teaches;[415] "which things we speak" (says the apostle) "not in the words which man's wisdom teacheth, but which the Holy Spirit teacheth, comparing spiritual things with spiritual (1 Corinthians 2:13)." The Holy Spirit – speaking to us in plain places – discovers to us all that is necessary to be known and believed for our eternal salvation,[416] and thereby gives us so much light as that we may sufficiently

---

[413] Legislator judicat αυτοκρατορικός; Minister Publicus υπηρετικους; Christianus privatus ιδιώτης. Vide Reverend. Dr. Davenant de judice ac Normâ fidei. cap. 3. p. 3. learned Dr. Rainolds' Confer. with Hart c. 2. 4, 5, 6.

[414] Vide Aug. lib. de doctrinâ christiana & Enchir. ad Laurentium.

[415] Doctrina nostra est publica, quia est Doctrina Spiritus sancti in Scripturis publice loquentis.

[416] Vide Optatū contra Parmen. lib. 5. in Prin. & Tertul. de Anima Quis revelabit quod Deus texit? Praestat per Deum nescirc quia non revelaverit, quàm per hominem scire quia ipse praesumpserit. Caeli mysterium doceat me Deus ipse qui condidit, non homo qui seipsum ignoravit. Ambr. Ep. l. 5. Ep. 31. Ez 1. 30. 19, 20, 21. ver. Vide Damas. de orth. fid. lib. 1. c. 1. In fraudem legis facit qui salvis verbis legis sententiam ejus circumvenit. Contra Dig. Leg. Senatusque consultis. Ama Ecclesiasticas legere literas, & non multa invenies quae requiras ex me—ipso magis inspirante quam hominum aliquo commonente perdisces, Aug. Ep. 120.

understand hard places, if we pray as we should, compare and search the Scriptures as we ought in the spirit of faith and modesty, (James 1:5, John. 5:39, Matthew 7:7; 1 John. 5:14, Romans 2:2-3) and practice what we know before (John. 7:17, Philippians 3:15-16), for we shall at least learn so much wisdom as not to expound hard places of Scripture in any sense that is contrary to the mind of the Spirit clearly delivered in plain places of Scripture.

If we expound hard places according to the analogy of faith clearly delivered in other places, though we should make mistakes in the application, yet the Spirit so far interposes as to keep us from falling into heresy. And if we meet with no plain places to expound a hard place by, there is then no danger of heresy, because all things necessary to salvation are set down clearly in the plain places of Scripture. This conference of Scriptures is an excellent means to bring us acquainted with all book-cases, the determinations which the Spirit has made in Scripture,[417] and left there upon record in those sacred rolls (which are the treasury of the church) for the direction of the saints. And whether we make use of this ordinance in our private reading, or in the public ministry, the Spirit delivers his judgment authoritatively and infallibly in the holy Scriptures, and we may come to be acquainted with the mind and judgment of the Spirit by both ordinances. "Thine eyes shall see thy teachers, and thine ears shall hear a word behind thee saying, This is the way" (this and not that, behold a clear direction),[418] "walk ye in it, continue, and go forward in it, do not forsake it; when we are wavering and even turning out of our way on one hand or the other, when ye turn to the right hand, and when ye turn to the left," then,

---

[417] Damasc. de orth. fid. lib. 1. cap. 1, 2. Aug. de Doct. Christ. lib 1. cap. 35, 36, 37, & 40. lib. 3. cap. 2. Aug. de Trinitate lib. 1. cap. 2. & 4. & lib. 5. cap. 26. Aquin. part. 1. qu. 36. art. 2. Aug. in Epist. 1 Ioh. Tract. 3.

[418] Nos Ecclesiae Ministerium in honore habemus, internas persuasiones sine externo verbo tanquam Satanae ludibria cavemus; ex Scripturis sapimus, cum Scripturis sentimus, propter Scripturas credimus: Whitaker de Authoritate Script. lib. 1. cap. 10. prope finem. & Controv. 1. de Script. interpret. qu. 5. cap. 4, 5.

even then, does the Spirit resolve us, and put us out of doubt.[419] When we are disputing, and even yielding up the truth in a controversy, we have a clear, certain, and infallible direction from the Holy Spirit (Isaiah 30:20-21).

The Holy Spirit exhorts the Jews to compare the dimmer light of the prophets with the clearer light of the apostles that so the sun of righteousness may shine in its strength with its healing beams into their hearts; and then tells them that no prophecy of the Scripture is of private interpretation,[420] because prophets spake (as the apostles also did) not as the will of man did move, or the fancy of man directed; but according to the mind and will of the Holy Spirit.[421]

And therefore since all the Scriptures were indited, all are to be expounded by the Holy Spirit speaking in the Scriptures thus compared,[422] for the Holy Spirit did move all the holy men, apostles as well as prophets to write, and teach them what they should write. And though we have no extraordinary revelations now by a voice from the excellent glory for our direction, yet we have that which is better: the writings of the prophets and apostles to compare together. The prophecies are dark, yet they are sure – more sure than those voices which may be more easily counterfeited. Though the prophecies are dark, yet the Spirit who did indite them, will if you compare them with the writings of the apostles,[423] give light to both, and deliver his judgment as clearly in all necessary points as if it were written with a sunbeam. This I take to be the scope of the Holy Spirit in that excellent discourse (2 Peter 1:16 to the end of the chapter). And I have

---

[419] Item de Catechis. rudibus. cap 3, 4, 6, 7, &c.

[420] Verbum Dei est lux, lucerna, lumen ad Deum dirigens in Agendis, Credendis, Sperandis, amandis.

[421] Psalm 19, Psalm 119; 2 Peter 1:16, 19

[422] Vide Chamier. de Veritate Canonis, Interior Magister docet, Christus docet, inspiratio ipsius docet. Aug. Tract. 3. in Epist. Iohan. Non dicit meliorem sed Certiorem Aug. de verbis Apostoli Serm. 27. cap. 4.
Praevidens Dominus Iesus Christus impios quosdam futuros qui miraculis ejus Calumniarentur magicis artibus ea tribuendo, prophetas ante praemisit, Aug Tract. 35. in Iohan. Vide D. Davenant. de judice & Norma fidei, & D. Gomarum.

[423] Chamier de Interpret. lib. Canon.

consulted the most judicious and experienced writers upon that place, though I cite but few in the margin, because I do not have time to peruse them again.[424]

True it is that we are not to believe every spirit, and therefore are permitted to try the spirits whether they are of God or not (1 John 4:1). But in this trial, the Holy Spirit speaking in the Scriptures is the supreme judge, and the Holy Spirit condemns all erroneous and fantastical spirits who forsake old truths, and pretend to follow new light.[425] The Holy Spirit constantly teaches the same truth in the holy Scriptures; for he does not change his mind, or contradict himself. We (says the apostle) having the same Spirit of faith according as it is written, I believed and therefore have I spoken, we also believe and therefore speak (2 Corinthians 4:13).[426] The same Spirit leads all the faithful into all truth necessary to salvation, not absolutely and at once, but by degrees. For we see the apostles themselves were for a time guilty of gross errors (Mark 10:37, 41, Acts 1:6). But the faithful cannot obstinately hold and continue in such odious and damnable errors as do directly overthrow the foundation of faith. And for the time in which they do err, they hearken to their own spirits so far as they are carnal, and do not as they ought, search, and pray, and wait for the direction of the Holy Spirit.[427] It is not the spirit of faith which speaks in them, when they dissent from such as receive the public testimony of the Holy Spirit speaking in the holy Scriptures.[428] And therefore the Spirit teaches us to try the spirits

---

[424] Dr. Rainolds, in his learned conference with Hart chap. 2. Divis. 2. pag. 46. Mr. Hildersham in his 145 Lecture upon the 51 Psal. pag. 697. Dr. Alting. Loc. com.

[425] Erroneous and fantastical spirits are condemned by the Holy Spirit. Vide D. Whitaker, controv. 1. de Script. Interpret. qu. 5. cap. 4, & de Authoritate Scripturae lib. 1. cap. 10. in calce capitis.

[426] 2 Cor. 4:13 Ingenue fatemur non esse nunc novas revelationes expectandas, sive à summo pontifice sive a Concilio sive ab Ecclesiâ totâ. Canus lib. 2. cap. 7.

[427] Mark 10:37, 41

[428] Acts 1:6. Aristot. Ethic lib. 5. cap. 7. Non eritijs matutina lux. Isa. 8. 20. Judices ejus lupi vespertini, sacerdotes ejus polluerunt sanctum; injuste egerunt contra legem. Soph. 3. 3. Omnis potestas judicis ministerialis Legibus adstricta est; unicus autem summus Judex est, Isa. 32. 22. Iacobi 4. 12. qui quidem νομοθετικός solus judicat.

and doctrines of men by the Scriptures. If they speak not according to this Word, it is not because they have new light from the Spirit, but because they have no light, no morning light, heavenly light conveyed unto them in that point wherein they dissent,[429] or they have not as yet received it; the Spirit has not as yet sealed that portion of truth to their consciences, or written it in their hearts. For the Spirit does not whisper one thing in private to my conscience, and declare the contrary in his public testimony delivered in the Word. "Behold," (says the wisdom of God) "I will pour out my spirit unto you, I will make known my words unto you (Proverbs 1:23)." For this is the covenant of God: that his Word and Spirit should go together, and the Spirit should deliver his public testimony authoritatively as it becomes his supremacy and sovereignty in the holy Scriptures.[430] "This is my covenant with them saith the Lord, my spirit that is upon thee, and my word," etc. (Isaiah 59:21).

And by attendance on the ministry of the gospel in the church of Christ we receive the Spirit (Galatians 3:2).[431] By hearing the doctrine of faith preached in the gospel they received the Spirit, and therefore the ministry of the gospel is called "the ministration of the Spirit (2 Corinthians 3:8)." And for these reasons, we try the doctrines and spirits of men by the word of God, because the Spirit who is the author of Scripture everywhere agrees with himself, and there is a friendly relation between the truth of the party witnessing, and the truth of the thing witnessed.[432]

---

[429] Revelatio mihi in conscientiâ meâ facta est Privata ex parte Subjecti, Publica verò ex parte Objecti.

[430] Ecclesia Instrumen taliter commovet sed non sola movet; movent ipsae Scripturae movet Spiritus, & Principaliter movent. Whitakerus.

[431] Non potest Deus nisi per Deum intelligi, sicut nec honorem a nobis Deus nisi per Deum accipit—non cogitando aut dispatando veritatem homo assèqui potest, sed audiendo ab eo qui solus docere potest, Hilarius de Trinitate lib. 5. Vide D. Whitaker de Sacra Scriptura controv. 1. qu. 3. c. 8.

[432] Judicium practicae Discretionis a dono coele sli pendet, ex infuso lumine Spiritus Sancti oritur, non ex privato sensu aut phantasmate, & ad normam verbi exigitur simul & dirigitur. Distinguit ita{que} D. Davenantius inter Iudicium Discretionis, & Iudicium Praecipitationis. Non ad enthysiasmos itaque fanaticos, vel asslatus

We do readily acknowledge that the world looks upon this public testimony of the Spirit in the word as a private testimony, and are apt to scoff at them who receive it, as at men led by their own private spirit; but the true reason is because this testimony of the Spirit is not manifest to them who have not the Spirit. But it is so manifest to those who have had this public testimony sealed up to their consciences, that they will hold fast this testimony though it cost them their lives. "I saw under the altar the souls of them that were slain for the word of God, and for the testimony which they held (Revelation 6:9)." The testimony which they held is no other than that public testimony which the Spirit delivers in the Word, and had privately sealed up to their spirits. They were slain for the Word of God, and for the testimony which they held according to that Word. They were martyred because they gave testimony of that truth, which they had learnt in the Word of God.

I am willing to dwell longer upon this subject, because it is *fundamentum fundamentorum*, and therefore we will for our better satisfaction descend from handling the point in general unto some very weighty points in particular, and show how the Spirit persuades the hearts and consciences of men to receive his testimony in particular controversies, which have been raised and disputed by men of great wit and spirit.

In the great controversies between us and the papists, they do, as several heretics have done before them, urge visions, miracles, traditions, successions, prudential motives, and sometimes councils, fathers, and for a fairer pretense, the holy Scriptures.[433] But when they are beaten off from

---

Anabaptisticos fideles remittimus. vide D. Daven. de judice & Normà Fidei. Mr. Hildersham his Lectures upon the 51 Psal. Mr. Ball in his larger Catechism. Dr. Rainolds' conference with Hart. Dr. Whitaker above cited. Et Rev. D. Rainolds Academiae Oxon. Procancellarii in Concione de Animali homine hoc anno 1649. habitâ.

[433] Aug. de unitate Ecclesiae, cap. 16. in Johan. Tra. 13. Iren. adv haereses, lib. 3. cap. 2. 12. Euseb. Hi. Eccles. lib. 5. cap. 14. Socrat. lib. 4. cap. 23. Theod. Histo. lib. 1. Cap. 16. Aug contra Max. Arian. lib. 1. De Bapt. contra Donatistas, lib. 3. cap. 2. Epist, 165. ad Generosun.

their pretending to councils and fathers by our learned Whitaker, Jewel, Abbot, Ussher, Rainolds, not to name Chamier and other worthies, what lamentable shifts do they make when they are pressed to stand to the public testimony and judgment of the Holy Spirit delivered in the holy Scriptures! We do therefore in compassion to their poor souls entreat them to hearken to the Spirit of Christ, and not to the spirit of Antichrist,[434] because the right sense of the Scripture expounded by the Scripture is the sword of God's Spirit wherewith all heresies whatsoever are overcome by all those good soldiers, who add the shield of faith to the sword of the Spirit. But when men neglect the Scriptures, and idolize human inventions they spend their strength in vain, and are like the blind men of Sodom who wearied themselves to find the door.

The great point of the pope's infallible supremacy can never be proven by the original, universal, and perpetual tradition of the church of Christ in all ages; no, nor by the unanimous consent of all learned men now living in communion with the present church of Rome.

The Sorbonne doctors cannot believe that the popes of Rome are not subject to the sins and passions of other men. If the succession of popes which they brag of were to be tried by fame, celebrity, antiquity, consent; it is most evident to all that are acquainted with pure antiquity, and impartial history, that the supremacy of the popes and papacy would be sufficiently condemned.[435] But if the pope's infallible supremacy comes to be tried by the Holy Spirit, speaking in the holy Scriptures, the popes and papacy will be infallibly condemned by the Supreme Judge.

The learned papists do not agree concerning the infallible propounder of fundamental points,[436] for: (1) some say that the pope's proposal *ex cathedra* is sufficient, but Galatians 1:8. (2) Others say a council without the pope. (3)

---

[434] 1 Corinthians 2:13. Ephesians 6:16-17.
[435] Read the Protestation of learned Protestants, repeated by Bishop Jewel, and Doctor Rainolds in his conference with Hart, Chapter 8, First Division, pag 393.
[436] Vide Frācis. Pic. Mirandul. Theor. in expos. Theor. 4ti. Thom. Waldens. Tom. 3. de Sacramentalibus, Doct. 3. pag. 5.

Others, the pope and council both together. It seems the pope is not sent as Peter to strengthen his brethren, but his brethren must be sent to strengthen him. (4) Some say both together is not sufficient, either in point of manners, or matter of faith, unless the acceptation of the church universal be superadded. (5) We are not able to reckon up the number of those who deny the infallibility of the present church and pope of Rome. (6) They cannot give us a perfect inventory of all written verities, unwritten traditions, and church definitions,[437] which the whole succession of popes have upon the credit of their infallibility determined to be necessary for all Christians to know and believe.[438]

I need say nothing of the papal reservations, provisions, mandates, and all postnate [*subsequent*] dictates, and decrees which bishops and metropolitans, are by their oath made to the pope at their confirmation, obliged to observe. Nor will I trouble my reader with the distinction of supremacy of knowledge in resolving church questions (because that they say belongs to the fathers, who excelled the popes in expounding of Scriptures) and supremacy of power to decide church causes.[439] For this latter supremacy, is that which popes and cardinals and all must live by in the court of Rome, and the former supremacy is purposely claimed for the support of this. But it was a long time before the popes presumed to challenge the power of deciding all the greater causes of the church throughout the world, for the bishops of Rome were at the first but bishops within their own city; then metropolitans within their own province, afterwards archbishops or patriarchs over metropolitans within their princely diocese; and last of all their pride and policy being crowned with success did

---

[437] Vide Formam juramenti prae stand ab Episcopo electo in Pontificali Romano parte primâ.

[438] Reservationes, provisiones, mandata Apostolica totis viribus observabo, & faciam ab alijs observari.

[439] Gratian. Decret. Distinct. 20. Vide Wolfgang Laz. comment. Reipub. Rom. [12]. cap. 2. Concil. Constan. 1 cap. 2. Theodos. & Valent. Epist. ad discor. in Concil. Chalced. Act 1. Theod. Hi. Ecel. l. 5. cap. 28. Gregor. Regist. l. 4. Epist. 34.

swell them up to be popes and lords over all the Christian, or rather anti-Christian world.

The ecclesiastical and temporal supremacy or sovereignty of popes is condemned by reason and history by fathers and councils as others have proven at large.[440] Let us not therefore be put off with that ridiculous piece of sophistry, which is so common – that the pope is infallible and supreme head of the church, and lord of the world, because the scriptures mean so; and the Scriptures mean so, because the pope says so. Who does not see that the Scriptures are only put in for a mere stale?[441] And therefore the argument had been as strong if they had proven the pope's infallible authority and princely supremacy by an *ipse dixit* at first. The pope says that he is infallible, ergo he is so. I am not at leisure to hear what the pope, who has endeavored to dethrone Christ, and depose the Holy Spirit, says on his own behalf at Rome, for if he once bring this great question to be resolved in his own consistory, he will soon bring all causes to be decided there also where he himself is plaintiff, witness and judge; only in prudence and modesty he has entertained a company of cardinals (who are to divide the spoils with him) for his grand inquest.[442]

The pope's supremacy is unwritten, and therefore he is a fit judge to decide all controversies amongst the traditionaries, whose faith is not written in either Testament.

But since the pope strives with the Holy Spirit for the chair, and Christ for the throne, let us hear what Christ and the Holy Spirit do both speak in the Holy Scriptures of truth, and we shall quickly decide this grand

---

[440] D. Ussher, Jewel, Rainolds, Whitaker, Abbot, Davenant, Bilson, Chamier, Gomarus.

[441] Vide. Aenc. Silv. de gestis Basil. Concil. lib. 1. Iaco. Almain. de authoritate Ecclesiae cap. 8. Summi Poncifices suas fimbrias nimis extendentes alios Papas adducunt in testes.

[442] Ask a thief or his fellow whether he is a thief. Vide L. nullus D. de testibus L. omnibus C. co. 4. 9. 2. & 3. c. si testes

controversy, and many more. Christ is the only pastor of his church; he is to continue so and have no successor.

We find in holy Scripture that Christ is the only head and Savior of his whole church (Ephesians 1:22, Colossians 2:19). He does and will continue with his church always, even unto the end of the world, to give life, sense, and motion to it, and to rule and govern the whole, and every member of it, by the effectual council and working of his Holy Spirit.[443]

The apostles were but ministerial heads, or principal members who had a preeminence over the inferior members for perfecting of the saints by the work of the ministry (1 Corinthians 12:2, 1:28). First apostles: this eminent ministry or headship did belong to all the apostles, and not to Peter only; the power of remitting and retaining sins was given to the other apostles as well as Peter (John 20:21, 22:23). We do not deny Peter to be the first apostle in time, as Andrew was the first disciple, and therefore Peter is first reckoned (Matthew 10:2). Nay, we will not deny him to be most eminent in grace,[444] and for both reasons grant him to be first in order, but we deny that he was chief in dignity or supreme in power, because we know the apostles had all equal power, for Christ sent them all as his Father sent him. They had all of them power to open heaven to believers, and shut it against unbelievers. The power of the keys was given upon the confession which Peter made in the name of all the rest (Matthew 16:16, 18) as he was wont to do (John 6:69). The confession was common to all, the promise common to all, the performance common to all (John 20:21-23). I need say no more but this.

(1) The papists do entitle Peter to that supreme sovereignty which belongs to Christ.[445] But Peter and the rest of the apostles were joint

---

[443] Christ is the only head of his whole church, Ephes. 1. 22. Col. 2. 19. Ioh. 10. 16. Per pastorem unicum intelligimus Christum non Papā Oecumenicum, Ioh. 10. 9. 14. 16 26, 27, 28. Sic per Davidem intelligimus Christum, Eze. 37. 22, 23. 24. Ezek. 34. 23. 1 Pet. 2. 25. Heb. 13. 20

[444] Cuncti claves regni Caelorū accipiant ex aequo. Hieronym advers. 10. vin. lib. 2. Vt Plato Princeps Philosophorum, ita Petrus Apostolorū Hieron. adver. Pelag. lib. 1.

[445] Vide Glos. extravagant. Ioh. 22. Potestas summa Pap. six. 4. Sac. Cerem. eccles. Rom. lib. 1. sect. 7. Leo's Sermons, Epistles, Rhemish annot, in Mat. 16. 18.

foundations built on Christ, the only proper head and foundation (Ephesians 2:20).

(2) They entitle the pope to that power which did belong to Peter, but Peter had no successor in his extraordinary and apostolic power. The pope is no apostle;[446] and when Peter speaks of his ordinary power, he tells the elders that he is their fellow presbyter. I who am also an elder, exhort the elders (1 Timothy 5:1).[447] But that Peter was an ordinary bishop of one city – first of Antioch for seven years, and then of Rome for twenty-five – cannot be proved by Scripture, no, nor by any credible historian. I know they rely upon Eusebius' testimony, but it is enough for me to reply, that Eusebius' history dissents from his chronicle, and his chronicle dissents from Scripture.

(3) Christ has many ministers to preach his gospel, but he has no catholic vicar besides his Spirit who can challenge the supreme sovereignty of deciding controversies by an infallible sentence: it is the Spirit that makes the word to be effectual (1 Corinthians 3:7).[448] As Christ works by his Spirit, he has no vicar, for he himself is with his disciples always to the end of the world (Matthew 20). Christ himself baptizes with the Holy Spirit; he himself did open the heart of Lydia.

(4) The pope challenges this power over the Gentiles, but Paul was the apostle of the Gentiles by the appointment of the Holy Spirit, and Peter's own consent (Romans 11:13, Acts 13:2, Galatians 2:9). Paul was chief and labored more abundantly than any in this service.

(5) Peter did never claim or exercise any such power over the princes and kingdoms of the world as the pope does (Luke 22:25-26, Matthew 20:25-26).

---

[446] Vide Annot. Romae excus. in Cyprian. De aequalitate. Apostolatus qui cum Apostolis morientibus cessavit nec ad Episcopos transijt.

[447] Vide Comarum parte 3. Disp. 22. de Petri Apostoli & Papae Romani repug. Dr. Rainolds in his conference with Hart Chap. 6. Division 3. pag. 209. 210, 211, 212.

[448] Act. 14. 23 Act. 20. 28 Tit. 1. 5 Phil. 1. 1. Pro Apostolis filij nati sunt; non Pater unicus papa Oecumenicus. Vide Aug. Enarrat, in Psal. 34. nec non in Psal. 44.

(6) If Peter had desired and usurped any supremacy over the rest of the apostles, he would have thereby degraded himself, and been last of all (Mark 9:34-35).

(7) If the vices of popes may make them supreme or their errors infallible, we are able to prove that by fraud, violence and such like black arts, they have usurped a power over the consciences of men to lead them into heresy, Antichristianism, and atheism.[449] For by endeavoring to prove their infallibility by the Scripture, and then venting gross errors as infallible truths upon the authority of the pope and church, they have tempted some to believe neither church nor pope nor Scripture. The pope has told them that they had as well believe nothing as not believe all, and therefore it is to be feared that too many believe nothing at all.

Let us then to the law and the testimony, and let Christ and his Spirit be heard speak in them, and we will proceed to trial with the papists upon what points they please. We will try all their new tutelar gods, whether angels or dead men, or their breaden god in the mass by the first commandment. Their picturing of God and worshiping of him by pictures by the second commandment.

Their superstitious benedictions, magical Incantations, exorcisms, and all those helps to salvation, which salt, wax, spittle, bells can afford, by the third commandment; and so I might proceed to the holy-days, masses, etc., or try their popes' usurpations, the cruelty of their inquisition, their allowance of fornication, forbidding to marry, their equivocations, [and their] rebellious concupiscence by the second table. We will – by the gospel of Christ – try the doctrine of justification by works, their public prayers in an unknown tongue, their denying of the testament of Christ's blood to the people; we will examine whether there be more sacrifices of Christ than one? Whether they that die in Christ rest from their labors? I might proceed to examine their doctrine, concerning the offices and benefits of Christ; concerning the

---

[449] Vna vetula potest esse perfectior ac major ipso Papâ perfectione Gratiae & amplitudinc Virtutum. Turrecrem In Summa de Eccles. lib. 2. c. 82.

nature and use of faith, and the doctrine of the Sacraments, and the rest of the points in controversy between us and the papists. And truly when I do read such questions as these I cannot but think of those texts of 1 Timothy 4:1-3: "Now the Spirit speaks expressly," etc. The Spirit so expressly condemns these seducing and erring spirits, that whosoever will be persuaded by the evident demonstrations of the Spirit, and be overruled by his positive definitions in Scripture, will confess that the papists were very wise in offering to be tried by unwritten traditions, or the pope and his adherents, in all points in question. It is clear that the popes have taught for doctrines the commandments of men. He that reads the epistles to the Romans and Galatians, 1 Corinthians 14, Colossians 2, 2 Thessalonians 2, and the plainer places of the book of the Revelation, will acknowledge the Spirit speaks expressly.

The pope must therefore be beholden to his Schoolmen to defend his doctrine, and to his canonists to keep up his discipline, and pretend no more to Scriptures or pure antiquity for his justification.

If the anti-Scripturists would but hearken to the Spirit speaking in the Scripture, they would say the Spirit has magnified both law and gospel, and made them honorable, precious and glorious in our eyes.

I will not insist upon those many convincing arguments whereby the Scriptures are undeniably proven to be the Word of God, but humbly desire all men to consider whether the true reason (why those arguments do not effectually persuade obstinate men) be not clearly this: because men do undervalue the testimony of the Holy Spirit, and resist, vex, grieve, or quench the Holy Spirit, whose office it is to seal up this and all other saving truths to our consciences and hearts.

True it is that the law of God is written in our hearts by nature, but our nature is corrupted, and we are blinded with pride, passion, prejudice, with self-conceitedness and self-love, and therefore it is requisite that the wrath of God should be revealed from heaven against pleasing gainful sins; nay, unnatural sins (Romans 1:18 to the end of the chapter). Moreover, it is to be sadly considered that the gospel is not written in our hearts by nature, nor can it be found out by any artificial demonstration, but it is discovered to us by divine revelation (Romans 1:16–17).

I know many learned men have used the testimony of human authors in a secondary and subservient way to confirm our faith in this point, but it is clear that we must rest our faith upon the authority of God in this and all other points, or else our faith will not be a divine faith.

God swears by himself, because he is the greatest, and bears witness to himself in his Word, nay, to his Word, in his Word, because he is the truest, for he is indeed the prime truth, the only infallible truth. And hence it is that the Scriptures are called the testimonies of God, and the testimony of the Spirit is so often produced: 1 Peter 1:11, Acts 5:32, and 1 John 5:6. It is no shame to adhere to the testimony of God in the weightiest point, Psalm 119:31, 46. Hence it is that the penmen do so often show their commission and cry: "Thus saith the Lord." And hence it is that God does so often own the Scriptures for his word. This is my word, says God, this came from my inspiration saith the Spirit (2 Timothy 3:16; 2 Peter 1:21). "This is my writing, says Jehovah, I will own it, and stand to it. "I have written to him the great things of my law," says God (Hosea 8:12). The Scriptures are the oracles of God (Romans 3:2). They contain the counsel of God (Acts 20:27). God has given us sufficient assurance that the law was written by his own finger, and all other books by his special command and inspiration. "All Scripture is given by inspiration of God (2 Timothy 3:16)." "Prophecy came not in old time" – the word is ποτε – "it came not at any time by the will of man but holy men of God spake as they were moved by the Holy Spirit (2 Peter 1:21)." Our Savior gives a full testimony to Moses, David, the rest of the penmen of the Psalms, and all the prophets (Luke 24:44). God has sealed the testimony of the penmen by miracles on men and devils, we need not expect new miracles to confirm this Old Testament and ancient gospel; both are confirmed by the old miracles which stand upon record in both. But if any man preaches a new gospel, we may well call upon him for new miracles. Nay, the very preservation of the Scriptures in spite of tyrants, heretics and devils is a convincing miracle. In a word, the testimony of the penmen is sealed: (1) by the oath of God, (2) by the blood of Christ, (3) by the testimony of the Spirit, and (4) by the efficacy of the Spirit.

The testimony and efficacy of the Spirit is that sweet subject which I am now more especially engaged to insist upon; the testimony of the Spirit to the heart and conscience of every true believer in particular is a convincing testimony.

But it will be said, that this is such an argument as none can take notice of and therefore altogether insufficient to persuade other men to believe, to whom no such testimony has been vouchsafed.

(1) I answer: this is an argument indeed whereby I cannot convince others, but this is an argument which makes all other arguments effectual to convince me.

(2) The efficacy of the Spirit in the word upon the hearts of enemies is very considerable. Their minds are enlightened, their judgments convinced, their consciences awakened,[450] terrified, their hearts smitten, because the very thoughts of their hearts are strangely and unexpectedly discovered,[451] their souls embowelled,[452] and their marrow as it were melted in their bones by this almighty Spirit speaking, testifying, working in and with the Word. The very letter kills them, the very savor confounds them, though bold atheists scoff at the Word, and do in their Jovial fits blaspheme the Spirit; yet sometimes their hearts quake their joints tremble, even as Belshazzar's did at the very sight of the handwriting, when they do but glance their eye upon some startling text. Their consciences do often join with the word and spirit against themselves against their wills; for though they be self-willed, yet they are – after some soul-searching admonition – self-confounded and self-condemned men (Titus 3:10-11).

---

[450] Hebrews 4:12-13
[451] 2 Corinthians 3:6
[452] 2 Corinthians 2:16

And though the malice of some men is too strong for their wit, reason, and conscience, yet it is not too strong for the Spirit in the Word. All the powers of hell in them are overpowered by this good Spirit; all the strongholds of Satan battered, and they themselves so confounded, that they seem to be even damned already, they think themselves in hell above-ground, when they are stung and bitten, they fall into the passion of the heart, and are taken with such hellish convulsion-sits that they do even foam at mouth, and gnash with their teeth.[453] They are cut to the soul, and tormented in their conscience,[454] they cry and howl and fight against the Spirit,[455] but all in vain, for even they are outwitted and overpowered, who are not converted by this stinging efficacy of the Almighty Spirit.

What shall we say to these things? If idols have been overthrown, oracles silenced, devils convinced by the majesty of the Spirit in the holy Scriptures, and so over awed by the Spirit that they have been forced to confess, nay believe these truths at which they tremble, then surely those bold theists are worse than devils who do not tremble at the Word because they do not believe the Spirit.

(3) Look upon a soul in its agony and pangs, in its throws and conflicts at its first conversion, or in its after-throws upon some sad relapse, and observe how the wit is captivated, reason conquered, conscience confounded, heart broken, and will turned, nay all the powers of corrupt nature overpowered and overturned by the Word and Spirit of God, and then you must cry out, "O the divine efficacy of Scripture, which turns a lion into a lamb, a goat into a sheep; a man, a beast, a devil into a saint, and persuades philosophers and courtiers, emperors and soldiers, publicans and harlots, mariners and politicians to embrace a religion, and run a course clean contrary to the carnal and devilish wisdom of their proud reason, contrary to the stubborn resolutions of their perverse wills; in a word,

---

[453] Acts 7:54
[454] Revelation 11:10
[455] Acts 5:39

contrary to their very nature, education, custom, contrary to dictates of policy and reasons of state, contrary to their passions, lusts, interests friends companions! O victorious Spirit! What aileth, what aileth thee, O thou man of war, and pride, thou secretary of nature, and advocate of the devil to hang the head and weep, to resign thy estate, lay down thy commission, and thy arms, burn thy conjuring-books, and sacrifice thy dearest life in the maintenance of that truth which thou hast formerly contemned?"

I must cry as he did: "Εύρηκα! Εύρηκα!" This is the power of the Word! Behold the efficacy of the Spirit in the word conquering and triumphing over the subtlety and obstinacy, the pride and malignity of carnal men. The promises of God are better than all the proffers of Satan. The devil shows us the glory of the world; the Scripture shows us the vanity of the world, and the conscience is convinced by the Word and Spirit that the reversion of Heaven is infinitely better than the possessions of earth. All the kingdoms of the world and glory of them are not worth one day's communion with Jesus Christ, nay, one day's comfort from the gospel and Spirit of Jesus Christ. Good reason have we then to believe the Spirit. Angels admire and devils tremble at the majesty of the word. Saints believe, obey, adore the majesty of the Spirit speaking in the word of truth and life, of grace and glory.

The Familists might learn by this sad discourse to believe the Spirit of God speaking in the word of God, and not believe their own natural, carnal, phantastical spirits which contradict the Word and Spirit of God. The Familists did learn of the papists to call orthodox Protestants *Scripture-men*, to scoff at them as Scripture-wise, and to say as Stapleton and several others do, that the most diligent conference of Scriptures is the ready way to the most damnable errors, that the fountains of Greek and Hebrew are neither pure nor necessary, and the like.[456] And yet Howlet in his Epistle to Queen Elizabeth did lay the sin of the Family of Love to the charge of the Protestants. But Dr. Rainolds, our learned champion in his conference with

---

[456] H. Nicolas' book entitled *The Gospel of the Kingdom*. Dr Rainolds' *Conference with Hart* cap. 1. divis 2. pag, 60. 61 Howlet's Epistle in Queen Elizabeth.

Hart, vindicates the Protestants, and makes it evident that such as were godly and learned in the Scripture, did detest Harry Nicolas, that imp of Satan and master of the Family of Love, and therefore they could not lay the Family's sin to our charge as if we did foster that venomous vipers brood (I keep to the doctor's own expressions, so that you may see how the zeal of that meek Moses was inflamed in this contest), which did march into the field with papists to strengthen their hands against Protestants.

The Anabaptists likewise might learn from hence to make the Spirit speaking in the word the judge of their pretended revelations, if they were not too conceited of their own inventions, and apt to fall in love with the dreams of their own feverish brain, with their weak arguments but strong delusions.

The Arminians – the constant enemies of the grace of God – should consider that the Pelagians – the advocates of free will and corrupt nature – were confounded with those plain Scriptures which were urged by the Councils of Carthage, Milevis, Orange, and holy Augustine in his fragrant works.[457]

The Socinians – the enemies of the only true God:[458] Father, Son, and Holy Spirit – should consider that the Arians were overthrown by the Scriptures in the Nicene council, and by the godly pastors of the church, who instead of broken Scriptures (which the Arians urged with as much fraud as the devil did; Matthew 4) produced plain Scriptures and the whole series of both Testaments, and so did invincibly refute their blasphemous errors.

The Libertines – who claim a liberty of publishing damnable heresies and blasphemies under pretense of prophesying – might learn, that where

---

[457] Vide Epist. ad Innoc. inter Epist. August. Epist. 90. & 92, Concil. Arausican. secundum, August. Tom. 7. Contra Pelagian.

[458] Vide Theodoret. Hist. lib. 1. cap. 7. Athanas. contra Arian. Basil contra Eunom. Nazianzen. Hilar & Aug. de Trinitate & contra Arian. Cyrill Alexand. Tom. 5. part. 1. & 2. Thesaurus &c.

the Spirit of the Lord is, there is liberty,⁴⁵⁹ true liberty, but nowhere else;⁴⁶⁰ for he who pretends to speak by the Holy Spirit, and yet denies Jesus to be the Lord, does at once blaspheme Christ and the Holy Spirit, and is an anti-spiritual liar, an anti-Christian blasphemer, and has neither Father, Son nor Spirit dwelling in him. For he who speaks by the Spirit does acknowledge Jesus to be the Lord (1 Corinthians 12:3). And he who denies the Son has not the Father. "Who is a liar but he who denies that Jesus is the Christ? He is Antichrist who denies the Father and the Son; whosoever denies the Son, the same hath not the Father (1 John 2:22-23)."

In like manner, "every spirit which confesseth not that Jesus Christ is come in the flesh, is not of God but of Antichrist (1 John 4:2-3)." This is that Vorstian liberty which has undone so many nations already, and is now idolized in England under the name of liberty of conscience, by such as have neither conscience nor liberty.⁴⁶¹ Reverend Dr. Sibbes did exceedingly cry out against this kind of liberty in his time.⁴⁶² He would not have way given to Vorstian lawless licentious liberty of prophecy: that everyone, as soon as he is big of some new conceit, should bring forth his abortive monster, for then the pillars of Christian faith will soon be shaken, and the church of God which is a house of order, will become a Babel: a house of confusion. The doleful issues of which pretended liberty, we see in Poland, Transylvania, and in countries nearer hand.

I might proceed, but this is sufficient for a taste, and if I should but name all the errors of this age and not confute them, I should abuse my reader, and therefore I desire to stop in time, and beseech all that are spiritually minded to hearken to the Spirit speaking in the word. Beloved, believe not every spirit, but believe the Holy Spirit, who is the author of the Scriptures, the author of faith, the judge of controversies, the interpreter of the Scriptures,

---

⁴⁵⁹ 2 Corinthians 3:17
⁴⁶⁰ 1 Corinthians 12:3
⁴⁶¹ Dr. Sibbes' judgment concerning liberty of prophecy.
⁴⁶² Dr, Sibbes' epistle before Mr. Baines' commentary upon Ephesians

the doctor and comforter of the elect, and he will lead you into all necessary truth for your present edification and everlasting salvation.

The Holy Spirit will assure you that the Scriptures of truth were all written by his own authority, and you may safely set to your seal, when you have received the infallible testimony of the Holy Spirit. We are witnesses of these things (says the apostle) and so is the Holy Spirit also (Acts 5:32). We shall never receive the word, as the Word of God, with joy, reverence, submission and assurance of faith, specially in times of affliction and temptation, unless we receive the witness of the Spirit, and ground our faith upon the wisdom and evident demonstration of the Spirit. When we look upon the word of God, and consider:[463]

[1] The wonderful consent of all those holy and self-denying men that penned it. [2] The marvelous fulfilling of all the strange prophecies in the fullness of time appointed by God. [3] The admirable providence of God in preserving the Scriptures notwithstanding all the rage and malice of heretics and persecutors. [4] The supernatural miracles wrought to confirm it. [5] The harmonious testimony that the church, martyrs, saints, have in all ages given to it. [6] The antiquity, majesty, and efficacy of it. [7] The divine and heavenly matter contained in it: {1} Mysteries above reason (1 Corinthians 2:9).[464] {2} Commands contrary to our corrupt nature, sent to all nations, and even to the greatest and proudest of men. {3} Threats beyond the strength of man to inflict, or the capacity of man to comprehend – a hard heart, a seared conscience, and yet a trembling spirit, a reprobate mind and sense, a spirit of madness, giddiness, horror or slumber, an everlasting worm, eternal fire, and torments with the devil and his angels. {4} Promises and rewards beyond the power of man to bestow, or wisdom of angels to comprehend (1 Peter 1:12, Ephesians 3:10). {5} The fall, corruption,

---

[463] See Mr. Hildersham upon Psalm 51:7, his 145th Lecture. Mr. Ball's larger Catechism. Master Hieron of the Dignity of the Scriptures. Reverend Mr. White in his book newly printed called *The Way to the Tree of Life*, the second and third chapters.

[464] Psalm 119:129

redemption, salvation of man wonderfully declared in the holy Scriptures: the inward frame and disposition of man's heart, his secret thoughts and most intimate projects, his reserved wishes, desires, ends, and purposes undeniably discovered for his conviction, even to admiration and amazement (1 Corinthians 14:25). Then the reason of man is even confounded, the obstinacy of man's heart subdued, all the pride of human glory stained, and the Scriptures appear to be the word of God.

But now all these arguments and many more which I could name, will not be effectual for our regeneration and conversion, until the Spirit be pleased to set all home upon the heart by his own irresistible efficacy, and seal this truth to the conscience by his own infallible testimony. But when the Spirit speaks to and works upon our spirits, then we do assent and consent to all the proposals of God, our very thoughts are captivated and subdued unto the obedience of Christ (2 Corinthians 10:5).[465] Our conscience is convinced swayed and undeniably obliged to believe what is promised, allow what is commanded, our will made willing to choose both, the affections to embrace both, our whole man to follow after both according to the directions of God for performing what is commanded, and obtaining of what is promised (Romans 7:12, 22, Psalm 119:106, 112-113, 127-128, 167, 173-174).

I must acknowledge my absolute total and universal dependence upon the infallible wisdom, infinite truth, power, majesty, greatness, and goodness of the Holy Spirit, and confess that he has sovereign right and divine authority to reveal and prescribe whatsoever he pleases upon the rewards and

---

[465] Vide Scholasticos de dono Discernendi credenda à non credendis. Lombard. lib. 3. dist. 34. Bonavent. sent. l. 3. d. 34. qu. 1. Argentin. Ib. Aquin. secund. q. 8. a 4. q. 9 a. 1. Parisiës. de Legibus cap. 21. Gerson. de exam. Doct. p. 1. con. 6. Mirandul. de fide & ordine credendi. Vide Sententiarios passim de Dono intellectus, Scientiae, & Consilii.

penalties of everlasting life and death.[466] And I am obliged to believe and embrace all that the Spirit teaches without any contradiction, though it seem never so improbable to my carnal reason, and be really contrary to my corrupt affections, ends, and designs. The Spirit teaches me how to apprehend and judge of spiritual things after a spiritual manner, for the Spirit teaches me what to approve, and what I should disallow (Philippians 1:9-10, 19). I must choose what the Spirit approves, and then prosecute what I have chosen with care, hope, desire, and embrace what I attain to with love and delight, and in a word rest satisfied with the love of the Father, the grace of the Son, and the communion of the Spirit, as my all-sufficient and satisfactory portion forevermore (Psalm 17:15, Psalm 63:5).[467]

Faith is that grace which enables and inclines us upon the divine testimony of the Spirit to depend on Christ for righteousness and life according to the tenor of the covenant of grace. The divine testimony of the Spirit is the true ground of justifying faith; but historical faith which may be in devils (James 2) and temporary faith which may be in reprobates (Luke 8) are not truly grounded on the testimony, wisdom, authority revelation, or demonstration of the Spirit.[468]

We read of a revelation of flesh and blood (Matthew 16:17), and the demonstration and revelation of the Spirit (1 Corinthians 2:4, 10, 14-15, Ephesians 1:17). A man who has nothing but sense and reason in him may have a historical or a temporary faith; but he who does upon the divine testimony of the Spirit believe that Jesus is the Christ, he is born of God, of

---

[466] Theologia est doctrina supernaturalis divinâ revelatione, non scientifica demonstratione tradita. Johan. 9. 29 Johan. 5. 47. Spiritus Prophetis & Apostolis imo & sibi ipsi in eis testimonium perhibuit. Vide Hen. Gandaveni. Sum. part. 1. ar. 9. q. 3. Greg. Homil. 19. in Ezek. Aug. Tract. 3. in Ep. Johan. Hilar. lib. 2. de Trin. prope. finem, & p. 174.
[467] Psalm 16:7
[468] Vide Origen. 4. [δει αρχών]. Simplicitas nec non majestas summa Evangelii cum efficacia conjuncta Philosophos, reges, mundum vicit. Vide Aug. l. 13. contra Faustum. c. 5. Gandav. sum. part. 1. art. 9. Q. 3. Scotum. in. 3. Dist. 23. q. 1. Occham. p. 1. l. 1. c. 4. Aug. l. 1. contra Ep. Fundamenti c. 5. Whitta. Disp. de Sacra Script. Contr. 1. q. 3. c. 8. Mr. White's *Way to the Tree of Life*.

the Spirit of God, and "hath the witness in himself (1 John 5:1, 6, 10)." For the regenerate – and they only – have a spiritual understanding in them to know him that is true when he is revealed unto them by the Spirit of truth (1 John 5:20; 1 Corinthians 2:14-15, Deuteronomy 29:4).[469]

For the demonstration of the Spirit is not understood by us until we are renewed in the spirit of our mind, so that we can look upon the divine truths testified by the Spirit with a spiritual eye, and discern them after a spiritual manner (1 Corinthians 2:14). And therefore the testimony of the Spirit is not received but by our renewed spirits (Romans 8:16). Before we are regenerate, we receive divine truths only because we judge them reasonable, or because we find them in the Scriptures, and we believe the Scriptures upon a human testimony, and therefore only with a human, not a divine faith.[470] But the spiritual man believes all upon the testimony of the Spirit, and does constantly beg the direction of the good Spirit. "O thy Spirit is good," says David, "teach me, lead me, quicken me by thy Spirit (Psalm 143:10-11)."

Finally, this good Spirit discovers to a man before he believes [1] his want of Christ, [2] the worth of Christ. His want of Christ by reason of {1} his heinous sins which are inexcusable, damnable, {2} his spiritual wants which are innumerable, and {3} his present misery, and slavery, which are unspeakable, unsupportable.

The worth of Christ, because he is an all-sufficient Savior, and only Savior. The Spirit discovers the treasures of free grace, the mysteries of divine faith, which even angels admire, the unsearchable riches of Christ, the fullness of God, able to satiate the soul with heavenly, glorious, everlasting

---

[469] Vide Chrysostom. Homil. 57. in Johan. 9. [και ουν ειπαι ημεις ηχουσαμεν αλλα οτι οιδαμεν] Biel. 3. Sent dist. 23. qu. 2. art. l. Majus lumen in Scientiâ, majus robur in fide Spiritus rationem dirigit, voluntatem determinat, fidem infundit vide etiam Aqu. secundae qu. 2. art. 3. & pag. 1. qu. 1. Almain. in 3. sent. Dis. 24. qu. unica. August. lib. 3. contra Petil. cap. 6. & Retract. lib. 1. cap. 14. Chrysost. Homil. 46. ad. Pop. Antioch.

[470] Tam certo scimus novum instrumentum esse divinum ac Judaei sciebant vetus instrumentum esse Divinum. Joh. 9. 29. Joh. 5. 47. Joh. 5. 39.

happiness, and even infinite content. Then the soul is convinced by the Spirit of God, not only of the truth, but goodness of the Covenant made by God with man in Christ, and that there are better things laid up for believers in Christ than any are or can be bestowed by Satan upon his greatest agents, and dearest favorites, the darlings of the flesh and world, and upon this account the soul is persuaded by this demonstration of the spirit, to close with Christ, and deny itself, to have no ability, wisdom, righteousness, will of its own, but to seek wisdom, righteousness, sanctification, and redemption in Christ (1 Corinthians 1:30). In a word to deny its own will, and take the will of Christ for its rule and compass, to do or suffer anything for Christ, to lose or sell all for him.

The good Spirit persuades us: [1] to prize Christ highly, even above all the kingdoms of the world, and glory of them.[471] [2] To believe in Christ steadfastly. [3] To love Christ dearly, better than ourselves,[472] or dearest friends, better than worldly treasures, sensual joy, or any carnal contentments whatsoever. [4] To follow Christ fully, so that we may enjoy him eternally as our crown, our happiness, our heaven. And to this end and purpose to set up the word of God in our consciences as our only rule for to direct us:[473] {1} in all points of faith, {2} in all parts of worship, and {3} in all passages of our life and conversation, so that we may cast out the world, the devil, nay, flesh and self and all to make room for Christ.

Now when the Spirit has by his own evidence, testimony, authority, wisdom and efficacy wrought faith in the soul, to carry it into the arms of Jesus Christ, Christ bids it welcome,[474] embraces, kisses it, and takes this young believer by the hand,[475] and puts him into his Father's bosom.[476] And when we are thus brought to believe in Father, Son, and Holy Spirit, then

---

[471] Psalm 119:103, 111-112, 127-128, 140
[472] Philippians 3:8
[473] Psalm 73:26, 28
[474] Romans 5:2
[475] Ephesians 2:18
[476] John 14:6

we are fitted and prepared to worship and obey all three glorious persons as one God blessed forever. And therefore, I may now proceed to speak of the worship of all three, and then of our obedience to all three.

He takes the name of Father, Son, and Holy Spirit in vain, and does not make that holy use which he should of the titles, properties, works and ordinances of all three, who does not with knowledge, faith, reverence, sincerity and spiritual joy worship all three, for this is true gospel-worship. And therefore, I would entreat my reader diligently to consider what I have delivered in the fourth, and fifth chapters of this treatise concerning the divine nature, titles, properties, works of all three in order to worship for the glory of the thrice illustrious, and yet single Godhead. And then if he will study the scope of the first table of the holy law of God, and the substance of gospel-worship, he will acknowledge that everyone who believes in all three persons will find his faith obliging and inclining him to worship all three glorious persons as one God blessed forever.

[1] God the Father is to be worshiped under the gospel as the Father of our Lord Jesus Christ, and our Father in him. I have touched this point already, and because it is not much controverted by our grand enemies, I shall not insist long upon it.

All the knowledge of God which we gain by the Scriptures of truth is revealed to us on purpose for our direction in the worship of God.[477] We must not worship God according to our own devices, but according to that discovery which God has made of himself to us in his holy word,[478] not only in respect of his divine nature (as when our Savior says "God is a Spirit," and from thence concludes, that God is to be worshiped "in spirit and truth"), but in respect of the divine persons also.[479]

---

[477] See learned Mr. Randoll's great mystery of godliness.
[478] Dr. Downham on the Lord's Prayer
[479] Mr. Burroughs of Gospel-worship, and Gospel-conversation.

We are to worship God as a creator, as the first of causes, last of ends, best of beings, to whom we owe our being, and our well-being;[480] but we must worship God the Father as God, and look upon him as the Father of our Lord Jesus Christ, and as our Father reconciled to us in Christ. This is that worship which becomes the gospel,[481] and therefore we ought to worship God the Father considered after this evangelical manner, so that he may be glorified, and we moved and affected with those endearing expressions: "O God the Father of our Lord Jesus Christ, and our Father in him."

Such expressions as these do beget in us: {1} holy boldness mixed with reverence.[482] {2} Christian confidence: our Father will supply the wants of his children out of his rich treasure, for he commands heaven and earth. {3} Filial love, and cheerful obedience, which are even connatural to our new man upon due consideration of this sweet relation between God and us (Jeremiah 3:19). {4} A thankful acknowledgement of God's fatherly bounty, even unto admiration: "Behold what manner of love the Father hath bestowed upon us, that we should be called the sons of God (1 John 3:1)." Nay, "heirs of God (Romans 8:17).' What are we vile wretches, worms and no men, yea by reason of our filthiness, dogs, and devils, that we should be adopted into the family of God, married to the Son of God, and made co-heirs with the Lord of glory! When the spirit of a man is raised by such thankful acknowledgements unto a holy admiration, then it is brought into a gospel frame, and by such high and sweet thoughts of God's fatherly love and bounty fitted for filial and gospel worship.

But it will be said that the whole Trinity is our Father, and therefore all three persons are to be worshiped under that fatherly consideration, and in that dear relation. To this, I answer:

---

[480] Mr. Thomas Goodwin's *Triumph of Faith*

[481] Distinguendum est inter objectum considerationis, & objectum adorationis; inter objectum, adorationis materiale & formale. Pater enim quà Pater abstractà ratione Deitatis non est adorandus; ipsa enim Deitas est ratio formalis adorationis.

[482] Ephesians 3:12 παρρησιαν και την προσαγωγην εν πεποιθησει

(i) That when the word *Father* is attributed unto God essentially, though all creatures are excluded, yet all the three divine persons are included, because they are co-equal, they have one nature, will and worship; they are one and the same God, and they are one Father also in opposition to images (Jeremiah 2:27) and to saints (Isaiah 63:16): "Doubtless thou art our Father,[483] though Abraham be ignorant of us, and Israel acknowledge us not.[484] Thou O LORD art our Father, our Redeemer, thy name is from everlasting." And in opposition to all creatures (Matthew 23:9), and in the Lord's Prayer, Father, Son, and Holy Spirit are all called upon as our Father.

(ii) The word *Father* is sometimes taken personally, and attributed to a single person of the Godhead. More frequently, and more peculiarly to God the Father, who is the first principle of subsisting life (even in respect of his own natural and coessential Son, as has been proven at large in this treatise) and is to be reckoned first in order; and finally in regard of our adoption and the mysterious and divine economy and dispensation vouchsafed for the salvation of man; and yet these peculiar notions do not exclude the other persons from being God, as has been proven above in the fourth chapter, nor do they exclude them from being our Father in the common notion of Father in opposition to creatures and idols; nay all three persons have a fatherly care of us, and love to us, and therefore Christ is called our Father (Isaiah 9:6, Hebrews 2:13-14). And it is the proper office of the Holy Spirit to regenerate us, as it is of the Father to adopt us. But then the Father adopts us in Christ who is a Father to us, though a Son to God the Father, and the Holy Spirit is the Spirit of regeneration and adoption, and therefore all three coessential persons are our Father.

(iii) We may direct our prayers to any one person, as Stephen directed his to the Lord Jesus (Acts 7:59). "Lord Jesus, receive my Spirit."

---

[483] Deuteronomy 32:6
[484] Jeremiah 31:9

(iv) We may direct our Prayers expressly unto two of the divine persons. "Now God himself and our Father, and our Lord Jesus Christ direct our way unto you (1 Thessalonians 3:11)."

(v) We may direct our prayers unto all three, as we do in the administration of baptism, and in that fundamental benediction of 2 Corinthians 13:14.

(vi) When we direct our prayers to one of the divine persons, we exclude none, because the persons are in one another; the Father is in the Son, and they are all three coessential, coequal; They are one God, and therefore are to be worshiped with that self same religious and divine worship which is due to their single and undivided Godhead.

(vii) When we direct our prayer to the Father of our Lord Jesus Christ, the term *Father* is taken in a peculiar notion, not in the common notion, and the apostle directs his prayer after this peculiar manner in Ephesians 3:14-15: "For this cause I bow my knees unto the Father of our Lord Jesus Christ, of whom the whole family in heaven and earth is named." God the Father looks upon us poor worms as part of his family, nay, as his dear children whilst we are here on earth, as well as he looks upon his other children, the glorious saints, who are made perfect in heaven. Oh what a quickening consideration is this, to bring us upon our knees at a throne of grace before Christ's Father, and our Father, that we may have a child's portion, and be prepared for that place which Christ is now preparing for us! We are part of the family numbered amongst those of the best rank; we are children, and have the same Father that Christ and the saints in heaven have (John 20:17, Ephesians 3:14), and therefore shall come to be co-heirs with Christ and them. Here is heavenly encouragement unto gospel-worship, and gospel-conversation.[485]

It is no wonder then if that gospel-worship be frequently performed to God under this endearing consideration and in this sweet and comfortable

---

[485] 1 Timothy 1; 2 Timothy 1:2, Titus 1:4, Philemon 3, Romans 1:7

relation.[486] The apostle wishes us grace and peace from God our Father, and the Lord Jesus Christ in Romans 1:7, and in like manner in 1 Corinthians 1:3 and 2 Corinthians 1:2.[487] Observe that solemn form of thanksgiving. "Blessed be God, even the Father of our Lord Jesus Christ the Father of mercies, and the God of all comfort (2 Corinthians 1:3)."[488] Oh how willingly and cheerfully do we run to the God of all mercies and comfort in a time of temptation and affliction (2 Corinthians 1:4)![489] For the Father discovers his bowels of mercy on purpose to invite us to him. The Father himself loves you (John 16:27). All spiritual glorious eternal blessings, our election, redemption, salvation, are ascribed to this Father of all grace, mercy, comfort, glory. Christ redeems us according to the will of God and our Father (Galatians 1:4, John 10:17-18). "Blessed be the God and Father of our Lord Jesus, who hath blessed us with all spiritual blessings in heavenly things in Christ according as he hath chosen us (Ephesians 1:3, 4, 11)." Much more might be said to this purpose; but this may suffice. It is now time to proceed to my next point, which is that:

---

[486] 1 Corinthians 1:3
[487] 2 Corinthians 1:2, Colossians 1:3, Ephesians 1:2-3, Philippians 1:2, Colossians 1:2
[488] Colossians 1:2, Ephesians 1:2-3; 1 Thessalonians 1:2; 2 Thessalonians 1:2
[489] John 16:27; 1 Peter 1:3

(2) Divine worship is due to the second person of this coessential Trinity, to Jesus Christ our Lord and God.

There is but one immediate formal proper adequate and fundamental reason of divine worship or adorability (as the Schools speak) and that is the Sovereign supreme singular majesty, independent and infinite excellency of the eternal Godhead. There is a peculiar and singular esteem, faith, love, and worship due to Father, Son, and Holy Spirit, who are one God, the only true God. These three are the only object of religion, and therefore the only Object of religious adoration. There is but one kind of divine worship, and that worship and all degrees of it is due to this one God, Father, Son, and Holy Spirit; this truth is made good against the papists as well as against the Socinians, and divers others, whom I need not name, the Ubiquitists and Arminians, by a clear stating of the point in controversy, and invincible demonstrations to confirm the truth.

First, for the clear stating of this point, we must look a little into the rise of this controversy, and consider how far it has been discussed by learned men, and stated by such as are orthodox and prudent men, since the Socinians, Ubiquitists, and Arminians have endeavored to make the question more perplexed, and the truth more obscure.

(1) The papists are deeply engaged to prove that religious honor may be given to a creature, at least in some degree. Their distinctions are so well known that I need not insist upon them.[490] Cardinal Perron exceeds them all for sophistical distinctions, which he who is at leisure may read in Book 5 Chapter 20 of his answer to King James. But Smiglecius – being engaged against the Socinians, states the point rightly: he distinguishes between Christ's natural power as he is the natural and coessential Son of God, and his

---

[490] Cultus latriae, duliae & hyperduliae precatio est directa vel indirecta. Absoluta aut relativa; Suprema vel subalterna; transitoria velfinalis; oblatoria aut extra oblationem. Card. Perron. in responso ad Regem M. Britan. l. 5. c. 20. Smigl. de Monstris Arrianorum. c. 9. Vide sis Cajetanū, Suarez. Valent. in Thomam. part. 3. q. 25. art. 1. & 2.

delegated power which he has as mediator, and concludes that Christ is to be worshiped as he is the natural Son of God with divine worship, because his natural power is his divine nature. But, he says, Christ is not to be worshiped in the second consideration with divine worship. Doctor Rainolds, in his book *De Idololatria Romana*, has abundantly refuted all that the papists bring to excuse their idolatry, and proves clearly that it is idolatry to give religious honor to any creature. I shall not therefore trouble my reader with any set dispute upon that argument.

(2) The Socinians tell us that the Father is the only absolute, supreme, independent God, but Christ is a dependent and subordinate God, and therefore may be worshiped as he is mediator with a relative and subordinate worship, which they are not afraid to call divine worship.[491] But they confess that they worship the Father only as the supreme cause, the first efficient, and the last end. But they worship Christ as the second or middle cause of our salvation, and the intermediate end of religion. The ground and formal reason of this subordinate worship is (as they conceive) Christ's mediatory office, the new subordinate Godhead, and Lordship over us bestowed upon him for his obedience unto death, which they say, is the mediate, as his exaltation is the immediate, cause of this subordinate glory.[492]

(3) The Arminians – in their apology and other writings – endeavor to excuse and gratify the Socinians, for they deny that our grand argument taken from the divine honor and worship of Christ, sufficiently proves his nature to be divine, and Christ to be one God with his Father.[493] This argument, say they, is not invincible, and irrefragable, nay, they call it a leaden argument, because this divine honor is given to him by his Father's gratification in time.

---

[491] Vide Crellium de uno Deo Patre sect. 1. sect. 36, 37.
[492] Socin. de Adorat. Christi cum Christiano. Franken. & Fran.—Dav. & Antithes. Francisci—Davidis, Ostorod. Instit. cap. 10.
[493] Remonst. Apolog. c. 2. & 16. p. 153. Rhapsod. l. 1. c. 9.

(4) Some Lutherans are very much to blame in this point, for they say that the divine majesty, worship, glory, omnipotence, omnipresence of the Son of God are communicated to Christ as man – but enough of that.

(5) Several learned, orthodox, judicious doctors of the church have given the enemy too much advantage by their unwary expressions in this point, and the vigilant enemy has taken that advantage and made a very unhappy use of it, to the great prejudice of Christianity.[494] *Uno absurdo dato mille sequuntur; Error parvus in principio fit magnus in fine.* I do therefore entreat the most accurate and nice reader at his best leisure to read Junius, Chamier, Polanus, Polyander, Pareus, Cameron, Maccovius, Cluto, Beza, Heidan, Diest, Zanchius, Voetius, Altingius, and other late writers upon this point, who have observed every turn, ward, shift of the enemy, and have given a very fair account of all.

For the present state of the question be pleased seriously to consider these plain and weighty conclusions following.

(1) Divine excellency, infinite majesty, and perfection, are the formal and adequate ground and reason of divine worship.[495] For by divine worship we do acknowledge and declare the infinite majesty, truth, wisdom, goodness and glory of our blessed God. We do not esteem anything worthy of divine honor and worship which has but a finite and created glory; because divine honor is proper and peculiar to the only true God, who will not give his glory to any other who is not God. God alone is the adequate object of divine faith, hope, love, and worship, because these graces are all

---

[494] Securius locuti sunt viri gravissimi ante exor. tum Arrium, Nestorium Pelagium, &c. sic & nonnulli qui inter reveren dissimos merito recensentur ante enatas controversias Socinianas Remonstranticas, &c. Junius defens. Trinit. contra Samosat. p. 3. pag. 190. Exam. Grat. Prosp. part. 2. sect. 5. Chamier. tom. 2. l. 1. c. 4. Polan. Syntag. l. 2. c. 31. Polyand. prima concert contra Socin. c. 21. Paraeus Iren. c. 28. Method controv. ubi{que} c. 31. Camer. tom. 3. Praelect. pag. 173. Maccov. misc. q. 5. Disp. 35, 36, 37. Clut. Id. Disp. 3. 4. 40. Beza. Col. momp. part. 1. pag. 196, 197. Zanch. de 3. Elohim cap. 12. l. 1. Epist. 9. Voet. de Adorat. Christi.

[495] Roman. 1. 21. ad 25. Lactant. Instit. l. 1. c. 19. Si honos idem tribuitur aliis, ipse comnino non colitur, cujus religio est illum esse unum ac solum Deum credere.

exercised, and this worship performed in acknowledgement of his infinite perfection, and independent excellency, and therefore no such worship can be due to anything below God. But the most glorious and excellent creatures are all below God, and therefore that point is clear.[496]

(2) The Father, Son, and Holy Spirit are one and the same God, as has been proven in the fourth chapter of this treatise, and therefore one and the same worship is due to all three, because they are coessential, coequal, coeternal; they have one and the same divine nature, excellency, perfection, and essential glory; and therefore the same acknowledgement is due to all three both from men and angels.

There is not one kind of divine honor due to the Father, and another to the Son, nor one degree of honor due to the Father, and another to the Son; for there can be no degrees imaginable in one and the same excellency, which is single because infinite; and what is infinite excels and transcends all degrees and bounds. And if there are no degrees in the ground and adequate reason of divine worship, there can be no ground or reason of a difference of degrees in the worship itself.

The Father and Son are one (John 10:30): one in power, excellency, nature; one God, and therefore are to be honored with the same worship (John 5:23). All men should honor the Son, even as they honor the Father; every tongue must confess that Jesus Christ who is man, is God also, and therefore equal to his Father. And it can be no robbery, no derogation to the Father's honor for us to give equal honor to him, and his coequal Son, who subsists in the form of God, in the nature of God (Philippians 2:6, 11). You see the divine nature, the infinite excellency of Jesus Christ, is an undeniable ground of this coequal honor, and therefore the worship due to Christ as

---

[496] Cyprian. ad Fortunat. de exhort. mart. c. 2. Tertul. de Idol. c. 1. Idololatria Dei honorificentiam usurpat, & vendicat creaturae. Ambros. in Epist. ad Ephes. c. 5. Greg. Nyss Orat. in laudem Bas. mag. Gr. Naz. Orat. in Christi Nativit. Aquin. in Epist. ad Ephes. cap. 5. lect. 3.

God, the same God with his Father, is the very same worship both for kind and degree which is due to the Father.

(3) This divine honor was due to Jesus Christ, before there was any creature to give him his due. Christ was adorable, worshipable, that is worthy of divine worship before there was any man or angel to adore, to perform actual worship, that divine worship which was due to him for his infinite excellency from all eternity.[497]

(4) When Jesus Christ was declared to the world, God did command even the most glorious angels to worship him, as his natural and coessential Son, who was begotten from the days of eternity in the unity of the Godhead. "For when he brought in his first-begotten, and only begotten Son into the world, he said, and let all the angels of God worship him (Hebrews 1:6)."

(5) If man had never fallen, never stood in any need of Christ's blood, yet all men would have worshiped the natural and coessential Son of God, as one and the same God with his Father, and therefore with the same divine worship as soon as his Godhead had been sufficiently revealed to them from heaven, or else that very neglect would have been their fall and ruin.

(6) The office of Christ, his discharge of his office, by his active and passive obedience, and glorious benefits which we receive thereby, are excellent motives to excite us to give that divine worship to Jesus Christ, which is due unto him for his own infinite excellency, but his infinite excellency is the formal, proper and adequate ground, reason and cause of all the divine worship which we perform to Jesus Christ, and that for these reasons:

---

[497] Adorabilitas est Attributum Dei absolutū, sive essentialis proprietas. Adoratio autem supponit aliquam creaturae actionem. Deus sine Adorabilitate non est Deus, fuit autem Deus ab aeterno sine actuali adoratione. Vide Zanchium lib. 1. de incarnatione. Voetium qu. An Christus quà mediator sit adorandus.

[1] Because if man had never fallen, and Christ had never died for man's redemption, this divine worship would have been due unto him for his infinite and eternal excellency, as has been proven.

[2] Because the Father and the Spirit are not mediators as Christ is, and that office which is not common to all three persons cannot be the prime, immediate, proper, formal cause, ground or reason of that divine honor and worship which is due to all three as one God blessed forever; nay, no office whatsoever can be the proper cause of divine honor.[498]

[3] Because this divine honor was due to Jesus Christ from all eternity, before his incarnation, passion, etc., and therefore this divine honor is not bestowed upon him as a reward of his active or passive obedience, for no worship or thing can be before its formal cause.[499]

[4] Because Jesus Christ is a mediator according to both natures. Therefore according to his human nature as well as his divine nature; but all the honor due to Christ according to his divine nature was due from all eternity, and there is no divine honor due to him for and by reason of his human nature, or any perfection which truly and properly belongs to Christ as man. He who was born of Mary, is to be adored with divine worship, but not for that reason, because he was born of Mary, but because he is God, the coessential and eternal Son of God. We must distinguish between the material and formal object of worship.[500]

---

[498] Unicum tantum est Religionis & religiosae Adorationis objectum, unus nempe verus Deus, Pater Filius & Spiritus Sanct. Vide Molin. in novitate Papis. Riv. Dec. ad pri. Praecept.

[499] Omnis Ratio Formalis in Objecto naturâ prior est omni actione in objectum illud tendente: passio Christi autem posterior est Adorabilitate, imò & ipsa adoratione filii Dei.

[500] Maturam humanam assumpsit persona divina, & divinae suae naturae univit; manet itaque unica Christi persona duabus constans naturis. Totam Christi personam itaque adoramus, non totum Personae; natura enim assumpta est creatura: totum Personae duas Christi naturas significat.

{1} The material object of worship is Christ, who is both God and man, the son of David, the son of Mary, the Son of God, the mediator and savior of his people from their sins.

{2} The formal object discovers to us the prime formal adequate ground and reason of his divine worship: the coessential and eternal Son of God, who is one and the same God with the Father and the Holy Spirit – he is worshiped for his infinite and divine excellency.[501] Christ is worshiped as God with this divine worship; his mediatory office, servile suffering, cannot be the prime and immediate foundation, the ultimate and terminating object of divine worship due to the Father, Son, and Holy Spirit. Therefore, we must conclude that the formal and proper reason of the divine worship due and given to Jesus Christ our mediator, is the divine nature and infinite excellency of our mediator, which alone is of itself and for itself capable of divine worship. I should make a tedious digression if I should declare what great Cyril of Alexandria, noble Athanasius, the Ephesian Council of old, and very learned and accurate writers of late have delivered upon this argument with great dexterity and circumspection. They would not be mistaken as if they did divide the two natures of Christ, or remove any glorious adjuncts from the eternal Word, the second person of the Godhead; and yet desire you to put a difference between that which Christ assumed by the most free decree of God, and grace of hypostatic union, And that which belongs to him as he is one God with the Father and the Holy Spirit.

Finally, they entreat you to put a difference between the gracious motives to worship Christ, and the prime, formal, adequate proper ground and reason of that worship, as I have done, and profess that they worship

---

[501] Vide Cl. DD. Prof. Leidens. in Censura Confess. Remonstr. cap. 16. In adoratione objectum Formale & causa propria seu Terminus (ut Scholae loquūtur) est divina tantum natura quae hujus cultus per se tantum est capax. Vide Cyrilli Thesaur. de Incarnat. Unig. c. 26. l. 2. in Joh. c. 92. Athan. contra Arrianos Orat. 5. Dialog. 3. Humanitas Christi non adoratur καθ' ἑαυτόν nec δι ἑαυτόν. Adoratio Mediatoris non resolvitur ultimò in munus Mediatorium sed in Deitatem. Vide Professor. Leid. ubi supra. cap. 16. D. Voetium de Adorat, Christi. p. 536. Pareum Irenic. cap. 28. Cyrill. ad Theodos; de recta fide lib. 1.

their whole mediator with one entire worship which is not mixed but purely divine, and therefore is not founded upon any temporary office, service, benefit, nor any external denomination or relation, but upon his infinite excellency, his eternal Godhead.

And if these considerations will not give men satisfaction, I hope to satisfy them farther yet before I conclude this chapter.[502] For the point is very clear and plain to me. If Jesus Christ were worshiped as mediator, so that his mediatory office or actual mediation should be laid as the first foundation, or assigned as the formal reason of our worship, then this fourth argument – which I am still improving and enforcing for the proof of the point – will plainly discover that the mediation of Christ having respect to the human nature, and will make the human nature at least in part the ground, reason and cause of this divine worship, which I leave to all sober divines to consider, before they admit.

And it is further to be considered that Jesus Christ as mediator condescends to an office and employment which subjects him to God as a head: "the head of Christ is God" (1 Corinthians 11:3).[503] And hence it is that he is called "the servant of God," in respect of that service which he was to perform as mediator (Isaiah 42:1-4). Nothing is more clear than that there are some offices to be performed by Christ as a mediator, which cannot be performed by Christ as God, because they do import some subjection, as prayer unto God does, though it is true that Christ being the natural Son of God intercedes after an authoritative manner. We may for the further clearing of this point resolve that grand question, what the meaning of that request is, when we say "Lord Jesus, pray for me," the great doubt is whether this request be presented to Christ as God, or as man.

---

[502] Zan. de. 3. Elohim. l. 3. cap. 12.

[503] Vide Chamier. Panstrat. Tom. 2. lib. 1. c. 4 Junius Defens. 2. de S. Trinitate Sect. 7. pag. 88, 89 Christus est aequalis Patri secundum Deitatem personamque divinam, Christus ut θεάνθρωπος lecundum voluntariam gratiae dispensationem Patri subjectus est—& pag. 100. propter certas causas se ultrò demiserit salvo naturali jure ut Dispensative inferius regnum procuret per gratiam.

The answer is, that if we look upon this petition as a duty performed by us, this duty of prayer is directed unto Jesus Christ as God, for all divine worship is due to God alone, as has been proven.[504] But if we look not upon the duty of prayer, but the matter of this prayer, it is clear that the business which we recommend to Christ is to be performed by him as man. For it is proper to him as man to pray to the Father; yet because we desire him to intercede in an authoritative way to the Father, we do likewise request him to intercede as it becomes the natural and coessential Son of God. And therefore if we look upon the whole business of intercession, we conclude that he intercedes θεανδρικῶς, as it becomes God-man; because he is our mediator according to both natures, divine and human. But then we must remember to reserve what is proper and peculiar to each nature, for though we grant that there is a communication of all properties belonging to both natures unto the person of Christ, yet we must not attribute anything to the human nature which is proper and peculiar to the divine. And it has been undeniably proved that divine worship is proper and peculiar to the divine nature.

[5] The office of our mediator has a special respect to God's chosen people by God's most free decree, but the relation and external denomination arising from thence cannot be the prime, fundamental and immediate ground, formal reason, or adequate cause of divine worship. For if Christ had not been God, he could not have been capable of that office, because nothing could satisfy the justice of God but the blood of God, and whatever arises from the free decree of God, was not necessary in itself, but sure I am, divine worship must be founded upon what is absolutely necessary

---

[504] Vide D. Voetium de Adoratione Christi pa. 5 36. Distingue ipsam Petitionem Formaliter ut est actus noster, à repetitâ. Petitio dirigitur ad personam Mediatoris & ea terminatur in quâ Deitas habet se ut Ratio Formalis illius tendentiae seu motus cordis nostri in Christum. Res Petita est actio Christi Mediatoris qua mediatoris, agenda sc. secundum naturam humanam quae est Immediatum precationis subjectum.

and infinitely perfect, and therefore not upon external relations or denominations, but upon the Godhead itself.

[6] The actual mediation of Christ cannot be the prime and fundamental ground of divine worship, for Christ was not only worshipable, but worshiped with divine honor before he did actually mediate as God-man.

[7] The office of our mediator is to bring us to himself, his Father, and Holy Spirit as to one God blessed forever, in whom all our blessedness consists; and therefore our faith does not rest simply and finally in Christ as he is our mediator, God and man, but as he is one God with the Father and the Holy Spirit. For by the ministry and mediation of Christ as God-man, we are brought to believe in God, that our faith and hope might be in God (1 Peter 1:21). Christ is God by nature, he is mediator by institution, by a voluntary and gracious dispensation unto which he did condescend for our salvation.[505] Upon this account, learned Junius told the subtle Samosatenian, that Jesus Christ as mediator brings us to himself as God. And Doctor Voetius says that Christ as mediator is an inferior cause, in whose name, and by whose mediation we make towards God our chiefest good, in whom we believe, and whom we do worship and adore as the first cause and last end (John 14:6). And Christ is said to save them to the uttermost by his intercession who come unto God by him (Hebrews 7:25).

"We worship Christ and pray unto him," says judicious Pareus, "as one God with the Father and the Spirit the only true God, and this worship is absolute and divine; for it is the absolute worship of the Godhead. But then we call upon God in the name of Christ, because he is our mediator, and we

---

[505] Christus est Deus Naturâ, Mediator autē instituto O eco nomico, & dispensatione voluntaria. Nemo igitur Deum Patrem adit fine mediatore: ac ne Christum quidem, cum idem sit Mediator & Deus. Junius de S. Trinitate Defens. 2. pag. 114. D. Voet. De Adoratione Christi pag. 5 29. Christus non est objectum Formale fidei qua Mediator, non est primum Efficiens, & ultimus finis,—sed est causa inferior, tum Procataractica, seu meritoria, tum Instrumentalis & hac ratione collator bonorum, in cujus nomine, per quem & propter quem tendimus in summum bonum, Deum sel. inque eum credimus, in eum speramus, eum colimus & adoramus. Joh. 14. 6. Pareus in Method. Controv. ubique cap. 31.

desire to be heard for the satisfaction and intercession of that person who is God-man."⁵⁰⁶

But the Socinians conclude that if Christ is not to be worshiped with divine honor as mediator, then there is only a subordinate honor and worship due unto him.

To which we answer that Christ may be considered in four manner of ways:

{1} According to his Godhead and divine person, and it has been proven at large in this treatise, that there is divine honor due unto the Godhead and divine person of Jesus Christ, and this is his essential infinite glory.

{2} Christ may be considered as mediator according to both natures, as God-man (by a gracious condescension and personal union), and so we say there is a mediatory glory due unto him, which is more illustrious in regard of its manifestation since the alteration of his condition from a state of humiliation to a state of exaltation.⁵⁰⁷ This glory outshines all the glory of saints and angels in heaven, but it is different from that natural and essential glory which is common to Father, Son, and Holy Spirit, as one God. For that essential glory cannot be communicated to the human nature – no, not since its assumption and Christ's exaltation.

This mediatory honor is very glorious, because Christ sits as a king at the right hand of the majesty on high, and everyone must confess that our royal mediator is not only man but God also; yet we must acknowledge that since the exaltation of our king, the glory of his divine nature, his essential glory, is only more manifested whereas it was eclipsed before in the state of

---

⁵⁰⁶ It was not immediately obvious from Cheynell's original 1650 edition where Pareus' quote ended.

⁵⁰⁷ Proprietates utriusque naturae toti Personae in concreto verè competunt. Filius hominis, qui est persona duabus constans naturis est omnipraesens, aeternus, adorabilis, adorandus, nempe secundum naturam divinam cujus haec sunt idiomata. Adoramus Deitatem incarnatam, ipsa autem Deitas est proprium & Absolutum divinae adorationis objectum.

humiliation; and the human nature assumed is only more perfected and not transubstantiated into the divine. The human nature is still a creature, though it has gained as much glory as it is capable of by the Grace of personal union, and glory of exaltation; and being a creature cannot be capable of divine and infinite perfection, which is the formal object of divine adoration – even as the divine nature of our mediator notwithstanding the personal union, is not capable of any human imperfection.[508] For there is a preservation and distinction of the two natures, notwithstanding their intimate and inseparable union in one person. The natures are united, ἀδιαιρέτως as the Greek church of old.[509]

The actions performed by our royal mediator flow from a double principle in this single person, because this person consists of two natures, and each nature performs its proper work. The divine nature does what is divine, and the human nature what is human. And therefore, though the person be but one, and the effect one, yet there are two different actions of two different natures united in one person that produce one and the same glorious effect, and we are to give to each nature what is properly due unto it.

Finally, the kingdom which is administered by our royal mediator God-man, in a glorious way is but a dispensatory kingdom, not his natural kingdom, an inferior and temporary kingdom, not his sovereign essential eternal kingdom; and therefore even in the very administration of it our mediator God-man, is in respect of order, and that gracious dispensation unto which he condescended for our salvation, employed in a kind of Subordinate way; and when he has accomplished that work for which he

---

[508] Humanitati Christi nec per μέθεξιν, nec per [ουδαχοῦ] communicata sunt Idiomata divina, quia Idiomata divina sunt ipsissima Deitas; humanitas autem Christi non fit Deitas Christi nec per gratiam unionis, nec per gloriam exaltationis. Humana enim natura charismata accepit gloriosa, non Idiomata divina. Vide Wendilin. Christian. Theolog. lib. 1. cap. 16. Smiglec. de monstris Novorum Arian. lib. 1. cap. 9. Polan. Syntag. lib. 2. cap. 31. Agit Christus secundum Humanitatem ut instrumentum assumptum in unitatem Personae. Iunius de Trinitate.

[509] Here Cheynell uses several Greek terms including ἀδιαιρέτως: without division.

undertook this royal office, he will refine this dispensatory kingdom, and become subject (as man, and as head of that body which he has purchased) to his Father, himself, and the Holy Spirit, as one God blessed forever, that God may be all in all (1 Corinthians 15:28). For as we are Christ's, so Christ is God's (1 Corinthians 3:23) in that safe sense and subordinate way which we have but even now declared, that the divinity of Christ (which humbled, and as it were emptied itself in the administration of this subordinate, temporary and dispensatory kingdom, yet with the preservation of its natural and eternal right) may be more gloriously manifested by the full possession, use, and enjoyment of that natural, divine, eternal kingdom, which belongs to Father, Son, and Holy Spirit. For all three coessential and coequal persons reign with the same power, majesty, and glory in the unity of the divine essence and common acts, in all, and over all, infinitely and immutably from everlasting, to everlasting;[510] although the natural reign of Jesus Christ will not be so fully and gloriously manifested until he has resigned his dispensatory kingdom, and brought all his elect, notwithstanding all their wants, sins, infirmities, temptations, trials, enemies, safe to heaven.

This dispensatory kingdom is administered principally by the Godhead, instrumentally by the manhood, absolutely and perfectly by the person of Christ acting in a divine way as God, and human way as man, that the properties of each nature may be reserved as peculiar to each, even whilst he mediates reigns, and judges according to both, and therefore divine honor is still reserved as proper and peculiar to the divine nature of our mediator, who is God-man in one person. This definite and dispensatory kingdom is

---

[510] Judicium respectu vario commune est Sanctae Trinitatis & Christi singulare. Commune respectu communis principij agentis, Patris, Filij & Spiritus Sancti; singulare autem respectu Christi; 1. Respectu Principalis termini secundùm naturam divinam illius. 2. Respectu naturae humanae ut Instrumenti adunati in unitatem Personae (ut ita dicam) singularissimum. Iun. de Trinitate, pag. 98, 99. Agit enim utraque forma cum alterius Communione quod proprium est, verbo scilicet operante quod verbi est, & carne exequente quod carnis est. Leo. Epist. 10. ad Flavianum. Utraque natura suum confert; divina quod divinum, & humana quod humanum est. Wendelinus.

changeable, terminable; it did begin with the first foundation, and will end with the perfection of the church of God.

Christ was a mediator from all eternity in the decree of God.[511] He was actually given to be a mediator as soon as necessity required,[512] he was manifested in the flesh in the fullness of time,[513] and will cease to be a king in this mediatory and dispensatory kingdom when he has finished his work,[514] and saved his church.[515] Now nothing is more clear than this: that Christ is now subject to his Father in all respects, in which he shall be declared to be subject when he gives up his dispensatory kingdom; and we are not to worship Jesus Christ with divine worship as he is subject to his Father, but as he is equal to his Father, as he is indeed one God with his Father and the Holy Spirit.[516]

{3} Christ may be considered as head of that body unto which he has united himself, and which he has purchased with his dearest blood; and so we know Christ the head, and his body the church make up one Christ mystical. The glory of Christ as a head is exceedingly great, and is excellently described in Ephesians 1:20-23. Christ is set at God's own right hand in heavenly places "far above all principality, power, and might, and dominion, and every name that is named not only in this world, but also in that which is to come. And hath put all things under his feet, and gave him to be the head over all things to the church, which is his body, the fullness of

---

[511] Ephesians 1:5-6
[512] Genesis 3:15, Revelation 13:8
[513] Galatians 4:4-5
[514] 1 Corinthians 15:28, 25
[515] Galatians 4:4-5
[516] πᾶσα ἐξουσία est Apotelesma Personale Mediatoris Mat. 28. 18, 19. collat. cum Marc. 16. 15, 16. & est potestas subordinata Act. 2. 36. 1 Cor. 15. 25, 27. Act. 5. 31. πασα δυναμις Sive Omnipotentia est proprietas essentialis Dei. Vide Dr Alting. Licet Pater major est donantis auctoritate, tamen filius minor non est cui unum cum Patre esse donatut. Hilarius lib 9. de Trinitate, Pater Filio tantum donat esse, quantus ipse est. Idem.

him that filleth all in all."⁵¹⁷ Now Christ mystical – the head and body, the whole Christ mystical – is to be subjected to God, when the mediatory and dispensatory kingdom is resigned; and therefore if you take Christ as the apostle does (1 Corinthians 12:12) for the head and body, for Christ mystical, we say that head and members are to be subject to Father, Son, and Holy Spirit, as one God blessed forever.⁵¹⁸

{4} Christ may be considered according to his human nature. And we are bold to say that there is an eminent and transcendent glory vouchsafed to the human nature of Christ by the grace of personal union, and the glory of its exaltation. The glory of Christ's divine nature was more manifested, but the human nature of Christ was fully perfected by his exaltation; and therefore the human nature was exalted in a peculiar sense. No nature, not the nature of the most glorious angel, was ever so highly preferred in these two respects:⁵¹⁹

(i) In respect of personal union with the Godhead (Acts 2:36).

(ii) In respect of royal mediation between God and man, none but Christ the son of Mary was ever so highly honored as to be taken into the society, and fellowship of the mediatory office with the Son of God.⁵²⁰ For there is but one mediator between God and men, the man Christ Jesus (1

---

⁵¹⁷ Quoties Christi nomen inter argumentandum producitur duplex fallacia cavenda est. 1. Vna utrum de Personâ Christi agatur in se an vero in mysterio.

⁵¹⁸ Altera si de Personâ Christi agatur inse, utrum secundum totum Personae, an vero secundum hanc aut illam naturam. Jun. de Trinitate pag. 101. Vide D. Alting. Loc. com. part. 2. de communicatione Proprietatum. Caput & corpus unus sunt Christus. Aug. Christus ille mysticus ex personâ Christi velut capitis omnia ανακεφαλαιωσαντος & corpore Ecclesiae per οπισυναγωγιω Christi in ipsum adunato constans subjicietur Patri. Junius.

⁵¹⁹ Vide D. Alting. loc. com. part. 2 de communicatione proprietatum, nec non Wendelinum. Nec honorem a nobis Deus nisi per Deum accipit, &c. Hilarius de Trinitate. l. 5

⁵²⁰ Christus humanitatem non a naturâ habuit ab aeterno quia Filius Dei est, sed ex voluntate assumpsit ad dispensationem salutis nostrae; atque haec humanitas non in se proprie gloriam divinam habet, sed in personâ ex unionis gratiâ: in se vero divinae proximam ex habituali gratiâ, Angelorumque gloriam longissimè superantem. Gloria itaque humanitatis est habitualis & dispensativa per personalis unionis gratiam. Vide Iunium de S. Trinitate Defens. 2. pag. 69, 98, 99, 100, 101, 102.

Timothy 2:5), who is God as well as man. *Nec honorem a nobis Deus nisi per Deum accipit.*

But it is most evident that the human nature remains a creature still even after its assumption, and exaltation, and therefore we hold fast our first conclusion: that the divine and infinite excellency of the coessential Son of God is the prime and fundamental ground, the formal reason and cause of that divine worship which is due to our mediator Jesus Christ – Jesus Christ our only Savior by doctrine, merit and efficacy, by confirmation and communication.[521]

True it is, that the majesty of God considered in itself is terrible,[522] it is a light not to be approached unto, and therefore the Word was made man, that we might have encouragement to come unto God[523] – not only by the mediation of a man full of grace and truth, but by the mediation of him who is God blessed forever, because a mere man, though free from corruption, and filled with grace could not by reason of such natural infirmities as are not sinful, perform the office of a foundation, head, and spouse in upholding,[524] quickening and preserving of his church (Acts 20:28, Ephesians 1:23 and 1 Thessalonians 1:10, Hebrews 9:14-15).

That Jesus Christ and the Holy Spirit are one and the same eternal God with the Father, has been proven at large in this treatise, and therefore divine honor and worship is due to Christ and the Holy Spirit as well as to the Father himself, because all three are coessential, coequal, and coeternal.

---

[521] Christus est servator confirente Socino.

[522] 1. Annunciatione quia est Propheta.

[523] 2. Confirmatione vitae inculpatae exemplo, miraculis, passione, nec non resurrectione.

[524] 3. Communicatione, quia credentibus pro data sibi potestate vitam aeternam communicat. Nos autem, ulterius agnoscimus Christum servatorem nostrum esse, 1. Merito, quia pro peccatis nostris Deo satisfecit, nobisque remissionem peccatorum, justitiam & vitàm aeternam acquisivit. 2 Efficaciâ dando fidem, resipiscentiam, remissionem, effundendo spiritum, donando vitam aeternam. Merito ut Sacerdos, efficaciâ ut Rex. Heb. 10. 12. Act. 2. 36, Act. 5 31.

When the seven electors of the empire met at Frankfurt about the election of Maximilian II,[525] some of them, being strict Protestants, went out of the place of worship when the mass began, because they would not be present at that idolatrous service, but came in again when they sang "Come Holy Spirit, eternal God." We being then convinced by clear Scriptures that Christ and the Holy Spirit are one and the same God with the Father, we must glorify all three persons as one God blessed forever.

(1) We must not do any divine service to them who are not gods by nature (Galatians 4:8).[526] But the three divine persons have the self-same divine nature, and therefore the very same divine worship and service both for kind and degree is due to all three coessential persons. We must not conceive otherwise of God than he has revealed himself in his Word, for then we shall not worship the true God, but a mere fantastical idol of our own brain. "Ye worship ye know not what," says Christ of the Samaritans (John 4:22). The Samaritans served their own gods, who were not gods by nature, but false gods. 2 Kings 17:29:33.

(2) Nor must we give Father, Son, and Holy Spirit the only true God, any other kind of worship than what is prescribed in his Word. Israel is said to be without the true God when they were without the law, without a priest to teach them how to worship God according to his law 2 Chronicles 15:3 reads: "Now for a long season Israel has been without the true God, and without a teaching priest, and without law." The divine kind of worship prescribed both in law and gospel is spiritual worship (Mark 12:33, Hebrews 12:28, Psalm 51:6, 16, Deuteronomy 6:5, 1 Corinthians 5:8, 1 Chronicles 28:9, Philippians 3:3, John 4:23-24).

(3) The worship of God is either natural or instituted worship. The instituted worship has been changed, for it was different before the law, under the law, and under the gospel. But the natural worship and service of

---

[525] Vide Hist. de Maxim. 2. in Rom. Regem. Elect. hist. Simonii Schardi. Tom. 3.
[526] Galatians 4:8; 1 Thessalonians 1:9-10, Acts 5:59; 2 Corinthians 13:14, Matthew 28:19

God is perpetual and eternal, it is to be continued in heaven, both by saints and angels for evermore.

Natural worship is due to Jesus Christ and the Holy Spirit, because they have one and the self-same divine nature with God the Father. angels are called upon to give this natural worship to Jesus Christ. And let all the angels of God worship him (Hebrews 1:6).

(4) Instituted worship is subservient, as I may so speak to this natural worship, for when we worship God with those mean helps and actions which he himself has appointed and ordained, we must worship him in spirit and truth. All ordinances of Christ are means of grace to beget knowledge, faith, hope, love, self-denial, gratitude, humility, sincerity, reverence, zeal, and all other graces in the soul, and to increase them in us, that we may exercise all these graces upon every opportunity, and give God that natural, spiritual, divine honor, which is due unto his singular majesty, infinite excellency, independent perfection, and eternal Godhead, in knowing, esteeming, admiring, believing, loving, obeying God that our souls may be delighted and satisfied with God as the chiefest good, as the crown of all our joys; an all-sufficient portion of our souls for evermore.

This is the full scope of the first table of the law, and this is the sum of the gospel. If the first table of the law did discover to us: [1] the object of worship, [2] the means of worship, [3] the time of worship; and did not also prescribe, require, enjoin [4] the manner of worship, we should be at a loss: the law would not be a perfect rule. Our worship would not be agreeable to the nature and will of God; God would be defrauded of his natural spiritual divine worship. Therefore, when our Savior delivers the full scope of all the four first commandments by reducing them to one commandment, he says, "Thou shalt love the Lord thy God with all thy heart, with all thy soul, and with all thy mind, this is the first and great commandment (Matthew 22:37-38, Deuteronomy 6:4-5)." This spiritual worship is taught us in every commandment of the first table, if we look upon the inside and spiritual compass of those commandments discovered to us by Moses, the Psalms, prophets, and the New Testament.

[1] In the first commandment, we are not barely required to take God for the object of our worship, but to give him spiritual worship also, because we are required in mind, heart, will, affection and the effects of all these to take the true God – Father, Son, and Holy Spirit; God in Christ by the assistance of the Spirit – to be our God, to know, esteem, admire, trust, love, reverence, adore, and serve him with hope, humility, self-denial, patience, joy and thankfulness, zeal, and constancy.[527] This is the inside and spiritual compass of the first commandment.

[2] In the second commandment, we are required to worship God purely according to his will in every ordinance, without any carnal imagination or affections. The papists will grant that we are by the use of ordinances (and as they dream images also) to carry our hearts to God and Christ in obedience to the second commandment.[528] The more learned papists will confess that it is a sin against the first commandment to terminate our worship in any image,[529] because no image is Jehovah.[530] But they worship images relative (though not terminative) as visible helps to devotion to carry their hearts to God in worship;[531] and it is clear that the Jews and heathens of old intended no more. Therefore, there is as much to be said for heathen and Jewish as there is for Romish idolatry.[532]

---

[527] The spiritual compass of the first commandment: Isaiah 43:10, Deuteronomy 4:39, Jeremiah 24:7, Micah 7:18, Psalm 89:6; 2 Chronicles 20:20, Deuteronomy 6:5, Matthew 10:37, Romans 15:30, Psalm 2:11, Revelation 5; 1 Thessalonians 5:17, Psalm 43:4.

[528] Deuteronomy 4:15-18, 23-24

[529] Isaiah 40:17-18, 25

[530] Acts 17:29

[531] Quam siguram ponetis ei qui Spiritus est. Hier. in Isa. c. 40.

[532] Vide Dr. Rainold de Idololatriâ l. 2. Mr Shepheard in his Treatise of the morality of the Sabbath. Mr. Ball's larger catechism. Bishop Jewel's apology. Aug. contra Manich. lib. 20. c. 5. Chrys. in Epist. 1. ad Cor. Hom. 20. What is meant by love and hatred of God in the second commandment.

This then is the great sin of the Antichristian worshippers at Rome (who endeavor to defend this relative worship of images): that they conceive, that the heart of man will be better carried to God and Christ by human inventions (such as images, crucifixes, relics, etc.) than by divine institutions – and this sin is called a hatred of God in the second commandment.

And in the very letter of this commandment, we are directed how to express our love to God, namely, by seeking of him, and closing with him in his own ordinances, and institutions with an ingenuous contempt of human inventions in divine worship, and service. Though legal ordinances are not only changeable, but actually changed and abolished; yet there is something moral and unchangeable in this second commandment, which is attendance upon, and observance of the institutions and appointments of God.

It is an immutable law that we should give God that worship which is due unto him, express our faith in him, and love to him by a spiritual use of such means and ordinances as he himself should from time to time appoint. The due acknowledgement of God's immensity and infinite majesty in our attendance on the instituted means of worship is clearly opposed to the image-worship in Isaiah 40 and Romans 1, and therefore the inside and compass of this second commandment is spiritual, though the words of it are so comprehensive as to take in ceremonial as well as evangelical worship. For reverend divines have made it clear, that though the second commandment be moral in regard of its substance and general nature which contains the immutable law above mentioned, yet in regard to its particular application to those significant ceremonies, sacrifices and sacraments which God did appoint, we say, all ceremonial institutions are referred unto, and comprehended under the second moral commandment of God. See Mr. Shepherd in his excellent treatise of the morality of the sabbath, on pages 24 and 40-41.

[3] The third commandment prescribes a reverend use of all the titles, properties, works, and ordinances of God with spiritual understanding and

affection, with faith, reverence, love, joy, sincerity and thankfulness in thought, word, and life.

[4] In the fourth commandment, we are not only required to rest, but to sanctify a rest to Jehovah. If then we find the titles, properties, works of Jehovah given to Christ and his Holy Spirit in the Old and New Testament, we must conclude that Christ and his Holy Spirit are to be worshiped in the same ordinances with the same spiritual and divine worship, which is due to God the Father.

The scope of law and gospel is to bring us unto God by the mediation of Christ and assistance of the Spirit, that we may rest upon Christ for justification, walk and grow up in Christ in the progress of our sanctification for our everlasting satisfaction. Our business therefore is to avoid those two dangerous rocks upon which so many split and suffer shipwreck in this tempestuous age, namely the rock of neglecting duties in the course of our sanctification, and the rock of resting in duties which overthrows our justification.

We must labor by all means appointed by God to gain a spiritual, practical, experimental knowledge of the love of Jesus Christ, a knowledge which surpasses all intellectual knowledge, an affectionate knowledge which is felt in the heart,[533] but cannot be comprehended in the brain.[534] This is the right evangelical knowledge, which prepares a man for spiritual and evangelical worship,[535] for heavenly communion with Father, Son, and Holy Spirit in all gospel dispensations and gospel-conversation,[536] that he may come to be enriched with the unsearchable riches of Christ, and filled with all the fullness of God.

"For this cause," (says the apostle, and well he might) "I bow my knees unto the Father of our Lord Jesus Christ." Mark the strain, it is purely

---

[533] Ephesians 3:19
[534] Philippians 3:8, 10
[535] Philippians 1:9-11
[536] Galatians 2:20

evangelical: "that *he* would grant you according to the riches of his glory to be strengthened with might by his *Spirit*, that *Christ* may dwell in your hearts." Here are all the three co-essential persons; but how may this be obtained? And to know the love of Christ which passes knowledge: to know it in my heart, to believe it with my heart, to feel it in my heart, because the love of God is shed abroad in my heart by the Holy Spirit. But what shall I gain by this?

Why, the apostle goes on: "that ye may be filled with all the fullness of God." In Ephesians 3:14, 16-17, 19, the great design of the apostle was to be found in Christ, having the righteousness which is of God through the faith of Christ (without pleading his own righteousness, which is of the law) for his justification. And to have a spiritual and practical knowledge of Christ grounded upon a deep and affectionate experience of the virtue of Christ's death, and resurrection in his own soul (Philippians 3:9-10) that he might be thereby encouraged and provoked to press forward in the course of sanctification, toward the mark for the prize of the high calling of God in Christ Jesus (Philippians 3:14) so that his faith might act in all holy services. Justifying faith is the principle of evangelical worship, and gospel-conversation.[537] "Grace be to you, and peace from him which is, which was, and which is to come, and from the seven spirits which are before his throne, and from Jesus Christ, who loved us and washed us from our sins in his own blood: And hath made us kings and priests unto God, and his Father; to him be glory and dominion forever and ever. Amen (Revelation 1:4-6)."[538]

The hearts of true believers are golden vials full of odors and incense, faith and love, sincerity and zeal, self-denial and thankfulness, humility and godly reverence; and the belief of their redemption by the blood of Christ moves them to acknowledge the divine power of their Redeemer, and to

---

[537] Revelation 5:8-10, 13
[538] Bona Theologia non fert ut gratia & pax Evangelica ab Angelis postuletur Alcasar. Col. 2. 18. Rev 19. 10 Rev. 22. 9.

give him divine worship. The angels, elders, people all join, even ten thousand times ten thousand, and thousands of thousands in this acknowledgement: "Worthy is the lamb that was slain to receive power, and riches, and wisdom, and strength, and honor, and glory, and blessing. And every creature which is in heaven, and on the earth, and under the earth, and such as are in the sea, and all that are in them heard I saying, Blessing, glory, honor, and power be unto him that sits upon the throne, and unto the lamb forever and ever. And the four beasts said Amen, And the four and twenty elders fell down and worshiped him that liveth forever and ever (Revelation 5:8-14)."

We must be brought to the knowledge and faith of the Son of God before ever we can be wise unto salvation (2 Timothy 3:15, Isaiah 53:11, John. 3:14-15, Galatians 2:20). When once we come to believe the love of Christ, then we love, adore, obey Father, Son, and Holy Spirit after an evangelical manner. All the fundamental articles of our faith have reference unto Christ as the foundation, because they are all such as concern his Father, his Spirit, his incarnation, mediation, or his church, and the benefits which the church receives from him.[539] And in like manner, all our worship is directed unto Father, Son, and Spirit as one God by the mediation of Christ, and assistance of the Spirit. Ephesians 2:18; 2 Corinthians 13:14:1 Peter 2:5; 1 John 1:3, 4. Ephesians 4:15.

It is our happiness, our heaven upon earth to believe, adore, and live to Father, Son, and Holy Spirit by maintaining a holy communion with all three as one God, and our God, in the use of all ordinances and duties required of us. This is the mystery of godliness, the art of living unto God; this is the lesson which all members of the church universal must learn; the four beasts (who join with angels and presbyters in adoring the lamb) are (as learned Mr. Mede, and several others conceive) the catholic church of Christ in the four quarters of the world professing and embracing the doctrine of

---

[539] See Dr. Ussher's learned sermon of the unity of faith.

the four evangelists. These beasts are full of eyes, full of the knowledge of the mysteries of Christ, and their spiritual experimental knowledge moves them to worship Jesus Christ.

Mr. Mede makes this interpretation the key to open very many types in the book of the Revelation, and doubts not but everyone who seriously perpends the old castrametation [*measuring out a military camp*] in the wilderness, and compares it with the apocalyptic types, will subscribe to this interpretation.

I know several learned men do conceive that the four beasts are four angels, and some presume to name the angels,[540] but I cannot embrace their opinion, because I find that the chorus is made up of angels, beasts and elders; and these three sorts are clearly distinguished. Revelation 5:11 reads: "And I beheld and I heard the voice of many angels round about the throne, and the beasts, and the elders." That the angels do join with the beasts in worship is granted. That the angels do protect these beasts with eyes in all quarters of the world – east, west, north and south – is likewise granted.[541] But that the beasts are angels, that is it which is, and must be denied, and therefore I do conceive that Mr. Mede is in the right, and the good man was sorry that he had not time to clear that point at large; and therefore I am the more willing to proceed upon this argument, and perform that service to the church, which he would have done with more dexterity. Let us then consider:

[1] That upon Christ's mediation, his Father gave him the heathen for his inheritance, and the uttermost parts of the earth for his possession. "Ask of me and I will give thee the heathen, etc. (Psalm 2:8)."

[2] Let us consider that promise made to the church the mystical body of Christ in Isaiah 43: "Fear not, for I have redeemed thee, I have called thee by

---

[540] Michael, Gabriel, Raphael, Uriel.
[541] The four beasts represent the Church universal. Formae quatuor animalium diversae collectionem novae Ecclesiae ex quatuor orbis plagis diversisque nationibus, populis, linguis significant. Pareus in Com. in c. 4. Apocalyp

thy name, thou art mine; – I am Jehovah thy God, the Holy One of Israel thy Savior; – Since thou wast precious in my sight thou hast been honorable, and I have loved thee, – fear not, for I am with thee; I will bring thy seed from the east, and gather thee from the west. I will say to the north give up, and to the south keep not back, bring my sons from far, and my daughters from the ends of the earth, even everyone that is called by my name." This is the substance of the seven first verses of Isaiah 43. Behold the church universal gathered from all parts of the world into one mystical body, so that all may be united unto Christ the head by faith, and to one another by love, that so they may all join in believing, adoring and obeying the Lord Jesus, his Father, and the Holy Spirit.

[3] Consider how these precious promises are fulfilled by gospel dispensations and Christian exercises. For by one Spirit are we all baptized into one body, whether we be Jews or Gentiles, bond or free, and have been all made to drink into one Spirit (1 Corinthians 12:13). Christ did grace the solemnity of his triumphant ascension with that choice gift of the ministry, for the edifying and perfecting of saints, "till we *all*" – even all the members of the church universal – "come in the unity of the faith, and of the knowledge of the Son of God, unto a perfect man, unto the measure of the stature of the fullness of Christ (Ephesians 4:8, 11, 13)."

Christ mystical is deficient until the saints are gathered from all quarters into the unity of faith, and knowledge of the Son of God, because this is a fundamental point. For Christ built his church upon that fundamental confession: "Thou art Christ the Son of the living God" (Matthew 16:16, 18) and "other foundation can none lay (1 Corinthians 3:11)." And the superstruction must be agreeable to the foundation, that we may attain unto the measure of the stature of the fullness of Christ, every part making some considerable supply for the increase of the body, by growing up in all things into Christ the head (Ephesians 4:13, 15-16). Christ is the only head and mediator, and therefore Jews and Gentiles both have access through Christ by one Spirit to the Father (Ephesians 2:18). Here's an acknowledgement of the blessed Trinunity made by the catholic church in gospel worship. And the apostle directs his epistle to the church of God at Corinth, "with all that in every place call upon the name of Christ our Lord both theirs and ours (1 Corinthians 1:2)," and concludes his second epistle with "The grace," etc. (2 Corinthians 13:14).

[4] Compare what has been spoken with the song of angels, presbyters and saints full of eyes in the book of the Revelation.[542] These four beasts were in the midst of the throne and round about the throne (Revelation 4:6). The form of the throne is quadrangular, and one beast placed in the middle of everyone of the four sides. Mr. Mede shows how these four beasts observe what is done by God in the four quarters of the world, and how they speak in order upon the opening of the four first seals (Revelation 6:1-7), and a voice proceeds from the midst of the four beasts, (Revelation 6:6). Finally, the virgin church (Revelation 14) sings the same song that the four beasts did, which is called "a new song," sung in the praise of the lamb and his Father. And in some copies which are of credit, we read that the virgins had the lamb's name – as well as his Father's – written in their foreheads (Revelation 14:1), and they are the firstfruits to God and to the lamb (Revelation 14:4).[543]

[5] This new song which is sung to the lamb and his Father, contains in it the mystery of gospel-worship, because in it redemption, power, riches, wisdom, strength, honor, glory and blessing are ascribed unto him who sits upon the throne, and to the lamb (Revelation 5:12-14): "Worthy is the lamb that was slain to receive power," etc. (Revelation 5:12). They fall down before the lamb and sing a new song (Revelation 5:8-9): "Thou art worthy, etc. for thou wast slain, and hast redeemed us to God by thy blood."

---

[542] Thronus iste in medio Presbyterorum & Animalium positus est Templum aut Tabernaculum. Quid aliud innuere volunt Quatuor cornua altaris aurei in conspectu Dei? Apoc. 9. 13. Templum Tabernaculi Testimonii apertum in Coelo. Apocal. 15. 5 M. Mede Com. ad cap. 4. pag. 6, 7.

[543] Habentes nomen Agni. Primasius, Aretas, Andreas, Syrus In|terpres, &c. Vide M. Mede Com. ad cap. 14. pag. 215.

[6] This pattern of gospel-worship comes from heaven; the angels sing this song,[544] and the saints, the followers of the lamb, they glorify the lamb and his Father on earth as the angels do in heaven; according to that request in the lamb's prayer, the Lord's prayer: "Our Father which art in heaven, let thy will be done on earth as it is in heaven." We receive this directory for gospel-worship from Christ and his angels.

[7] All the virgin-church, all that follow the lamb whithersoever he goes, into all or any quarter of the world. They, and they only, learn this song.

[8] These redeemed virgins refuse to receive the beast's mark, they renounce the dragon and his angels, all his pomps, vanities, worship, and all the furniture of his worship, all the errors and idols of the false prophets, though they lose their trading, the comforts of their life, yea and life itself.[545] This is the lamb's mark.

[9] These redeemed virgins make a public profession of their faith in, and love to the lamb and his Father. They have the mark of both in their forehead, and they cry aloud, their voice is like the voice of thunder (Revelation 14:1-2, Revelation 5:12).[546] They are not ashamed or afraid to acknowledge Father, Son, and the Holy Spirit the only and adequate object of divine faith, and worship, and the sole cause of justification, sanctification, redemption, peace and glory, for all this is held forth to us clearly in this book of the Revelation, and there is a special blessing promised to such as "read and hear the words of this prophecy, and keep those things which are written therein (Revelation 1:3)."[547]

Amongst other blessings. they have the blessing of victory, and triumph vouchsafed them, they get victory over the beast,[548] over his image, his

---

[544] Idea cultus Evangelici aliunde quā à caelitibus peri nequit.
[545] Satanae Angelos, pompam, pultum, ocera, omnemque apparatum ejus Idololatricum respuo.
[546] Revelation 1:4-5
[547] Revelation 5:8-9, 12
[548] Revelation 14:4

mark,[549] and the number of his name (Revelation 15:2).[550] They defy the Roman errors and idols,[551] and are armed with faith and patience against this cruelty and tyranny of Antichrist.[552] They cannot be enticed by any rewards, seduced by any subtleties, terrified by any threats to embrace any doctrine, or form of worship derogatory to the honor of the Father, the lamb, or the Holy Spirit; for the Spirit in this book teaches the churches to come in to Christ, and defy the beast; and the churches hearken to the Spirit as the Fountain of truth, grace, peace, and glory.[553]

This is the mystery of gospel-worship:[554] we must believe, love, adore, obey the Father, the Lamb, and the Spirit of grace and peace, the Doctor and Comforter of all Christian churches throughout all the four quarters of the world:[555] east, west, north, south, that so the promise of Isaiah 43 may be exactly fulfilled. In Revelation 7:9-10, we read that a great multitude, an innumerable multitude of all nations cry: "Salvation to our God which sitteth upon the throne, and unto the lamb." The kingdoms of the world must become the kingdoms of the Lord, and of his Christ (Revelation 11:15).

And when the devil and his angels – who deceive the world, accuse the brethren, and blaspheme Christ – are cast forth, then there is a loud voice in heaven: "Now is come salvation, and strength, and the kingdom of our God, and the power of his Christ; for the accuser of our brethren is cast down, etc. (Revelation 12:9-10)." In a word, when the redeemed virgins and noble conquerors come to sing their triumphant song, that song contains the scope of the law, and the substance of the gospel; for they are to sing the song of Moses, and the song of the lamb (Revelation 15:3). And they who sing are such as do keep the commandments of God, and the testimony of Jesus

---

[549] Revelation 12:11
[550] Revelation 15:2-3
[551] Revelation 14:12
[552] Revelation 17:14
[553] Revelation 1:4-5
[554] Revelation 2:18, 29
[555] Revelation 5:13-14

(Revelation 12:17). And the testimony of Jesus is the testimony of the Spirit, delivered in the Word to the churches of Christ, (Revelation 2:7, 11). All three persons do deliver the same testimony (1 John 5:7),[556] but the Son and the Spirit do most eminently join in delivering their testimony (Revelation 2:11, 18, 29, Revelation 3:1, 6, 7, 13-14, 21- 22, Revelation 19:10).

{1} The Spirit encourages them to believe his testimony, and follow the lamb; and the martyrs are slain for the Word of God, and for the testimony which they held (Revelation 6:9). They overcome by the blood of the lamb, and by the word of their testimony (Revelation 12:11), the testimony of the Spirit, and the testimony of Jesus (Revelation 12:17). And when the Spirit has encouraged them to love Christ better than their lives (Revelation 12:11) and they have overcome by the testimony of the Spirit and the blood of the lamb, then the Spirit pronounces them blessed. "Blessed are the dead which die in the Lord— yea saith the Spirit (Revelation 14:13)." The church is begotten, instructed, persuaded, governed, upheld, and comforted by the Holy Spirit, as Babylon is the habitation of devils, and the hold of every foul spirit (Revelation 18:2).

{2} It is the Spirit which woos the church, and persuades her to be the wife of the lamb, and to make herself ready for the marriage. "And the Spirit and the bride say come (Revelation 22:17)." And that we may look upon this whole prophecy as coming from the Spirit as well as the lamb, the angel assures us that the testimony of Jesus is the spirit of prophecy (Revelation 19:10). The love of the Father,[557] and the grace of the Lord Jesus is communicated to us by the Holy Spirit. Therefore, although the grace of the Lord Jesus is alone expressed in the close of this book of the Revelation, yet the love of the Father, and communion of the Holy Spirit must be understood according to the prayer in the beginning of the book – Revelation 1:4-5: "Grace," etc.[558]

---

[556] Revelation 11:19
[557] 2 Corinthians 13:14
[558] Revelation 1:4-5 compared with Revelation 22:21

{3} The Spirit is worshiped in this book of the Revelation. "Grace be to you and peace from the seven spirits (Revelation 1:4)." It is not agreeable to the Christian faith to pray unto angels, and beg grace and peace of them. They do not hold the head, who worship angels (Colossians 2:18-19). angels are our fellow servants, and do forbid us to give that worship to them which is due to God only, and they refuse to be worshiped because it is contrary to the testimony of Jesus. Revelation 19:10 reads: "And I fell at his feet to worship him, and he said unto me, see thou do it not; I am thy fellow servant, and of thy brethren that have the testimony of Jesus; worship God."[559] This is the testimony of Jesus: "Thou shalt worship the Lord thy God, and him only shalt thou serve (Matthew 4:10)." The book of the Revelation contains several clear testimonies against worshiping of angels, "I am of them," (says the angel) "that keep the saying of this book: worship God (Revelation 22:9)." And therefore that place of Revelation 1:4 must be understood of the Holy Spirit. For God will not give his glory to another,[560] and good angels will not take it from him, but protest against this will-worship as idolatry.

The Holy Spirit is called "seven spirits" by an usual metalepsis of the effect for the cause: he pours forth various gifts. Seven is a note of perfection, and the Holy Spirit, one and the same Spirit is given to all the seven churches.[561] Every church has so much of the Holy Spirit as is necessary, and it runs as if each one of the seven churches had seven spirits, because each one has enough of the Spirit for their sanctification and salvation. The apostle therefore – begging grace and peace from this coessential Trinunity: the Father, the seven Spirits, and Jesus Christ – sufficiently instructs us in this

---

[559] Tertia interpretatio veterum & recētiorūs Doctorum solae Scripturae, & fidei Christianae analoga est. D Pareus Com. in Apoc. c. 1.
[560] Isaiah 42:8
[561] Gratiam precatur septem ecclesiis, quibus singulis unum eundem{que} spiritum sanctum quasi septem in solidum tribuit.

mystery of evangelical worship.⁵⁶² Some object that then the Spirit will be set before the Son; but the answer is easy, that there is a metathesis in the words; and it is observable that the Son is sometimes named before the Father (2 Corinthians 13:14), and sometimes the Spirit is named before the Son (Revelation 1:4 & 1 Peter 1:2). And sometimes the natural order is observed, the Father is named first, the Son second, and the Holy Spirit third. The natural order is not overthrown when the Father is named after the Son, or the Spirit before the Son, nor is the equality of persons overthrown when the natural order is observed, and therefore that objection is not considerable.

Natural worship is due to the Holy Spirit because he has the same divine nature with the Father and the Son. That divine faith is due to the Spirit has been proven at large. That divine love is due to him is clear (Romans 15:30): "I beseech you for the Lord Jesus Christ's sake, and for the love of the Spirit." The Spirit is the author and object of all those graces which are called divine *ex parte objecti*: faith, hope, and love (Romans 15:13, 16, 30).⁵⁶³

In a word, instituted worship is due to the Holy Spirit by virtue of both sacraments (Matthew 28:19). By one Spirit we are all baptized into one body, and have been all made to drink into one Spirit (1 Corinthians 12:13; 2 Corinthians 13:14; Matthew 3:11, John 5:5).

In hearing of the Word, we must hearken to the Spirit with the self-same attention, devotion as we do to the Father and the Son (Hebrews 3:7-8 compared with Psalm 95).⁵⁶⁴ The Holy Spirit forbids us to harden our hearts against himself speaking in the Word (Acts 7:51). We grieve the Spirit when we resist the Spirit and will not put our seal to the Word by a spiritual assent, and fiducial consent, and hinder the Spirit from sealing up our election and redemption to us. For though Christ makes the purchase, yet the Spirit makes the assurance (1 John 3:24, John 14:16-17, John 15:26).

---

⁵⁶² Votum Gratiae & pacis univocè concipit απο του ο ων και απο των επτα πνευματων και απο ιησου χριστου D. Parei Com. in Apoc. c. 1. Deus Trinunus gratiae Pacisq{que} causa adaequata integra.
⁵⁶³ 1 Corinthians 6:11
⁵⁶⁴ Revelation 2:11, 18, 19

In prayer, we are to call upon the Holy Spirit (2 Corinthians 13:14, Revelation 1:4) because the Holy Spirit is God (1 Corinthians 12:6, 11, Acts 5:3-4). I cannot but wonder at those who say that holy and spiritual worship is not due to the Holy Spirit, when the truth is that we can give no worship at all to the Father or the Son until we are enabled by the Holy Spirit (Romans 5:5; 1 Corinthians 12:3; 2 Corinthians 4:13, 13:14). And when by the communion of the Spirit we have communion with the Father and Son in gospel worship, we are the temples not only of the Holy Spirit, but of the coessential Trinity of Father, Son, and Holy Spirit, all three do dwell in us, walk in us, and abide in us. For when we receive the Spirit of truth, he abides with us, dwells in us, persuades and enables us to love God the Father, and the Lord Jesus, and then all three coessential persons make their abode with us, as is clearly held forth to us (John. 14:16-17, 23; 2 Corinthians 6:16, 18; 1 Corinthians 3:16, Ephesians 3:16-17).

But if a man has not the Spirit of Christ, he has no saving interest as yet in Jesus Christ (Romans 8:9) because he is not as yet the Son of God by regeneration or adoption, he is not a member of Jesus Christ, he is not the temple of the Holy Spirit, and he does not worship this coessential Trinity as he ought to do in Spirit and in truth. He who has the Spirit in him, does worship the Spirit in spirit and truth, because the Spirit is the power of the Highest, (even as Christ is the Son of the Highest) a personal power (Luke 1:32 & 35 compared). The Spirit is the *Spirit of Elohim* (Genesis 1:2), the *Spirit of Jehovah* (Isaiah 11:2), the God of Israel, (2 Samuel 23:2-3), The Spirit of God, and the Spirit which is God (1 Corinthians 2:11-12, Acts 5:3-4).

This point has been sufficiently proved in the fourth chapter, and therefore I need say no more, considering that the Socinians have no arguments which are considerable, when compared with these plain places of the Holy Scriptures, and those many places and proofs which have been formerly produced in this treatise.

If any desire to have their arguments (such as they be) answered at large, he may read Mr. Estwick's learned treatise concerning the Godhead of the

Holy Spirit, lately published. I proceed to the third part of godliness, which is obedience.

(3) *Obedience is due to the Father, Son, and Holy Spirit, all three coessential persons, because they are coessential, because they are one God blessed forever.*

(1) **Obedience is due to God the Father.**

This truth is generally acknowledged by all that are not atheists; the Jews and Socinians subscribe to it. If we do acknowledge God the Father to be the Father of our Lord Jesus Christ, and our Father in him, the inference will be immediate, clear and strong, that we ought to honor and obey our heavenly Father. For how shall God put us among his children, unless every one of us say unto him, "My Father, my Father, I do obey thee, and will not depart from thee?" "But I said, how shall I put thee among the children, and give thee a pleasant land, a goodly heritage of the hosts of nations? And I said, Thou shalt call me my Father, and shalt not turn away from me (Jeremiah 3:19)." And when God speaks to them as to children, they presently submit: "Return ye backsliding children, And I will heal your backslidings;" they presently reply: "Behold, we come unto thee, for thou art the LORD our God (Jeremiah 3:22)." "A son honoreth his father – if then I be a father, where is mine honor?" (Malachi 1:6, Malachi 2:16, Matthew 12:50, Matthew 23:9).

When God is considered under this endearing relation of a Father, we yield a filial obedience unto God, we perform a federal obedience, a sincere and evangelical obedience.[565] "I," says Jehovah, "will be your God, I will be your Father." "Having these promises," (says the apostle) "let us cleanse ourselves from all filthiness of the flesh,[566] and spirit,[567] perfecting holiness in the fear of God (2 Corinthians 6:16, 18; 2 Corinthians 7:1; 1 Peter 1:14, 17-18)."[568] As we are to worship God in this Fatherly relation (Matthew 6:9,

---

[565] Titus 2:14
[566] 1 John 4:16, 19
[567] Psalm 130:4
[568] Psalm 103:13

Galatians 4:6), so are we to obey him also: "Whosoever shall do the will of my Father, etc. (Matthew 12:50)."[569]

That all three coessential persons are our Father, has been proven already in this very chapter, and that God the Father is our Father in a peculiar consideration, and therefore I need not insist longer upon this point, since the Scriptures are clear, so clear that even very cavillers confess this truth. Christ himself as man obeyed the Father (John 4:34).[570]

(2) God the Son is to be obeyed.

"This is my beloved Son in whom I am well pleased, hear ye him (Matthew 17:5)." Hear him, believe him, obey him; the Godhead of Christ is the formal reason of our obedience;[571] but all his benefits are sweet encouragements to us to perform our duty.[572] "Be obedient as children," says the apostle, "and if ye call on the Father," etc., "pass the time of your sojourning here in fear;" "For as much as ye know ye were not redeemed – but with the precious blood of Christ (1 Peter 1:14, 17-19)." Why do the presbyters throw down their crowns at the feet of Christ, and fall down before the lamb, but to testify their subjection, and profess how ready they are to serve and obey Jesus Christ? (Revelation 4:10-11, Revelation 5:8).

Christ is the author of salvation to them that obey him (Hebrews 5:9). The life of a Christian is a living unto Christ, a life of faith, love, and obedience (Galatians 2:20; 2 Corinthians 5:14-15, Philippians 1:20-21). We are made new creatures in Christ, that we may perform new obedience to Christ (2 Corinthians 5:17). He who serves Christ is acceptable to God, and approved of men (Romans 14:18). We are under the law to Christ (1 Corinthians 9:21). All manner of obedience, inward and outward is due unto the Lord Jesus Christ.[573] Cursed is he that does not prize and love Christ

---

[569] Matthew 23:9, Hosea 3:5
[570] Ezekiel 16:63; 1 John 4:10
[571] Galatians 1:10, Hebrews 5:9
[572] Titus 2:14; 1 John 3:16
[573] Matthew 28:19-20, Colossians 3:23-24, Titus 2:14; 1 Corinthians 16:22

above all the kingdoms of the world and glory of them, above all the comforts of life, and life itself (1 Corinthians 16:22, Luke 14:26, 33, Matthew 13:44, 46, Philippians 3:7,-8, 10, Colossians 3:23-24, Ephesians 6:6-7, Ephesians 5:26-27, and Titus 2:14 compared together).

(3) God the Holy Spirit is to be obeyed.[574]

We are devoted to his service in baptism. Our bodies and souls are temples consecrated to his honor and service. The Spirit conquers our carnal reason, mortifies our corruptions, and subdues our hearts unto the obedience of himself, as well as to the obedience of the Father and the Lord Jesus.[575]

We are debtors to the Spirit.[576] We are his creatures. The Spirit of Elohim did form and fashion the rude mass, out of which all things were made (Genesis 1:2).[577] The renovation of all things by continued propagation is ascribed to the Spirit:[578] "Thou sendest forth thy Spirit, they are created, and thou renewest the face of the earth (Psalm 104:30)." Our souls are breathed into us by this Spirit of life (Genesis 2:7). Job 33:4 reads: "The Spirit of God hath made me, and the breath of the Almighty hath given me life." The soul is enabled and adorned with all abilities by the Spirit, that it may be qualified for all manner of service: in respect of counsel and government (Numbers 11:25), in respect of resolution and action (Judges 14:6). But that which is most endearing, is, that the Spirit is the Spirit of conviction, regeneration, conversion, sanctification, edification, and consolation (1 Peter 1:2; 2 Thessalonians 2:13, Galatians 5:22; 1 Corinthians 12:8-9). The Spirit is the God of all comfort, it is his special office to comfort mourners. The Spirit fitted the man Christ to be our mediator; as is most evident, because:

---

[574] Revelation 12:11
[575] Matthew 28:19, Acts 5:3-4, 32
[576] 1 Corinthians 3:16-17
[577] 2 Corinthians 13:14
[578] Revelation 1:4

[1] The Spirit formed the nature of man of the substance of the Virgin after an extraordinary manner (Luke 1:35 compared with Galatians 4:4) for the service of the Lord Christ.

[2] He sanctified the human nature which Christ assumed after such a perfect manner, that it was free from all sin in the very moment of conception (Luke 1:35).

[3] He united this pure human nature with the divine in the same person, the person of the Son of God (Luke 1:35 compared with Hebrews 10:5): "a body hast thou fitted unto me" – by the Holy Spirit. Our Savior was anointed with the Spirit above measure, that he might be a fit head and mediator for us, that we and his whole church might receive of his fullness,[579] graces answerable to his graces (John 1:16, John 3:34, John 1:14, Isaiah 61:1, Psalm 45:7 compared together, Acts 10:38, Luke 2:40, 52, Matthew 3:16-17, John 7:39).[580]

If we consider how the Spirit has manifested his divine power in garnishing heaven and earth (Job 26:13), in anointing Christ and Christians (1 John. 2:27), in ordering and regulating church affairs, and enabling ministers for all church-service, that the elect might be gathered, converted, perfected, saved by the efficacy of the Spirit in all ministerial dispensations, we shall see reason enough to acknowledge the divine power of the Spirit, by all spiritual and heavenly obedience. (1 Corinthians 12:4-6, 8-9, 11, 13, Isaiah 6:1, 9, Acts 28:25 compared).

If we harden our hearts against the precepts and exhortations of the Spirit speaking in the Word, if we vex, grieve, resist, and quench the Spirit, we are in a ready way to that black and unpardonable sin of doing despite to the Spirit of grace; and therefore unless we mean to proceed to total and final disobedience, it highly concerns us to obey the Holy Spirit, and answer the

---

[579] Christus est Messias Messiarum Christus Christorum. Joh. 20. 31.

[580] Dona ista absolutē & in se finita fuere, sicut & ipsa Christi natura finita est; nostri tamen respectu, sunt absque mensurâ. Vide D. Alting. exp. Catech. part. 2. & pag. 170, 171.

many calls and motions of the Spirit by sincere obedience, that our effectual vocation may evidence our election, and the Spirit may seal us up unto the day of redemption; for the same Spirit is the Spirit of sanctification and adoption, the spirit of revelation, mortification, vivification, consolation. The Spirit quickens, moves, enables, inclines, persuades us to believe in Christ, and to love one another, to keep all the commandments of God. Now this Spirit of faith, love, and obedience is the Spirit of sanctification; and if you find the Spirit of sanctification in you, be of good comfort; though the Spirit of adoption seem to withdraw, yet he is certainly present, nay, is not idle or silent, he speaks by his real works, and sweet fruits; for the spirit of sanctification is the Spirit of adoption, it is one and the self-same Spirit. "This is his commandment, that we should believe on the name of his Son Jesus Christ, and love one another as he gave us commandment. And he that keepeth his commandments dwelleth in him, and he in him, and hereby we know that he abideth in us, by the Spirit which he hath given us (1 John 3:23-24)." "And hereby we know that we dwell in him, and he in us, because he hath given us of his Spirit (1 John 4:13)." And therefore if there be a spirit of faith, love, and obedience in you, rejoice in it, lift up your heart to God in thankfulness for it; God be thanked that ye (who were the servants of sin) have obeyed from the heart that for me of doctrine which was delivered unto you by the Holy Spirit (Romans 6:17). Be much in supplication and thanksgiving, and the Spirit of supplication will be a Spirit of adoption, an oil of gladness (Hebrews 1:9). The Spirit will teach you to cry Abba, Father, with comfort (Galatians 4, Romans 8).

The Spirit will fill your souls with all joy, and peace in believing, and in obeying; the joy of the spirit shall be your strength, the comforts of the Almighty, even all the comforts of the kingdom of God (which consists in righteousness, and peace, and joy in the Holy Spirit)[581] shall be all-sufficient to revive and support your dejected spirit. All your fears and discomforts

---

[581] Romans 14:17

shall be dispelled, your wants supplied your wound, soars, infirmities healed, and you at last filled with all the fullness of God (Malachi 4:2, Ephesians 3:19).

Believe in the Spirit, obey the Spirit, and you shall be sealed with the Spirit (Ephesians 1:13). I beseech you by the tender mercies of God, by the meekness and gentleness of Christ, by the joy, and for the love of the Spirit, that you consider what has been said, that you receive this wholesome Word as it is in truth the Word of God, the Word of the Father, Son, and Holy Spirit, but testified after a more especial and immediate manner by the Holy Spirit that it may work effectually in all you who believe it (1 Thessalonians 2:13) – even unto spiritual and sincere obedience to Father, Son, and Holy Spirit. That it may be so, we must have a care to obey after the right manner, for Amaziah was to blame, though he did that which was right in itself, because he did it not with a perfect heart (2 Chronicles 25:2). Let us imitate our Savior, who did all as he was commanded (John 14:31).

Let us have:

{1} High thoughts of the majesty and greatness of God.

{2} Sweet thoughts of the rich grace and infinite goodness of God.

{3} An entire and universal respect to all the commands, and every work of God (John 6:28-29). Every work which God has given us to do (John 17:4) and ordained for us to walk in (Ephesians 2:10). For every command of God must have a divine authority over our consciences and hearts. (Psalm 119:6) and then Christ will account us his friends (John 15:14).

{4} A more special respect to the weightiest and greatest duties of religion, such as God has more especially enjoined, for instance: (i) the duties of inward worship and obedience (Matthew 22:37-38), the most reserved and intimate duties of religion. (ii) Duties of judgment, mercy, and fidelity towards all men (Matthew 23:23). Love to our enemies (Matthew 5:44-45). (iii) Duties of our particular callings and special relations, public duties, and family duties, especially such as are most private (Matthew 6:6. Zechariah

12:12).⁵⁸² (iv) The great work of faith, which is the sum of both Testaments, because all judicious and zealous love, all sincere and uniform obedience springs from faith.⁵⁸³ John 6:29 reads: "This is the work of God;" and unbelief is the work of the devil. Faith purifies our heart by applying the blood of Christ to our souls (Hebrews 9:14).⁵⁸⁴

The weighty matters of law and gospel may be referred to those four heads above mentioned;⁵⁸⁵ observe that excellent Scripture: God has "chosen the poor of this world *rich in faith* and heirs of that kingdom which he hath promised to them that *love him* (James 2:5)."⁵⁸⁶ Faith and love will make us constant in the performance of all the other weighty matters required of us both in law and gospel, and we have proved at large that faith and love is due to all three persons.⁵⁸⁷

We must perform all our duties: {1} as to a Father, a divine Father, as has been proven. {2} In the name of Christ. {3} In the strength of the Spirit. {4} At the command, and for the glory of all three co-essential persons, for all things are of the Father, by the Son, and through the Spirit.⁵⁸⁸ {5} With a willing mind, a perfect heart, a good conscience, and faith unfeigned.⁵⁸⁹ {6} With all self-denial, diligence, constancy.⁵⁹⁰ {7} With a humble desire that we and our obedience may be accepted in and for Christ according to the tenor of the covenant of grace.

Let us now put all together again, and observe what a sweet harmony, exact symmetry, and glorious uniformity there is in this whole mystery of faith, this mystery of the coessential Trinunity as reduced to practice by its effectual influence into the mystery and power of godliness.

---

[582] Psalm 101:2, 8, Zechariah 12:12-14
[583] Acts 26:18, Hebrews 9:14; 2 Peter 1:3-4, Ephesians 3:19
[584] Ephesians 6:16, Acts 15:9; 1 John 4:16, 19
[585] Magnes amoris amor
[586] 1 Timothy 1:5
[587] James 2:5; 1 John 5:3-4
[588] 1 Corinthians 8:6; 12:6, 11
[589] 1 Chronicles 28:9
[590] 1 Timothy 1:5

Beloved Christians, I look upon myself as the least of saints, and greatest of sinners, unworthy to be accounted a member, but far more unworthy to be a minister of Jesus Christ, because I know more evil by myself than I know by any member of Christ. But I thank God our Father, Christ Jesus our Lord, and the coessential Spirit the same God, who works all in all (1 Corinthians 12:6) that I have obtained mercy, and ability of all three for to be faithful, and to be counted faithful by them all; for they have all three in some measure enabled me, for that they counted me faithful, putting me into the ministry, for I am a minister of that gospel, which is revealed from heaven by Father, Son, and Holy Spirit. And I am a minister according to the gift of the grace of God given unto me by the effectual working of his power; unto me I say, who am less than the least of all saints in this grace given, that I should preach the love of the Father, the grace and unsearchable riches of Christ, the sweet communion, peace, and joy of the Holy Spirit, which is unspeakable and full of glory.

Be pleased then to take a view of the whole mystery of faith and godliness, and observe how this coessential Trinunity of Father, Son, and Holy Spirit, who are one God blessed forever, is the adequate object, author, and end of all religion.

(1) Look upon the grand mystery of our election unto grace, peace, and glory, and observe what practical inferences may be drawn from thence to raise our hearts to admire, believe, love, worship, obey Father, Son, and Holy Spirit.[591]

"Elect according to the foreknowledge of God the Father through sanctification of the Spirit, unto obedience and sprinkling of the blood of Jesus Christ: grace unto you and peace be multiplied. Blessed be the God and

---

[591] The grand mystery of our Election by Father, Son, and Holy Ghost reduced to Practice. Sicut ergo caetera praedicanda sunt, ut qui ea praedicat obedienter audiatur: ita praedestinationem suo tempore & loco praedicandam esse, ut qui obedienter haec audit, non in homine ac per hoc nec in seipso sed in Domino glorietur. Aug de Bono persev. l. 2. c. 24. Frustra ignorantium auribus ingeris nos Liberum Arbitrium condemnare; imò verò damnetur ille, qui damnat. Hieron. ad Cresiphontem.

Father of our Lord Jesus Christ, etc (1 Peter 1:2-4)." "God hath from the beginning chosen you to salvation through sanctification of the spirit, and belief of the truth, whereunto he called you by our gospel to the obtaining of the glory of the Lord Jesus Christ" – "Now our Lord Jesus Christ himself and God even our Father, etc. (2 Thessalonians 2:13-14, 16)." Here is the free will of the elect, but "Blessed be the God and Father of our Lord Jesus Christ, who hath blessed us with all spiritual blessings in heavenly places in Christ according as he hath, chosen us in him before the foundation of the world that we should be holy and unblameable before him in love, etc (Ephesians 1:3-5)."

Our thankfulness should be shown for this free grace to all three persons in our thanksgiving, believing, obeying, as is clear from these places,[592] and so our prayers should be answerable to our faith, love, and thankfulness,[593] and therefore it is observable that in the very same chapter, the apostle makes his address after this model: "That the God of our Lord Jesus Christ the Father of glory may give unto you the spirit of wisdom, and revelation in the acknowledgement of Christ (Ephesians 1:17. and so 2 Thessalonians 2, 16. Revelation 1:4, 5; 2 Corinthians 13:14)." Many other places may be urged which contain the mystery of faith, worship, and obedience, and if Christ and his Spirit are not always named in them, yet the benefits of Christ, the gifts, graces, fruits, comforts of the Spirit (which are named) do direct us to both. Moreover, when the name of God is used indefinitely, all three persons must be understood to be comprehended in that essential title, because they are one and the same God.[594]

Finally, one person subsists in another, and the same honor is due to all three, because all three have the same divine nature, which is single because infinite, and therefore there is enough discovered to prevent all scruples in

---

[592] Ephesians 1:3-5, 13, Colossians 3:12, John 15:16
[593] 2 Timothy 1:9
[594] Quoties Deinomen Indefinite ponitur, non minus Filium & Spiritum, quàm Patrem designat—retineatur unitas essentiae & habeatur ratio ordinis. Calvin Instit. lib. 1. cap. 13. sect. 20. Joh. 14. 10. Joh. 15. 26. Joh. 10. 30. 1 Joh. 5. 7.

the upright-hearted, and cavils in the contrary-minded. Read Colossians 3-4, and there you will see a very pregnant proof of this point:[595] "Put on therefore as the elect of God holy and beloved bowels of mercies, kindness, humbleness of mind – above all these things put on charity; let the peace of God rule in your hearts – do all in the name of the Lord Jesus, giving thanks to God and the Father by him; Whatever you do, do it heartily as to the Lord." And then the sum of all their requests is that they may stand perfect and complete in all the will of God. This takes in the full scope of law and gospel; whatever belongs to faith, worship, or obedience; whatever is just, and equal, or well-pleasing unto God (Colossians 3:20, Colossians 4:1).

And the epistle to the Ephesians runs parallel with this to the Colossians:[596] You are elected and therefore ye must be holy before all three coessential persons by whom you were elected; you must believe the Word of truth as the truth is in Jesus, that you may be sealed with the Spirit, and filled with all the fullness of God; you must bow your knees to the Father of our Lord Jesus Christ; you must study the unity of faith, and of the knowledge of the Son of God; you must keep the unity of the Spirit, you must grow up into Christ in all things; you must not grieve the Holy Spirit whereby ye are sealed unto the day of redemption, but maintain a fruitful fellowship with God in Christ by the communion of the Holy Spirit; for the fruit of the Spirit is in all goodness and righteousness and truth; you must be filled with the Spirit, giving thanks always for all things unto God and the Father in the name of our Lord Jesus Christ; you must do whatsoever is right

---

[595] Colos. 3. Pia sanctorum vigilantia non est ex ipsorum arbitrio sed ex dono gratiae in ipsis per gratiae media exuscitato. πεπληρωμενοι εν παντι θεληματι του θεου. Colossians 4:12. Confitemur neminem immeritò perdi, neminem meritò liberari. Prosp. The Epistle to the Ephesians. Fides est medium ad salutem, & tamen ipsius electionis Effectus.

[596] Impius sensus qui putat beatiorem esse hominem, cui Deus nihil dedecit, quam cui universa in Christo per Spiritum Sanctum secundum electionem gratuitam contulerit. Romans 11:5, 7, Matthew 20:16; 24:22, 24. electi sumus non meriti praerogativâ, non fati necessitate, non temeritate fortunae, sed altitudine divitiarum sapientiae & scientiae Dei quam non aperit sed clausam miratur Apostolus. Aug. Prosper. Eulgentius.

or equal (Ephesians 6:1). τουτο γαρ εστιν δικαιον: this is right, just, and equal. Put on the whole armor of God, take the sword of the Spirit, the shield of faith, pray always with all prayer and supplication in the Spirit. Peace be to the brethren, and love with faith from God the Father and the Lord Jesus Christ. Grace be with all them that love our Lord Jesus Christ in sincerity. I need make no inferences; the words are so plain, that they prove the point *in terminis terminantibus*, as we tend to say.

Consider the discourse of the apostle in the epistle to the Romans, where the apostle has even lost his reader in the depth of this mystery of the eternal counsel of Father, Son, and Holy Spirit.[597] He puts this question to all the busy disputants: "Who hath known the mind of the Lord, or who hath been his counselor?" and concludes that: "of him, and through him, and to him are all things, to whom be glory forever. Amen." We have mercy from him, faith and repentance from him by an effectual vocation according to his purpose of election (Romans 8, 28-29, Romans 9:11,15-16, 18, 23-24, 29-30, Romans 10:20, Romans 11:2, 5-7, 29-30, 32, 36). We have mercy, grace, and glory from all three, and therefore all honor and glory be to all three forever. Amen.

And the apostle beseeches the God of patience, and consolation, the God of hope, and the God of peace, to fill them with all joy and peace in believing that they may abound in hope through the power of the Holy Spirit, who is the God of hope, comfort and peace; for the kingdom of God consists in righteousness and peace, and joy in the Holy Spirit (Romans 14:17).[598] And if we serve Christ (who is God blessed forever: (Romans 9:5) in these things, we shall be acceptable to God, and approved of men (Romans 14:18).

---

[597] Amori Patris aeterno, gratiaeque Spiritus singulari nobis in Christo destinatae totum Salutis adscriptum videmus in Epistols ad Romanos: Contumeliam reddit justitia, honorem donat indebitum gratia. Aug.
[598] Ephesians 5:9, Augustine Epistle 105

The fruits of the Spirit in us are marks, because fruits of our election by God. The apostle, writing to the church of the Thessalonians, which is in God the Father, and in the Lord Jesus Christ, begs grace and peace for them from God our Father, and the Lord Jesus Christ; remembers their work of faith, labor of love, and patience of hope in our Lord Jesus Christ,[599] in the sight of God and our Father, and then concludes their election of God because the gospel came to them in power, and in the Holy Spirit; for they received the Word in much affliction, with joy of the Holy Spirit. The apostle exhorts them in everything to give thanks, because it is the will of God in Christ Jesus, and bids them beware of quenching the Spirit; and beseeches the Spirit, who is undeniably the God of peace, and by special office our Sanctifier and Comforter, to sanctify us wholly. "The very God of peace sanctify you wholly," etc.[600]

And the apostle discourses in like manner in 2 Timothy. "God," he says, "hath given us the spirit of power, of love, and of a sound mind, saved us and called us with an holy calling, according to his own purpose and grace, which was given us in Christ Jesus before the world began." And tells us that everyone who pretends to be elected, or presumes to call upon Christ and claim an interest in him, must depart from iniquity, be sanctified that he may be meet for the master's use, and prepared unto every good work.

I instance in some dark expressions, on purpose to show that even in them there is by interpretation an acknowledgment that we are elected by Father, Son and Holy Spirit to grace, peace and glory, and therefore ought to admire, believe, worship, love, obey all three persons as one, and the same God, blessed forever; we must be holy before them in faith and love.[601]

---

[599] Quae sit liberae discretionis in concilio Dei causa supra facultatem humanae cognitionis inquiritur & sine fidei diminutione nescitur, modo con fiteamur neminem immeritò perdi, neminē meritò liberari.

[600] Si omnes liberarentur, lateret quid peccato per justitiā deberetur; si nemo, quid gratia largiretur.

[601] Augustine, Epistle 105

(2) If we consider our creation, we are created by Father, Son, and Holy Spirit, as has been proven;[602] and therefore we were created for the worship and service of all three.[603] The Spirit of Elohim sat upon the waters, hatched the world and all the beauty and glory of it.[604]

(3) If we consider the vigorous providence of God, all things are preserved, upheld, maintained, ordered, governed, by Father, Son, and Holy Spirit. The Holy Spirit governs the church, and overrules the world also.[605]

(4) If we consider our fall, and therein our abominable sin, and the intolerable curse due unto it. [1] Our sin which we committed in Adam the first sin, it was a sin of cursed atheism, devilish pride, unbelief, rebellion, apostasy, a sinning sin, because it did disable, pollute, infect, poison both our souls and bodies with original and damnable corruption; all sins against Father, Son, and Holy Spirit proceed from this root of bitterness. [2] The curse due to this sin is intolerable, unavoidable, it is the curse of an omniscient and omnipotent God; a temporal, spiritual, eternal curse, the curse of the Father, Son, and Holy Spirit. Men and angels cannot help us, we cannot be pardoned, redeemed, sanctified, adopted, comforted, saved, but by the Father, Son, and Holy Spirit. Still this doctrine of the coessential Trinunity, must be preached and applied for our spiritual and eternal good, as will appear by our following discourse.

(5) If we consider our effectual vocation: the Father calls us in Christ by his Spirit speaking in law and gospel, and working powerfully upon our consciences and hearts. All three persons do jointly perform this saving work. Show which person can be spared![606]

---

[602] Genesis 1:2
[603] 1 Corinthians 8:6
[604] Job 33:4, 26:13
[605] Psalm 104:30, John 1:3, Zechariah 4:6-7; 1 Samuel 10:6; 2 Corinthians 3:6, Luke 1:35
[606] 1 Corinthians 1:9; 1 John 1:3; 2 Corinthians 13:14, Romans 15:16; 1 Thessalonians 1:5

(6) Our justification is by the free grace of the Father manifested in the covenant of grace, by the righteousness of Christ imputed by the Father, and applied by the Spirit. Our faith is grounded on the testimony of the Spirit, and wrought by the efficacy of the Spirit.[607]

(7) Our redemption is by the Father who gave us his Son: by Christ, who gave us himself; by the Spirit, who draws us unto Christ, and puts us into the arms and bosom of our Redeemer.[608] We are redeemed from the guilt and punishment of sin more eminently by Christ, but we are redeemed from the power and dominion of sin, from our vain conversation, from this present evil world, and tyranny of Satan, not only by the death, resurrection and intercession of Christ, but by the efficacy and power of the Holy Spirit.[609] And it is to be observed that though Christ makes the purchase, yet the Spirit makes and gives the assurance.

(8) Our adoption is by all three. The Father adopts us in Christ by the Spirit of adoption.[610]

(9) The covenant of grace is made and confirmed by all three.

(10) The church is gathered, instructed, preserved, saved by all three; the church enjoys and maintains spiritual and heavenly communion with all three in all ordinances and duties (2 Corinthians 13:4).

[1] In hearing the word, Father, Son and Holy Spirit, do all teach us, as has been proven at large (John 6:45; 1 Corinthians 2:13, Hebrews 1:1-2, Hebrews 3:7).

[2] We are baptized in the name of all three, devoted, dedicated, consecrated to the service of all three (1 Corinthians 12:12-13, Matthew 28:19, Titus 3:5-6; 1 Peter 3:21, Matthew 3:11, John 3:5, Romans 6:3-6). We are adopted into the family of God, that we may be married to the Son of God, and made coheirs with Christ in glory.

---

[607] Galatians 5:5, Titus 3:5-7; 1 Corinthians 6:11
[608] Ephesians 5:25-27, Galatians 1:3-4, Acts 26:18
[609] 1 Peter 1:18-19, 22-23; Romans 5:6, 8, 10, Ephesians 1:13, Romans 8:16
[610] Romans 8:15, Galatians 4:6

[3] In the Lord's Supper the Father invites, and entertains us, gives us his Son for our head, husband, savior, feast and all; Christ gives us his body and blood to nourish us,[611] and the Spirit enables us to receive this spiritual nourishment after a spiritual manner,[612] that we may thrive and grow thereby; the Spirit mortifies our lusts, strengthens our faith, renews our repentance, inflames our zeal, pacifies our conscience, purifies our heart, assures us of the favor and love of God, seals our pardon to us, and seals us up to the day of redemption.[613] The love of the Father, the grace of the Son, the communion and peace of the Spirit, are so plentifully vouchsafed to experimental Christians in this sacrament, that I may well subscribe *probatum est* [tried, tested, and proven].

[4] In prayer and thanksgiving we do manifestly hold communion with all three. Firstly, we pray to the Father in the name of Christ by the power of the Spirit of supplication (Ephesians 2:18, 1 Corinthians 1:2, 1 Thessalonians 3:11, Romans 8, Galatians 4; 2 Thessalonians 2:16, Revelation 1:4). Secondly, our thankful praises (Ephesians 3:21, Ephesians 5:18-20) are presented to all three.

[5] We keep a Sabbath to Father, Son, and Holy Spirit; all our fiducial breathings after God, all our penitential meltings before God, our obediential closing with God, our pangs of love, raptures of zeal, ecstasies of joy, do arise and spring from the belief and consideration of the rich grace, tender mercies, and sweetest love of our dear Father, our beloved Savior, and our sanctifying Comforter (Galatians 2:20, Colossians 1:12, Ephesians 1:3, 5-6, 11, 13, 17, Ephesians 2:4-6, 8; 1 Peter 1:8).

Every Lord's day – much more every sacrament-day – should be a sealing day, a sanctifying day, an edifying, saving sabbath.[614] God does, upon such days, take us wholly off from our own business, that we might make it

---

[611] 1 Corinthians 10:16
[612] 1 Corinthians 11:24-25
[613] 2 Corinthians 13:14
[614] Eheu nec fictis lachrymis dolendaest ista profanatio quae sub praetextu Libertatis Christianae in diei Dominici celebratione tanquam torrens irrupit.

our only business to serve and enjoy God by maintaining a holy communion with God in Christ by the effectual working of the Holy Spirit for a whole day together, that we may in the close of the day attain the end of our sabbath service, which is a rest of complacency, sweet content, and full satisfaction in the arms and bosom of a Father, a Savior, and a Comforter. This – this! – is to enjoy a Christian sabbath.

The heathens knew something of a sabbath.[615]

The Jewish holy days were appendices to the fourth commandment, and therefore might be well taken off again, the moral commandment remaining entire. For it is granted that they are taken off from the second commandment, and yet that remains entirely moral. And I believe it will be clear to any man that studies the point that the Jewish holy days did belong most properly and directly to the second commandment, and indirectly and but reductively to the fourth, because they were at most but appendices to the fourth commandment.

But even Jewish holy days, and the most solemn services upon them did in their primary and principal institution – as Walaeus himself does acknowledge – point at Christ and his benefits; and the point is clear by the Epistle to the Hebrews, and more especially by the ninth and tenth chapters of that epistle: Hebrews 9:10-11, 14, Hebrews 10:1, 4, 9-10, Luke 4:18-19; 1 Corinthians 5:7.[616]

The sabbath was instituted before the law was given on Mount Sinai, but the fall of man defaced the whole work of the first creation, and therefore it is no wonder if Christ, the Lord of the sabbath, require us to keep a sabbath in remembrance of the new creation by the work of redemption, which was actually finished by the resurrection of our blessed Lord upon the first day of the week.

---

[615] Sabbathū inter omnes mortales celebre. Vide Theophil. Antioch. lib. ad Attolycum. Joseph. lib. 2. adversus Appion. Phil. Iud. lib. 2 de vitâ Moysis.

[616] Vide Aug. Ep. 68. ad Casulanum. Chrysost. Homil. 10. in cap. 2. Gen. Phil. Iudae. lib. 3. de vitâ Moysis. Theod. Trad quaest. in Gen.

For Christ entered into his estate of rest in the day of his resurrection, though he did not enter into his place of rest in the third heavens till the day of his ascension, and the place is but accidental in respect of the state of rest, and rest itself. The will of our Lord was the instituting cause, the Rest of our Lord the moving cause. When God rested from the work of Creation he was refreshed (Exodus 31:17), and when Christ rested from the work of redemption he was refreshed, and his Father took delight in the work of the new creation, which he could not take in the old creation, which was so defaced, that he did repent of it (Genesis 6).[617] But God will never repent that he sent his Son to redeem, or his Spirit to sanctify his elect, but Father, Son, and Spirit will be refreshed and satisfied with all the sweet fruits of this new creation and renovation by the death, resurrection, and Spirit of the Lord Jesus (Matthew 17:5, John. 19:30, Isaiah 53:10-11, Romans 4:25. Romans 8:33-34, Romans 11:29, Hebrews 7:21-22).

The approved practice of the primitive Christians declares the doctrine of the apostles, and the doctrine of the apostles shows what was the command of Christ the Lord of the Sabbath concerning the sanctification of the first day of the week, which is therefore called the Lord's day, and the Christian sabbath.

The Jewish sabbath was the holy day or sabbath of Jehovah as creator, and all three coessential persons did create us.[618] The Christian sabbath is called *the Lord's day*, since the Lord Christ has been declared to be the Son of God by his resurrection (Romans 1:4) and the Lord of all (Romans 14:9, Matthew 28:17-18).

The ministry and sacraments under the New Testament are appointed by Christ, and therefore used by virtue of the second commandment though the outward worship be changed, and in like manner, the sabbath appointed

---

[617] See Master White of the morality of the 4th Commandment. Dr. Twisse, Mr. Cawdry, and Mr. Palmer, Mr. Shepheard, Dr. Ames Medulla Theol. Dr. Lakes Theses.

[618] The Jewish sabbath, Isaiah 58:13, the Christian sabbath

by Christ must be observed by virtue of the fourth commandment, though the day be changed, because this is the general scope both of the second and fourth commandments that we ought to observe all the institutions of God from time to time.

We are then obliged both by law and gospel to observe the Lord's day, and we may with confidence expect a blessing upon our observation of it, for he who sanctified the day did bless it also, that is, annex a blessing to the sanctification of it.[619] Read Peter Martyr upon Genesis 2 and the fourth commandment. When God rested from the works of creation he appointed a sabbath, although he did not rest from works of providence, and in like manner, Christ has appointed a Sabbath upon his resting from the work of redemption by price, although he does not rest from the work of redemption by power until all his enemies be vanquished and his elect saved.

These grounds being laid, it is most evident, that we are to keep a spiritual rest to Father, Son, and Holy Spirit upon the Lord's day. We are not only to draw near to the ordinances, but to God, and Christ in them by the power of the Holy Spirit, because all spiritual communion with God in Christ is maintained by the power of the Holy Spirit (2 Corinthians 13:14). And our communion with God upon the Lord's day ought to be more immediate and eminent, more spiritual and heavenly than at other times. Christians do enjoy God, not only in his creatures, providences, and works of their callings according to the variety of their occasions, but also in acts of immediate worship and service even upon the weekdays; but we are to do God some more eminent service on the Lord's day. We should not content ourselves with weekday prayers and praises. Our holiness and communion should be extraordinary upon this solemn day, and therefore:

---

[619] Rabbi Agnon dicit hanc benedictionem transire super sanctificantes Sabbatum ante legem in Sina datam. Cognitio & celebratio Dei Creatoris, & consideratio seria operum Creationis ac Redemptionis ad Ceremoniā referri nequeunt. D. Waelleus de Sabbatho. pag. 583.

(1) Eminent for the degree of it; there should be a sequestration of our minds and hearts from the world, and a consecration of them to the blessed Trinity in the highest degree, and after the most immediate manner in all exercises of religion with admiration, confidence, love, reverence, delight, and thankfulness, that we may come as near to God (who comes down on purpose to meet us in his ordinances with a full blessing) as it is possible for creatures that are clothed with flesh.[620] We must abstain not only from servile works, but servile thoughts, cares, and affections. The sacrifice was doubled on the sabbath to show that our holiness should be redoubled on that day (Numbers 28:9). The sabbath was called "holiness" (Exodus 31:15) and "the holy of Jehovah" (Isaiah 58:13) to show that we should be exceedingly holy upon this holy day. We should be transported beyond flesh and the world, and have our conversation in heaven that day, for the day requires some transcendent holiness.

(2) Our holiness and communion should be restorative. For we contract much soil, abate the vigor of our graces by converse with the world upon the weekdays, and now there should be *restauratio deperditi*. We should sadly review our experiences, and failings all the week, and make up all our defects upon this acceptable day, this season of grace, when God sits in state, and scatters treasures of grace amongst hungry, and thirsty saints that are poor in spirit, and wait for spiritual alms at a throne of grace.

(3) Constant communion. We should maintain a continued and uninterrupted communion with God in private, as well as public all the whole day together. It is lawful for us on the weekdays to go about our worldly occasions after we have been at prayer, but we find that when we have been well warmed by family duties, we are apt to catch cold again presently when company or worldly businesses break in upon us. But we must keep our hearts in a sabbath's day's frame all the Lord's day, yea, and at night also; when our bodies are wearied in service, we must not be weary of

---

[620] Read Mr. Shepherd's excellent treatise upon this subject in his fourth part of the sanctification of the sabbath.

service, but our hearts must be panting and working after more of God, and Christ, and the Holy Spirit.

(4) Soul-satiating communion. We must take delight in our converse with God, enjoyment of Christ, and walking in the Spirit all the day. We must enter into the rest of our beloved, and take a sweet complacency in the fruition of God, in the glimpse of his glory, in the taste of his love, in the kisses of his mouth, in all the testimonies of his favor, in all the love-tokens sent us from heaven. The joy of the Lord must be our strength, and in this strength we must go forth and mortify our corruptious, resist temptations, and go about our worldly business all the next week with heavenly minds.

I cannot stand to speak directly and fully to the particular duties of the sabbath, or extraordinary duties of evangelical fasting, and Christian feasting, for all which there should be a serious preparation, in all which there must be a prudent sequestration of our minds and hearts from the world, that there may be an entire consecration of them unto God, and a sincere sanctification of all these times to Father, Son, and Holy Spirit, as it becomes the Sons of God, the members of Christ, and temples of the Holy Spirit. We should get oil into our vessels, dress and trim our lamps, that we may meet the bridegroom of our souls in his appointed walks, in his own ordinances and exercises.

I should say something likewise of our penitential meltings before God. Thus in brief then, when our conscience has been wounded by the Spirit of bondage, and is renewed by the Spirit of regeneration, it will in due time be pacified by the Spirit of adoption, but even then the soul will melt into tears, nay, then it melts most kindly, and laments most affectionately:

"O I have sinned against the tender mercies of the bowels of God; I have kicked my Father upon the bowels; I have made a sport and pastime of those sins, which let out the heart blood of my dear Savior; I have grieved, vexed, and even quenched the Holy Spirit, my sweetest Comforter; I have sinned against all three, and so trebled all my sins; I fear I have (says the soul in its agony) even done despite to the Spirit of grace, and trampled on the blood of the Son of God; but I have learnt to submit, and believe, to rejoice, and tremble, to weep, and wait; for I wait upon a Father, upon him whom my soul loves; the Spirit of faith and love has taught me to come with a broken heart, and a bleeding conscience to a Father, to a Savior, to a Comforter. I desire to keep the wound open by renewed confessions, and sprinkle the cleansing blood of Christ upon it by a lively faith. Oh, it is sovereign blood, and must be fiducially sprinkled by a special application!" And it is the Spirit which makes this special application, and administers reviving cordials to broken hearts, and fainting souls in their swooning fits.

When the most ingenuous and refined sort of unregenerate men come to see that, notwithstanding all their civility and formality, they are in the gall of bitterness by reason of their impenitence and unbelief, their opposition to the power of godliness, their undervaluing of the mercies of God, the love of Christ, graces and comforts of the Holy Spirit, and feel these sins set home upon their hearts and consciences with stinging aggravations, they are even fired out of their natural estate, and by the preventing grace of the Spirit made sensible of sin, and hungry after grace and mercy. The dreadful impressions of God's infinite majesty, and damning wrath make all the sensual impressions of sin to be remembered with proportionable and self-condemning horror.

But when the most glorious treasures of God's sweetest mercies, and richest grace, folded up in his fatherly bowels, are opened to these ingenuous men, and the Spirit has touched their hearts to lament after Christ; then this ingenuous soul will cry out, "Oh what restless agonies, what stinging worms, what unquenchable floods of flaming brimstone, how many hells are there treasured up in one hell for such a wretch as I am, who have undervalued the riches of God's mercy, the love and merits of Christ, the graces and comforts of the Spirit! Heaven and earth may be astonished; men and angels amazed at my prodigious madness in undervaluing Christ and heaven!"

In the midst of this agony and conflict, prudent astonishment, and spiritual horror, the Holy Spirit urges invincible arguments which are sweetly compulsive to persuade and constrain the soul to long for Christ. For when the Spirit has made the threats both of law and gospel effectual to humble us, he fills the soul with despair of mercy if it continues in its former estate, in the gall of impenitence and bond of unbelief, but nevertheless assures the soul that there is plenteous redemption, and eternal salvation treasured up in Christ for penitent believers. Then the Spirit opens the mystery of free grace contained in a covenant sealed with the oath of God, and blood of Christ. He reveals the eternity, excellency, sweetness, freeness, fullness, infiniteness of God's mercy and grace, Christ's love and merits as so many motives and encouragements unto faith and repentance. The Spirit sets a pardon and a crown before us, acquaints us with the all-sufficient righteousness and unsearchable riches of Christ, and his own free and effectual grace, unspeakable comforts, and glorious joys, and then convinces us that we want this grace to sanctify us, this pardon and righteousness to justify us, this crown, and these joys to enrich and satisfy us. And upon this discovery, the soul is encouraged to give credit to the Holy Spirit to believe the love of the Father to depend upon Christ's satisfaction, and apply his righteousness, to prize the love of the Father, the merit of Christ, the grace and comforts of the Spirit above a world – in a word, to sell all for Christ, and give up all to Christ, resolving to be ruled by himself and his Spirit forevermore.

Now the soul has a new life put into it, it hungers and thirsts for a more intimate communion with Father, Son, and Holy Spirit, and this hungry soul sucks whilst the breast is open until it has filled itself with substantial nourishment and reviving cordials. This devout soul becomes (as Chrysostom styled Paul) an insatiable worshiper of Father, Son, and Holy Spirit. It desires to grow in grace, to press on towards perfection, to have Father, Son, and Holy Spirit to come sup with it, dwell in it, rule in it, that it may be enriched with the unsearchable riches of Christ, and filled with all the fullness of God.

This converted soul does – after these penitential meltings, fiducial breathings after Christ, and obediential closing with Father, Son, and Holy Spirit – differ as much from itself (when it was most ingenuous before its conversion) as an angel does from a devil. For the most ingenuous and refined sort of unregenerate men have nothing in them, which is more excellent than common grace, and common grace leaves them in the state of nature under the power of sin, and in the very suburbs of hell, wholly at the command of Satan; and if any man think otherwise, let him take heed that that very thought does not nail him fast to that unregenerate and cursed estate forevermore.

Believe it brethren, that historical faith and natural wisdom do but excite some pang of self-love, which makes us very solicitous how we may stop the mouth of our convinced conscience with some kind of ingenuous civilities, and outward formalities without any penitent acknowledgment of our sinful and cursed estate, any prudent esteem of Christ, whose blood, merit, righteousness, and grace ought to be prized above a world. We never seek Christ in earnest till he has first sought us, found us out, and brought us home by his preventing, quickening, saving grace. And when Christ dwells conquering and reigning in the soul, the soul is not content with civilities and formalities with common grace, or some low degree of special grace, but it aims at grace in perfection. The heart is kindly broken by faith and love; the soul is humble, thankful, zealous, merciful, diligent, constant in serving Christ, and Christians upon all occasions.

Civil and formal men may by legal terrors be brought to some kind of devotion, they may by a historical faith be brought to some kind of admiration of the gospel, to many good wishes and velleities, nay, to a reformation in many particulars, but because they undervalue the love of the Father, the grace of Christ, the communion of the Holy Spirit, and consequently the power of godliness, notwithstanding all their terrors, wishes, admiration, reformation, and hankerings after Christ and heaven, they perish in their unbelief, because they never had any hungry and thirsty desires, restless desires after Christ (such as would not be satisfied without him) wrought in their souls by the light of the gospel, power of the Spirit, and serious and seasonable offers of Christ. They never come to a deliberate choice and thankful acceptance of Christ to be their savior, husband, priest, prophet and king; but did indeed choose rather to be Satan's bondslaves, then Christ's spouse, they would not make a prudent exchange of Satan's fetters for Christ's yoke, and therefore are but dancing to hell with their fetters, in the fairest path that they can possibly find to the chambers of death.

They could never be persuaded to be content with Christ alone as their all-sufficient portion, and therefore refused to sell all for him, and give up all to him, but did upon mature deliberation, and in cool blood reject Christ, resist his Spirit, refuse a pardon of sin, and deed of heaven, purchased and sealed with the heart-blood of God; and this very consideration will sting the conscience and torment the soul of these everlasting Bedlams, when they lie in chains of darkness, cursing themselves to all eternity, and blaspheming God for torturing of them in the angry flames of hellish brimstone.

But that this mystery may be yet more freely discovered, take any man that is not guilty of the black and unpardonable sin of trampling on the blood of Christ, and doing despite to the Spirit of grace, and let him be one of the most desperate villains that ever served the devil, and I dare encourage this wretch, whom hell and Satan do even gape and groan for, to go to Christ for preventing grace, that the Holy Spirit may set home the curses of the law, and the more severe threatenings of the gospel, upon his obdurate heart in a saving way, and beseech him to knock early at heaven-gate, the sooner the better, because God gives Christ and his Spirit, a pardon and a crown, as fathers give lands to their children, only because they will give them, he gives all freely and royally.

Christ has gifts for the rebellious also, God shows mercy and gives grace to them that do deserve neither grace nor mercy. And if the Spirit does open the eyes and heart of this man, that the sense of his own devilish brutishness may move him to inquire after God and Christ (Proverbs 30:1-3) and gives him present support from falling under the weight of his own sin, and God's curse into despair, after illumination, conviction, terrors, before he come to hunger after Christ, submit to him, and close with him, as an all-sufficient Savior, and an only Savior, then this trembling soul may – in the midst of cares, and hopes, and terrors – be encouraged and enabled by a Spirit of regeneration, with all humility, joy and thankfulness to accept of Christ, and rest upon him for righteousness and life, by a faith of dependance, adherence, recumbence, and to submit and melt with evangelical repentance at a throne of grace. And when his heart is thus broken by faith and love, which do cast out unbelief, self-love and slavish fear which tends to despair, this even now very black soul – but now purified by the Spirit of regeneration, and revived by the Spirit of adoption, sprinkling the blood of Christ upon his conscience, and shedding the love of God abroad in his heart – will be encouraged to call God *Father*, and Christ *Savior*. The Father will meet, embrace, adorn him, wipe off his tears and filth, and kiss that prodigal mouth, which came from feeding with swine and kissing of harlots. Christ will bid this soul welcome, it shall be thrice welcome to this coessential Trinity.

For God who brought his pardoning mercy, preventing and effectual grace to us when we looked not after him, will surely bid us welcome when we come unto him with a prudent care, a lively faith, a son-like reverence, a penitent indignation against our sin and lusts, melting affections, and yearning bowels towards him, and flaming zeal in his service, and for his cause. He who ran and called after us when we looked not after him will not reject us when we come unto him out of tender respect, and hearty love to him and his service. He that has the Spirit, shall have Son, and Father also.

Let all churlish Nabals, proud Pharisees, politic Gallios, scoffing Ishmaels, impenitent formalists, and unbelieving atheists consider what has been said, and look upon themselves as guilty of eternal death. Let them hear with wonder and amazement, let them believe and tremble, and let all the enemies of the grace of God, Pelagians, papists, and so on, know that all preparatives are wrought by the Word and Spirit, and that it is one great preparative to abhor the thought of all meritoriousness in all or any of those preparatives which make way for the infusion of faith.

For faith is the free gift of God, and though there be many necessary preparatives to drive us to Christ, yet there are no meritorious qualifications in us to bribe God, allure Christ, or deserve grace. The Spirit works when, where, and as he pleases, and he who does not prize the love of the Father, the grace of Christ, and communion of the Holy Spirit above a world is not as yet acquainted with the mystery of faith, or the power of godliness, he has neither Father, Son, nor Spirit in him.

Chapter 10

Christians who have a Lively Sense & Sweet Experience of this Grand Mystery of Faith, & Practical Mystery of Godliness, are Afraid to hold Communion with such as Pretend to be Spiritual Christians, & yet Deny the Divine Nature & Distinct Subsistences of Christ & his Holy Spirit.

It is observed by a great statesman that he who follows truth too near at heels, may have his teeth beaten out, but I had rather lose my teeth than not teach, and profess the truth. He who presses this point in this licentious age, wherein skeptics in the highest points are called seekers, and heretics good Christians, had need beg the promise of the Father, that he may be endued with virtue from on high, that is, a magnanimous and more than a heroic spirit to preach the truth.[621]

We must not fear the face of man in the cause of God. If the devil might set up his church in England, wherein heresy is instead of a preacher, profaneness and ungodliness instead of ruling elders, yet I must be bold to say, that these seekers whom the Reformers called *libertines*, are as the fathers called them, but nullifidians, and atheists, professed atheists. For they are atheists, who will not believe and adore the only true God – Father, Son, and Holy Spirit – and such are the seekers whom I am to deal with, who deny the Lord Christ to be God; and I shall easily discover that this is atheism. Whether [this is] reigning atheism or not, let the Socinian seekers and deified atheists judge.[622]

---

[621] Luk. 24. 49 Magnitudo animi ad praedicandum Evangelium necessaria ex alto promittitur. D. Alting.
[622] An etiam Abnegatio Christi quae fit corde in Epicureismum prolapso sit peccatum in Spiritum Sanctum? Vide Scultetum in Ideis concionum ad cap 6. ad Hebraeos. Clamant Deificari Spiritus homunciones se nullum habere Deum, sed usque adeo se sibi esse mortuos, ac Deo unitos ut ipsimet Deus effecti sint; vide Joh. Ruys broch. in

"Whosoever transgresseth and abideth not in the doctrine of Christ *hath not God*; he who abideth in the doctrine of Christ, he hath both the Father and the Son (2 John 9)." "Who is a liar but he that denieth that Jesus is the Christ? He is antichrist that denieth the Father and the Son. Whosoever denieth the Son, the same hath not the Father (1 John 2:22-24)." He who has not the true God – Father, Son, and Holy Spirit – for his God, is an atheist, for if he do acknowledge a false god, a false god being no God, it must still be granted that no man can be excused from atheism by his acknowledgment or worship of anything that is not God.

I speak of such speculative atheism as does commonly run into practical atheism, and may consequently end in direct and downright atheism, or at least such affected atheism as will permit that radical and seminal atheism which was borne with them to sit quietly in their hearts as on a throne, so that they have no actual belief of the true God which amounts to a historical belief; much less any that can effectually overpower or dethrone their natural atheism. And yet I believe these atheistical libertines can never fully blot out all the natural notions of a Godhead written in their hearts by the finger of God, though many of them have made a very unhappy progress in this devilish study.[623] For the devils themselves have not attained to any atheistical πληροφορία or αναιθησια: the devils believe and tremble; but enough of that; the Socinians are interpretative atheists at the least.[624]

---

cap. 2. Apologiae. Nobilissimum Marnixium in Tract. contra Enthysiastas, & Calvinum de Libertinis in Gallia. Merceunum contra Deistas. De Atheismo subtili & palliato, vide D. Vedelium de Deo Synagogae. Casp. Barth. Adversar. lib 10. cap. 6. Cornel. à Lapide Comment ad Act. 17. 18. Sladum nec non Eglisemnium contra Vorstium. Atheus est qui fidem & cultum Dei directe aut indirecte à se aut ab aliis removet. D. Voetius de Atheismo.

[623] Vide John. Junium in Refutatione Praelect. Socini cap. 2. & D. Rivet. in Psal. 19.

[624] D. Voet. de Atheismo. Ignorans quis sit Deus ignorantiâ pravae dispositionis; & contra sensum numinis congenitum verum Deum negans, Atheus certè, nec immeritò, dicendus est. Nulli autem sunt Athei qui certò persuasi sunt non esse Deum. Vide Mersennum in Gen. 1. à pag. 235. usque ad pa. 279. & Voetium in Ther site. Sect. 2. cap. 4. & de Atheismo parte secundâ, & parte quarta pag. 189. Wigandum de Arianis in Polonia. Facilis est ab Atheismo Sociniano in directum Atheismum prolapsus. Vide Bedae notas in Ephes. 2. 14. & D. Vedelium de Deo

It is not enough for Christian communicants to attain to the first principle of natural theology, and confess that there is a God, but they must acknowledge the first principle of Christianity, which is indeed supernatural divinity, and acknowledge, that Father, Son, and Holy Spirit are the only true God; for else we go no further than Pharaoh that grand seeker did, when he asked: "Who is Jehovah that I should obey his voice?" (Exodus 5:2). Or then the Samaritans and Athenians did, who worshiped they knew not what (John 4:22, Acts 17:23). The Turks, the Pagans, and the Jews do acknowledge that there is a God; unless then we do intend to hold church-communion with Pagans, Jews, Mahometans, we must require somewhat more of those, whom we admit unto Christian Communion than a bare acknowledgment that there is a God, or that the Father is God.[625] For he who does deny the Godhead of the Son, does deny the Father also, and consequently has no God at all for his God, as has been proven already from 2 John 9 and 1 John 2:22-24. He that honors not the Son as highly as he honors the Father, he does not honor the Father, who sent his co-equal Son to give us life (John 5:21, 23). We must acknowledge the Son to be equal to the Father, for this redounds to the glory of God the Father (Philippians 2:6, 11).

We can have no Christian and spiritual communion with God the Father but in his natural Son, and by their coessential Spirit, as is manifest by comparing these texts together: 1 John. 1:3, 1 Corinthians 1:9, 2 Corinthians 13:14, Revelation 1:4-5, Matthew 28:19-20, Ephesians 2:18, 22; 1 Corinthians 12:3, 6, 8, 11, 13, and by the full scope of all my practical discourse in the ninth chapter of this treatise. "This is life eternal," etc. (John 17:3; 1 John 5:6-7, 11-13, 20). When Paul enlarges the bounds of Christian communion as far as he can, he writes thus: "Unto the church of God which

---

Synagogae. Atheismus interpretativè contradicens & directè blasphemans ferendus non est in civili hominum societate, quia bonum civile non consistit sine metu cultuque numinis. Vide Calvin. in Psal. 115. de Atheo blasphemante.

[625] Vide Arist. de coelo lib. 1. cap. 3. Aug. in Psal. 44. Senec. Epist. 1. 7. Damasc. de Orth. fid. lib. 1. c. 1. Ciceron. de naturâ Deorum.

is at Corinth, to them that are sanctified in Christ Jesus, called to be saints, with all that in every place call upon the name of Jesus Christ our Lord, both theirs and ours (1 Corinthians 1:2)."

We cannot maintain any Christian communion with such as deny the Godhead of Christ, for they must (as Francis David and David George, etc. did) deny that Christ is to be worshiped with divine faith and love, because (as they blasphemously said) he has not the same divine nature with God the Father; or else they must say as Socinus, who wrote against Francis David, said, that Christ is to be worshiped with divine worship. Then they will – if you put their principles together (as you may see them together in that Racovian Koran known as the Racovian Catechism) – be found to be even the very best of them, but a pack of blasphemous idolaters, with whom we ought not to hold communion.[626] For whilst they do blasphemously affirm that Christ is a mere man in glory, and the Son of God only in a metaphorical, not any proper sense, we must draw these conclusions. The best of the Socinians maintain:

(1) That Jesus Christ our Lord is but a mere man in glory, a very creature and no more.[627] Therefore, they are blasphemers; and so are all they who say, that they are as much God as Jesus Christ. For these are high swelling blasphemies, such as the deified atheists of the Family of Love (with whom I fear Mr. Fry has had too much acquaintance) do usually vent to the great dishonor of Christ and Christianity.[628]

(2) That a mere man, a very creature is to be worshiped with divine honor; and therefore they are idolaters. Master Fry must prove that he himself is to be worshiped with divine honor also, or else he cannot make

---

[626] Vide Epistolas Martini Seidelii Silesii apud Socinum de Adoratione Christiad versus Christian—Francken. & Franciscum Davidis. Catechis. Racov. The Socinians are blasphemous and Idolatrous Hereticks.

[627] The Family of love. H. Nicolaus Familiae Caritatis: Pater dixit, Ego sum Deus. Vide Theodor.

[628] Cornhert in Specimine injustitiae Deificati Hen Nicolai Praefat. Mr. Fry's Bellows. pag. 16.

good his proud assertions in his blasphemous pamphlet; or else he must say as David George did, that Christ is not to be worshiped with divine honor.

Now then, the question is: what respect is to be shown, or communion ought to be held, with blasphemous and idolatrous heretics, who are seducers also, and do zealously endeavor to poison souls, as it does well become apostatizing renegades?

Those who are acquainted with ecclesiastical writers[629] know what respect was shown or communion held with Arians and others who did deny the Godhead of Christ, though they did maintain that Christ was to be worshiped with divine honor.[630] I shall not tell long stories of Cerinthus, Ebion, Photinus, Arius, and their adherents, but it is clear and evident that the Arians were condemned because they were a pack of blasphemous and idolatrous heretics, seducers, apostates, upon the grounds which I shall presently relate and such as are above mentioned. They did deny the divine nature of Christ, and yet acknowledged that divine worship was due unto him. But I had rather produce proofs than tell stories, and therefore I shall give you the true grounds and reasons why they are rejected from Christian communion, and why even civil respect is denied to such, who – upon mature deliberation, after more admonitions than one – deny the Godhead of Christ, and the Holy Spirit.

I shall begin with Christian communion, because that makes most for my purpose.

(1) These vain men are rejected from Christian communion for these reasons:

[1] Because they do not agree with Christians in the common unity of the Christian faith, for all who are come into the unity of the faith are come into the knowledge of the Son of God (Ephesians 4:13), and into the knowledge of the Holy Spirit, because these are the baptismal principles of

---

[629] Vide Gomarum, Voetium, Zanchium, Polanum de Trinitate. Jod.
[630] Coc. Thesaur. Cathol. lib. 1. Goldast. in Imperial. constit. Tom. 3. Elmenhorst. com. ad Gennadium.

the doctrine of Christ (Acts 19:2-3, Hebrews 6:1-2, 4, Matthew 28:19, John. 14:17; 1 Corinthians 2:1, 4, 12-13; 1 Corinthians 12:13, Ephesians 4:4-6).

[2] They do not agree with Christians concerning the adequate object of divine and evangelical worship. The Father, Son, and Holy Spirit are the adequate object of divine and evangelical worship, of divine faith, hope, and love (1 John 5:6-7; 2 Corinthians 13:14, Revelation 1:4-5, Matthew 28:19, John 14:1, John 5:23, Romans 15:30; 1 Corinthians 3:16, 17; 1 Corinthians 6:19-20; 1 Corinthians 12:6, 8, 11). They may well go join with Pagans, Jews, and Mahometans in worship, who say that Christ is a mere man. Mahomet did collect his Koran with great dexterity out of such common principles as that he might take in Jews and Christians.[631] And Socinus followed Mahomet's instructions, saying that Arians and Calvinists may be both saved, so they do but live morally. Barlaeus says that Jews may be very pious towards God in their religion, though they do deny and reject Jesus Christ, as Videlius shows in his book de *De Deo Synagogae*. And this, as Barlaeus is pleased to call it, is accounted the most accurate divinity of the high-flying mercuries.

Beza, in his epistle to Petrus Statorius, has given our great wits a fair warning. I have read of one Nuserus, a minister in the Palatinate, who did first fall away to the Socinians and deny the Trinity, and afterwards turned to the Turks, and did solemnly profess himself to be a Mahometan at Constantinople. And the like is written by authors of good credit, concerning that schoolmaster who fell away to Judaism, and wrote letters from Thessalonica that the reason why he went off from the Christian profession was because he could not digest the mystery of the Trinity. We that are Christians, worship the only true God, Father, Son, and Holy Spirit;

---

[631] Vide Epistolas Seidelii apud Socinum de Adoratione christi. Videl. de Deo synagogae. lib. 1. cap. 2. socinismus ex Mahumetismo oritur, & in eundem resolvitur. Stegman. Photin. Socinismus est recta ad Judaismi, Turcismi, nec non Atheismi via. Exempla dabant Neuserus & Pafradus viri non indocti, quorum ille minister in Palatinatu, hic praeceptor Classicus Scholae Marpurgensis. Vide D. Voetii Antidota Generalia adversus Socin. pag. 437. 438. Abrah. Calovium

and therefore we must be true to our religion, and beware of such impostors, who would seduce us to worship a mere man instead of the great God, and our Savior Jesus Christ.

My heart rises with just indignation against Mr. Fry's blasphemous pamphlet, when I read there that according to his understanding of the word *subsistence*, he may be said to be God too, as well as Jesus Christ (page 16). I know he will wrangle about the word *subsistence*, but that word is found in Scripture, and applied unto the Father (Hebrews 1:3), and we read of the being, or subsisting of the Son in the form, that is, the nature of God; he thought it not robbery to be equal with God.[632] Sure Master Fry ought to think it robbery to make himself equal with Christ in subsistence, when Christ is equal to his Father, and has no human, but a divine subsistence only,[633] which upholds the human nature which Christ has assumed; and all Christianity is built upon the divine subsistence of Christ, God-man, as has been shown, and shall be yet more clearly manifested.

In like manner, they that receive not the Holy Spirit cannot be received by us whose happiness it is to believe, adore, and obey the Spirit – as has been shown at large.

[3] They do not agree with Christians concerning the substance of the gospel, and the covenant of grace. Whatsoever we receive in point of religion ought to be received upon the credit of all three persons, but more especially upon the divine testimony of the Spirit of Christ, the holy and eternal Spirit sent down from heaven (1 Peter 1:11-12; 1 Corinthians 2:1, 4-5, 12-13). They then who reject the Spirit and deny his testimony to be divine because his nature (as they blasphemously maintain) is not divine, do indeed reject both Testaments, and therefore reject the whole gospel and covenant of grace. Moreover, this covenant is made by all three persons, for the covenant contains the love of the Father, the grace of Christ, and the

---

[632] εν μορφη θεου υπαρχων Philippians 2:6
[633] Error Personae fatalis error est.

communion of the Holy Spirit.[634] The Father of our Lord Jesus Christ enters into covenant to be our Father in the Lord Christ. The covenant is established upon the satisfaction and righteousness of God-man; and therefore they who deny the Godhead of Christ, must rest upon their own righteousness and obedience for justification, and salvation, as the Socinians do, and then Christ will profit them nothing, because they overthrow the new covenant and are fallen from grace (Galatians 5:4-5).[635] The covenant is sealed with the blood of Christ, who is not only the Son of Mary, but the natural Son of God. This is the substance of the gospel: the same person is God and man, the son of Mary is the true Messiah, the Lord Christ, the only Son of God, equal to his Father, the head and savior of the church, the true God, the blessed God, the great God, the mighty God. We are redeemed with the blood of Christ, the blood of God, the blood of Christ who is God. The covenant is to quicken and cure us.

{1} To quicken us, for we were dead before the medicine came, and Christ and his Spirit raise us from death, and give us a spiritual life.

{2} To cure us, for when our physician has restored us to life, he can more easily restore us to health. In the covenant, God promises to give us himself, his Son, and his Spirit. The bond of the federal and mystical union on God's part is the Spirit, and on our part faith, which is wrought in us by the same coessential Spirit. And Christ is the only mediator of this covenant.

(i) We have but one mediator and surely of this covenant (1 Timothy 2:5; 1 Corinthians 8:6).

(ii) This one mediator is God and man in one person: the Son of man (Matthew 16:13), the Son of God (Matthew 16:16-17, Romans 1:3-4, Romans 9:5, Hebrews 7:3, John 8:58, Acts 20:28; 1 John 1:1, Ephesians 4:10, John 3:13, John 6:62, John 1:14, Philippians 2:6). He for whom are all things,

---

[634] Galatians 5:5; 2 Corinthians 13:14, Ephesians 2:18.

[635] Socinismus est haeresis pestilentissima, divinitatem Christi spiritus{que} abnegans, viamque per propriam vitae obedientiam ad coelum affectans. Socinianism overthrows the covenant of grace. Socinismus divinam Christi essentiam, personam, satisfactionem negans, objectum fidei cultusque tollit, Christianismum evertit.

and by whom are all things, even he himself and not another person; he also himself took part of the same flesh and blood whereof we are partakers (Hebrews 2:10, 14).

I hope by this time it is evident that the covenant is made in Christ the natural and coessential Son of God, who is God and man in one person, and therefore we cannot close with them who will not close with this saving truth; for this is an article of everlasting life (Matthew 16:16-18, John 17:3; 1 John 5:20, Ephesians 4:13). I humbly entreat Mr. Fry to consider what has been said, so that he may repent and retract his unhappy opinion, namely, that the word subsistence holds forth no more of Christ his being in the Godhead than may be affirmed of every creature, that whatsoever the head did partake of, that did the members also.[636] And that according to his understanding of the word *subsistence*, Mr. Fry himself might be said to be God too as well as Jesus Christ (pages 15-16). This is the unsavory breath of Mr. Fry's blasphemous bellows printed at Addle Hill in February 1648. If his confutation be as public as he thought fit to make his blasphemous error (which he accounts but a molehill on page 17), he may thank himself.

I might add many other reasons, but I must be brief.

[4] I might argue from the very nature of Christian communion, which is a Christian and spiritual communion with the Father, in the Son, by the Spirit; but I have said enough of that already in this very chapter, and handled it practically and at large in the ninth chapter of this treatise.[637]

[5] I might argue from the sacraments of communion, and seals of that covenant of grace, which they who do deny the Trinity overthrow, as has been proven.

{1} In baptism, we Christians are devoted and consecrated to the belief, worship, and service of God the Father, God the Son, and God the Holy Spirit, who are all three one and the same God, the only true God blessed forever. Therefore, those who do not believe and worship God the Son, and

---

[636] Mr Fry in his Bellows, printed at Addle-hill. pag. 15, 16, 17.
[637] 2 Corinthians 13:14, Ephesians 2:18

God the Holy Spirit as the same God with the Father, do indeed renounce the faith and baptism of Christians; they take away the adequate object of Christian faith and evangelical worship.[638] God promises to be a Father, Savior, and a Comforter to us; he seals his promise to us by baptism and fulfills his promise by giving us his Son for our Savior, and his Spirit for our Sanctifier and Comforter; for he shows himself to be a Father to us in Christ by sending the Spirit of regeneration and adoption into our hearts.[639] We are regenerated by the Spirit of God, adopted into the family of God, and married to the Son of God, so that we may be heirs and coheirs with Christ the King of heaven, and Lord of glory – and all this is to oblige and encourage us in the belief, worship, and service of Father, Son, and Holy Spirit.

{2} In the sacrament of the Lord's Supper, we Christians sanctify the name of Christ the natural Son of God, and the name of the coessential Spirit; the everlasting counsels of God's Fatherly love, the riches of his free grace, all the treasures of the covenant and Spirit of grace, all the sufferings of our crucified redeemer, the Lord of glory, are in this great ordinance evidently set before the eye of our faith, that by the grace of Christ, assistance and fellowship of the Holy Spirit, we may have a more intimate communion with God; for this sweet communion with the Father of our Lord Jesus Christ is by the communion of the blood of God (Acts 20:28. compared with 1 Corinthians 10:16) and of the Spirit of God (2 Corinthians 13:14). This is the grand ordinance for the highest, sweetest, strongest communion with the Father, in the Son, and by the Spirit, that can be attained whilst we are clothed with flesh. The gospel is appointed both for the begetting and increase of grace; this ordinance is annexed to the gospel, that the gospel and this ordinance both together may (by the power of Christ and his Holy Spirit) be effectual according to the counsel of God's will for bringing of lost sinners into a saving communion, nay, a growing,

---

[638] Matthew 28:19, Ephesians 2:18; 2 Corinthians 13:14, Acts 2:38-39
[639] 2 Corinthians 6:18, 7:1, Galatians 4:5-6.

thriving communion with Father, Son, and Holy Spirit, that we may come to be enriched at last with the unsearchable riches of Christ, and filled with all the fullness of God.

(i) When we see the bread and wine consecrated and set apart for this holy use, we should consider the unspeakable love of God the Father, setting his co-essential Son Jesus Christ apart in his secret and eternal counsel in order to be the surety and Savior of his chosen people. This is the great mystery, which the very angels desire to look into, and which will be the subject of all the praises and hallelujahs both of saints and angels to all eternity in the highest heavens.

(ii) When we see the bread broken and wine poured out, we must remember the love of Christ, whose body was broken and blood shed for our sins.

(iii) When the bread and wine are distributed and divided, we should meditate upon the application of Christ crucified to everyone of our own souls in particular. Now this special application is made by the assistance and communion of the Holy Spirit.

And therefore this mystery of the coessential Trinunity must be acknowledged by all who are admitted to this sacrament, because this is the greatest confirmation of the great bond of the highest communion which we can have with Father, Son, and Holy Spirit, and with the most precious Christians, who are sound in faith and holy in life.

We can never understand the presence, institution, and mind of Christ in this ordinance, unless we believe the cursed condition of men in their natural estate, the divine nature and person of Christ, the greatness of the price that was paid for the satisfaction of God's justice, and appeasing of God's wrath, who did not spare his own coessential Son, but manifested his hatred against sin, and love to his elect in not sparing his Son, but breaking his body and shedding of his blood so that we might be redeemed by the blood of God.

This is the mystery which is made sensible in the sacrament, and is really evident to the eye of faith (Galatians 3:1). And whosoever looks upon these great mysteries of the gospel as fancies, and does not believe them to be real things truly exhibited, really presented to believers in a sacramental, mystical, and spiritual way in this ordinance, has not yet learnt the truth as it is in Jesus; and is not prepared for such high communion.[640]

We Christians do not come with hungry and thirsty souls longing after further communion with Christ for mortifying of our lusts, and increase of all our graces by his spirit, until we believe this grand mystery of faith; and we are then experimentally acquainted with the mystery of godliness when we have been made drink into one Spirit with Christ and his members, when we look upon him whom we have pierced by our sins, and acknowledge him to be the natural and coessential Son of God. There can be none of those fiducial breathings after Christ, penitential meltings before him, or obediential closings with him – as is evident by our ninth chapter – until we do in some measure believe this mystery of faith, and understand the substance of the covenant of grace, which is sealed in this sacrament by God, and must be actually renewed by every good communicant. Our meditations, faith, love, repentance, joy, thankfulness, will not be rightly placed or exercised, if this grand mystery of faith and godliness be rejected by us.

[6] I might argue from all the offices of Christ; they who do not believe the divine nature of Christ, do utterly disable Jesus Christ from being a mediator, a priest, a prophet, and a king for the saving of his people to the uttermost.

They who deny the divine essence and person of Christ, do deny his satisfaction to be all-sufficient on our behalf. They depose Christ from that spiritual and heavenly kingdom which he has by nature; and render him incapable of that mediatory kingdom, which is delegated to Christ:

---

[640] John 6:55, 63

God-man by the decree of the coessential Trinunity. But I have said enough of that in the former part of this book.

I pass on to inquire what civil respect is due to such as do deny the divine nature of Christ and his Holy Spirit. That one text to my apprehension – 2 John 9:10, 11 – contains a very full and satisfactory answer: "Whosoever transgresseth and abideth not in the doctrine of Christ, hath not God; he that abideth in the doctrine of Christ he hath both the Father and the Son. If there come any unto you and bring not this doctrine, receive him not into your house neither bid him God speed. For he that biddeth him God speed, is partaker of his evil deeds."

But that this point may be more clearly stated, and all mistakes prevented, be pleased to consider,

(1) That such points of religion and worship as are necessary to be known and believed for the maintenance of Christian, spiritual, saving communion with Father, Son, and Holy Spirit, are clearly delivered in the holy Scriptures of truth.

(2) That if men who were formerly unblameable in their life and conversation, be seduced into any error which contradicts or subverts such fundamental points, they ought to be instructed with the spirit of meekness in a Christian and brotherly way.

(3) They are to be admonished with all faithfulness and meekness of wisdom twice or thrice, that they may understand the importance of the truth which is denied, the danger of the error maintained, the sad consequences of both, that if their conscience be not feared, they may return from their beloved and damned errors.

(4) If after all this meekness, patience, and forbearance, all Christian instructions, and brotherly admonitions, they do (as men that are judicially blinded for sinning against conscience): [1] persist in their error, [2] reject and revile the truth of God in these high and necessary points, [3] fall from the grace of God, frustrate the grace and covenant of God, evacuate the death of Christ, depose Christ and his Spirit from their throne and Godhead,

[4] seduce and poison others (Matthew 21:38), [5] deny and overthrow the foundation of divine faith, hope, love, and justification by faith, and the adequate object also of all Christian faith, evangelical worship, and sincere obedience, then these bold atheists (for they deny the only true God, Father, Son, and Holy Spirit) may without any scruple be rejected from Christian communion.[641] For there is certainly some lust or other which hinders them from seeing the truth, or professing that they do see it, and therefore it may be taken for granted that these men are obstinate, self-condemned men, men that combine with their wills and lusts against their own conscience, and clear shining Scriptures.[642] And therefore these men cannot complain that they are punished for their conscience, when they are indeed punished for sinning against their conscience; because they are condemned by their own conscience.

But it will be said that there are scarce any such men to be found as I have described.

To which I answer:

(1) Be pleased but to consider what has been delivered in this very chapter already, and compare it with the foregoing chapters, and with the many blasphemous pamphlets which do pass up and down without control in this licentious age (in which men adventure upon the very language of hell under pretense of exercising their Christian liberty, and speaking according to their new light) and this point will be too clear. For we do already grant that no man ought to be troubled for following the dictates of his conscience rightly informed, but for following pernicious errors which are contrary to his own conscience, unless he be judicially blinded by God for his customary sinning against light of conscience in former times.

---

[641] Titus 3:10-11

[642] He who persists in dangerous error after two admonitions wisely and faithfully dispensed, is condemned of himself, that is, of his own conscience. Read Reverend Mr. Cotton's Answer to Mr. Williams p. 26, 27. and so on to p. 35.

(2) Nothing is more common than for men to speak out of the abundance of that natural atheism which lurks in their hearts, contrary to the dictates of their natural conscience.

(3) Though conscience may be quiet whilst men are exercising their wits to maintain some error which is contrary to those mysteries of faith, which transcend natural reason, and are repugnant to the corruption of reason, especially, if they (are engaged in multitudes of business, connived at by such as sit at stern, and) do thrive and prosper in the world; yet conscience will find a time to speak when it may be heard, and then it will scourge these Mercurial vaporers with scorpions, and set all their errors and blasphemies in order before them with stinging aggravations, and prove them to be inward heretics.[643]

(4) We must distinguish between speculative atheists, such as libertines and enthusiasts usually are;[644] and practical atheists, such as sensual men are known to be; for I am bold to call these heretics atheists who deny the Son and Holy Spirit to be God after frequent instructions, and wholesome admonitions in cool blood and studied discourses;[645] for I do not speak of such as talk vainly and blasphemously also in the heat of disputation, or in a sudden paroxysm of temptation.[646] But he who does – upon mature deliberation, after the application of so many gracious remedies (with such meekness of wisdom as has been said)[647] – deny the Godhead of Christ after it has been made plain to him that if he holds this error, he overthrows the foundation of the Christian faith, and denies the adequate object of evangelical worship, because he does but believe in a creature, and so trust in an arm of flesh; and that he worships a mere creature, and therefore is an

---

[643] Quidisputat contra internum sensum & naturale conscientiae dictamen, est Heraeticus Interior.
[644] Vide Bezam. Annot. ad Eph. 2. 12. 1 The. 4. 5, Tit 1. 16. Ps. 10. 11, 13.
[645] Psalm 14, 36; Job 21:14-15
[646] 1 Corinthians 15:32, 34
[647] A subverted heretick (Titus 3:11) Εξεστραπται is quite thrown ess from the foundation, and turned upside down. See Mr Cotton against Mr Williams, cap. 13. pag. 30.

idolater; that a mere creature cannot satisfy the infinite justice of God for the sin of man, and consequently that we are not redeemed, and cannot be justified by Christ, if he is (as they blasphemously say he is) a mere man in glory. Finally, that if all his faith be carnal confidence, and all his worship idolatry, it is impossible for him to be saved if he continue in that vain faith and worship all his life.

Of such a man as this, who has made a profession of Christianity, and lived in an external conformity, it is no breach of charity to say, he is a subverted and self-condemned heretic, an apostate idolater, blasphemer, etc.[648] Therefore, we may safely reject him from Christian communion, and deny all civil respect unto him: for it is to be feared he is of their strain who said (Matthew 21:38): "This is the heir," etc.

The princes and states of Germany in their 100 grievances, Erastus, and some others would have church censures passed upon heretics, apostates, etc., but they desired that profane persons and those living scandalous lives might be spared – a doctrine fit to be preached amongst cyclops, men that have no sense or care of piety, a doctrine fit to usher in atheism or popery.[649] For they say the pope may be deposed for heresy, but not for a profane or scandalous life.[650] Grotius on the other side, and some of his followers would have scandalous persons excommunicated, but those (whom the Reformed churches have convicted of heresy) spared.[651] But I fear that there are too many in England who would have all the poison of Erastus and Grotius put together in a directory for church government, so that men might hold what they list, and live as they please. What a strange syncretism, what a promiscuous communion, what a church shall I say, nay, what a hell would there be in such an atheistical communion as these mercurial grandees affect.

---

[648] Titus 3:9-11; 2 John 9-11

[649] Atheismus dicitur Synecdochice Cyclopismus, quod Cyclopum instar nullam pietatis, & honestatis curam habeant. D. Voetius de Atheismo. pag. 117.

[650] Aen. Syl. de gestis Concil. Basil. l. 1.

[651] Grot. Annot. in. Luc. 6. 22. The Atheistical Syncrctisme.

If we had but another Cassander, and another Acontius to compose a new confession of faith; another Erastus, and another Grotius to join their malignity together to make a new directory for church government, the devil would then have good hopes to reign visibly in England in heretical, profane, and scandalous combinations.

I believe some may wonder to read what I write of Acontius, but those words did not fall as a blot upon the man from my running pen, and therefore I am ready for more reasons than one to give a fair and an ingenuous account of this deliberate and premeditated censure.

Acontius came forth of Italy (as Alciate, Blandrate, Gibrald, and both the Sozzinis, Laelius, and Faustus did) and lived in the time of Socinus the Elder and Younger also. The elder Socinus died 1562. and printed nothing. About three years after his death, Acontius published his book of *Stratagems*, in which he gives the right hand of brotherly fellowship to the Socinians.[652] When the followers of Socinus did begin to seduce, up starts Acontius and pleads for the seducers. When the Arminians do enlarge the bounds of communion so far, as to take the Socinians into Christian communion, they constantly urge the authority of Acontius in their apology, and in their answer to the reverend professors of Leyden.[653] Acontius thought fit to lay aside the ancient confessions of faith, and compose a new creed, which Socinians may subscribe. He came into England under a fair pretense of being banished for Christ's sake; but certainly his greatest danger was of being called into question for his intimate confederacy with such as were no great friends to Jesus Christ. Judicious Pareus looked upon him as a sneaking solicitor for the Socinians, and as fast a friend to them as Bonfinius himself. The learned professors of Leyden, Peltius, Videlius, Voetius, and a whole synod of discerning Reformers, have set a brand upon him. His book of *Stratagems* printed in the year 1565 was printed again in the year 1610. And as I remember, in the year 1616, I find that he himself was living in the year

---

[652] In the year 1565

[653] Vide Remonstran. Apol. p. 11. & Respon. ad Profes. Leydens. pag. 65.

1613. In the year 1631, his book was printed here at Oxford, but generally condemned by such as were learned and orthodox at that time in this University; they thought it more fit for the fire than the press.

About the beginning of March 1647, there was some part of his *Stratagems* (translated into English) published in print at London. I confess I was amazed at it, but could not learn who was the translator of it. We were at that time required to look after all books that were pernicious or dangerous, and I did complain to the reverend assembly sitting at Westminster, that there was such a book lately published, dedicated to both Houses of Parliament. to the general, and lieutenant general of all the forces raised for the defense of the commonwealth, and recommended to the parliament, army, and city as a book fit to direct them how to distinguish truth from error in that juncture of time.

Moreover, the translator in his epistle to the parliament acknowledged that the book never endeavored to speak English before, but if his essay did find acceptance, it was his intention to go in hand with the remaining books, which all who have read, know, contains the quintessence of those poisonous dregs which are in his third book (now Englished) not so generally observed by unwary readers. Whereupon the reverend Assembly chose a committee to peruse the book, and report their judgment of it to the Assembly with all convenient speed. Upon perusal of the book we found that the author was recommended by Peter Ramus, but we did not much wonder at that.

(1) Because the book is written with much art, and the malignity of it very closely couched.

(2) There are many plausible pretenses, fair insinuations, and several religious expressions in it.[654] The man was master of his passions as well as art, or else he had not been such an excellent agent and solicitor in so bad a cause, and so complete a courtier as indeed he was.

---

[654] 2 Peter 2:3, πλαστοις λογοις. Colossians 2:4, εν πιθανολογια.

(3) Acontius spent a great part of his time in the study of mathematics, he was excellent in the art of fortification, and therefore Peter Ramus might set the higher price upon him.

(4) He has many excellent passages which are of great use against the papists.

But that which we admired at, was that a member of our own assembly should recommend the book. It was therefore desired that Mr. Dury might be added to that committee. When Mr. Dury came amongst us, and saw that he had given too fair a testimony to that subtle piece, he dealt as ingenuously with us as we had dealt with him, and assured us that he would be ready to make his retractation as public, as his recommendation had been made without his consent, because he clearly saw that they practiced upon his passionate love of peace to the great prejudice of truth, and that he was merely drawn in to promote a syncretism beyond the orthodox lines of communication.[655] For in all syncretisms and interimisms between Protestants and papists, or between the Reformed and the Lutherans, the Socinians were ever banished out of the lines of Christian communication. And therefore Dr. Voetius does in the very same breath commend Mr. Dury for leaving out the Socinians in his proposals for peace, and condemn Acontius for taking of them into his *Syncretism*. His words are these:[656]

"*Si percurrantur Historiae, and sexcenti libelli (ut vocantur) Pacifici (quorum Catalogi editi cum consultatione Cassandri, and nuper cum libello Johannes Duraei de pace Ecclesiasticât inter Evangelicos procurandâ) non invenies communi pace quae petitur, aut praetenditur, Anti-Trinitanos comprehendi. Fidem etiam faciunt illa, quae anno 1635 Socinianis in Poloniâ ad Collationem de religion and oblita consilia Pacis se offerentibus, unus and solus Tractatus Acontii imprudentioribus nonnullis imposuit*, etc. Dr Voetius, *De Necessitate et Util. Trin*. (pages 494-495)."

---

[655] Aliudest scribere uni, aliud omnibus.
[656] D. Voet. Tract. de necessitate, & utilitate Dogmatis de Sacrosancta Trinitate. p. 494, 495.

That acute and learned divine does in very many places set forth Acontius in his right colors, and says that the Arminians made great use of him, and that he was but one remove from a Socinian, or guilty of a Socinian syncretism at least,[657] because he does exclude the Sabellians only, and does not obscurely include the Photinians within the compass of his catholic creed,[658] in which there is a snake lurks, which does not hiss, but sting;[659] for this moderate man did never say that it was necessary for our salvation to know and believe that the Father, Son, and Holy Spirit are one and the same God who is the only true God blessed forever.

And yet it is his main business and design in his third book, which is now in English, and in his seventh, which I hope will never be Englished, to show what are the only points necessary to be believed for the attainment of salvation. But Acontius is not very modest when he comes to pass sentence upon the ancients who were rigidly orthodox, and faithfully severe in requiring men to believe those grand articles of faith which are necessary to salvation. For when he discourses of the faith of the man sick of the palsy, he says, "*Credebat enim (ut par est) hominem eum qui Jesus diceretur,*" etc. For he believed (in all probability, says the translator) that that same man whose name was Jesus came from God, and was in favor with God; and therefore he hoped that by this means he might recover his health. But that he knew all those things which the church has for a long time accounted as articles of

---

[657] Voet. de Atheismo parte 3. pag. 160. Quamlongé autem abfuerit Acontius ab occulto Socinismo, aut saltem Syncretismo cum eo, discipotest, quòd Sabellianorum haeresin Praecisé excludat, Photinianorum verò minime; imo eos Symbolo suo (lib. 7. p. 341.) non obscure includit.

[658] Sabelliani ab Acontio extra novum ipsius Catholicum Sym|bolum & communionem seu Syncretismum collocantur, quia statuunt filium esse eandem personam cum Patre. D. Voet. de Trinitate. pag. 496.

[659] Quod ad Acontium dicimus eum meritò in hoc negotio suspectum esse—videantur modo l. 3. p. 114, 123. & lib. 7. p. 341. edit Basil. 1610. & judicetur quis anguis in herba latuerit, quod hic vir in fundamentalibus assertionibus nunquam το ὁμοούσιον trium Personarum statuerit, nec adversarios Samosarenum, Photinum, Arrium, Eunomium, Pneumatomachos, aut corum errores rejecerit, contentus solos, illos rejectos qui negarent filium non esse alium à Patre. D. Voet de Trinitate. pag. 501.

faith necessary to be believed to salvation, how likely a matter it is, I leave it to every man to judge.[660] There are likewise many other texts to the very same purpose.

Concerning the faith of Abraham, he speaks somewhat like an Arminian, and an Anabaptist, but concludes like a Socinian, that Abraham did believe: (1) that he should be the father of many nations, (2) that the nations should be happy by his seed, and (3) somewhat concerning the Land of Canaan.

But (he says) of those points of religion which it is judged everybody is bound to know upon pain of damnation, we read not a word. Yea, and the mystery of salvation itself by his seed is very closely and obscurely promised.

I know that Acontius does acknowledge Christ to be the Son of God, and to be God, and so do the Socinians in some sense, as we have shown, but then Acontius qualifies all with a pretty diversion.

Many things (he says) may be reckoned up, which that we might be saved, ought both to be, and to be performed:[661] as that our sins were to be abolished, and that by a man void of all sin, and of infinite virtue and power, and he therefore to be the Son of God, yea, God and the like.[662] And then he presently mixes some things of less consequence, and concludes thus.[663]

Doubtless that it may evidently appear to us that these things are likewise necessary to be known, either we must have a plain text of Scripture that shall pronounce, whatsoever is necessary to be done, that also (to attain salvation) must necessarily be believed. But there is no testimony of Scripture that I know which pronounces, that whatever ought to be done ought to be believed.

By this one taste you may plainly see that, though it should be granted necessary unto salvation that Christ should be God, abolish sin, etc. yet

---

[660] Read Acontius in Latine p. 115, 116. in English pag. 79.
[661] Acontius in English page 70
[662] Per hominem peccati omnis expertem, virtute immensas proptereáque Dei filium itemque Deum, & similia. Acont. Strat. pag. 103.
[663] Acontius in English pages 70-71

Acontius will not grant that this is necessary to be believed for the attainment of salvation; and therefore he left it out of his catholic creed, and syncretism, and yet condemns the Sabellians, who did not deny the Godhead of Christ, but said that he was one God (and somewhat which they should not have said, or believed, that he was one person) with God the Father. You may hereby understand the modesty of the man and cry out as he did, "*En modestiam satis perfrictam, usque ad os impudentiae perfrictam.*" But if his seventh book (which the translator did not dare adventure to English until he saw how this would take) had been translated, I need not have said anymore for the discovery of this subtle sir. Judicious Pareus, and the Synod of Lublin were able to detect him for all his courtship and hypocrisy,[664] and Dr. Voetius assures us, that if the Reformed churches had taken Acontius' third and seventh books into their consideration, they would have rejected Acontius from communion with them, unless he would have declared himself more plainly, and made it evident, that coming out of Italy under pretense of reformation, he had not brought the same errors with him which Alciate, Blandrate, Gribald, or Socinus the uncle, and the nephew, brought from thence.[665]

Those who are acquainted with ecclesiastical writers can readily declare what difficulties they wrestled with, and what persecutions they did undergo rather than they would consent to any syncretism with the Arians when it was obtruded, or yield to any agreement, when it was offered to them upon plausible and tempting conditions.[666] Those who have read the acts of the

---

[664] Pareus Epist. ad N. N. Martii. 1. 1613. Arminium vestrum Sociniani in Poloniâ expresse ut suum nuper nominarunt, unà cum quodam Bonfinio, & Acōtio clandestinis asseclis, quorum authoritate postularunt à fratribus Orthodoxis fraternitatem, isti verò fortiter recusarunt. [Acta] ad me misit Synodus Lublinensis.

[665] Siquidem innotuisset Ecclesiis Reformatis quod tectè innuit lib. 3. p. 114. 123. & lib. 7. pag. 341. edente Jo. Grassero. 1616. Bas. utique in communione suâ illum non retinuissent, nisi a pertius declarasset, se ex Italia praetextu Reformationis non attulisse quod populares ejus Alciatus, Blandrata, Gribaldus, Socinus uterque, &c. D. Voetius de Trinitate. p. 495.

[666] SVide Acta concilii Niceni, Concil. Syrmiensis, anno 357. utriusque Ariminēsis, anno 358. Athanasium de Synodis Oratione 2. contra Arianos, & ad Seraplonem

Nicene, Syrmiensian, and both the Ariminensian Councils, Athanasius, Hilary, Epiphanius, Nicetas, Socrates, Sozomen, Theodoret, Augustine, know this to be as clear as if it were written with a sunbeam. Was there not an anathema denounced against Liberius by great Hilary for yielding to such a syncretism with the Arians, as Acontius did propound for an accommodation between Christians and Socinians? Pardon the harshness of that expression; I am not in passion, or in haste, but follow the example of the orthodox doctors of the church, who did use the name of Christians in opposition to the Arians, to show that they did not acknowledge the Arians for to be Christians, because they denied the true Christ, who is God-man, the only mediator and Savior of his people from their sins.

Melancthon and Bucer were men of great prudence, modesty, and moderation, as well as piety and learning, but they never offered to conclude a peace with any of these new Arians.[667] They would not admit any into Christian Communion with them, unless they would subscribe to the confessions of faith received in the four first general councils. They who deny the Godhead of our Savior, and the Holy Spirit, are Antichristian, anti-spiritual men: their idolatry in worshiping Christ, whom they look upon as a mere creature, their impiety in denying worship to the Holy Spirit, their horrid blasphemies to the dishonor of Christ and Christianity,

---

Disput. prima & secunda contra Arrianos. Epiphan. haeres. 65. & 73. Anathema tibi Liberi inquit Hilarius. Vide Hilar. de Synodis Nicet. Thesaur. Orth. fid. lib. 4. haeresi. 32. Socrat. Hist. l. 1. c. 6. & 2. c. 29. 52. Sozom. lib. 4. c. 5. Epist. Synod. Sardic. apud Theodoret. Aug. de Haeres. c. 14. serm. 129. Baronii Annales ad annum 357. & 358. Photium in Epist. Philost. Alcuinum de Trinitate, Gomarum, Chamierum, Voetium, Zanchium de Trinitate.

[667] Vide Melanct. Loc com. Examen Theologicum. Consilia. Profess. Leidens. in specimine Exceptorum. Vedel. in Arcan. Arm. Pezel. in Disp. de Trinitate. Schevica. de Trinit. Jun. in Antapolog. Jodoc. Cocc. Thesaur. Cathol. l. 1. Elmen. horst. in Comment. ad Gennad. Ambros. Praef. ad lib. de Sacro Sancto. Goldast. in Constit. Imperial. T. 3. Theod. Hist. lib. 5. cap. 16. Ecthes. Heraclii de Trinitate & fide Catholica. Edicta Constantini. Decreta Ord. Gen. 1598. de combustione librorum Socini & ejectione Ostorodi & Voidovii ex Provinciis unitis. Socinismum cum Turcismo & Judaismo comparant Trelcatius Senior Gomarus, Vedelius, Voetius. Anti-Trinitarios δευτερος ιυδαιους appellat Epiphanius.

their poisoning of souls, and their disturbing of Christian societies, should all be laid to heart by all Christian magistrates, all ministers and members of Jesus Christ; and therefore this Acontian syncretism is abominable.

Upon these and various other considerations I was desired to make a report to the reverend assembly concerning the danger of translating and printing of Acontius in English. The heads of the report were briefly these.

The Report made to the Reverend Assembly.
March 8th, 1647–48.
By Mr. Cheynell.

We humbly conceive that Acontius' enumeration of points necessary to be known and believed for the attainment of salvation is very defective.[668]

(1) Because in the creed which Acontius framed, there is no mention made either of the Godhead of Jesus Christ, or of the Godhead of the Holy Spirit. And,

(2) Although Acontius does acknowledge Christ to be truly the Son of God, yet he does not in his creed declare him to be the natural Son of God.[669]

That these points are necessary to be known and believed for the attainment of salvation, is in our judgment clearly expressed in the holy Scriptures (1 John 5:7, 20 compared with John 17:3).

We do therefore conceive that Acontius was justly condemned[670] because he maintains that the points of doctrine which he mentions are the

---

[668] Variatur fides, auge, tur vel diminuitur—non ratione primae veritatis, quae est unica inomnibus, sed ex parte credendorum, dispositionum, personarum, & temporum. Reyn. Pant. de Fide cap. 12. Qui Trinitatem negat, negat Baptismum. negat Christianismum. Tota enim Ecclesia christiana quae Deum in tribus personis colit, Mysterium Trinitatis in vero Scripturarum sensu pro necessario habet; Arianos, Photinianos, χρισομαχος, πνευματομαχος, & proinde Socinianos damnat. Vide censuram cl. Theol. Profess. in Confes. Remon. instit. c. 3. de sacro-sancta Trinitate. Frustra sunt qui loco Patris Filii & spiritus sancti unius veri Dei Idolum colunt.

[669] Sociniani Christum verum Dei filium esse agnoscunt, verum Deum esse negant. Vide D. Alting. Loc. com. parte secundâ pag. 367. Vide etiam Acta Concil. Niceni. Symb. Nicen. Symb. Athanas. Epistolam Eusebii apud Socratem lib. 1. Hist. cap. 8. Theodor. lib. 1. cap. 12. D. Vedel. Arcan. Arminianismi. Stegman. Photin. Smiglecium de Naturali Dei filio. Symb. Constant. apud Theodor. lib. 5. cap. 9. Epiph. in αγκυρωτ. Videl. de Deo Synagogae. D. Voetium de Atheismo, de Symb. de sancta Trinitate, ubi supra. Pelt. Harmon. Praefat. Melanct. Loc. com. exam. Theol. & consilia ejusdem. D. Voet. de Trinitate p. 501. Acontius το ομοούσιον trium personarum in fundamentalibus assertionibus non statuit.

[670] Regula fidei pusillis magnisque communis

only points which are necessary to be known and believed, and did not hold forth or mention the points aforesaid as necessary to salvation.[671]

And we esteem him to be the more worthy of censure, because he lived in an age when the Photinian heresy was revived, and yet spared the Photinians, though he condemned the Sabellians.

Finally, Acontius cautiously declines the orthodox expressions of the ancient church, in the four first general synods; and delivers his Creed in

---

[671] Aug. Epist. 57. vide Sym. apud Epiph. in haeresi 72. & quae de consil. Chalced habentur apud Evagrium lib. 2. Hist. c. 4. praesertim de spiritu sancto. Consulantur Scholastici de iis, quae necessaria sunt Necessitate medii vel finis. Bannes in secundam secundae quest. 2. art. 8. Greg. Val. Tom. 3. com. The. quest. 2. punct. 2. Scot. Suarez. Ocham Lorca, &c. Vide Aug. contra Pelag. & Celest. lib 2. c. 24. Ecclesia una dicitur propter unitatem fidei. Hieronym. in Psal. 23. Baptismus est Sacramentum fidei Aug. epist. 23. Vide Basil. de spiritu sancto lib 1. cap. 2. Tertul. de praescript. cap. 14, 20. Iren. l. 1. cap. 2. Parker. de desc. ad Inferos. Fides nostra secundū Christi doctrinam est in Patre & Filio, & spiritu sancto. Mat. 28 19. Eph. 4. 5. concil. Ancyran. de spiritu sancto 2. Sym. Antioch. apud Socrat. l. 1. cap 8. [Vide] Concil. Constant. Epist. apud Theod. l. 5. Hist. cap. 9. Sct D. Ussher's learned answer to the Jesuit's challenge, p. 311, 312. And his excellent Sermon of the unity of Faith, where he gives a satisfactory account of the faith of the Eastern and Western Churches. Mr Rous his Catholique charity. cap. 10, 11. D. Voetius de Symb. Apost. D. Potter his Answer to charity mistaken. sect 7. lod. Coc. Thesaur. Cathol. l. 1. art. 4. Acta Consilii Niceni. Athanas. de Synodis, Hilar. de Synodis. Epiph. haeres. 73. Socrat. Hist. lib. 1. cap. 6. Baronii Annales ad an, 357, 358. Alcuinum de Trinitate. Nicet. Thesaur. Orthod. fid. l. 4. haeres. 32. Videlium de Deo Synagogae. Gomarum de Trinitate. Atheus est juxta religionem Christianam, qui Christum ut Deum non colit. Vide sis, orationem D. Jac. Arminii de componendo dissidio Religionis inter Christianos. Arii Symbolum explodendum statuimus; nam si ab aeterno Deus est Pater, Filius quoque Patri coaeternus necessario statuitur. D. S. Glassius de Deitate Filii. Vide Tilenum de Deo Patre & Filio, D. Sohnium de Trinitate. Zanchium, Bezam, Calvinum, Junium, Trelcatium Seniorem, D. Altingium, Maccovium, Synop. Purioris Theol. Polanum, Chamierum, Libertinismus introducit Socinismum, Socinismus destruit Christianismum. Socinus, Acontius, Barleus, nec non Semi-Iudaizantes Arminiani pietatem fovent parum Christianam. Vide Stegmannum, Voetium, Videlium de prudentia veteris ecclesiae l. 2. cap. 5, 6. de Deo synagogae, de Arcanis Arminianismi, de finibus Arminianismi lib. 1. cap. 1, 2. Comnenus reclamantibus Orthodoxis dixit Turcas colere verum Deum, ut videre est apud Nicetam Choniatem in Manuele Comneno lib. 7. Qui quaerere Deum se profitentur extra Christum quem abominantur ut Turcae & Iudaei, neque verum Deum, neque verum cultum habent. Nam sine Christo nec verus Deus cognoscitur, nec colitur. D. Rivet. Comment. in Hos. 3. p. 116.

such general expressions, that as we conceive the Socinians may subscribe it, and yet retain the worst of their blasphemous errors.

The promises being humbly presented, we leave it to the judgment of this reverend Assembly whether Acontius' *Stratagems* was a book fit to be translated into English, and recommended to the parliament, army, and city to direct them how to distinguish truth from error in this juncture of time.

Upon these few heads of the report I discoursed somewhat affectionately and freely, according to the weight and moment of the point in question. And thereupon the reverend assembly did unanimously desire the prolocutor to persuade me to print something about that argument, as soon as the heat of our employment at Oxford was over for the satisfaction of the kingdom. I am very willing to obey the commands of that assembly famous for learning and piety, even to the admiration of those great scholars whose hearts were once espoused to another interest. If the debates of that reverend assembly upon several articles of faith were printed and published to the world, all ingenuous enemies of piety would blush at the remembrance of those bitter censures which have been passed upon men of whom this age is unworthy. But I must hasten, for my book begins to swell beyond its just proportion, and I am called away to another service, which cannot be performed at any other time.

Acontius has invented very pretty diversions instead of excuses to abate our zeal against the most dangerous errors. He says that heretics do not intend to make Christ a liar. The controversy between them and us is not concerning the truth, but concerning the meaning of the words of Christ.

To which I answer, that he who believes the words of Christ in the sense of Antichrist, and rejects the sense of Christ and his Spirit, is not a Christian, but is in deed and truth Antichristian.[672] The sense of Scripture is the Scripture, and therefore if men be permitted in these great and weighty articles to impose a new sense upon the church of Christ, they do clearly

---

[672] See Dr. Rainolds' learned conference with Hart.

impose a new creed, a new gospel upon us, and deserve that anathema (Galatians 1:8-9), though they should pretend to apostolical authority, or angelical purity: "Although we or an angel from heaven preach any other gospel unto you, than that which we have preached unto you, let him be accursed. As we said before, so say I now again, if any man preach any other gospel unto you than that you have received, let him be accursed." Grotius in the days of his modesty refused to solicit on the behalf of the Socinians, and professed that he did not know a man in the grand Assembly in Holland, that would not pronounce the Socinians accursed.[673] The distinguishing question, which was then put, was the old question: "Do you believe that Christ is God by nature? If you do not, you are an Arian; and if you are an Arian, you are no Christian."

Acontius reckons up some things as necessary to believe which are expressed in Scripture, and some other things which are necessarily inferred from what is expressed, but he does not reckon up the Godhead of Christ, or the Holy Spirit in his catalog of things that are plainly expressed, or necessarily inferred, as is most evident by his whole discourse in his third book which is now in English.

Finally, the Socinians take away the right foundation of faith, hope, worship, justification, as has been proven, and lay a wrong foundation; they bring in a new Christ, a mere man, and a new gospel, a new judge in the highest matters and mysteries of religion, their own reason, which they might infallibly know to be not only fallible, but corrupt. They deny the true causes and means of salvation, and the right application of them. Their impiety in not worshiping the Spirit, their idolatry in worshiping one whom

---

[673] Grotius in Pietate Ord. p. 13. &c. Hic ego optima fide profiteor, neminem me nosse in omni Hollandiae Conventu, qui non istis opinionibus, & omnibus, & singulis dicturus sit Anathema. Christus est [Ουσια Θεου], credis vel non? si non, Arianus es, Christianus non es. Vide etiam Nicet. Thesaur. Orthod. Fid. lib. 4. haeresi 32. Athanas. ad Serap. Orat. 2. Disp. 1. & 2. contra Arianos. Photium in Epitome. Philost. Canones Concil. Nicen. Epiph. haeres. 65. & 73. Socrat. Hist. l. 1. c. 6. Baronii Annales ad annum 357, & 358. Anathema tibi Liberi inquit Hilarius. Vide Photii Nomocan. Tit. 1. c. 1. Alcuinum de Trinitate.

they esteem to be a mere man, and refusing to be washed and purged with the blood of the covenant, will justify all that reject them and their confederates from Christian communion.

I am not at leisure to handle the magistrate's duty in this point, nor are many of them at leisure to consider all that is fit to be considered in that weighty point. But for the present satisfaction of such as know not how to study in these busy times, I shall point at some unquestionable truths for the ending of that unhappy and fatal controversy in the church of Christ.

(1) There is no warrant given in the Word to any minister of the state, or Officer of the church to molest, oppress, or persecute any man for Righteousness' sake. He who persecutes a man for following his conscience when rightly informed by the Word and Spirit of the Lord Jesus, does certainly persecute the Lord Jesus Christ. "Saul, Saul, why persecutest thou me? I am Jesus whom thou persecutest," it is a fit text to be preached on the day of February 22nd, 1649.[674] But I am now learning another lesson, which is to suffer persecution patiently for righteousness sake, and pray for such benefactors, who do besides their intention, and against their will, make Christians happy by endeavoring to make them miserable in their outward man by an unexpected persecution. Yet I could not but take notice of the seasonableness of this truth, and put down the day, the month, and the year, as the prophet did. Ezekiel 8:1 reads: "And it came to pass in the sixth year, in the sixth month, in the fifth day of the month, as I sat in mine house, and the elders of Judah (the princes of the people) sat before me," etc. The great statesmen were at leisure now in the time of the captivity to hear the prophet. If they would have heard, believed, obeyed before, they had never gone into captivity, for the misusing of the prophets, and despising of their message was the sin against the most sovereign remedy, and when there was no other remedy, then God sent them away captive, etc (2 Chronicles

---

[674] Acts 9:4–5

36:16-17). Let all such consider this, who are posting on in the high-way to captivity.

(2) No man ought to be punished for following his misinformed conscience, until he has been better informed and spiritually admonished (as we have formerly shown) twice or thrice, and is so unconscionable as to despise good information, reject prudent and faithful admonitions contrary to the doctrine of godliness and all good conscience, for of such a man the apostle says not only that he is perverted, but he is subverted (Titus 3:10).[675]

(3) The ministers of God, the civil magistrates, and the ministers of Christ, and all church officers whatsoever must join together and uphold one another in the discharge of their several duties, that they may be in a capacity to revenge all disobedience, and execute the judgment that is written (Romans 13:4; 2 Corinthians 10:6; 1 Corinthians 4:21, Deuteronomy 13:10-11).

(4) Heretical seducers, blasphemous apostates, and idolaters (of whom we have discoursed at large) are wolves that subvert whole houses (Titus 1:11), churches (Galatians 5:10, 12, Acts 15:24), states, and kingdoms; and therefore they must be driven from the sheepfold, lest the very vitals of Christianity be corrupted, religion destroyed, many souls poisoned, God extremely dishonored, the church and state endangered, as is fully declared unto us in the holy Scriptures of truth.

(5) God works by these legal terrors and executions of vengeance sometimes upon the party punished; the false prophet converted by the Spirit of God working in this great ordinance, does in the day of his visitation confess the justice and charity of those officers, who did stigmatize him with wounds in his hands (Zechariah 13:6), as Mr. Cotton observes in the ninth chapter of his *Answer to Mr. Williams*, pages 20-21. Moreover, it is most clear that God does make use of the magistrate as his minister and instrument for

---

[675] Non tantùm διεςραπται sed & εξεστραπται; haereticus post unam alteramque admonitionem repellendus itaque est eversus haereticus, ut qui suopte judicio sit condemnatus.

the overawing of the people by inflicting exemplary punishment on such as do speak lies in the name of the Lord, blaspheme the name, truth, person of Christ, and seduce (or thrust) men away from the only true God: Father, Son, and Holy Spirit (Deuteronomy 13:6, 8-11).

The moral equity of this command is very evident for the punishing of such as do entice men from the true religion, because there is a reason given which is of general and perpetual equity. "Thou shalt stone him, because he has sought to thrust thee away from Jehovah thy God." It is now certainly as great a fault to seduce men from Father, Son, and Holy Spirit; nay, a greater fault now, because it is a sin committed against clearer light. And it is of general and public concern to have such great examples made in a nation to make the generality of men affected with an awful regard of the truth, goodness, majesty, and justice of God. For this is God's ordinance: to strike the people with such a reverence as shall at least restrain them from this sin. "And all Israel shall hear and fear, and shall do no more any such wickedness (Deuteronomy 13:11)." The Lord is acquainted with the frame of our hearts and spirits, and he propounds such remedies as are proper and suitable to our distempers; and he who ordains such remedies will make them effectual by his own Spirit, who often sanctifies legal terrors and outward afflictions, and makes them subservient to spiritual purposes, and therefore these outward weapons are spiritually used, and are of a spiritual efficacy according to the counsel of God's will.

When the magistrate as a minister of God draws the sword in the cause of God for the honor of God, according to the ordinance of God expressed in Deuteronomy 13, Zechariah 13, and Romans 13, the sword that is thus drawn is not the sword of Gideon only, the sword of man, but the sword of God.

And it is certainly most proper to restrain them by the sword, who will not be restrained by any other ordinance of God. Men that have seared consciences have strong passions, and exemplary punishments will work effectually upon the passion of fear in a self condemned man, when no spiritual physic will work upon him, because all wholesome admonitions are rejected by him.

Carnal men are ready to pursue a new interest without any new light or direction from the Word of God, and there is no way to balance these men who are swayed by worldly hopes, but by affrighting them with legal terrors from all those sins, unto which they are tempted by self interest in this tempting age. Men that will not be ruled by law or gospel, or conscience rightly informed by both but do indeed sear their consciences, and harden their hearts both against law and gospel, must be restrained by the sword, because they are unconscionable. Shame and fear will work upon men that have any manner of ingenuity remaining in them.

(6) We must distinguish between the object and the end of the magistrate's power.

[1] The immediate object of the magistrate's power is external, the body and outward goods of his subjects.

[2] The immediate end of the magistrate's power is to preserve and promote the peace and welfare of a nation in its civil society, but the ultimate end is for the support and furtherance of godliness and honesty. No Christian magistrate ought to aim lower in any nation, unto which the means of grace has been offered by the special providence and favor of God. Put all together and you have the adequate end of the civil power of Christian magistrates over all in their dominions, who have given up their names to Jesus Christ. The apostles themselves, and the churches planted by them, begged this favor of God for kings in their time (when you know who they were that governed the world) that God would so far overrule their rulers, that the Christians might lead a quiet and peaceable life in all godliness and honesty (1 Timothy 2:2).[676] But it is readily acknowledged that there are some magistrates who are ignorant of truth and godliness, and

---

[676] See Reverend Master White's *Way to the Tree of Life* concerning human authority. Mr. Cotton in his *Bloody Tenent Washed White*, chapter 70.

therefore are not able to perform the whole duty of magistrates. But our next conclusion is;

(7) All magistrates ought to study the truth and worship of Jesus Christ, that they may be instructed in the principles of Christianity, and made wise enough to discern between fundamental truths, and damnable errors, that they may not by following their own blind and erroneous consciences countenance heresy and apostasy, and persecute truth and fidelity.

"Be wise therefore O ye Kings; be instructed ye judges of the earth; serve the Lord with fear, and rejoice with trembling; kiss the Son lest he be angry and ye perish from the way," etc. (Psalm 2:10-12 compared with Deuteronomy 17:17-20 and 1 Timothy 2:20).

And surely it is then no great task for any magistrate who has given up his name to Christ, to learn the principles of the Christian religion, whereby he hopes for to be saved, that he may be able to judge and punish such blasphemous and seducing heretics as endeavor to subvert the Christian faith.

(8) God freely reveals and communicates himself to all true-hearted magistrates who seek unto him in his own way for direction and instruction in those weighty points which they are bound to know both as servants, (and as civil ministers) of God for their own, and their subjects everlasting good. Hezekiah did prevent the priests and Levites, and for ought we read, the whole church also, in discovering the right way of reformation in matters of religion after that general apostasy in the days of Ahaz; read 2 Chronicles 29:4-12. And it is generally conceived that David was the first that did discover that great disorder in carrying the ark of God in a cart. Read the fifteen first verses of 1 Chronicles 15 and take special notice of verses 2, 12, 13, and 15: "None ought to carry the ark of God but the Levites, for them hath the Lord chosen to carry the ark of God, and to minister to him forever," etc.

(9) Christian magistrates have no other rule of civil righteousness prescribed unto them by God than that which God gave by Moses, and such as have expounded Moses in the Scriptures of truth. This one proposition

fully explained and confirmed would put an end to this unhappy controversy between all judicious and ingenuous men. We cannot in equity extend the law of Moses to such as never entered into any covenant with God, nor to any that are led away in their simplicity before they have been better instructed and admonished once and again; nor to such as do in a Christian and peaceable way dissent from their brethren in points of less consequence. But we extend the law of Moses to seducing apostates, blasphemous heretics, and idolaters, who are obstinate against light and admonition, and poison others, or endeavor to poison them with doctrines which do subvert faith and holiness in heart or life, that they may be punished according to their several demerits.[677]

I need not say anything of such disturbances of the civil peace as tend to the destruction of the lives or souls of men. Jerome tells us that because Arius, who was but a spark of fire in Alexandria, was not quenched presently, he kindled a flame which devoured almost the whole Christian world.[678] And yet it is clear that the church had done their part against him, for he was twice excommunicated out of the church of Alexandria, as Socrates, Sozomen, and several others of the ancient writers relate. And therefore when spiritual instructions, admonitions, censures, will do no good upon these self-condemned persons they are even ripe for civil censures. When the wolves come into the sheepfold, the sheep run to the shepherd. The magistrate is a civil shepherd (as is confessed by all) and the civil shepherd has some dogs at his command to hunt away these wolves, at least out of the sheepfold, lest they worry and destroy the sheep.

(10) Toleration of seducing apostates, blasphemous heretics, and idolaters by the civil powers, has exceedingly strengthened the hands of Antichrist, and been very prejudicial to the church of Christ. I am not at

---

[677] Deuteronomy 13:10

[678] Arius in Alexandriâ una scintilla fuit, sed quia non statim oppressa est, totum orbem ejus flamma de populata est. Hieronymus. Mirabatur se totus mundus factum Arrianum.

leisure now to relate the mischiefs which happened in the days of Constantius, Valens, Julian, and others, who were patrons of seducing apostates and blaspheming heretics. Julian thought that a toleration of heresies, and a suppression of the schools of learning (that none of the Christians might be able to confute them) was the most speedy and effectual course to blot out the Christian name from under heaven. For this sacrilegious liberty (as Augustine well observes) would soon overthrow the power of Christianity.[679]

(11) The toleration of blasphemous heretics, seducing apostates and gross idolators has too often introduced a persecution of saints. Apostates are of all others the most keen and bloody persecutors, witness Julian. And when subtle seducers are tolerated, they will quickly be countenanced, employed, preferred; and then woe be to all orthodox saints, I mean men sound in the faith, holy in life, and peaceable in their conversation.[680] The toleration of seducers made the world turn Arian, as ecclesiastical writers show; and the toleration of seducers made the world Antichristian, as Mr. Cotton proves. And how the Christian world has been not only shaken, but even broken by the Arian, and Eutychian persecutions, by the insurrection of the Macedonians in Greece, and by the Antichristian wars and persecutions for many hundred years, is evidently proved by sad and experimental demonstrations.[681]

When King James did tolerate papists, he did persecute Puritans, as they then called men that were seriously and invincibly pious. When seducers get

---

[679] Julianus desertor Christi, & inimicus, Haereticis libertatem perditionis permisit, & tum Basilicas haereticis reddidit, quando Templa Daemoniis. Eo modo putans Christianum nomen posse pertre de terris si unitati Ecclesiae, de quâ lapsus fuerat, invideret, & sacrilegas dissensiones liberas esse permitteret. Epist. 166. Toleration of Heretikes in Doctrine, and Idolatours in worship made the world Antichristian; See Reverend Mr. Cotton in his answer to Mr. Williams' Bloody Tenent. Chap. 61. pag 131-132.
[680] Vide Athanas. Apolog. Socrat. Hist. lib. 1. cap. 25. lib. 2. cap. 22.
[681] Vict. de per. sec. vandal. lib. 3. Euseb. in vitâ Const. lib. 3 ca. 4. Sulpit. Sever. Sozom. Evagr. Pau Diacon. Baron. Annal. Hieronym orat. de non crad. Basil.

head, they strengthen their party by force as well as fraud, and oppose such as dissent from their damnable errors, as the Circumcellians did with clubs and swords, or as Zedekiah did Micaiah with his fists. Muncer, Becold etc., who were so tender and careful to preserve the tares, would not suffer the wheat to grow till harvest.

(12) We must distinguish (as judicious Davenant did) between tolerable and intolerable errors; simple, and [complex] errors, as others speak.[682] There are corrigible and incorrigible heretics, some heretics are but perverted and they are teachable; others are subverted, men that are smitten with a spirit of obstinacy, impenitent and self-condemned men, condemned formally by their own conscience, or virtually by their proud and stubborn contempt of Christian admonition, and their voluntary rejection of plain truths, that they may enjoy their beloved errors and their heretical lusts; men whose lives are as full of atheism as their assertions of blasphemy; seducing heretics, who endeavor to thrust away others from the belief or worship of the only true God, Father, Son, and Holy Spirit. The Calvinists do not say that anyone ought to be put to death for simple heresy, as the reverend and learned professors of Leyden show in their censure of the Arminian confession. And on the other side, the Lutherans grant that seditious blasphemous seducing heretics, idolaters, and apostates are, when they grow incorrigible, to be punished with death, as well as sorcerers, traitors or adulterers.[683] Let them name one of us (says Beza) if they can, who says that all heretics ought to be put to death, or that calls everyone a heretic who dissents from him in some

---

[682] Esterror amoris, est & Amor erroris. Errores sunt vel praeter, vel circa, vel contra fundamentum. Est error pervertens est & error, animam subvertens, fidem ever. tens, pacem Ecclesiae nec non Reip. Christianae perturbans. Hereticidium autē ob simplicem & nudam hae. resin, nemo nostrûm simpliciter asseruit. D. Profess. Leyd. Censur. c. 24. p. 318. Calvin. Epist. p. 197. Calvin. Refut. err: Michaelis Serveti inter opuscula pag. 694. Scimus tres esse errorum gradus &c. Pelargus in Deut. 13. Bullinger. Beza &c. Mr. Rutherfurd against pretended liberty. pag. 184.

[683] Vide Brochman. de Magist. Pal. cap. 2. qu. 3. dub. 2. Meisner. Philosoph. sobr. sect. 2. cap. 4. Haereticum leditiosum & blasphenium capitali supplicio dignam nemo ex nostris facile impugnabit. Tota quaestio est de Haeretico Simplici.

profitable, but not fundamental points.⁶⁸⁴ Servetus (says Mr. Calvin) might have saved his life, if he had been a modest heretic.⁶⁸⁵ Master Cotton approves the decree of the Senate of Geneva for punishing Servetus with death.⁶⁸⁶

No judicious Protestant will affirm that errors are to be confuted with fire and faggot, but with meekness of wisdom expressed in faithful instructions and admonitions. Our reasons are spiritual, and if the magistrate draw the sword in God's name, it is not to punish simple error; but to smite some intolerable error, that is, twisted and complicated with blasphemy, apostasy, obstinacy, or some such sins as are eminent in seducing heretics, and destructive to the souls, religion, and peace of Christians. Some erroneous persons have the itch, and some the plague; some of them are melancholic, and some of them are mad, and madmen must be bound, or at least not permitted to walk abroad without their keeper. The itch and the plague are both infectious, but they are not both alike dangerous; and nothing is more clear in the point of civil government than that magistrates should not suffer any to go about with plague-sores running on them. Seducing apostates, blasphemous heretics, and gross idolaters do not only subvert order and peace, but faith and piety. They infect, nay, poison souls.

(12) The glory of God, the good of souls, and the happiness of Christian societies are irresistible motives to quicken the magistrate to act (against such dangerous persons as we have described according to the law of judgment, and their different demerits) in faith and love.

[1] In faith: for the Christian magistrate does not act like himself if he does not perform acts of civil justice in faith. And it is clear that if there be no moral equity in any of the judicial laws in the Old Testament, and there

---

⁶⁸⁴ Ergo si potest, vel unum nominet qui aut omnes Haereticus censuerit interficiendos, aut ita sibi placuerit ut alios omnes diversum sentientes pro Haereticis habuerit. Vide Bezam contra Bellium, & Monfortium, & Tract. de Haereticis puniendis.
⁶⁸⁵ Calvin in opposition to Servetus
⁶⁸⁶ Mr. Cotton often in his Answer to Master Williams' *Bloody Tenent*. p. 126, 181.

are none at all extant in the New, then the Christian magistrate cannot perform any act of civil justice in faith, But it is indeed too evident to be denied, that all divine laws which concern the punishment of moral transgressions are of perpetual obligation, and therefore still remain in force according to their substance and general equity, abstracted from special circumstances, typical accessories, and the old forms of Mosaic polity,[687] for:

{1} These divine laws are not expired in their own nature.

{2} They are not repealed by God.

{3} The authority of the lawgiver is the same under both administrations, old and new; the consciences of Christians as well as Jews, are subject to his sovereign and perpetual jurisdiction.

{4} The matter of the laws is moral, and very agreeable to the Dictates of nature, as appear by the several laws and decrees of heathens (Daniel 3:29, Ezra 7:23, 25-27, Ezra 10:3, 5, 8 compared with Numbers 15:30-31, Leviticus 24:15-16, Deuteronomy 13:8-9, Zechariah 13:3, 6). Seducing, poisoning, and slaying of souls is by the law of nature and nations the worst of injuries.

{5} The reason for these divine laws is immutable, and that reason is sometimes expressed and declared, but it is not necessary that there should be any express ratification of every moral law in the New Testament which is plainly delivered in the Old.[688]

{6} These divine laws are independent of the will of man, and therefore indispensable by man's authority.

[2] The magistrate is to act in Christian love and charity against these dangerous men. It is mercy to drive away the wolf, and cruelty to spare him. There must be so much fatherly love shown to the souls of Christians to the little flock, as to preserve them from wolves and foxes. He who loves Christ, the Christian religion, the souls and peace of Christians, will not bear the

---

[687] See Piscator on Exodus

[688] See Master Palmer and Mr. Cawdrey *of the Sabbath*. Chap. 2.

sword in vain; his head, heart, hand, bowels will keep time in working according to the written rule.

(14) The happiness of civil societies as well as church assemblies does much depend upon the punishing of antichristian heretics, seducing apostates, etc. according to the nature and measure of their offenses. In all civil states whose acts are recorded in sacred or profane stories, the magistrates were to have a care, not only of justice and honesty, but of that religion also which they esteemed divine for the good and happiness of their civil state, though it is no wonder if the heathens did misapply this zealous instinct of nature, to the maintenance of superstition and idolatry, of a false religion and false gods. Socrates, Theodorus, and Protagoras – famous philosophers – were all three condemned at Athens by the law against irreligion. But let us look into Christian states.

When the means of instruction and reformation have been vouchsafed to a people that are in covenant with God, and they corrupt the truth and worship of God, the Lord does not only punish degenerate churches, but even civil states, princes, and people for this spiritual pollution. The Turk was let loose from the River Euphrates to punish the worshippers of images (Revelation 9:14, 20). The flourishing of religion, is the flourishing of the civil state; and the decay of religion, the decay and ruin of the civil state, according to the ordinary dispensations of God.

When Christ had ridden through the Roman state on the white horse of his gospel of grace and was rejected, then followed the red horse of war, the black horse of famine, and the pale horse of pestilence and other deadly plagues (Revelation 6:2-8). Can any Christian state hope upon Scripture grounds, that it shall enjoy honor, health, riches, peace, safety, settlement, if faith and piety be overthrown by the indulgence of that state, if seducers be permitted to poison souls, to teach damnable doctrines, and persuade men to deny the Lord that bought them, to deny his divine nature and subsistence, his offices and the efficacy of them; nay, his very redemption by way of purchase, by way of proper and all-sufficient satisfaction as the Socimans do?

The patience and bounty of God – acting as it were by prerogative – is gloriously manifested in our days, but surely no Christian state can be secured by a council or an army which permits men to live without Christ, without God in the world, without any spiritual communion with God in his coeternal Son by his coessential Spirit. Woe be to us if we neglect so great salvation as is yet offered to us in this day of grace.

(15) The church as a church has no sword; it does therefore belong to the magistrate to smite with the sword, but the church may exhort the magistrate to do his duty (1 Kings 18:40).

(16) We must distinguish between Christian forbearance, vouchsafed to weak brethren, that they may live quietly in all godliness and honesty: and antichristian indulgence extended to blasphemous heretics and seducing apostates, that they may live quietly in all ungodliness and dishonesty to the infection and seduction of others. The kings shall be rewarded for burning, and God praised for judging the seducing whore. But judicious Mr. Cotton is afraid that the antichristian whore will steal in at the backdoor of a toleration.

(17) Gospel dispensations are as spiritual for the conversion of sorcerers, adulterers, murderers, as for recovery of blasphemous heretics and seducing apostates, and therefore they who plead for the toleration of these obstinate persons in hope of their conversion, do indeed proclaim a general pardon for all malefactors, save such only as sin against the Holy Spirit.

(18) They who permit men to deny supernatural principles, do permit them to overthrow the gospel, which is not written in our hearts by nature as the law is. And yet it should be considered that those who deny the gospel do consequently sin against the light of nature, because they make God a liar by rejecting the testimony of God concerning his Son (1 John 5:10). They who did seduce men from the belief and worship of God as revealed in the Old Testament were to die the death, and yet the Old Testament is as divine and supernatural a revelation as the New Testament itself. And it is clear that God did reveal himself in Christ, even in the Old Testament, for there is

much gospel in the law and the prophets; because all the law and the prophets bare witness of Christ, and "Moses," says our Savior, "wrote of me." If then there is an indulgence granted to such as deny supernatural truths, men may overthrow both the Old and New Testament, and be anti-Scripturists without control.

Nay it will if this absurdity be granted, clearly follow, that the magistrate may punish such severely who deny the truths which are written in Aristotle, but must not touch them who deny all the supernatural mysteries of faith written in the book of God. Blush ye heavens, and be ashamed, O earth, at the atheistical libertinism of this licentious age! Seducers, who did thrust men out of the way which the Lord commanded them by his written word to walk in, were put to death (Deuteronomy 13:5, 10) though they were directed by a supernatural Revelation, to walk in that way reverend Mr. Burroughs often acknowledges in his *Irenicum* that such as profess Christianity are justly punished for sinning against the common light of Christianity.[689]

For it is not conscience, but the devil in the conscience, which moves Christians to maintain errors against the light of Christianity, errors that are destructive to the Christian religion; and if any man has a mind to be an advocate for the devil, I dare not be an advocate for him; only I desire him to beware how he hearkens to the devil in Samuel's mantle, and beseech him to cry mightily to him who alone can cast out devils, to cast the devil out of his conscience, and place himself there as on a throne, that he may rule the conscience, and command the whole man by his Word and Spirit.[690]

(19) He that by seducing seeks to thrust men away from the belief and worship of the only true God, Father, Son, and Holy Spirit, deserves to be punished for his very attempt and endeavor to subvert souls, though he does not prevail with one soul to depart from God. "Because he hath sought to

---

[689] Mr. Burrough's *Heart Divisions*. page 35.
[690] The very attempt of killing a soul deserves death. See Master Cotton's *Tenent Washed White*, page 175.

thrust thee away from Jehovah thy God (Deuteronomy 13:10)." The very murderous attempt of killing a soul by abusing an ordinance of God, corrupting of religion, telling lies in the name of the Lord, fathering our own damnable lies upon the Holy Spirit, is a capital crime.

(20) Christians are in a worse condition than the Jews were, if men may seduce our wives and children into such opinions and practices as will certainly undo their souls to all eternity, and we must only entreat them not to seduce our friends to hell, and the Christian magistrate has no power to punish these soul-murdering seducers. This argument is affectionately pressed by sweet Mr. Burroughs in his book of *Heart Divisions* (pages 23-24).

I have much more to deliver upon this weighty point; but I remember what Hugo said: that it is best at some time to say nothing, at every time to say enough, but at no time to say all.

FINIS.

www.ingramcontent.com/pod-product-compliance
Lightning Source LLC
Chambersburg PA
CBHW021146060526
44107CB00146B/1365/J